A GREAT RURAL SISTERHOOD

Madge Robertson Watt and the ACWW

CW01498560

As the founding president of the Associated Country Women of the World (ACWW), Madge Robertson Watt (1868–1948) turned imperialism on its head. During the First World War, Watt imported the "made-in-Canada" concept of Women's Institutes – voluntary associations of rural women – to the British countryside. In the interwar years, she capitalized on the success of the institutes to help create the ACWW, a global organization of rural women. A feminist imperialist and a liberal internationalist, Watt was central to the establishment of two organizations which remain active around the world today.

In *A Great Rural Sisterhood*, Linda M. Ambrose uses a wealth of archival materials from both sides of the Atlantic to tell the story of Watt's remarkable life, from her early years as a Toronto journalist to her retirement and memorialization after the Second World War.

LINDA M. AMBROSE is a professor in the Department of History at Laurentian University.

A Great Rural Sisterhood

Madge Robertson Watt and the ACWW

LINDA M. AMBROSE

UNIVERSITY OF TORONTO PRESS
Toronto Buffalo London

© University of Toronto Press 2015
Toronto Buffalo London
www.utppublishing.com
Printed in the U.S.A.

ISBN 978-1-4426-4772-5 (cloth)
ISBN 978-1-4426-1579-3 (paper)

Printed on acid-free paper with vegetable-based inks

Library and Archives Canada Cataloguing in Publication

Ambrose, Linda McGuire, 1960–, author
A great rural sisterhood : Madge Robertson Watt and the ACWW /
Linda M. Ambrose.

Includes bibliographical references and index.
ISBN 978-1-4426-4772-5 (bound). ISBN 978-1-4426-1579-3 (pbk.)

1. Watt, Madge Robertson, 1868–1948.   2. Associated Country Women
of the World – History.   3. Rural women – Social conditions.   4. Rural
women – Societies and clubs.   5. Women social reformers – Canada –
Biography.   6. Feminists – Canada – Biography.   I. Title.

HQ1122.A43 2015   305.4209173'4   C2014-906272-9

University of Toronto Press acknowledges the financial assistance to its
publishing program of the Canada Council for the Arts and the Ontario
Arts Council, an agency of the Government of Ontario.

   Canada Council   Conseil des Arts
                        for the Arts   du Canada

University of Toronto Press acknowledges the financial support of the
Government of Canada through the Canada Book Fund for its publishing
activities.

This book has been published with the help of a grant from the Federation
for the Humanities and Social Sciences, through the Awards to Scholarly
Publications Program, using funds provided by the Social Sciences and
Humanities Research Council of Canada.

Contents

Acknowledgments

Many wonderful people have crossed my path in the process of research-ing and writing this book, but I want to begin by acknowledging the members of the Ontario Women's Institutes who were the first ones to encourage me to study Madge Watt. It all began while I was writing the centennial history of the Ontario Women's Institutes in the early 1990s, and WI members, with their continued interest in this project, have been a constant encouragement. Exchanging emails with Mary Janes, Margaret Eberle, and Marion Egerter helped me to remember that there were readers eagerly waiting to hold this book in their hands, even after all these years. Women of the WI are masters of networking, and my Ontario contacts soon branched over to other provinces. It was the women of the BCWI who initiated the move to have Madge Watt recognized as a person of national historical significance, and I was pleased to accept their invitation to be part of their centennial celebra-tions in Duncan, BC, in 2008. Beyond the provincial WIs, I found many more cheerleaders for this project among the national networks of the Federated Women's Institutes of Canada.

When I attended a triennial conference of the Associated Country Women of the World in Tasmania in 2004, I was graciously welcomed to the gathering and encouraged in my work by Hilda Stewart, the ACWW world president at the time. Hilda personally went through some of the ACWW records in the London office to see what she could find for me, and I am grateful for her generosity to me. It was in Hobart where I had the great good fortune to begin my friendship with Bethan Williams, a WI member from Wales. Bethan deserves special thanks for all that she has done for me, including putting important sources into my hands, introducing me to her friends (especially Audrey Jones), playing tour guide through North Wales, and being a tireless promoter for this project, calling attention to it with unflagging enthusiasm through her WI contacts in the UK and ACWW circles in Europe. Like everyone else with an interest in the history of the WI in the UK, I owe a huge debt of gratitude to Anne Stamper for her work in organizing and depositing the records of the National Federation of Women's Institutes in the Women's Library in London. Anne has been very generous with me in our correspondence, and it was a delight to finally meet her in person and spend a day together at Denman College.

I am grateful for the funding that made this project possible. The Social Sciences and Humanities Research Council of Canada provided me with a general research grant from 2003 to 2006. Without it, I could not have funded the student research assistants or the ambitious travel schedule that gave me opportunities for archival research across Canada and in the United States, the UK, and Australia. That funding also meant that I could attend conferences and present my work-in-progress to academic colleagues. Laurentian University Research Fund also provided important funds to prepare for the initial SSHRC grant and to bring the project to completion. I want to thank Len Husband at University of Toronto Press and the anonymous reviewers who read the manuscript and made insightful suggestions. It was a pleasure to work with Catherine Plear, whose skilled copy-editing work made this a better book.

A helpful librarian or archivist can be a historian's best friend. In the course of this project, many enthusiastic archivists and record keepers have proven to be important friends to me and to this project. Ashley Thomson, of the Laurentian University library, is the most enthusiastic librarian I have ever met, and I still remember my conversation with him on the day I first became convinced that Madge's life was worthy of much more than a short entry in the *Dictionary of National Biography*. Staff members at the Collingwood Public Library (along with local history and genealogy enthusiasts there) were pleased to help me trace the Robertson family history through their resources, as were the helpful folks at the Simcoe County Archives, the Meaford Public Library, and the Grey Roots Museum and Archives in Owen Sound. The staff of the Collingwood Museum, especially Anita Miles, Melissa Shaw, and Susan Warner, were most helpful, not only as they gave me access to the records I knew I would want to consult, but especially for bringing to my attention the ones I didn't even know existed. I will never forget that phone call from the museum in the summer of 2003 telling me that they had just uncovered a scrapbook belonging to the Robertson family and they thought I should have a look at it. What a find! Time spent at the University of Toronto Archives and in the Robarts Library reading the *Varsity* to piece together important clues about Madge and Alfred's student days was pleasant work indeed. At the Archives and Records Office of the Presbyterian Church in Canada, Kim Arnold and Bob Anger helped me to find the sources I needed to understand Bethia Robertson's work with the church's missionary society.

In the summer of 2001 I worked in the archives of the New York State College of Home Economics, housed in the Carl A. Kroch Library at Cornell University in Ithaca. There I was happy to find correspondence that led to a more complete understanding of Watt's relationships with Flora Rose and Ruby Green Smith as well as the infamous misunderstandings that surrounded Watt's plan to move the ACWW to America for the duration of World War Two. At the time of my visit, the Cornell library was hosting an exhibit on the history of home economics that made me think about the broader context of Watt's work with rural women.

The Women's Library (now at the London School of Economics) holds the records of the NFWI, and while I worked on this project, it was housed at the Metropolitan University in London in a wonderful facility. The staff there were a terrific help, especially Vicky Wylde, who first brought several Madge Watt photographs to my attention. I returned to that pleasant reading room on Old Castle Street, Aldgate, London, on several occasions during the life of this project, but the most unforgettable visit was in July 2005 when the staff in that reading room literally encouraged all of us to "keep calm and carry on" as the sirens roared outside during the second interruption that month to the London transit system.

In BC, the University of Victoria Archives and BC Archives were treasure troves of records with multiple clues about Madge's many activities as an elite member of Victoria's influential social network. In a serendipitous turn of events, I had the good fortune to visit inside the walls of the William Head Institution, and I am grateful to David Clouston, assistant warden, for granting me access to the site and its archives. The day I spent "on the inside" becoming familiar with the grounds and the records of the quarantine station, now a federal penitentiary, was unforgettable. On that same visit to the Metchosin area, Daisy and Johnny Bligh were gracious hosts and advisors about the local history and community where the Watts had lived nearby to the quarantine station.

I have been blessed by the assistance of several capable and congenial research assistants through the life of this project. Their professionalism and camaraderie have been a source of encouragement, and as they have gone on to graduate studies, careers, and other adventures, they have remained friends, and I have followed their successes with pride and interest. I want.to thank: Heather Barkey-Laing, Lee-Ann Fielding, Kristin Hall, Kristin Ireland, Debra Mann, Kathryn McLeod, Stephanie McPherson, and Tanya Touhimaa. Leda Culliford was a supportive writing coach whose advice made the manuscript better. Kristin Hall became a collaborator, and publishing an article with her was a highlight of this process. Rosemary Ambrose tracked down several important details and documents about the Robertson and Watt families as only a skilled genealogist could do. As the project was wrapping up, I received an email from Madge Watt's great niece in Australia, Helen Geissinger, and it was a joy for me to finally make contact with a member of Madge's extended family when I thought there were no relatives still living. I hope this biography helps you to understand your famous aunt a little more fully.

Laurentian University's history department has provided me with a great academic home, and I have great colleagues there. In particular, I thank my good friends Joel Belliveau, Amélie Bourbeau, Matt Bray, Sara Burke, Guy Gaudreau, Mark Kuhlberg, Dave Leeson, Janice Liedl, Andrew Smith, and Todd Webb. My friend and colleague, Sara Burke, deserves special mention because she generously agreed that while she was doing her own work on co-education at the University of Toronto Archives, she would have an initial look at the press-clipping files there to see what they might hold about Madge Robertson and Alfred Watt. Her find alerted me to the nature of Dr. Watt's tragic death and set me on a whole new course of inquiry. Rose-May Demoré is at the heart of our department, and how we would ever manage without her I cannot fathom. When I was department chair, she not only helped me manage the department's affairs, but also encouraged me to guard the time I needed for research and writing. I also have a very special bond with two other women at LU: Linda Brisson and Carole Germain-Chiswell, with whom I worked very closely in 2008–9. Their laughter is like good medicine to me. The other source of inspiration for continuing momentum on this project has been my colleagues in the Laurentian writing group, with whom I have spent many pleasant hours in coffee shops and cafés writing, revising, and editing this manuscript. Our academic disciplines are various, but we have shared lots of time on many different writing projects, discussion about the episodes of academic life, and sometimes just knitting. Thank you to all those writing friends, but especially the regulars: Kristin Hall, Alicia Hawkins, Gina Comeau, Joel Belliveau, Shelley Watson, and our former colleague, Alexis Shotwell, who helped the group to launch in the first place. Margaret Kechnie, recently retired from Thorneloe University, also a historian who has studied the Women's Institutes, is my friend and collaborator. Over the years ever since I first moved to Sudbury, she has been my pleasant travel companion, friendly debater, and wise mentor. I want to thank Margaret for the laughter, the hospitality, and for the trailblazing that she did for me and so many other women coming after her at Laurentian.

Friends and family have been my constant supporters through the many years that I have lived with the Madge project. Some of my dear friends who heard more than their share of my Madge adventures include Valerie Carlson, Debra Humbert, and Rod and Sharon Koski, and the Wednesday night gang. I appreciate how you always listened patiently with interest through the ups and downs of this project. Gordon and Rosemary Ambrose are wonderful second parents and they have been tireless in their support as I recounted my research adventures and the tales and details of academic life. Moreover, they have always made me feel like a daughter, and I am thankful to have them in my life. My own mother, Doreen McGuire, has my great respect. She made so many sacrifices for me, and though it seems that my world is so different from hers, we have a very special bond. Her support and love mean the world to me.

My children, Meredith and Meghan, grew up with Madge. Or so it seems. As this project stretched out through their years at secondary school and university, they became accustomed to my periodic absences when I went away because of Madge. But there were perks of shared travel adventures too: from the gorges of Ithaca, New York, to the historic sights of London, retracing Madge's steps sometimes led to great family adventures. As the project drew to a close, Chad and Garnet joined our family, and shortly after, Jaedyn Elizabeth, Avah Hazel Jean, and Benjamin Robert arrived. Now, as we all wait to meet Baby H, these lovely little people are filling us all with unspeakable joy. I thank each of you for your encouragement and love and for always reminding me about what really matters most.

Rob has always believed in me and supported me with his constant encouragement and love. There are definite advantages for a historian like me to live with an IT expert like him, and several times Rob rescued me from the kind of computer glitches that can be terrifying to a writer. His constant companionship is a delight, and we have shared many happy travel adventures that began around the Madge project but ended up as unforgettable memories. After more than thirty years you are still the love of my life, and every day I feel thankful and blessed because of you.

A portion of chapter 3 was published as Linda M. Ambrose, "Quarantine in Question: The 1913 Investigation at William Head, B.C.," *Canadian Bulletin of Medical History/Bulletin canadien d'histoire de la medicine* 22, 1 (2005): 139–54; portions of chapter 2 and 3 were published as Linda M. Ambrose and Kristin Hall, "A New Woman in Print and Practice: The Canadian Literary Career of Madge Robertson Watt, 1890–1907," *History of Intellectual Culture* 7, 1 (2007): 1–19; and part of chapter 3 was published as Linda M. Ambrose, "The New Woman in Rural British Columbia: Madge Robertson Watt and the Women's Institutes, 1893–1913," *Pacific Northwest Quarterly* 105 (Winter 2013/14): 3–11. Used with permission of the journals.

Sudbury, Ontario
August 2014

A GREAT RURAL SISTERHOOD

Madge Robertson Watt and the ACWW

Framing the Life of Madge Robertson Watt

In the 1980s, one researcher who attempted to write a full-length biography of Madge Robertson Watt gave up in frustration. In her words, "after searching for her life story for about three years and finding very little, one can only think of a high diver who rises in the air, twists, turns, swirls and twirls then disappears into the water with hardly a splash."[1] It is true that despite an impressive literary reputation among her North American contemporaries in the late nineteenth-century world of popular writing, and despite the fact that she went on to become the founding president of one of the world's largest international women's organizations, Madge Watt's name is not at all well known today in Canada or elsewhere. This is surprising because her writing appeared in some very well-known publications including *Vogue*, *Life*, and *Leslie's Weekly*, and one of the organizations she helped to found is the Associated Countrywomen of the World (ACWW), a group that currently has consultative status with the United Nations and represents approximately nine million members in seventy different countries.[2] Given those accomplishments, one would expect that her name might be more widely recognized, but it was not until 2007, after careful research and deliberation, that the Historic Sites and Monuments Board of Canada agreed with a proposal submitted by a group of Women's Institute members from British Columbia that Margaret "Madge" Robertson Watt should be designated as "a person of national significance worthy of commemoration."[3] That official recognition of her historic significance notwithstanding, no complete biography of Watt's life has ever been written. Such a project is long overdue because Watt is significant, not only to Canada, but also to the history of international women's movements.

The metaphor of the diver seems particularly apt for Watt because she skillfully performed many intricate twists and turns during the course of her life (1868–1948), making her story a most interesting one. In a period when co-education was still in its controversial development stage in Canada, she was among the first women to graduate from the University of Toronto, and the first woman to complete a graduate degree (master of arts) there in 1890. After her graduation Robertson worked as a journalist in Toronto and New York, entertaining readers with her quick-witted depictions of the emerging "New Woman." In 1893 she married Dr. Alfred Tennyson Watt; within a few years, he was posted to a British Columbia quarantine station on rural Vancouver Island. There Watt raised two sons, continued her writing career, and began to organize Women's Institutes to help BC's rural women overcome their isolation. After her husband's premature death in 1913, Watt moved to England, where she is credited with establishing the Women's Institute movement in hundreds of rural villages and communities throughout the UK during the First World War. Twenty years later, in 1933, she was named the first world president of the newly formed ACWW. Her role in bringing international rural women together in a global cooperative effort is an important part of Canadian women's history that deserves to be told; it is on the strength of this claim that the Historic Sites and Monuments Board of Canada agreed to commemorate her historical significance. Madge Watt's wider significance lies in the fact that she was a transitional character who represented a number of emerging trends in the early twentieth century: While she embraced the ideal of the New Woman, she firmly maintained a great emphasis on respectability and conventionality. She was a proud Canadian with unabashed loyalty to the Empire. She is known for exporting a Canadian idea to the mother country – Women's Institutes, an organization for rural women, which she succeeded in transplanting to England and Wales. Her unwavering commitment to internationalist ideals meant that she tirelessly promoted worldwide collaborations among rural women, yet on a personal level, she was a frustratingly uncooperative co-worker and a surprisingly relentless self-promoter.

Reaching a consensus on an accepted interpretation of any historical subject is a complex process, but in the case of Madge Watt, the problem is magnified because sources about her life and work are so fragmented and scattered that it seems her life's performance ended like that of a skilled diver, barely making a splash in the pool of history. As this book project has demonstrated, reconstructing Watt's life has been a time-consuming task. There is no central collection of her personal papers because, as a Women's Institute researcher noted, "Madge was not a gatherer";[4] gathering sources about her, therefore, was an important first step. While she did not amass sources in one central place, she certainly spawned a great number of them, and evidence of her involvements can be found in a surprisingly large number of locations. Over a ten-year period of research, I traced her activities, and in the process, I covered a lot of territory that involved travel both within Canada and internationally. I began in the local public library and museum in Watt's hometown of Collingwood, Ontario, where town records, genealogical files, and a family scrapbook were consulted.

In Toronto, Ontario, the alumni records, the student newspaper, and press clippings in the archives of the University of Toronto provided important clues about Watt's student days and subsequent career. Collecting an extensive file of Madge Robertson Watt's publications involved piecing together the clues from the family scrapbook, collections in the Library and Archives of Canada, newspaper microfilm, and extensive online searches through digitized newspapers and periodicals where her short stories and columns appeared. Time spent in British Columbia included research at the provincial archives in Victoria, where the records of the British Columbia Women's Institute and the Provincial Advisory Board on Women's Institutes were consulted, and at the University of Victoria Archives, where records of the local chapter of the University Women's Club revealed that Watt was a charter member. While in BC I also made an unexpected site visit to the former William Head quarantine station which houses archival records from the period when Watt's husband was the federal inspector of quarantine. The National Archives of Canada include papers from the Federated Women's Institutes of Canada, and within them there is a surprising amount of material about Watt and her work with the ACWW. While Watt left no personal diaries or journals behind, one of her personal assistants during the 1930s was none other than Elizabeth Smart, who later became a very well-known author. Smart kept a daily record of her travels when she accompanied Watt on their world tour, and as a result, the Smart papers at Library and Archives Canada in Ottawa provide rare glimpses into that part of Watt's life and personality.

Throughout this project, I have enjoyed the wonderful privilege of extensive international travel, and the research adventures that unfolded abroad have proven to be an indispensable part of the process of gathering materials and reconstructing Watt's story. One of the highlights of the research process was a series of trips to the UK, where I spent several weeks in the pleasant surroundings of the Women's Library in London poring over the records of the National Federation of Women's Institutes (NFWI) while digging for clues about Watt's role in establishing the British WI and the ACWW. On one of those occasions, in 2008, I was graciously hosted by members of the Welsh WI, who treated me to afternoon tea in the WI hall at Llanfairpwll, Isle of Anglesey, where the very first WI in the UK was established in 1915. On that same occasion, we took a whirlwind tour of historic sites throughout northern Wales that helped me to understand the context of Watt's early work there. Four years earlier I had the unforgettable experience of speaking with dozens of members of the ACWW when I shared a week with them during their 2004 triennial convention in Tasmania. Meeting those women gathered in the city of Hobart from literally dozens of countries around the world, I gained a whole new appreciation for the legacy that Watt left behind through her vision of providing an international network for rural women. A visit to the Cornell University Archives in Ithaca, New York, helped me to piece together Watt's attempt to relocate the offices of the ACWW to North America during the Second World War. Gathering the materials from all these varied locations included visits to local libraries, museums, and community halls and time spent in university, provincial, and national archives in Canada, the United States, and the United Kingdom. The scope of those travels serves to reinforce not only the fact that Watt had an amazingly wide influence, but also underscores the level of detective work that was necessary in order to track down the details of both her public and private lives.

After overcoming the hurdle of locating the sources, the task of trying to make an interpretation of Watt's life still presented an incredibly challenging task because of the conflicting views that exist about her and the significance of her work. To members of the Canadian Women's Institutes, she is a hero who is credited with almost single-handedly establishing a remarkable network of rural women's organizations worldwide; indeed, to Canadians, her work in Britain can be seen (and celebrated) as a kind of reverse colonialism because she successfully transported the idea of the WI to England and Wales, and that made-in-Canada model played a significant role not only in spreading the gospel of women's organizations, but also in assisting the mother country to win the Great War. To others, particularly historians of the British Women's Institutes and the Associated Country Women of the World, she is commemorated as a nationally historically significant figure, worthy of inclusion in the *Dictionary of National Biography*[5] because of the significant work she conducted among rural women. Yet those who worked closely with her also remember her as a difficult personality who enjoyed the limelight but was really only one player among many when it came to the leadership of rural women. Therefore those in the UK who know about Watt's contributions usually recognize them in a more muted manner than do her admirers in Canada.

The fact that Watt worked on both sides of the Atlantic means that her life story must be understood in the context of the history of imperialism. Historians Phillip Buckner and R. Douglas Francis argue that World War One "strengthened rather than weakened a sense of imperial identity among those who served on both the overseas and the home front and reinforced the belief in the existence of a British world."[6] Madge Watt was among those for whom the Great War strengthened commitment to the Empire and contributed to what Buckner has called "the long goodbye" in Canada's imperial relations.[7] Watt's role as a colonial woman who founded the British Women's Institutes based on a "made-in-Canada" model makes her of particular interest in that ongoing discussion. It is useful to remember that Watt's life and work sprang from the same milieu that gave rise to groups like the Imperial Order Daughters of the Empire, who were motivated by what Katie Pickles describes as "female imperialism."[8] As one of the earliest university-educated women in Canada, Watt subscribed to feminist ideals, albeit conservative ones, and she was an enthusiastic imperialist, but what set her apart from her contemporaries was her ongoing work among rural women. Adele Perry points out that "one of the enduring lessons of what is being dubbed 'the new imperial history' is surely the importance of the local and particular,"[9] and one could argue that the history of particular individuals is an important part of that undertaking. By looking at the lives of transitional colonial women like Madge Watt, one is reminded that not only did imperialism have an enduring appeal for Canadians, but also the nature of how the imperial/colonial relationship operated was "rarely in an uncomplicated fashion."[10]

Biographies of women have received increasing attention from scholars as the field of women's history has expanded over the past forty years.[11] Carolyn Heilbrun's ruminations about feminist approaches to biography address the problem of writing about women who, like Margaret Watt, were privileged. Surprisingly, perhaps, Heilbrun's feminist instincts did not lead her to abandon exploring the lives of such women. Instead, she suggests that like those privileged women in the past, feminist historians of today "should make use of our security, our seniority, to take risks, to make noise, to be courageous, to become unpopular."[12] This model provides a useful theoretical framework for the biography of Margaret Watt. As a privileged woman, Watt occupied some very unorthodox roles, not only as a university student and journalist before such experiences were common to women, but also later in her life, when in widowhood she was recognized for her leadership among rural British women during World War One. Later, she was celebrated because her dream of creating an international organization for rural women was realized in her lifetime.

While biography has always been a popular form of historical writing for the general reader, recently there has been a renewed interest in biography among academic historians and in biographies of women in particular.[13] Biographies of women tend to fall into three different categories of approach. First, a biographer might take up the individual achievement of a woman, as Elisabeth Griffith did when she wrote the life of Elizabeth Cady Stanton. That book, which Griffith herself described as "unabashedly a 'great woman biography,'" employs a psychological approach known as "social learning theory," to trace out the early influences that shaped Stanton into the famous crusader for women's rights that she became.[14] Debates rage over the value and the reliability of psychoanalytical biography, and while there is no question that a psychological approach to Watt would be fascinating, because she left no diaries or journals behind, it is virtually impossible for any biographer to do for her what Griffith did for Stanton. Moreover, while it is important to continue our task of adding women to the record of our national histories, and while the case can be made that Watt's accomplishments are commendable and her life was extraordinary in many ways, the value of the "great woman" approach to history is limited. Beyond her impressive list of accomplishments, there is a complexity to Madge Watt that would be left untold if one approached her life story by concentrating solely on aspects of her "greatness" or limited the tale simply to the celebratory elements of her life.

A second way to approach biography is to emulate what Barbara Tuchman called for when she argued that biography at its best provides a "prism" through which to gain new perspectives on the political and social history that formed the context and backdrop of the subject's life; a synthesis as it were, of good narrative and careful contextualization.[15] As the biographer's light is cast on Madge Robertson Watt, the refraction that emerges brings rich colour to a broad spectrum of themes because her life touches many different aspects of Canadian women's history that provide the context for her experiences. These include the history of co-education; the establishment of Canadian writers and publishers; the roles and definitions of the "New Woman" at the turn of the twentieth century; the social dynamics between urban and rural communities; the establishment and spread of Canadian rural women's organizations; the enduring place of imperialism in Canadian society in the first half of the twentieth century; and the transnational exchanges that occurred among international women's organizations created in the interwar years. With that list (and there are probably others), Tuchman's "prism" metaphor seems to be a particularly effective way to examine Watt's life.

Biography that draws upon the work of historians influenced by cultural theorists provides a third useful approach. Several Canadian historians have explored how historical heroes are made and remade through a series of reinterpretations that prove useful to those who commemorate them. Cecilia Morgan has examined the textual portrayals of a Canadian heroine, Laura Secord, in order to better understand how Secord had been made and remade, going from "profound obscurity, to mythological heroine, to questionable woman, to symbol for a movement."[16] Norman Knowles's study of the Ontario Loyalists and Alan Gordon's study of Jacques Cartier are two more examples of the same idea; that is, that history is often written to reflect and serve the needs of the present.[17] Although Margaret Robertson Watt is not as well known as Secord, the Loyalists, or Cartier, there certainly are parallels: within rural women's circles, Watt has been variously recast as a symbol for the international rural women's movement. Therefore, this so-called "new biography" approach seems particularly appropriate for the present study. In her book, *The New Biography: Performing Femininity in Nineteenth-Century France*, Jo Burr Margadant asserts that

> the subject of biography is no longer the coherent self but rather a self that
> is performed to create an impression of coherence or an individual with
> multiple selves whose different manifestations reflect the passage of time,
> the demands and options of different settings, or the varieties of ways that
> others seek to represent that person.[18]

This approach to biography is clearly informed by cultural theorists' attention to the idea of self-representation, and specifically by Judith Butler's gender theory of the performed self.[19]

The idea of the performed self is an appropriate and useful approach for a study of Madge Robertson Watt because, as Margadant suggests, Watt is a prime example of "an individual with multiple selves," and the various ways that she cast herself into different roles seemed to depend very much on her current context and circumstances. Ever conscious of the demands and options that faced her in any given phase of her life, she responded to her circumstances by making choices and adjusting her personae to capitalize on the opportunities that presented themselves to her. Not all of those circumstances were pleasant ones; as we shall see, in at least two instances the death of a very close loved one was the critical event that catapulted her into an entirely new set of circumstances as she chose to relocate and remake herself once again. Her choices did not always achieve the goals she hoped for, as her experiences during World War Two demonstrate, and yet even then, at one of the lowest points of her professional life, she did not admit defeat but instead rallied to exert her influence in ways that she thought would benefit her cause and her reputation. That tenacity of spirit can be variously understood: either as a remarkable mix of adaptability, endurance, and optimism, or as a frustratingly stubborn refusal to accept reality, admit defeat, and bow out gracefully.

Watt occupied a variety of roles during her lifetime and consciously remade her image numerous times. It comes as no surprise then that those who have reflected on her life and her achievements have arrived at different conclusions. As Canadian pride in Watt's accomplishments demonstrates, national myth-making is a factor in this process of attaching meaning to her life, and so too is the process of creating an "imagined community." At certain points in her life, and in certain circles, Watt cast herself as a rural woman, a vulnerable widow with two small sons who could relate to the rural "everywoman" facing isolation and the accompanying challenges of country living. At other times Watt highlighted her university education, her successful and lucrative publishing career, and her extensive social networks as a clubwoman. The representation seemed to depend upon the message that needed to be communicated.

Indeed, there is a chameleon-like quality to Watt which makes her difficult to pin down, in part because of the distinct stages of her life and the various roles she played, but even more so because of the competing representations that have been constructed, both by her and about her. In attempting to trace her life, it is quite likely that those who know about one phase of her experiences might find the other parts almost unrecognizable. Growing up in a small town in southern Ontario, she also lived for a time in New York City, but seemed to be equally at home in rural parts of Vancouver Island, where she lived for twenty years, albeit with frequent and sometimes extended visits to the provincial capital, where she enjoyed the comforts and attractions that city life in Victoria could offer, such as the famed Empress Hotel. When she lived in England, she enjoyed a similar melding of urban and rural existence, making her home in rural Sussex but also spending time in London, where she frequently travelled for business meetings.

The story of Madge Watt's life belongs in the context of the literature on rural women's history, in particular sources that deal with rural women's organizations. It was while she lived in British Columbia as a wife, mother, socialite, and author that she first cast herself as a "rural" woman concerned for the women who were living in isolation without access to good reading materials, regular social interaction, or continuing educational opportunities. As academic historians have also taken up the subject of rural women's organizations, the literature has become rich.[20] In western Canada, studies such as those of Carol Dennison in British Columbia have explored how these rural groups can be understood in the context of the social reform efforts that so many urban women took up at the turn of the century. Catherine Cole and Ann Milovic in Alberta and Georgina Taylor in Saskatchewan have considered the appeal of these female groups for women's community organizational efforts and their own social and emotional needs. In Quebec, Gail Cuthbert Brandt and Naomi Black have compared rural women's associations with those in France, while Yolande Cohen has explored women's motivations for their involvement with groups known as the Cercles de Fermières. In Ontario, Margaret Kechnie's work has concentrated on the government's role up to 1919 in encouraging the formation of the early Women's Institutes of Ontario. She argues that the membership of the Women's Institutes included many small-town women, not just farm women, and that the provincial government hoped to use the WI to curb rural depopulation by imposing middle-class values on rural women. My own work takes a woman-centred approach to explore how women used these rural organizations for personal development, educational opportunities, and community organization.

The study of rural women's organizations like the Women's Institutes and Homemaker Clubs is quite closely associated with explorations of domestic science instruction, such as the work of Ruby Heap,[21] because that was one of the key emphases of the groups, both here in Canada and abroad. The fact that they focused so much attention on improved homemaking skills might lead to the conclusion that these groups were anything but feminist. However, Monda Halpern and Louise Carbert challenge that view, each arguing that rural women's groups should indeed be considered feminist in their orientation because of the economic and legal issues they championed and the forum they provided for farm women to make their voices heard.[22] The life of Madge Watt clearly reinforces these interpretations because throughout her life and work with rural women, she concentrated on promoting female empowerment, but she did so within the forum of socially conservative groups like the Women's Institutes, the organization that British historian Maggie Andrews has characterized as "the acceptable face of feminism."[23]

Not only was Watt a rural organizer; she was also an accomplished author, and her published writing also reflects the nimble way in which she occupied a variety of roles. Her first publications appeared while she was a coed at the University of Toronto from 1886 to 1890 writing under the pen name of "Greta" in both the campus and the city papers. After her graduation, from 1890 to 1893, she launched a successful writing career, publishing a variety of works in Toronto and New York, even spending some time as the editor of a widely read weekly women's newspaper at a time when women rarely climbed to the position of editor, and certainly not at such a young age. After her marriage, she continued to sell her writing to a number of publishers and became a literary reviewer, writing from her rural home on Vancouver Island in British Columbia. When she moved to England, her writing took the form of speeches and papers delivered to audiences of rural women in Canada, the United States, Britain, and beyond, and were designed to encourage them in their domestic work and their organizational lives. In leadership with the ACWW, her dynamic public speaking skills were continually noted, and she was instrumental in encouraging the publication of reports about rural women's groups worldwide, so that the far-flung members of the organization could learn about each other's activities.[24]

There is a pattern to Watt's life that has a familiar core of privilege and activism. Invariably, she worked from a position of privilege and most often she used her influence to argue for and work on behalf of groups of women that she cared about, women with whom she had close associations and whom she felt were misunderstood or disadvantaged in some way. When she was a student, for example, she used her excellent writing and speaking skills to defend female students at a time and place when co-education was not yet widely accepted. As a single woman, she published her views about women's roles in the pages of widely read magazines, most often using humour and a folk-like charm to disarm critics and argue for women's rights to education, paid work, and a sense of empowerment in their relationships, all the while straddling a fine and subversive line between Victorian propriety and emerging modern notions about new womanhood. When she took up the task of organizing rural women's clubs, first in British Columbia and then in Britain during World War One, she divided her time between influencing policy makers through her role as a member of the British Columbia Provincial Advisory Committee, often taking afternoon tea with dignitaries at Government House or the Empress Hotel in Victoria, and visiting remote rural communities. In England she enjoyed life in the commodious setting of her friend's country home in Sussex, which provided her a base from which she mixed with elite women, and she frequently travelled to London, where she strategized with and reported to the national leaders of the Women's Institutes. Her itinerary, however, also took her on a marathon of travels to hundreds of rural communities throughout the English and Welsh countrysides, where she was a much-loved leader and an inspiring speaker who motivated countless rural women to organize around their common interests.

With a strong sense of her own accomplishments and pragmatic about where her credentials could take her, Watt proudly displayed the letters MA, MBE after her name. On the strength of those designations, she moved in two worlds at the same time: that of urban privilege and titles, and that of rural women living in isolation who would benefit from the groups she promoted. Both in Canada and in Britain, she used her connections to people with money and influence to take her place at the tea tables of the rich and influential who had the power to make the changes and to establish the organizations she envisioned. She also, however, drank her share of tea in much more humble circumstances (and sometimes in very distant ones as she travelled the globe), while comparing notes and personal experiences with rural women about raising children, keeping bees, tending gardens, raising livestock, and overcoming the obstacles that country living posed for them.

The fact that Watt had associations with rural organizations for women beyond her own countries makes her life of particular interest to the emerging comparative international literature on rural women. In the United States, researchers associated with the Rural Women's

Studies Association who turn their attention to farm and rural women's organizations suggest that useful comparative work should be done between American organizations such as those operated by the various state extension services and their Canadian counterparts such as the provincial Women's Institutes. Agricultural historian Dorothy Schwieder has researched the Iowa State University Extension Service, and as a senior American scholar, she suggests that useful collaboration on these themes is overdue. Other American scholars such as Mary Neth, Deborah Fink, and Debra Reid have studied state farm women's groups and concluded that the tension between state policymakers and grassroots participants is a useful line of inquiry.[25] Deborah Stiles, at the Agricultural Campus of Dalhousie University in Truro, Nova Scotia, is making links between rural women in that province and those in Kentucky.[26] Kate Hunter from New Zealand, Margreet van der Burg from the Netherlands, and Elizabeth Teather from Australia, all of whose works concentrate on the countrywomen's groups in those countries, have also suggested that it is time for more comparative work to be done that crosses national borders.[27]

In answer to these calls for comparative work, a biographical study of Watt is a logical place to begin because of her involvement in Canada, the United States, and Britain. A fuller understanding of Watt's life story expands upon previously published discussions of her role, such as the popular version published by Mrs. Neve Scarborough in the 1953 official history of the ACWW. My biography of Watt considers and contextualizes the competing versions of Watt's contributions. It also provides important clues about the early years of cooperative effort as international rural women's groups began to seek formal affiliation and create their own association.

Leila Rupp has written about the history of transnational women's organizations, giving attention to the period from the first-wave women's movement until the Second World War. Rupp set out to explore "how women committed to internationalism forged bonds not only despite but in fact through conflict over nearly every aspect of organizing."[28] Rupp's work, like that of Julia Bush, Angela Woollacott, and others, raises important questions about participation in these organizations by privileged women whose concerns about class, race, and Empire dominated.[29] Madge Watt moved in those circles of privilege, but as we shall see, she was not typical of other elite women because she did not enjoy great personal wealth like most of the others. Moreover, her efforts to encourage women to mingle across the boundaries of class, particularly in the British countryside, are noteworthy. By focusing on Watt's work among rural women, her story brings attention to a previously untold aspect of the history of international women's groups.

The life of Margaret Robertson Watt is a story best told in two parts, with 1913 marking a critical divide between her early years in Canada and her later work in England and other areas. This biography is organized into a series of chapters that reflect the roles that she played at various stages of her life. We begin with an exploration of her early years. Chapter one, entitled "Formative Years: Family Influences and University Life," argues that her family of origin provides important clues that help to explain how young Madge was shaped for her later experiences by her parents and their various civic and church activities. Madge Robertson was immersed in a family that prided itself on demonstrating middle-class propriety; observing her parents take their places in a variety of public roles in her hometown, she learned early on that leadership roles in fraternal organizations and mission circles lent not only an air of respectability but opportunities for great influence. Hailing from that prosperous middle-class family, Madge Robertson enjoyed the unusual privilege of a university education when the idea of women attending postsecondary institutions was still a novelty in late nineteenth-century Ontario. She took up her role as a "coed" with great enthusiasm, entered fully into campus life, and distinguished herself from other female students by becoming the first among them to be granted a graduate degree from the University of Toronto in 1890.

After her graduation from the provincial university, Robertson at first followed a path that was not uncommon to single women in the period, trying her hand at school teaching. While the sources are not entirely clear about the reasons she did not pursue that path for a longer period, after only one year she abandoned the school-teacher role. She then made the decision to follow her passion for writing, and as a young woman with notable literary talent, she quickly established herself as a popular author who enjoyed some extraordinary experiences as a female journalist in Toronto and New York. That work, which included the rare opportunity to edit a popular weekly women's paper with a circulation of more than 25,000 readers, is the subject of chapter two, "Scripting the New Woman: Writer and Editor." In the absence of personal papers from this period of her life, her published works provide an opportunity to explore the ideas and values that she shared with her readers and the role of social commentator that she occupied as a journalist. Her writing reflects the fact that Robertson was very much a product of her times, as she explored a variety of "New Woman" themes, promoting feminist ideas about women's emerging roles in education, sports, and paid work, and arguing that women should not be passive in their personal relationships. With a sharp wit, she used her columns and short stories to feed her readers a steady diet of these progressive ideas, and there are several indications that much of her writing was highly autobiographical.

Some of Madge Robertson's favourite literary topics were romance, engagement, and marriage, and after three years of making her living as a journalist, she married a man she had first met during their university years in Toronto. By the time of her marriage to Alfred Tennyson Watt in December 1893, he had established a successful medical practice in Victoria, BC, and the couple made their home in that province for the next twenty years. Chapter three, "Playing Multiple Parts: Family, Society, and Sorrow," explores how Madge Watt continued her writing career and added the titles of socialite, wife, mother, and activist to her expanding repertoire of roles. From the beginning of their marriage the Watts' stature in Victoria's elite circles meant that they enjoyed a very active social life, and their activities were regularly featured in the society columns of the local newspaper. While she was keeping a very busy schedule with women's groups, cultural activities, alumni association, and press club, her husband accepted a government appointment as the medical inspector of quarantine for British Columbia at William Head, BC. In that isolated setting outside Victoria, Watt got her first taste of country living. She entered into the pleasures of living in the countryside, raising her sons, tending to her gardens, making preserves, and continuing her avid reading and writing. It was in that idyllic environment that Watt first cast herself as "rural," although her financial security, material comforts, and continued frequent visits to the city (sometimes for extended stays) meant that she was hardly living the life of a typical Canadian farm woman. Nevertheless, from her home near Metchosin, BC, Watt caught a vision of what she could bring to rural women throughout the province, and she took a leading role in establishing numerous branches of the Women's Institutes.

Madge Watt's ideal life was shattered in the summer of 1913 with the tragic death of her husband. To escape the national media attention that came in the wake of her husband's highly publicized suicide, she promptly left rural British Columbia to seek a quiet place in which to recover from her shock and get through the grieving process. She was spending time at the country home of her friend in Sussex, England, when war broke out the following summer and she answered the call to serve the Empire. Chapter four, "Role Reversal: From Colonial Widow to Imperial War Hero," explains how, in an act of reverse colonialism, Madge Watt introduced the Canadian idea of Women's Institutes to the United Kingdom, suggesting that if rural women were organized into a systematic scheme for planting victory gardens, the challenge of ensuring a domestic food supply for the duration of the war would be solved. Her ideas were not immediately accepted, but between 1915 and the end of the war, Women's Institutes became an extremely popular phenomenon, and hundreds of local branches were established, due in no small part to Watt's indefatigable travels from county to county. Analyzing how Watt performed in her role as an organizer of rural women, one is struck by the strategies she employed to negotiate her way through the challenges that presented themselves to her in Britain where, even for a Canadian who had great loyalty to the Empire, the cultural differences between her new setting and her homeland were significant.

At the end of the First World War Watt returned to Canada as a Member of the Order of the British Empire (MBE) and received a hero's welcome for her war work. Buoyed up by the success she had seen with her organizational work, and influenced by the spirit of interwar efforts to achieve lasting peace, Watt turned her attention to the possibilities that existed for organizing rural women on an international scale. Chapter five, "On the World Stage: Forging International Networks," begins with Watt's experiences upon her return to Canada in 1919. For a period of two years she travelled extensively in Canada, and although most of the initiatives she personally tried to introduce during that time met with limited success, her time back home gave her the opportunity to observe how WI groups were forging links across great distances to create a Canadian federation. Inspired by that model, she returned to England in 1921 with a renewed confidence that she had a pivotal role to play in bringing rural women together internationally. Watt's efforts reveal that she was working within a broader context of internationalism that was characteristic of the interwar years. She hoped that her personal contacts and enthusiasm for travel would inspire support for her dream of creating a worldwide federation of rural women. Her efforts were frustrated by a series of complications that might have defeated a less determined individual. After Lady Aberdeen offered her support for the idea of an international gathering of rural women, real progress was made, and the Associated Country Women of the World emerged as an offshoot of the

International Council of Women. Watt occupied the office of world president during the early years of ACWW activity when meetings were held on a triennial basis in Stockholm (1933), Washington, DC (1936), and London, England (1939). In that important first decade of the ACWW's existence, Watt made tireless efforts on behalf of the organization, and her dogged determination to promote the work at any cost meant that while her worldwide travels resulted in a legacy of impressive achievements, they also came at the cost of some serious personal misunderstandings and dire financial consequences that crippled the group in the years to come. While she inspired her audiences of rural women, behind the scenes, she was becoming increasingly difficult to work with, and ironically, in her efforts to unite rural women worldwide, she caused some deep divisions within the organization itself.

The conflicts between Watt and her colleagues in the London office of the ACWW were reinforced even further when, in the fall of 1939, she found herself in North America, unable to return to England because of wartime conditions and lack of finances. In an effort to maintain influence despite the physical and social distance that separated her from the other leaders of the organization, Watt proposed that the offices of the ACWW should relocate to New York State, where she planned to run the operation from a temporary location provided by Cornell University. Chapter six, "Sidelined by War: Waning Influence, Denial, and Death" takes up the story of the battle for control of the ACWW and reveals that even in her declining years, Watt still considered herself to be the real leader of the movement. It is difficult to say whether she ever really accepted the fact that she had lost control of the organization that she helped to found; indeed, she carried on with her campaigns as though she was still very much in charge. Of course the real heart of the operation was back in London where, in the midst of bombings and blackouts, her counterparts were struggling to keep the ACWW alive and to help it recover from the precarious financial situation that resulted from Watt's expensive travels and grandiose publishing plans. Her insistence that she was an elder stateswoman because of her experiences with organizing rural women in the previous war creates a sense of déjà vu about the way she attempted to negotiate with government officials for funding to support her efforts, claiming that she had strategies that would help the cause of the allied forces. The war years deepened the misunderstandings on both sides of the ocean and cast a cloud over the legacy of Watt's leadership. Given the fact that the last years of Watt's life were marked by these conflicts, it is not surprising that controversy arose both at the time of her death and afterward on the question of how her memory should be honoured. For her contemporaries, reactions to Watt (both in life and in death) ranged from fondness and admiration on the part of those who respected her accomplishments and found her persuasive speeches inspiring, to frustration and exasperation on the part of those who worked closely enough with her to bear the brunt of her uncompromising tenacity.

Commemorating such a colourful character as Madge Watt is no easy task, nor is it a simple question to answer why her life has historical significance. The final chapter, "Conclusion: Interpreting the Significance of Madge Watt," reveals the challenges that have arisen for Canadian Women's Institute members over three sites of commemoration where historical representations have been made about the meaning of Watt's life and work. How history is packaged and presented for public consumption is a fascinating question, and the life of Madge Watt presents an intriguing case study on how interpretations change over time and how commemorations serve to construct and reinforce particular social meanings. By treating Watt as a historical hero, Canadian rural women have inscribed her life with particular meanings that are relevant to their own organizations.

Beyond the membership of rural women's groups, the significance of Madge Watt's life is tied not only to her leadership in those organizations, but also to her commitment to imperialism and her passion for the internationalist ideal. In each chapter of her story, Watt performed a variety of roles, adding layers to the complexity of her life. Peeling back those layers, the life of Madge Robertson Watt reveals a woman whose experiences shed light on several aspects of Canadian women's history and helps to explain the roots of international women's organizations. In a 1918 talk she gave to train British Women's Institute leaders for their work, Watt urged her listeners to imagine the potential of their collective influence, reminding them that when a rural woman joined an organization such as theirs, she became "a member of a great rural sisterhood, not only here, but all over the Empire."[30] That "great rural sisterhood" was complex and multifaceted, springing up in the context of early twentieth-century transnationalism. Understanding Madge Watt and her international work with women helps us to better understand the rural sisterhood itself.

Chapter One

Formative Years: Family Influences and University Life

"Every social location offers a limited number of possibilities from which individuals can create a possible self."[1] While postmodern biographers make such claims about the ways that individuals consciously and unconsciously make and remake themselves, historians still debate to what extent individuals are shaped by their circumstances and to what extent they shape themselves by accepting and rejecting various influences around them. Either way, one thing is certain: the historic context in which one finds oneself has a bearing on that person.

Growing up as the privileged daughter of a lawyer and a church-woman in Collingwood, Ontario, in the last quarter of the nineteenth century, Margaret Rose Robertson enjoyed certain social advantages. Many influences acted on the young Madge during her early years, but her family experiences and her educational privileges are particularly noteworthy. The Robertson family's status in the town where the young Madge grew up was a formative factor for her, as were her father's municipal and fraternal involvements and her mother's church work and literary pleasures. Moreover, the position that the family enjoyed meant that she benefitted from the rare opportunity of a university education – something only a handful of Canadian women in her cohort would obtain, and something that she was afforded partly because she had no brothers. All these elements acted on the young Miss Robertson as she chose the path she would follow in her life – a path of public involvement, literary pursuits, and global interests.

Margaret Rose Robertson was born on June 4, 1868, in Collingwood, Ontario, a thriving nineteenth-century town located approximately one hundred miles north of Toronto. The local business community indulged in shameless boosterism of their town, promoting the vast potential of this marine community. As the end of the line on the Northern Railway, part of the Grand Trunk railway system, and a key shipping port on the Great Lakes waterway, Collingwood enjoyed a very healthy economy during the second half of the nineteenth century. As one local historian explains, "Collingwood would never have existed as we know it without the railway. The same is true for communities as is true for real estate: location, location, location. Collingwood's location as the terminus of a major rail line resulted in its boom."[2] The railway first came to Collingwood in 1855, when the population of what was then called "Hen and Chickens Harbour" was only about fifty people. This transportation link was an integral part of the town's success in later decades. Three years after the railway's arrival, the town of Collingwood was incorporated, in 1858. The continued growth of its economy relied heavily on revenue generated by the shipyards established there in 1870. By the turn of the century, the population was approximately 5,000, with almost 1,000 employed in shipbuilding.

Collingwood's rapid growth and success were so noteworthy that the town began to be called "the Chicago of the North." The 1893 annual report of the local board of trade claimed that

> [t]o the young man of brains, who possesses a "Push" and a little capital, there is no place on the continent that offers more favorable inducements for business success than Collingwood does, for sooner or later, she will be a grand distributing point for every conceivable kind of manufacture that will be required in the great North West. Examine a map; you will be convinced.[3]

Having examined that map, one young man with "brains, 'push,' and capital" who rose to prominence in Collingwood during this boom time was Henry Robertson, a young lawyer who graduated from the University of Toronto in 1861 and was called to the bar the same year.[4] Robertson was born in 1840 in York County, Ontario, and although sources vary in their estimates about when he actually arrived in Collingwood, it is clear that he was involved in town affairs perhaps as early as 1856.[5] By 1872, the promoters' predictions about how well a young man might do for himself seemed to have come true for Robertson and his family. As one of the leading families, the Robertsons were at the centre of the local business and social scene. The annual reports of the Collingwood Board of Trade frequently featured the name of Henry Robertson because of the professional, political, and social leadership he lent to his community.

Robertson married Bethia Rose, the third daughter of John Rose of Brantford, Ontario, in 1866, and the couple was living on Maple Street in Collingwood when their first child, Margaret Rose Robertson, was born in 1868. Some time later, they moved to an elegant brick home on Third Street west of Hurontario, which they called "the Struan." Their neighbours included the leading citizens of the town: the chief of police, the police magistrate, the manager of the Bank of Toronto, the town clerk, the mayor, and the president of the board of trade. *The Annual Report of the Collingwood Board of Trade for 1893* suggested that "a short drive, a spin up Third St., westward from Hurontario ... will introduce the tourist to a very handsome part of the town, there being situated along this avenue some the finest private residences in the county; many of them being surrounded with well-kept grounds and velvety lawns." The *Report* also suggested that the grand homes of Third Street, such as that of Henry Robertson, were comprised of "buildings and grounds [that] will give the beholder pleasure to see."[6] Robertson's property was a source of pleasure to passersby on Third Street because of his avid interests in gardening, botany, and birdwatching.

Robertson's social standing meant that he could afford to spend leisure time occupied with a variety of interests, including golf, playing cards, swimming, sailing, bicycling, skating, curling, and strenuous hiking excursions. The coach house on the property housed the family's horses, and the menagerie was completed by the large dogs that also lived at Struan. One of them was a mastiff named Marquis, who was supposed to guard the house. According to local folklore, "When Henry walked down town, he sometimes met Marquis there, the dog having gotten downtown via the back lanes. The dog would not acknowledge his master on these occasions."[7]

Despite this tranquil domestic picture of the prosperity afforded to them through their comfortable middle-class existence, a visit to the local Presbyterian cemetery just outside of town provides a dramatic reminder of the fact that the Robertson family was not immune to the Victorian realities of infant mortality and premature death for women.[8] Henry and Bethia had four children, but only two of them survived past infancy. Madge, christened Margaret Rose, had one sister, Katherine (Katie) Leonora,[9] two years her junior. Madge and Katie had two baby brothers: Frederick, born in 1872, who lived to only two months of age; and Henry, born in 1877, who lived to only eight months of age.

While these tragic losses marked Robertson's private life, he ran a very successful law practice from his main-street office, and there are several indicators of the good fortune he enjoyed in his business life. First, to those arriving in this boom town with less than enough capital, Robertson advertised through the *Gazetteer and Directory of the County of Simcoe, 1872–73* that he had "money to lend."[10] Another sign of the success of his business is the investment he made in 1886, when telephone service first became available in the town: Robertson's law office was one of the first subscribers, appearing on a list of only forty business and residential subscribers.[11] A more enduring sign of success is the fact that Robertson was honoured with the designation of Queen's Counsel.[12] Robertson continued his law practice for a number of years, until the age of sixty-one, when in 1901 the local newspaper announced the creation of a new law firm: "Mr. Hy. Robertson, K.C. has formed a partnership with Mr. E.G. Morris, barrister, of Toronto, and it is expected that Mr. Robertson's already large legal connection will be considerably extended by the addition of new blood. Mr. Morris has already taken up residence in town."[13]

While there is no direct evidence to support the assertion that Robertson worked harder in an effort to forget the sorrow he suffered at the loss of his two sons, there is a great deal of evidence to show that Robertson's public life was very full. When Madge faced personal tragedy later in her own life, it was perhaps her father's model of a busy work life and varied civic involvements that helped her to rebuild her life and go on.

Henry Robertson used his position of privilege in the town for civic purposes, and one of his passions was the library. According to his obituary in the local newspaper, "He always took a warm personal interest in educational matters and was the founder of the Mechanics Institute, now the Public Library, and held the record of being a continuous trustee for 66 years."[14] The library was a source of pride not only for Robertson himself, but also for the town, which boasted in 1893 that after almost forty years of building its collection, "today Collingwood possesses the largest and most useful library of any town in this broad Dominion."[15] Given Henry Robertson's close involvement in supporting his local library, it comes as no surprise that his own family benefited from a growing collection of literature. Bethia Robertson read extensively, and it is very likely that Madge Robertson's love of books and her passion for literature were things she enjoyed with her mother and father from early childhood. As the town's promoters claimed, "This is quite a resort for the young people and is usually well patronized. The fees of membership to the Institute are very small and within the reach of any one."[16] Although money was no object for young Madge, having a wealth of books available to her through this well-appointed library was a definite advantage.

With such civic mindedness it is not surprising that Robertson took on leadership roles in the realm of municipal politics, running for various offices on more than one occasion. Indeed, the list of offices he held, and his attempts to win office, is long and impressive. The family scrapbook records his political forays in detail; a list entitled "Municipal Record [of] H. Robertson,"[17] includes twenty-three occasions between 1864 and 1904 where he ran for office (successfully or not), was appointed or acclaimed to some office, school board, or council.

In his bid to become Mayor in 1889, Robertson published a notice in the local newspaper announcing his candidacy in the upcoming election. He explained that "the growing importance of our Town demands the exercise of the best energy and ability that can be obtained, in order to further its interests and to secure for it all the advantages that its situation calls for." Making his personal plea for votes, he promised that

> [s]hould I be honored with your confidence, I shall try to deserve it to the best of my ability. I am not the candidate of any party or clique, and my aim shall be to act impartially towards all, and to endeavor to have *an honest administration* of the affairs of the Town, with a *due regard to economy* in the management of the public funds. As it will be impossible for me to make a personal canvas, I take this method of requesting your vote and influence on my behalf.[18]

One week later, the published results of the election showed that Robertson won 301 votes, but lost the election to his competitor Andrew Lockerbie, who garnered 404 votes. The total number of votes, 705, was the largest that had ever been polled in Collingwood's history.[19]

Growing up in a political family, even though her father's aspirations were limited to the local level, meant that Madge Robertson understood some of what was involved in campaigning, presenting a public persona, strategizing about networks, and changing course when a chosen path did not lead where one had hoped. While success in local politics proved to be somewhat elusive for her father, Madge Robertson caught his enthusiasm for public life and watched his successes in other fields, particularly his organizational life.

Though his mayoral aspirations were never realized, Robertson was definitely an important figure through his involvement in fraternal organizations, which gained him national recognition. He was an active member of two such organizations in the town of Collingwood: the Freemasons and the Independent Order of Odd Fellows (IOOF). According to the 1887 *Jubilee History of the Town of Collingwood*, when the Freemasons established a branch in Collingwood in 1866, Robertson was elected as an officer, and later went on to hold the highest office in the country when he was elected grand master of the Grand Lodge of Canada two years in a row in 1886 and 1887.[20] At the same time, the Independent Order of Odd Fellows established its local lodge in 1869 with Roberston as one of its officers;[21] again, he rose to occupy the highest office in the Canadian Odd Fellows Lodge in the same period, from 1886 to 1888. As the *Enterprise and Collingwood Messenger* newspaper accurately noted, "Mr. Robertson has been unusually honored by secret societies."[22]

In addition, Robertson wrote a nationally recognized book on the Masonic Lodge, *Masonic Jurisprudence*.[23] Historian Mary Ann Clawson argues that "the Freemasons were the accepted elite of the fraternal world, priding themselves in their venerable traditions, their greater selectivity, and their resistance to the recruiting practices employed by other orders."[24] With his service record and publications, and as a member and grand master of both the Oddfellows and the Masons, Robertson was unquestionably regarded as significant among the elite of Collingwood and the fraternal orders.

When *Masonic Jurisprudence* was published in its second edition in 1889, the *Toronto Empire* claimed that "the former edition of this work has been recognized as a valuable acquisition to Masonic literature of the practical kind outside the Canadian jurisdiction, and it has also been quoted as a standard book of reference on questions involving the written and unwritten laws and landmarks." The Toronto paper went on to say that this publication was a reflection of Robertson's long-time involvement in the organization "and his knowledge of common law [has] enabled him to produce a work of much interest and practical use to members of the craft the world over."[25] The reviewer noted that the Masons owed Robertson "a great debt of gratitude," and suggested that "Mr. Robertson's book should be in the hands of every Mason in Canada."[26]

As the author of the Canadian rulebook for Masons, Robertson occupied a privileged position in the organization. His expertise in civil law prepared him for the detailed work of compiling this authoritative guide for Masons, but his commitment to the core values of the organization was equally important. Historian Lynn Dumenil argues that among Masons, attention to the detail of their written codes was paramount,

> with carefully outlined procedures governing evidence, trials, and appeals. Masons could be tried for a variety of "crimes" – drunkenness, sexual transgression, embezzlement and fraud, atheism, and disobedience to Masters. Leaders constantly reminded Masons to be diligent in using the force of Masonic law to keep the order pure and its reputation spotless.[27]

To maintain the respectability of the Masonic order, legal procedures for the group were very highly valued. The rules that Robertson spelled out in his book for Canadian Masons were absolutely essential in order to uphold standardized practices among the membership.[28] Henry Robertson thus occupied an important position as a gatekeeper for the lodge at the national level. He was the expert to whom all members referred when questions about procedure surfaced. As a result, he was central to maintaining the propriety that Masonic life valued so highly among its membership. The internal codes of discipline, such as those that Robertson documented in his book, "demanded, in effect, a recognition of the lodge's right to define and demand the respectability of its members."[29] By setting those rules down for the membership, Robertson the lawyer became the final authority, in effect judge and jury, for matters of Masonic jurisprudence.

Her father's role in establishing and maintaining respectability was a model that Madge Robertson observed closely in the life of her father's fraternal involvements. His lodge memberships, particularly his Masonic ties, represented a complex package of civic leadership, social control, and status. Robertson himself came to personify the values of the Masonic order, and when he dressed in his formal lodge regalia, his small physical stature was more than compensated for by the weight of authority that he carried. As Dumenil contends, the symbolism of the Masonic rituals and regalia was very rich, and "the square and compass dangling from a watch chain stood for temperance, sobriety, honesty, industry, and self-restraint – it was the Mason's badge of respectability."[30] Henry Robertson represented all these virtues in spades. He was no ordinary Mason, but one of those that Dumenil described as "the most Masonic of Masons."[31] Henry Robertson's elder daughter watched her father as he rose through the ranks of the Masonic lodge, and from him she caught both his love for the symbols and the hierarchy associated with fraternal life, and the authority that came from being a published author and celebrated authority figure.

More than anything else, perhaps, Madge was imbued by her father's value system. Though of a different generation, she shared many of the beliefs that were explicitly expressed by her father and his lodge mates. Among the fragmented family sources that remain, there is much evidence that father and daughter shared a special bond. One of the most telling is the family scrapbook, where he carefully tracked her rising career as a writer and organizer of women. At their core though, both father and daughter valued family and community. When Henry Robertson excelled at his lodge commitments, he was not abandoning his family but expressing his social leadership, extending his fatherly role beyond his own household to that of the community at large.[32]

The Collingwood branches of the lodges, both the Odd Fellows and the Masons, met in the Masonic Temple on the main street of town.[33] During Robertson's time in office, a grand new three-storey Temple building was completed. Reflecting Robertson's twin involvements in both the Masons and the Independent Order of Odd Fellows, the new facility would house both fraternal orders. On an occasion to mark the beginning of construction in May 1890, members of the fraternal orders gathered with visiting dignitaries from across the country. According to the author of *Collingwood: Historic Homes and Buildings*, "the Grand Master of the Oddfellows said the construction of the building 'was evidence of the prosperity of the Order here and would be a benefit and an ornament to the town.'"[34] The local paper reported in October 1890 that "this magnificent building ... adds much to the appearance of the main street and is one of the sights of the town for visitors to see.[35] The new temple was a physical reminder of the historically significant role that the Masons, and indeed Robertson himself, occupied in the town. Robertson's close association with the construction of the Collingwood temple building firmly established the contribution that he was making to the town. Significantly, in the year that Robertson turned fifty, the new temple also marked that Collingwood had reached a certain stature of maturity and stability. Dumenil argues that Masonic temples "stood as imposing symbols of the wealth and permanency of Masonry," and that for members like Robertson, "access to the Masonic Temple, along with the right to participate in Masonic ceremonies and acquisition of Masonic secrets, set a man apart from the outside world."[36] Clearly, Henry Robertson was leaving his mark on the town through the symbol of the Masonic temple.

Historians of gender have been intrigued by the Masonic lodge and the rituals that reinforced a particular kind of masculinity. Tracing out those characteristics, there are four that seem particularly noteworthy: the networking, the gender exclusivity, the commitment to Empire, and the emphasis on toleration and inclusiveness. Madge Robertson observed her father's fraternal involvements continuously, and as she did, she saw certain characteristics of his public life constantly on display. They are worth exploring in some detail because one can see that all four would eventually figure largely in Madge's later involvement with women's organizations.

First, the Masons provided an extensive web of networking. As historian Roger Burt has argued, with the Masonic lodges, "members could exchange information, seek credit, arrange capital movements, organize contracts, find employment, exercise influence, and ensure benevolent support against the unexpected."[37] The networking that Henry Robertson enjoyed because of his Masonic lodge not only gave him connections within the town of Collingwood, but also across the country and, indeed, across the continent.[38] Given her father's strong propensity for this kind of networking, Madge Robertson would later come to duplicate it when she promoted the possibilities that existed for women in creating a web of organizational ties for rural women that would span communities, countries, and oceans.

The second noteworthy characteristic of these fraternal organizations that captured Henry Robertson's time and energy was their gender exclusivity. Some studies of fraternal organizations emphasize how important it was for men at the end of the nineteenth century to have an all-male alternative to the female-dominated spaces that organized religion provided. Clifford Putney, historian of masculinity, argues that "for fraternalists, this female monopoly on virtue proved unacceptable … the lodge hall [was] a male haven for fun, faith, and fellowship. Fraternal ritualism grew to provide what liberal Protestantism lacked: a celebration of the 'male' virtues (strength, courage, etc) …"[39] The inscription on Henry Robertson's own tombstone bears witness to the fact that he valued these male virtues, declaring, "His characteristics were virtue honor mercy."[40] While providing men with an entirely masculine space such as they were not finding in mainline churches by the end of the nineteenth century, Masonry did not enter into competition with religion, instead providing its members with a complementary experience. The Masonic lodges were not overtly religious, but they did insist that members confess a commitment to theism, and they did emphasize a morality congruent with Protestant values.[41] Henry Robertson's lodge was not in competition with his Presbyterian church; rather, his lodge involvement seemed to be a logical extension of what an open-minded Presbyterian man might do: "In the universalist view, then, far from competing with churches, Masonry served them and society by promoting religiosity and taking a firm stand against immorality and atheism."[42]

As Madge Robertson watched her father's life in the lodge with interest, she saw an organization that provided many advantages for men. It was broader than the church, yet not in obvious contravention of or competition with the church. Here was an organizational model that might appeal to women who were looking for something in addition to, or as an alternative to, their traditional church involvements.

A third characteristic of Freemasons' networks was their emphasis on the importance of the British Empire. According to Jessica Harland-Jacobs,

> Freemasonry was one institution that contributed to the development of these intracultural connections in the British Empire. By creating a global network that had both practical functions and ideological dimensions, Freemasonry played a critical role in building, consolidating, and perpetuating the empire.[43]

The fact that the Robertson household was dominated by a concern for the Empire through Henry's involvement with the Masons would prove to be a strong influence on Madge Robertson in the work she would take up on behalf of the Empire during World War One. Long after the formal ties ended, the sense of loyalty to the Empire lived on in the hearts and minds of people like the Robertsons of Collingwood.[44] As we shall see in later chapters, Madge Robertson was explicit about her motivation to serve the Empire during World War I, and that sentiment was in lockstep with Canadian Freemasons like her father.[45]

The fourth characteristic of Freemasonry that had a compelling influence on Madge Robertson was its overt emphasis on toleration and inclusiveness, twin values that she would champion in her later work with rural women the world over. How real that tolerance and inclusiveness really was can be debated, but the rhetoric of it is inescapable. Dumenil notes that while "Masons insisted that their order was committed to the principle of *universality*, [italics in original] ... the fraternity was, in fact, predominantly a white, native, Protestant, middle-class organization."[46]

The implicit contradiction in the Masons' inclusiveness was the irony that while it claimed to be cosmopolitan in outlook, it actually reinforced a British hegemony. In other words, "the Masonic network, it seems, could be global, but not universal."[47] The same could be said for international women's organizations such as those that Rupp has studied.[48] As for the Women's Institutes and the Associated Country Women of the World, a form of inclusiveness, though mostly imagined, was clearly at work in their documents and constitutions, which emphasized that no politics, no class differences, and no exclusion of any kind would be tolerated.

Not only were the Masons mostly composed of those who reinforced British hegemony; they were also well-to-do. Belonging to the Masonic lodge was an expensive pastime. Dumenil addresses this in her study of American Freemasonry, asserting that Masonic exclusivity was partly financial because "the higher degrees were expensive. York Rite total fees for all degrees were $75 in New York, $100 in Chicago, and $230 in San Francisco ... Uniforms and jewelry brought the total up substantially. Relatively few Masons made this expenditure."[49] Photographic evidence demonstrates that Henry Robertson was one who did spend the money, and he wore his Masonic regalia with pride. The vestments suggested a certain status, and Robertson's rise through the ranks of both the Masonic and Odd Fellows Orders demonstrates that he welcomed these physical signs of his status. His daughter shared her father's enjoyment of the finer things in life, and because of her upbringing in a home where status symbols were celebrated, she felt at home among the elite in society, whether in her hometown of Collingwood, or Victoria, British Columbia, where she lived for twenty years of her married life, or later, in London, England, where she mixed freely with women of title.

While Madge's father influenced her through his involvements in a very visible public role in local politics, business, and fraternal organizations, her mother also had an impact upon her as a dedicated homemaker, church member, and society woman. Bethia Robertson was a devout Presbyterian, and her obituary emphasized how fully she took up her tasks as a Victorian wife and mother of some social standing. According to the *Enterprise and Collingwood Messenger* newspaper, Mrs. Robertson

faithfully fulfilled the duties of her station in life, and always took an active part in all movements for the good. In church circles she was specially [sic] prominent, and socially she was distinguished as a hostess of gracious hospitality. Few women were so gifted as congregationalists, and her extensive reading gave her talk a particular charm.[50]

The Robertsons' home was only steps away from the Presbyterian church, and Bethia Robertson often walked that short distance between her home at the corner of Cedar and Third Streets and her beloved church at Maple and Third. Had the family resided in a larger urban centre, perhaps Mrs. Robertson's involvements might have included groups like the National Council of Women, but in her small-town setting, the church missionary society offered women like her an opportunity to broaden their horizons. As historian Patricia Hill argues, "Missionary work ... provides women with food for thought more wholesome than a steady diet of village gossip. Petty personal troubles recede when a woman reflects on the utter degradation of her heathen sisters. Thus missionary work broadens a woman's interior horizons."[51]

Mrs. Robertson's involvement in church circles seems to have fit these broadened horizons because her missionary work was not limited to the local congregation. Instead, she played a very prominent role in her denomination's Women's Foreign Missionary Society (WFMS), serving as president both of her local WFMS auxiliary, and from 1887 until 1892 as the president of the WFMS for the Barrie Presbytery WFMS. In this capacity, Bethia Robertson was part of a broad network of women who worked to enlarge their own sphere and also to improve the lives of women around the world. While Collingwood did not offer as many opportunities for women to be involved in club work as a larger centre would have, Robertson may have chosen church work quite deliberately because of its appeal to the Victorian sense of propriety concerning the appropriate roles she should occupy as a leading woman in her community.

On this question, Hill argues that church work was more popular than other forms of club work among some women because it seemed more virtuous than movements that emphasized civic reforms and self-culture.[52] Missionary work appealed to "woman's nature, her tenderness and motherliness responding to the appeal of her own sex."[53] Moreover, mission work among women offered them the opportunity to expand their influence without challenging the domestic sphere. Groups like the WFMS offered members "a role in a worldwide enterprise that claimed ultimate significance yet was entirely consistent with their ideology of home and motherhood and their theology of sacrificial service." As Hill goes on to argue, "despite the self-sacrificial character of their rhetoric, evangelical women were not wholly altruistic in their mission to their heathen sisters; they fully expected that in the process ... they would improve the quality of their own spiritual lives."[54]

Some of the improvements that mission work offered to women were not entirely spiritual ones. Wendy Mitchinson has argued that work in women's missionary societies provided women with an important means of gaining skills in the public sphere. Involvement with fundraising, learning to operate according to parliamentary procedure, and the keeping of minute books and membership lists introduced middle-class women like Bethia Robertson to the skills they would need to participate fully in public life.[55] While women of her generation took up those skills and pushed for expanded roles for women in Canadian society at large, their daughters grew to emulate the idea that it was natural for women to occupy public space and to have a voice outside the domestic realm. Mrs. Robertson was clearly an important model and mentor to her daughters. While there is little record of Bethia's own views about women's roles, it is clear that she enjoyed the broadened outlook that her mission work made possible. She travelled around Simcoe County, and probably visited Toronto for national conventions, promoting the work and connecting with women in other communities to encourage them to establish WFMS branches in their congregations.

The extent of Bethia Robertson's feminism is hard to gauge, but her somewhat progressive views were certainly mixed with a great deal of conservatism. This fact is well-illustrated through Bethia's travel writings when she had the opportunity to accompany her husband on a six-week trip to California in the fall of 1888 so that Henry could attend the meeting of the Grand Lodge of the IOOF. Bethia made careful observations throughout her trip, which she later reported through a series of newspaper entries entitled "A Lady's Notes of a Trip to the Pacific." In one of her serialized reports, Bethia commented on the young women she saw in Santa Fe:

> In the purely Mexican district we found the young ladies smoking cigarettes, much to my satisfaction, as I pointed out to the senior representative there were places where women took their rights, and it was comforting to know that there are girls who have as good a time as their brothers – other folks' girls I mean.[56]

Obviously there were limits to the liberation that Bethia Robertson thought was appropriate for young women, especially her own daughters.

Yet Bethia clearly had an impact on her own children and their widened world views. Many years later, when Madge was reflecting on the wide scope of her own activities and achievements, including the international travel that she had enjoyed, she remarked on the smallness of the life that her mother had lived. "[She] only had her missions work … Not the great opportunities we have today …"[57] One must wonder if Madge misjudged the size of her mother's world and the impact of the work that Bethia and women like her were accomplishing. It is true that during her own lifetime, Madge Robertson witnessed many changes and a widened sphere of influence, but in her day, her mother Bethia enjoyed a much wider set of experiences than the average woman did at the end of the nineteenth century. For Madge it was international work among rural women that became her passion, but she was no doubt introduced to the idea of women exercising broad influence through the life that her mother lived as she carried on her work among the WFMS.

That close mother-daughter relationship was severed prematurely when Bethia Robertson died at 49 years of age, in the spring of 1893. She had been ill for a number of months, and Madge returned home to Collingwood to be with her mother during the illness. The Collingwood newspaper announced her death in an article entitled "Death's Heavy Hand," saying,

> tribute may justly be paid to the amiable and accomplished lady just departed. She faithfully fulfilled the duties of her station in life, and always took an active part in all movements for good … Mrs. Robertson will long live in the affectionate remembrance of many friends, who entertain for the afflicted husband and his family deep and respectful sympathy."[58]

In the spring of 1894, the WFMS executive of the Barrie Presbyterial announced her passing with regret to the annual meeting of the WFMS held in Ottawa, giving her this tribute: "Death has been among us and taken one well known to us all – our late President, Mrs. Robertson (of Collingwood), who, for six years was our Presbyterial President. To the constant energy of this 'Mother in Israel' our Society owes much of its present status."[59] The term "Mother in Israel," both in biblical times and after, was one that was reserved for women of outstanding reputation.[60] The fact that Bethia Robertson's peers designated her as a "Mother in Israel," means that she was highly regarded as a woman who played roles outside the usual realm of female activity. She was among those women whom Mitchinson has described as "fortunate enough to have the leisure time to participate … with the opportunity to develop their abilities in leadership and administration."[61] For Bethia Robertson, like so many others, her involvement in the work of supporting foreign missions widened her concerns and her outlook.

Mrs. Robertson's model was significant for her daughters. More than forty-five years later, when Madge reflected on her mother's church work, she drew comparisons between her mother's involvement with the WFMS and her own international activities on behalf of women. In the daughter's estimation, her mother's work had at best, a very limited sphere:

> My mother, a most brilliant and feeling woman, died when I was a young girl without ever having known the joys of the humanitarian effort so wonderfully open to us today. She longed to work for humanity and her only outlet was a missionary society. The returns for her work were limited and meager so far as her own life was concerned, and she lived and died without ever knowing the joys of wider service. [62]

In this 1939 speech, Madge Watt was invoking the memory of her mother's work to make the point that her own mid-twentieth-century opportunities were much more broad than her mother's had been. Watt went on to say, "The whole field of human endeavour is open to us. I cannot but feel that if there is any part of our membership which does not rise to this wonderful opportunity, a great moment for them has gone by."[63]

Madge Robertson was only twenty-five years old when her mother died and she may not have realized the full extent of what her mother's WFMS involvements meant to her. As historian Ruth Compton Brouwer explains, there was much more going on at the church women's meetings than meets the eye:

> What *did* the WFMS offer to women within their own congregations? Though they varied a good deal from place to place, and over time, the regular auxiliary meetings ... offered certain unchanging attractions: the opportunity to come together in a good cause, to enjoy a sense of sisterhood, and to turn for a time from mundane household responsibilities to the exotic challenges of a faraway world. Especially in rural areas, the monthly missionary meeting was often one of the few outings available in a narrow social existence, and many women made extraordinary efforts to attend. "The meeting" was also a source of local leadership opportunities and intellectual stimulus. Such duties as serving on an executive, preparing a paper on an assigned missionary topic, reading appropriate scripture passages, and leading a group in prayer might well prove daunting to the congregation's most timid and least educated women, but they undoubtedly appealed to those desiring an outlet for skills and ambitions unused at home.[64]

While Bethia Robertson did not travel widely herself, her concerns broadened beyond her local setting because of her involvement with the WFMS, and one assumes that she gained a degree of personal satisfaction from her involvements.[65] As Mitchinson argues, "Protestant women's missionary societies ... broadened the outlook of many women and introduced them to the power of organization." [66] Madge's somewhat dismissive attitude towards her mother's church work only serves to reinforce Mitchinson's observation that "ironically, the members of the missionary societies did not consider themselves participants in the women's movement. Nevertheless, their efforts to establish a place for themselves in the church made them a part of the larger effort to expand woman's role in Canadian society."[67] Bethia Robertson was active in the WFMS both in her own congregation and at the next level, the Barrie Presbytery. The kind of skills that she and other women gained from their involvement with missionary societies was important, not only for themselves, but also for younger women like Madge who came after them.

When Madge Robertson lamented the limited expanse of her mother's involvements, she may have been referring specifically to the highly conservative nature of the WFMS. Mitchinson points out that of all the main Protestant women's missionary societies, the Presbyterians were perhaps the most conservative since their missionary society decided not to join the National Council of Women. According to Mitchinson, this may have been due to something beyond a deeply conservative outlook. The fact that WFMS women felt themselves to be very privileged compared to women in other parts of the world they heard about meant that they hesitated to work for improvements on their own behalf: "Compared to what they knew of the position of women in the mission fields of such countries as India, Japan and Burma, their own positions appeared envious [sic]. They felt no need to question the values of their own society concerning women."[68] Madge would have agreed with her mother on the fact that she did enjoy certain privileges because of their comfortable lifestyle. Like her mother, Madge too worked to improve women's conditions, though she did not limit herself to church work; nor did she concentrate solely on foreign fields.

The WFMS auxiliary in Collingwood, founded in 1883, was one of Simcoe County's most active and successful. As Table 1, below, illustrates, during the years that Bethia Robertson led it, Collingwood Presbyterian's WFMS had an active membership of up to three dozen women who made significant contributions of money and parcels sent to home mission locations in the north west. This local group was part of something much bigger, and involvement with it offered women a chance to broaden their own horizons and hone their skills. Mitchinson argues that "the woman's missionary societies of the Protestant churches offered tens of thousands of Canadian women an outlet for their abilities and energies. No other woman's organization worked on such a scale."[69]

Bethia Robertson's involvement in foreign missions work was something that Madge's sister, Katherine, also took up. For young women, usually the daughters of auxiliary members, a junior version of the local auxiliary existed, known as the Mission Band. Collingwood's Mission Band was very active in its own right, and Katie Robertson served faithfully on its executive. As Table 2 illustrates, in the earliest years of its existence the membership of the Mission Band outpaced the adult auxiliary with more than twice the membership of the parent organization.

The funds that WFMS groups raised are significant, not only for the amounts of money they collected, but also for the way in which they did so. Mitchinson explains that "unlike charity and benevolent organizations, dependent on the donations and the social influence of their members to raise money, missionary societies largely subsisted on the minimal weekly contributions of their members and what money they could save

Table 1. Collingwood Presbyterian WFMS Auxiliary Membership and Contributions, 1885–1892[70]

Year	Membership	Members of general society	Average attendance at meetings	Contribution ($)	Value sent to the north west ($)
1885	36	7	–	43.00	–
1886	29	5	–	50.00	–
1887	28	5	–	54.00	–
1888	35	12	15	80.67	N.V.
1889	30	14	16	62.69	25.00
1890				103.12	
1891	34*	12	18	81.00	45.00
1892	32	15	13	99.00	13.75

*Includes one life member.

Table 2. Collingwood Presbyterian WFMS Mission Band Membership and Contributions, 1887–1892[71]

Year	Membership	Members of general society	Average attendance at meetings	Contribution ($)	Value sent to the north west ($)
1887	65	–	–	–	–
1888	60	–	30	22	N.V.
1889	12	–	7	20.04	7
1890				23.04	
1891	15	–	9	30.33	–
1892	13	6	6	55.00	10.75

and raise in addition to this."[72] Collecting small amounts of money from across a broad base of the membership provided impressive amounts of money and caused women from various backgrounds to feel that they had an investment in the success of the missionary society. This model of funding sounds very much like the Women's Institutes with which Madge Robertson would become very involved during her married life and later. Her familiarity with the low membership fees and wide canvassing of the membership of the WFMS meant that she was familiar with the model of the WI and, later on, the Associated Country Women of the World, which were largely financed by the small contributions of a large number of members through an initiative known as the "Pennies for Friendship" scheme. Although Madge's sister Katie was much more directly involved in their mother's WFMS activities, it seems that Madge may have picked up on some of the genius of the funding model that the WFMS used.

Involvement with the WFMS was very much a family affair, as the case of Bethia and Katie Robertson illustrates. Madge, the elder daughter, was away at university from 1886 and continued living in Toronto even after her graduation, the period when the Robertson women were most heavily involved. However, Madge still felt that the WFMS was very much a part of her life; in the spring of 1892, Madge mentioned that she had been contacted by a lady who would be attending the annual meeting of the WFMS to be held that year in Toronto. In her capacity as editor of a Toronto women's magazine, Robertson related her familiarity with this Presbyterian institution to her readers:

"I am coming to stay with you," wrote a dear lady from the country, "because you are nicely convenient to the Annual Meeting." Do you ask "what Annual Meeting?" Oh, but the editor knows. Has she not grown up with W.F.M.S.? Bless your heart, Auxiliaries and mission Presbyterials and General Meetings are all as every-day terms to her. She is a perfect walking encyclopedia in regard to all that concerns the highly respectable organization known as the Woman's Foreign Missionary Society of the Presbyterian Church in Canada.[73]

Madge Robertson actually attended the WFMS annual meeting with her guest and as she continued to describe the gathering with gentle humour, she poked fun at her family's church traditions:

As I was remarking, nobody would mistake these thousand women for anything else than they are. One can always tell what denomination a congregation belongs to. The way they regard the service for one thing. With Presbyterian congregations there is reverence, to be sure, throughout all the service, but the congregation is not fairly settled down until the sermon begins. That is the real business of the day. Whatever else they may be at any other part of "divine worship" they are fully awake when the minister expounds or preaches. A Presbyterian minister takes his life in his hands when he ascends a pulpit. The congregation are not exactly on the lookout for unorthodoxy nowadays, but the critical faculty is not dormant. You hear a great deal about the sermon as you descend the church steps, and afterwards at the dinner table.[74]

While Robertson felt free to gently mock the Presbyterian women who were gathering for the WFMS annual meeting, a sense of humour that she apparently shared with her mother, she drew definite boundaries for herself about what she deemed to be proper humour, and particularly when it came to mother-daughter relationships. Writing about the kind of humour that was current among writers of her day, Robertson revealed the deep respect she held for her own mother. Just two weeks after the WFMS meetings, she wrote a column with a personal "rant" about "mother-in-law" jokes. Reporting that she had read through "half a dozen comic papers," she claimed to have found 132 mother-in-law jokes. Explaining her opposition to that particular kind of humour, Robertson built her case:

To begin with, I do not think the subject appropriate for joking. If there is one relationship more sacred and tender than another it is that of mother and daughter ... No mother, certainly, can regard this sort of witticism with any degree of tenderness. The very suggestion of such a horrible state of affairs is unpleasant in the extreme.[75]

While it is clear that Robertson did not follow exactly in her mother's footsteps, she held a great respect for her mother, and whether she realized it or not, one could argue that with her mother so heavily involved in women's organizations, albeit religious ones, Madge was unwittingly influenced.

The Robertson home would have been on the mailing lists of Henry's fraternal organizations' publications such as *The Odd Fellow* and also Bethia's WFMS publications such as the *Monthly Letter Leaflet*. This is significant because even as a young woman, Robertson learned how important it was for organizations to communicate with their membership. As American historian Patricia Hill has written, "By conceiving of their missionary magazines as intimate friends visiting women in their homes, the editors created a personal relationship between auxiliary members and a society's printed voice."[76] An avid reader herself, Madge Robertson would certainly have leafed through these publications, and her later writing and organizational careers may have been influenced by the fact that she was familiar with such publications. The idea of creating an imagined community through publications is something at which Robertson later excelled, both as editor of a women's magazine in Toronto in 1892, and later, as the organizer of rural women's groups in the UK and around the world. Before Madge Robertson launched her career as a writer and organizer of women, however, she went off to university.

It is clear from this portrait of her parents' civic, fraternal, and religious involvements that Madge Robertson hailed from a prominent and privileged family, one that was well acquainted with the prosperity and comfort afforded to the elite of Ontario's booming late nineteenth-century urban economy. For the very fortunate, like her, that privilege included the luxury of higher education. As an undergraduate entering her first year in 1885, Madge Robertson, a small-town Presbyterian lawyer's daughter, was not an atypical student. Apart from the novelty of being a female undergraduate (it was only the second year that women were admitted to University College) Robertson shared many things in common with her classmates. As historian Charles Levi has demonstrated, the majority of students attending University College at the time were the children of either prosperous farmers or professionals, most of them having grown up outside of Toronto itself. As for religion, Presbyterian women dominated the early coeds at Toronto.[77] In other words, Robertson had much in common with her classmates, though the student newspaper, the *Varsity*, made clear in 1887 that those who were privileged enough to attend university were set apart from the majority of the population. Using American statistics, students were informed that only "one-half of one per cent of the young men of the country are college graduates; 65 per cent of the presidents of the United States have been college graduates, vice-presidents, 50 per cent; speakers of the House of Representatives, 50 per cent; members of the Senate, 46 per cent; associate justices Supreme Court, 73 per cent; chief justices, 83 per cent; cabinet officers, 54 per cent. Draw your own conclusions as to the value of a college education."[78] Robertson's enrolment at the university meant that she was among those who were most likely to shape their society through public involvement.

As the elder daughter in a family with no male children, Margaret Robertson was the one who was afforded the privilege of a postsecondary education at a time when such an experience was rare, and rarer still for a woman. Robertson earned her BA with honours from University College at the University of Toronto in June 1889, and the local newspaper back home reported, "The young lady deserves the hearty congratulations of her friends in Collingwood, who will be pleased to hear of her brilliant success."[79]

Higher education for women was still highly contested in Canada at the time. It was only one year before Robertson began attending that the Ontario government had "passed an order-in-council admitting women to University College, the non-denominational arts college at Toronto."[80] That decision, which marked the beginning of co-educational opportunities for women in Ontario at the postsecondary level, would not go uncontested and, as historian Sara Burke points out, "the early history of women at the University of Toronto was an uneasy one, characterized not by triumphant progress but rather by an ongoing pattern of advancement and retreat."[81] Burke notes that "although women gained strength at the university in the late nineteenth century, detractors feared that their increase in numbers would result in the deterioration of both academic and moral standards."[82]

Evidently many people, both on and off the university campus, were not entirely comfortable with young women like Madge Robertson who made their way through the system to graduate alongside their male peers. As Burke argues, "it was the fluid definition of gender ... that charge[d] the debates over co-education."[83] Because of the continuing controversies that swirled around the women who attended the University of Toronto in those early days, the biographical experiences of individual students like Madge Robertson are important to trace. This is particularly the case because, as historians such as Jo LaPierre have demonstrated, it is difficult to explore the academic experiences of individual women because of their relative invisibility.[84]

According to an 1889 article published in *Life*, among the fourth-year students at University of Toronto

> Miss Madge R. Robertson is perhaps the best known of the ladies. She is a nice-looking brunette and quite young in appearance. Her talents are most versatile. In Modern Languages she has stood well since her first year. Outside her course she is best-known for her blue-stocking proclivities being a frequent contributor to The Varsity and also to some down town papers. Her non-de-plume [sic] is Greta.[85]

With that short description, *Life* provided many clues to the experience that Robertson lived out at University College from 1885 to 1889. Hardly invisible, she studied Modern Languages, as did the majority of the female students in the early years; her scholastic performance was strong; she was publishing her writing both in the campus newspaper and in the city papers; and she had "blue-stocking proclivities." These characteristics need to be unpacked and considered individually.

In the case of Robertson's talents and academic standing, it is clear that she performed well at her studies. She consistently stood near the top of her class in the Modern Languages program. At the end of her third year, her name appeared five times on the "Third Year Honour List" published in the *Varsity*.[86] Although she did not take first place in any of her subjects, she was honoured for outstanding performances in English, History, French, German, and Spanish.

As a well-rounded student, Robertson filled her days with more than simply her course work. The *Varsity* reveals that she took an active interest in extracurricular activities on the campus. Not all of the student clubs and societies on campus were open to women and therefore joining the longstanding Literary and Scientific Society (better known as "The Lit.") was not an option for Robertson and her female peers. Instead, Robertson's major extracurricular involvement was with one of the Lit.'s rivals, the Modern Languages Club, where she regularly socialized with like-minded students of literature, both men and women.[87] At regular monthly meetings of the club, Robertson heard other students present their papers, and she offered several of her own as well. In February 1886, during her first year, Robertson presented a paper on the life of Elizabeth Barrett Browning at a regular meeting of the Modern Languages Club. That paper was well received, and the following year, Robertson was invited to give the same paper again when the club held its first-ever public meeting. On that occasion the *Varsity* reported that "Miss M. Robertson read an essay on Mrs. Browning, reviewing her works and relating the incidents of her life."[88]

It is interesting that while Robertson studied the poetry of a great writer like Browning, she also wrote poetry herself, and one of her original poems was published in the student newspaper during her first year. On February 13, 1886, her work entitled "An Unfinished Dream" appeared: [89]

AN UNFINISHED DREAM

Vaguely feeling a strange unrest
That fills my soul with sadness;
Wearily asking "Is life then blest
Or worst?"
"Have my days been spent for the best
Or worst?"
"The measure of joy, of gladness
Is filled," the merciless answer pressed;
"They are gone, the hours, in idle jest
Dispersed."
"Alas! I dare not think," I cried at last,
And surging memories of a wasted past
In silent, hopeless woe are eddying fast
And bow my head with sorrow.
And ever anon the sad refrain,
"For thee there is naught but grief and pain
And bitter tears to weep in vain
In all life's dreary morrow."

Madge R. Robertson
University College, Toronto

Robertson's flair for public speaking was something she demonstrated early on, and a skill she continued to use throughout her life. During her second year, she prepared and presented a paper to the Modern Languages Club on the work of American humorist, James

Russell Lowell. This essay on *The Biglow Papers* was said to be "written in her usual terse and interesting style, and read with éclat."[90] During these busy student years, Robertson not only experimented with poetry writing, but went on to write many short stories and other humorous pieces. It is significant to know that she studied the work of contemporary humorists such as Lowell, who was well known for his works of political satire.[91] While Lowell satirized American politics, Robertson invoked satire to critique the gender politics of co-education on her own campus, as we shall see in a piece she published in the *Varsity* during her fourth year. She would go on to use similar techniques in the short fictional works that she published after her graduation on the politics of courtship, marriage, and employment prospects for women.

In the fall of her third year, another poem appeared in the *Varsity*, this one attributed to "Greta." Demonstrating Robertson's abilities as a language major, this work was a translation from French of a poem by Marceline Desbordes-Valmore entitled, "S'il avait su."[92]

S'IL AVAIT SU

(From the French of Madame Valmore [sic].)

If he had known the soul he has wounded.
If he had seen yon tears of the heart!
If he had known my heart's voice was silent
In loving too well, ah! not now apart
Estranged would we walk, my glad life days over.
He surely had yielded to Love's gentle arm,
And cherished the hope he deceived I all cunning,
If he had known!

If he had known what depths of true feeling
A glowing child-soul, awakened above
Deep buries; his soul knew not mine in its passion;
As he inspired it, he might have known Love
My eyelids, low drooping, concealed all my longing;
Ah! sweet sweeping lashes, read he that Love strove
With your pride? A secret all worth his divining,
If he had know!

If he had know how I into bondage
Was sold, when I looked into tenderest eyes,

As free as the air, the soft breeze of summer;
My days I'd have born under other fair skies
Alas! now too late to live my life over.
A sweet hope deceived, a prayer, then one dies.
Will he say in pity, my life-sorrow guessing:
"If I had known!"

Greta.

Not only was the poem a demonstration of her ability to translate from French – this work also represented one of Robertson's earliest published pieces dealing with the complicated negotiations of emotional relationships. This was a theme that would dominate her future work, most commonly in the form of short stories and often with humorous twists of irony and satire.

Robertson read a paper in the fall of her fourth year to the Modern Languages Club at a meeting devoted to "George Eliot and Her Works," and the *Varsity* reported that "the attendance, especially of the lady members, was large." The report continued, "Miss Robertson's essay was perhaps the most enjoyable read before the club this year. It dealt with 'The Mill on the Floss,' giving a good resume of the plot and an excellent analysis of several of the characters."[93] The other paper presented that evening by a male student also dealt with one of Eliot's works, though it did not seem to capture the listeners in the same way. "Mr. Dockray's paper on 'Adam Bede,' though short, was well written and interesting." In the charged atmosphere of debates about gender and co-education, the controversial life and writing of George Eliot was probably particularly intriguing for Robertson and her peers.

The rules for the Modern Languages Club spelled out that papers read before the group were to be submitted voluntarily by members, and that "the essays be made as original as possible [so] as [to] take not longer than 10 minutes to read, in the French and German; and 15 minutes in the English subjects; and also to be read as distinctly as possible." These were not assignments that were taken from course work and repackaged; indeed, members were instructed "[t]hat the essays be written in the summer holidays, and that the members also read as many as possible of the authors" from the list that was distributed in the Spring of each year.[94] Clearly, Robertson welcomed the challenge of the summer reading lists, titles she may have purchased or borrowed from the well-appointed public library her father had helped to establish in Collingwood. She easily rose to the challenge of reading widely and presenting such short and entertaining papers.

Beyond planning occasions for the entertainment of the membership, the Modern Languages Club also addressed some serious academic questions during Robertson's student years. Curriculum reform was one of the causes that they took up, submitting suggestions to the university senate about how the program requirements should be changed in order to even the workload and provide students with viable options for course selection.[95]

Another ongoing issue that the club tackled was a very deliberate attempt to develop a distinct Canadian literature by encouraging young Canadian writers to be original in their compositions, rather than imitative. It is significant to recognize that by the late 1880s, the members of the Modern Languages Club at the University of Toronto were already consciously trying to promote the emergence of a distinct Canadian literary culture. Touting the importance of homegrown Canadian creative efforts, such proponents told readers of the *Varsity*,

> [w]e should like to see fewer critical essays from our young writers and more original sketches based upon personal observation and personal experience. If Canada is ever going to have a national literature, it will be made up of work of this kind. We can only write well what we know well, and our best knowledge is gained at first hand. To this end our topics should be Canadian and our treatment of them individual and characteristic. If our native writers cannot find literary subjects or natural beauties, or interesting personal experiences at home, then their writing must be done under artificial conditions and is necessarily dead and profitless. But originality and enthusiasm, even if dealing with a common Canadian every-day scene or event, is sure to inspire interest and admiration. Let us be ourselves, and not Europe or America.[96]

Robertson's contributions to the "down town papers" came in the form of social columns on special campus events such as the annual "Conversazione." On February 16, 1889, "Greta" wrote a witty and critical review in one of the "downtown" papers of "Much Ado about Nothing," which was playing at the Grand Theatre. She found that Rhea, the actress who played the lead role, had a voice that was "a trifle too ponderous for a piquant, saucy Beatrice." In the review she quotes George Eliot and reflects on Matthew Arnold's observation that the French are non-appreciative of Shakespeare. She also, however, takes the opportunity to make quips about the behaviour of two young French men who attended the performance and slipped out at the intermission to imbibe a little too much.[97] Reflecting on this incident, Greta showed herself to be a woman who took note of men and assessed their character based on her educated opinions about national traits and her observations of their comportment in public settings.

Robertson's "blue-stocking proclivities" led her into controversial terrain on campus. Backed by her very publicly-minded parents and undaunted by the controversies that swirled around her and her fellow female students, she took up the challenge of defending women students and justifying her own place on the campus. In the January 1889 issue of the *Varsity*, Robertson, again using her pen name "Greta," argued that women had every right to be on the campus and she urged those who were uncomfortable with the idea to adjust their thinking and catch up with the times. In an article entitled "The Higher Education," she defended women's participation in postsecondary institutions. "Greta" wanted readers to recognize that

> the super-sentimental side of a girl's nature is not developed by her college course. She says that they do not carry notebooks of a color to match their dresses, and that "the charms of lunch are sometimes even greater to the average college girl than the charm of posing for admiring students." [98]

Then the author quipped, "We thought that they were too ethereal even to eat."[99] In this feature article, "Greta" was responding to a November 1888 article published in *The Varsity*, where a male student using the name "Old Roman," had argued that women had no place on the campus.[100] Although her real identity was probably not a well-kept secret, "Greta's" main tactic was to critique "Old Roman's" writing style; in doing so, she gave further clues about her own identity as a female student who was a very able writer. Concluding her argument with overt sarcasm, "Greta" suggested that if she were pressed to offer her own ideas about co-education, this is how she would respond: "It is a delicate matter and one that must not be harshly dealt with. But if it came to the actual question, and I had to answer what I would do, I think, yes, I am sure, I should reply that I would leave the talk to an abler writer."[101]

Besides her involvement with the Modern Languages Club and her other provocative writing, Robertson also entered fully into campus life by becoming an enthusiastic fan of varsity sports. This kind of interest on her part was yet another reason for opponents of co-education to worry about women and men on campus mixing too freely. The *Varsity* reported on a rugby game in the fall of 1887 (Robertson's third year) that "the Varsity's second fifteen went up to Hamilton on Thursday to play the second fifteen of the champions of the town series. Some half-dozen enthusiasts, including the brothers Senkler, accompanied the team." The report continues, naming some of the spectators. "Among the Varsity men and maidens who witnessed the game were A.F. Carpenter, B.A., A.W. Strat[sic] and Miss Madge Robertson."[102] It is unlikely that Robertson was indeed the only woman who accompanied the team on this road trip, but it is significant that she was named. This is further proof that, from a very early date, female undergraduates were taking their place alongside their male peers and that when it came to extracurricular activities, they were perhaps not as wary nor invisible as some earlier studies have suggested.[103]

Robertson had a particular interest in the game of rugby, or rather in one of varsity's star players, a student of medicine named Alfred Tennyson Watt, whose family hailed from Meaford, Ontario, in Grey County, only about twenty miles from her home town of Collingwood. Alfred Watt was regularly named as one of the outstanding players on the varsity team, playing as a forward. Reports of Watt's athletic prowess were featured in the pages of the *Varsity* with the same frequency as those on Robertson's interests in writing and the Modern Languages Club.[104] Watt, who would graduate with his MD degree in 1890, was elected to serve on the executive of the Rugby Football Club as the second-year representative in 1887, and the following year became treasurer of the Athletic Sports' Association.[105] It is not clear when the romance between Robertson and Watt began, but it is quite likely that Watt was among the spectators who travelled to Hamilton on the same occasion that Robertson accompanied the team.

The same year that Alfred Watt graduated with his medical degree, Madge Robertson distinguished herself even further from other female students by becoming the first woman to graduate from the provincial university with a graduate degree – the Master of Arts in Pedagogy and History. The *Collingwood Bulletin* newspaper proudly celebrated its hometown girl's accomplishment:

CONGRATULATORY – We notice with much pleasure that Miss Madge Robertson, B.A. ... received the degree of M.A. at the Convocation of the University of Toronto on Tuesday ... The distinction is, indeed, one that very few ladies are likely ever to attain, and to be the first to attain such a standing is an honor both to Miss Robertson and to her native town.[106]

While the local community support was no doubt welcome, the actual value of the MA degree was debatable. Martin Friedland, in his history of the University of Toronto, explains that in the early years

the degree was not highly regarded. No special courses were provided, nor was residence at the University required. In the early period, the thesis was actually written in an examination hall "without reference to books, or to other aids."[107]

Critics exposed the fact that the university granted the degree "for work done entirely in absentia, and on the submitting of a thesis which he can construct in from one to three months, without even having done any original research worthy of mention."[108] It is not clear whether Robertson sat to write an examination or whether she submitted a thesis, but having completed her undergraduate studies in 1889, she did complete the requirements of the MA within one year and did so while she was working as a teacher at the Parkdale Collegiate. In 1887 the *Varsity* explained the controversy this way:

> Every one knows that the Bachelor's Degree really represents the hard work supposed to be necessary to its attainment, and that the Master's Degree is more or less meaningless. And since no one can attain the higher, who had not already taken the lower degree, no great harm is done by changing the "B" to an "M" if one is willing to pay for the luxury."[109]

One is left to wonder then, if the MA degree that Madge Robertson proudly achieved was actually a noteworthy academic accomplishment or simply a "luxury" purchased on her behalf by her proud parents. Whichever it was, Robertson proudly displayed the designation of MA after her name for the rest of her life. Knowing how rare it was for a woman to have that designation, she used it to open doors for herself.

Madge Robertson and Alfred Watt would eventually marry, though not until three years after her graduation. Dr. Watt moved to British Columbia with the goal of establishing a medical practice, and Miss Robertson pursued her writing career based in Toronto and New York rather than settling back into the comfortable life that her family enjoyed in Collingwood. The next chapter considers Robertson's writing career, in order to explore what her writing reveals about her own thinking and how she expressed herself in her role as a writer for women.

Chapter Two

Scripting the New Woman: Writer and Editor

In July 1891, a short story by Madge Robertson entitled "The Heart Knoweth" appeared in a Saturday edition of the Toronto newspaper, the *Globe*. As the title suggests, it was a love story, and in typical Victorian prose, it told the tale of a young man named Edmund travelling overseas who was completely preoccupied with thoughts of the young woman, Margaret, whom he had left behind in her hometown of Collingwood, Ontario. The young woman had fallen hopelessly in love with the man, but he, fearful of making a commitment to her, had ended the relationship abruptly to pursue his travels in Europe, where he could not get the heroine of the story out of his mind. The author waxed eloquent in describing young Edmund's loneliness: "In snow-clad mountains he saw her purity and in honey-breathing valleys he felt her sweetness. The waves of foreign seas crooned her name in the twilight and the face of his beloved was near him in his dreams."[1] He tried unsuccessfully to assuage his desire in a relationship with a woman of dubious character in Paris. She, however, had a total lack of respect for him, and one day bluntly told him so. "I think you are like the rest of your selfish sex ... deceitful, fickle, weak and unworthy of the love of any good woman ... But good enough for me, you know."[2] After this indictment of his character, the young man came to his senses, and decided to make his way back to his first love to attempt to re-establish their relationship.

At this point, the plot of this otherwise predictable story takes a surprising turn. When the young man returned to find the object of his affection, he was shocked to learn that although she was not romantically involved with anyone else, and despite his pleadings, Margaret refused to take him back. When he tried to kiss her, she told him firmly, "You should not do that. How dare you!" and she went on to tell him to "be content with my forgiveness and leave me to work out my life labor. My sorrow was hard enough to bear, and now you come to bring back the old pain again. Oh leave me, please – please."[3] Clearly this heroine was a strong woman asserting that she would not take rejection lightly nor would she stand by pining for reconciliation. Despite that strong resolve, the narrator reported that after a long illness, and a bout with cynicism and then with anger, the heroine had expressed a sense of "incompleteness." When a friend suggested Edmund "as a completion," Margaret laughed and said, "I have plenty of missionary work at hand." The narrator retorted, "but no such attractive heathen as Edmund." The story ends with the hint of tears in the eyes of the young woman and the narrator resolving to write Edmund a letter, to encourage him to try again in his pursuit of Margaret, one assumes.

The ambiguity of the young woman's response is intriguing, and although it might be mere coincidence that the heroine of the story was named Margaret, and that the story was set in Collingwood, Ontario, there is no question that the author was none other than Madge Robertson. Speculating about the degree of autobiographical details in one story can only lead so far, but looking at the larger body of Robertson's writing does lead to important clues about her life and her thinking in the years between university and marriage. In the absence of other primary sources for this period of her life, using dozens of examples of Robertson's published writing in the years following her graduation from the University of Toronto, one gains insight into Robertson's experiences and ideas.[4] It is not unreasonable to think that in the years before her marriage in 1893 to Alfred Tennyson Watt, the young varsity athlete and medical student she had met at the University of Toronto, some aspects of the fictional separation story may have been very close to Madge Robertson's own heart. Certainly the themes of romance, courtship, and marriage were common ones in her writing, as were those of women and higher education, paid work, sports, homemaking, and motherhood. When historian Jean Barman wrote about Canadian journalist and writer Constance Lindsay Skinner, she commented that as she pieced together that biography, some of "the most tantalizing hints come through her writing."[5] The same thing can be said for Robertson. In the absence of any personal correspondence or journals from this stage of her life, her writing speaks volumes about the issues and ideas that dominated her thinking.

Instead of returning after her graduation to a secure and quiet life as a privileged daughter in a small town, from 1890 to 1893 Robertson took on a number of new challenges in an attempt to find meaningful employment in Toronto and other urban settings. Many trailblazing women like Robertson who had graduated from university in this period sought paid employment after graduation. Their most common path to employment was teaching, which was deemed to be an appropriate gendered choice, although a few celebrated individuals made more radical choices, pursuing careers in the male-dominated fields of law and medicine. Robertson tried teaching for a short time, but it was a short-lived choice, which she apparently did not enjoy. Her real passion was writing, and for three years after her graduation, she spent the bulk of her time pursuing opportunities to publish her work. Already accustomed to having her name appear in print in the Toronto papers since her student days, it is not surprising that in January 1892 a Toronto newspaper announced that

> Miss Madge Robertson, a graduate of Toronto University, and a bright, clever writer, has been appointed editor of the *Ladies Pictorial Weekly*, a position that she is well fitted to fill. Miss Robertson is already known as a contributor to the *Globe* and other journals, and it is safe to say that in her sphere of labour she will soon win a wider recognition of her literary ability.[6]

What is remarkable is that at the age of only twenty-four years, Robertson was propelled to the position of editor, with the power to choose which authors and articles would appear in print and which would not. According to historian of journalism Margaret Beetham, it was quite rare for women to become editors – even though the women's press was expanding in this period. It was rarer still for one so young to sit in the editor's chair.[7] Robertson was clearly launched on an exceptional career path.

Less than one year later, Robertson resigned from the editorship of the *Ladies Pictorial Weekly* to take up what seemed to be a very promising career opportunity in New York. The press clipping in her alumni file at the University of Toronto Archives reveals that

> Miss Madge Robertson, M.A., one of the cleverest of the literary women of Canada, has gone to New York to take a position on the staff of *Frank Leslie's Weekly*. Miss Robertson has been a contributor to many of the American and Canadian magazines, and is achieving for herself a high literary reputation.[8]

Clearly Robertson was an exceptional writer in her day, and the fact that her writing career actually led her into the rare position of editor of a ladies' weekly, and quickly after that into a position as staff writer for *Frank Leslie's Weekly* in New York, is noteworthy indeed.[9]

Scholars of literary criticism writing about women writers in the last years of the nineteenth and early twentieth centuries highlight strains of writing that they identify as "new woman" writing. Carroll Smith-Rosenberg defined "new women" this way: "In short, the New Women, rejecting conventional female roles and asserting their right to a career, to a public voice, to visible power, laid claim to the rights and privileges customarily accorded bourgeois men."[10] It is interesting to examine how Robertson's writing could be considered part of the "New Woman" genre because she asserted women's entitlement to the elements Smith-Rosenberg listed, including careers, public voice, power, rights and privileges. Robertson expressed many of the ideas that were typical of New Woman writers, but compared to the better-known New Woman novelists of the 1890s,[11] her writing was at once both more popular and more conservative. Her ideas represent what historian Clarence Karr called "a transitional stage, which provided a bridge between the Victorian era and the subsequent decades of the twentieth century."[12] Yet for Robertson, the conservative elements of her writing came out even more clearly after 1893, as we shall see in the next chapter.

The term "New Woman" was always contested, even as it emerged in the 1890s: "By 1895, 'New Woman' – like 'politically correct' a century later – had become a wildly skewed, reductive media construct."[13] In 1895, Hugh Stutfield coined an unforgettable image of a "literary bicyclist" when he wrote that the New Woman "covers a vast extent of ground, and sometimes her machine takes her along some sadly muddy roads, where her petticoats – or her knickerbockers – are apt to get soiled."[14] There are four subject areas that constitute the kind of "muddy ground" that Robertson and other new women authors covered. First, New Women believed that access to higher education – and in particular co-education, not simply a woman-specific curriculum of domestic science – was of paramount importance. Also, New Women argued that a woman should have access to the career of her choice even though this might mean that men in her chosen field would be uncomfortable with her presence there. Third, New Women promoted sporting activities for women because they believed that women should lead physically active lives, enjoying organized sport even though this would necessitate some controversial dress-reform measures. The fourth pillar of New Woman beliefs was the most contested:

marriage. New Woman writing served to problematize marriage from various perspectives along a spectrum of different views about the marriage question. Lyn Pykett has argued that

> in the latter half of the century, the Marriage Question not only appeared to be increasingly problematic, it also became more polarized. At one extreme marriage was seen (by both feminist and anti-feminists) as woman's highest and most natural calling. At the other it was a form of slavery or legalized prostitution.[15]

Most New Woman writers placed themselves somewhere between these two extremes, and Madge Robertson was no exception. In fact, she wrote about all four of these New Woman themes; by analyzing her positions on these questions, one can see how her views were shaped by the context of her own circumstances and life stage.

It was during her student years at the University of Toronto that Robertson expressed her views about postsecondary education for women most clearly. Her articulate defence of women's place on the campus and her demonstrated excellence as an award-winning author of essays and reviews offer convincing proof that she did indeed subscribe to New Woman ideas. After she left campus life behind her, Robertson was poised to take her place among the growing number of well-educated, quick-witted coeds, a Canadian parallel to the American Gibson Girl or the British Girton Girl.

In 1892, within just two years of her graduation, Robertson assumed the position of editor of the *Ladies Pictorial Weekly*, a Toronto-based women's interest magazine with a circulation of over 25,000 copies per week.[16] On page two of each issue that she edited, Robertson included an editorial column entitled "Inner Sanctum," where she wrote in a conversational tone to express her views on a variety of topics and to invite readers to interact with her ideas. The publication included features on marriage, child-rearing, religion, homemaking, cooking, literature, leisure, society news, and health issues. From February 1892 until July that same year, Robertson accepted and vetted submissions; she also wrote her own weekly editorials and feature articles for the paper. Madge Robertson exerted control over the content and tone of the *Ladies Pictorial Weekly*, which translated into a great deal of cultural influence for such a young female professional in Canada.

Middle-class women had been finding employment in journalism since the late 1880s; however, metropolitan, middle-class men retained the balance of power within the industry as editors.[17] As writers, women could essentially write about any topic they wished, which provided them a certain degree of freedom, but whether their work was published depended entirely on the male editors who evaluated their work. As a female editing her own periodical, Robertson was fortunate to bypass male censorship.

As editor, Robertson had a great deal of freedom in editing the *Ladies Pictorial Weekly*, but she also had to consider factors such as raising funds through the sale of copies and advertisement space to ensure the survival of her periodical. Because not all of her readers would share her New Woman sympathies, Robertson recognized that her own beliefs and those of some of her readers were not the same, meaning that she had to write and edit carefully if she wanted to perpetuate her own ideas without offending more conservative readers. The same may be said of those who advertised with the *Ladies Pictorial Weekly*. Robertson likely realized that they advertised within women's interest magazines because they recognized that females were the primary consumers within Canadian households and wanted to reach their target market,[18] not because they wanted to support the woman's rights campaign.

Robertson assumed an editorial stance that, like Karr's authors, straddled between traditional propriety and New Woman modernity.[19] She was careful to edit and write articles for *Ladies Pictorial Weekly* that reflected Victorian female gender norms yet also incorporated her own New Woman ideas. This was especially the case in articles pertaining to higher education for women, women and work, and love and marriage.

In the February 13, 1892, *Ladies Pictorial Weekly* article entitled "Let Us Live," Robertson reinforced assertions she had first made in the *Varsity* when she stubbornly argued that women belonged in institutions of higher education. She also reasoned that it was inexcusable that modern women be expected to put household duties above education:

> [i]t is a human being, then, merely a machine, whose chief use is to mend clothing and sew buttons! Shall a bit of mending be exalted before a thousand other duties, privileges or opportunities of life ... there are plenty of other things to be done by an intelligent girl.[20]

To further substantiate her argument, Robertson claimed that

> [w]e have fallen on times when the force of educated women is largely needed in the higher ministrations of life. She must become a home-keeper

not a house-keeper. There is a vast difference. Or, if she is in the life of art, or professions, or social work, her best strength must go to her especial work.[21]

Significantly though, Robertson argued for higher education for women while still asserting that women's place in life should lie primarily within the home, clear evidence of her stance as a transitional thinker. By listing various possible vocations for women outside the home, she extended the *Pictorial*'s appeal to New Woman readers, but at the same time she disarmingly appealed to more conservative views. As literary scholar Ann Ardis suggests in her 1999 work "Organizing Women: New Woman Writers, New Woman readers, and Suffrage Feminism," many New Woman writers such as Robertson composed their work in a way that would allow readers to "ignore that with which she cannot identify, to fail to hear/read whatever messages miss her mark" and to identify with those elements which she recognized as reflective of her world-view.[22] This allowed larger audiences to consume Robertson's work as certain elements appealed to conservative readers while others appealed to New Woman readers.

Though primarily advocating women's right to higher education, the article "Let Us Live" also demonstrated Robertson's second prevalent New Woman theme: women and work (both paid and unpaid). A first impression of Robertson's periodical might lead one to believe that any article pertaining to women and work would only discuss women's unpaid work within the home and glorify domesticity. That impression would be understandable due to the fact that aside from providing the title, the masthead also boasted a hand-drawn illustration of Queen Victoria and a quote from writer George Eliot which read "A woman's rank lies in the fulness of her womanhood: therein alone is she royal [sic]."[23] During the Victorian era, the only socially sanctioned measures of womanhood were the tenets of the cult of true womanhood, which included domesticity. Appealing to that view, Robertson incorporated section headings within the paper such as "Practical Information for the Housewife," "Culinary," and "Mother's Corner" to indicate the prevalence and the perceived importance of domesticity in the lives of Canadian women. Notably, there was no section heading related to women's paid work outside the home.[24]

"Practical Information for the Housewife" was a regular feature of the *Ladies Pictorial Weekly* that included advice on how best to care for one's home. The quote atop the housewifery section originally proclaimed

"Nothing lovelier can be found in woman than to study household good,"[25] but beginning in April 1892, Robertson changed it to "[a] hint is often all that is needed,"[26] indicating that because women were inherently capable in the domestic realm, all they would ever need would be hints here and there, and not outright directions. The articles within this section suggested that women's domestic work largely centred on cleaning and decorating the home, highlighting the importance of creating an aesthetically pleasing, comfortable home for one's family.[27] Though these articles suggested ways to save time or make household tasks easier, they were specifically directed at women, emphasizing that this was the type of work they should be dedicated to performing.

Within this section, women's role as household consumer was also underscored in articles such as "What to Try," "Home Hints," and "Useful Household Suggestions."[28] By providing women with lists of items needed within the home and disclosing where they could be purchased, these articles reinforced that women were expected to be responsible for allocating the resources needed to run an efficient household.[29] This meant that women had to venture into the public sphere to procure goods, but it is crucial to consider that they were only expected to do so to fulfil their duties within the domestic realm. The "Culinary" section provided women with lists of goods that were needed to prepare meals for their families and guests while entertaining. The recipes were detailed and time-consuming, with preparation and cooking time taking up to three hours in some cases.[30] This meant that not only would women have to remain within the home while preparing them, but they would have had to shop for the necessary ingredients prior to preparing these recipes.

Robertson recognized that for her readers, aside from caring for the home, shopping for household goods, and cooking family meals, childrearing was an important priority. Some of the articles in *Ladies Pictorial Weekly* advocated traditional Victorian childrearing including instilling moral and religious values and idealizing motherhood as women's ultimate responsibility.[31] Yet, as further evidence of her transitional thinking, Robertson wrote and published articles that capitalized upon common child-rearing dilemmas and offered solutions that advanced her own personal beliefs. It is significant that Robertson used "Mother's Corner" to covertly advance New Woman ideas. The article "Teach Your Children Self-Reliance," found in "Mother's Corner" in the February 13, 1892, issue provides an example of how Robertson applied this strategy.[32] She took up the question of "creating proper self-reliance" in children, asserting that it was a difficult thing for parents to know how "to give the child this confidence and still avoid boldness and impudence," but she offered her advice on how best to do so.[33] To those who were raising a daughter she suggested that

[w]hen a girl is of nine or ten years of age and has good health it is well for her to have some household duty to perform regularly … let her select the work providing it is something suited to her age and strength … You may find it a good plan to pay her a sum of money for the work she does … As she grows older her work should be gradually increased, at the same time paying her more if possible. Daughters who receive some compensation regularly, without having to go to mother or father to ask for it, usually are more contented and happy, and take greater pride in their work and do it better.[34]

Though Robertson was not suggesting female children should be exempt from traditional domestic duties, she put forward the idea that young women should be given the opportunity to choose the type of work they did and that they should be remunerated for their work. Thus, Robertson was able to skillfully promote change in the next generation of women without disturbing the status quo.

Robertson discussed her reformist ideas more explicitly when she published a commentary discussing women's work entitled "Woman – A Bird's Eye View." In it, Robertson praised women's traditional domestic role, yet maintained that some women longed to work outside the home and should be compensated justly if they chose to work for pay.[35] Having established that, essentially, without women in the domestic realm, society could not function, Robertson insisted that

[n]ot all daughters and sisters, and mothers, however, can remain in the dear hut called home. A woman frequently finds that she must be somebody on her own account, and no longer does she strive to get along on the reputation of her ancestors, and of her brothers and father.[36]

After making this radical statement, especially the inclusion of mothers in her list of women who might want to work outside the home, Robertson distanced herself from her comments. She wrote "[t]here are occupations and professions we would *not* like her to follow, new powers and new empires *we* would not wish for her." The emphasis on the word "we" would indicate to readers that Robertson did not necessarily condone all forms of work for women. Nevertheless, she made her argument regarding women's pay, claiming that "[w]here she is admitted, however, as man's equal in point of quality and quantity of labour, we cannot, within the range of our minds, find a shadow of reason for her remuneration being a half, a fifth of that he receives."[37]

The article "Women of the South," found in the February 6, 1892, edition, also incorporated this dual-edged approach to New Woman ideas regarding paid employment.[38] In the commentary, women from the southern United States were commended for being "the best match to man in business matters of any woman you can find." The author also praised southern women for demanding the wages she felt they deserved, regardless of sex,

> [w]ith the offer of her services comes the sum of money she expects for it. While the employer haws and hedges – as he is sure to do – she hums Dixie … She knows he'll take her terms, and she means to give him full return for what she gets.[39]

First Robertson praised attributes that would be considered desirable only to New Women, then she made an appeal to the Victorian sensibilities of readers by emphasizing that women entering the paid workforce, such as these southern women, need not reject respectable femininity for

> [s]he works royally, but she never for an instant relinquishes her belief that no woman ought to work. She still looks up to a man as a god-like and superior creature, and never accepts the fact that a woman should ride in anything but her own carriage, go out after dark without an escort, or open the door for herself. And it's a good belief.[40]

Once again, Robertson was able to discuss New Woman ideas while retaining an air of respectability by pointing out southern women's business skills and insisting that they not use them unless it was necessary.

Another means by which Robertson promoted her own ideas relating to paid employment was to allow firms looking for female employees to purchase space and publish want ads in the *Ladies Pictorial Weekly*. Companies such as Brown Bros. Co. published ads reading "Lady Agents Wanted: Special inducements now. Good pay weekly. Experience unnecessary. Pleasant light work. Can devote all or part time.

Terms and outfits free. Brown Bros Co. Toronto."[41] These, along with other advertisements from companies such as Platt-Owen, a company looking for women to sell hand-painted crafts, and *House & Home*, a women's magazine seeking female sales agents, allowed Robertson to not only promote the idea of paid work outside the home for women, but to facilitate their access to it as well.[42]

These advertisements combined elements of traditional thinking and used them to justify the respectability of the work to be performed, which is reflective of the strategy Robertson used to propagate her ideas concerning women and paid work. A June 18, 1892, Platt-Owen advertisement exemplifies this approach: "$15 PER WEEK IS A GOOD SALARY! We will pay to any lady who wants respectable employment and can sell our goods … Light, pleasant, profitable and respectable employment."[43] Though the advertisement sought women for paid employment, the company asserted that because the work was light and pleasant, women who performed it would retain their respectability and make a profit.

While Robertson coyly maintained the air of Victorian propriety around the question of women and paid employment in the pages of the *Ladies Pictorial Weekly*, she was less covert about her New Woman ideas in other publications. In addition to her work as the editor of the *Ladies Pictorial Weekly*, this was the period when she established herself as a writer of fiction. Analysts of New Woman writing point out that the dissemination of New Woman ideals occurred through one of two forms: either novels or more popular literature such as commercial publications, particularly short stories. Robertson never wrote a book-length work of fiction; she wrote only for the commercial market by selling her stories and columns to widely read magazines and journals. Although one might conclude that this made her a less serious contributor to the genre, recent scholarship in Britain suggests that by popularizing some of the strains of New Woman thinking, authors like Robertson served to soften the message and spread feminist ideals more broadly than the radical feminist stance taken in novels. For example, Chris Willis, a scholar of New Woman literature, has argued that the New Woman in commercial fiction was "scaled down and prettied up for popular consumption in a variety of novels and stories which possibly did as much for women's rights as did the more serious fiction produced by the campaigners."[44] One can conclude, therefore, that given her popular audience, Madge Robertson enjoyed an influence among readers that was both widespread and significant.

The best examples of her writing on the subject of careers for women are found in a series of columns entitled "By the Fireside," which she published in the *Globe* in Toronto in the winter of 1893. For that series, Robertson created a cast of fictional characters who discussed the pros and cons of various careers for women. As Barman reminds us, when biographers consider texts written by their subjects, they take up the task of "reimagining the author as a gendered human being whose texts reflect key cultural conditions."[45] The characters that Robertson created to meet regularly by the fireside were debating topics that were very much on the minds of readers as middle-class women took to the public sphere during this era of reform. There is no doubt that these fictional discussions were at least somewhat autobiographical, as the characters took up the topics of women in teaching and women in newspaper work, two fields where Robertson's own experience coincided closely with that of her characters' career choices. Literary scholar Ann Heilmann makes the argument that "in its most typical form, New Woman fiction is feminist fiction written by women, and deals with middle-class heroines who in some way re-enact autobiographical dilemmas faced by the writers themselves … [it is] a genre at the interface between auto/biography, fiction and feminist propaganda."[46] Reading Robertson's writing in this phase of her life, one can see that like most other authors, her texts "reveal the preoccupations, anxieties and confidences of our debates and disputes from the time we live in."[47]

As a former teacher herself,[48] Robertson wrote one character into "By the Fireside" who found that teaching was too constraining: the woman's whole life was under close surveillance regarding such things as her housing arrangements. Moreover, teaching across the broad range of curriculum, including physical education, was very stressful, though certainly not beyond a woman's mental capacity. These insights about the drawbacks of a teaching career might serve to explain why Robertson made a hasty exit from teaching when the Parkdale Collegiate Institute closed, in order to devote herself to writing full-time. Close scrutiny over the details of a teacher's private life did not suit Robertson's fictional character; as a promoter of the New Woman's right to personal freedoms, it seems entirely plausible that the author's own personal views were very close to those of her characters.

The autobiographical nature of those columns was reinforced again when Robertson turned to the topic of women and "newspaper life."[49] Here she recounted that successful women writers were answering a calling in their lives:

If a girl can write she will write, and nothing can ever stop her. But if there is any question of choosing in the matter, that is, if she hesitates between writing and any other profession, by all means let her take the other. The muse is as hard a mistress as art, and wants your whole soul or nothing. If the girls feels called to write she will not be able to keep from it.[50]

The remainder of the discussion about newspaper work was anything but a romantic picture. Robertson pointed out that until they became established writers, the pay was insufficient for women to make a living. Opportunities for full-time work on the staff of a newspaper were extremely rare for Canadian women, because "only half a dozen daily papers employ women at all, and then only, as a rule, one on each paper."[51]

The American situation was somewhat better, Robertson explained, but "you have your work cut out for you if you want to keep up with the newspaper times in New York." The problem, she explained, was the jaded nature of the American reading public, and the competition and pressure associated with writing for the daily press. It is quite conceivable that Robertson was speaking from her own experiences here, given the fact that these "By the Fireside" columns appeared several months after the announcement of her move to New York to work on the staff of *Frank Leslie's Weekly*. This particular instalment of "By the Fireside" explained that a woman who aspired to make money by writing had to understand how the writing business really worked. Some women, Robertson explained, "supply the big syndicates with fiction and miscellaneous matter concerning women ... The best off of all, I suppose, are the novelists or short story writers for the influential magazines."[52] While this column provided a good overview of the writing business in the 1890s, it also speaks volumes about the career path on which Robertson herself was well launched. The difficulties Robertson described were typical of those encountered by other Canadian female journalists and writers.[53]

Even if the life of a female journalist was not an easy one, Robertson did not lose her sense of humour. She devoted one column of "By the Fireside" to the raging debates about phrenology in which she humorously pointed out that while men's brains weighed more than women's, other mammals, including elephants and whales, had brains that were bigger still! She reached a conclusion about female superiority when she reasoned that "in comparison with the weight of her body the average woman has more brain, ounce for ounce, than the average man, in proportion to the weight of his body."[54] She applied this reasoning to the question of suitable career choices for each sex and concluded that because of their greater physical strength, men were better suited to nursing and heavy housework than women were. How much of this gender reversal she intended for serious consideration and how much for humour one is left to ponder.

Certainly Robertson would have argued that differences of physical strength had been overemphasized when it came to participation in sports; this was obvious in a series of columns entitled "Sports for Women," which she published in 1893 and 1894 through Tillotson's Newspaper Literature, a British syndication agency with a New York office.[55] Tillotson's distributed several features that Robertson wrote on a variety of sports, including skating, snowshoeing, golf, basketball, house boating, canoeing, tennis, and golf. This list of topics is further evidence that Robertson's writing was squarely within the New Woman genre. In her 1976 book, *Women and Marriage in Victorian Fiction*, Jenni Calder argues that the New Woman "wanted to do more in the open air, take more exercise, ride a bicycle, climb mountains and swim ... There was in fact a substantial body of opinion in favour of more exercise and fresh air for girls, and this necessarily involved new ideas about suitable clothes."[56] In each one of her sports columns, Robertson explained the rules of the sport, appropriate clothing for the sport, and gave humorous accounts of how she had played the sport with other women. Injecting humour into these columns, Robertson appealed to her popular audience. Writing in the first person, she made it clear that such physical activities were completely suited to female participation. Yet by adopting the light-hearted tone that was often typical of New Woman writing for the commercial market, Robertson conceded that not all women were adept at these sporting activities.[57]

Robertson also used Tillotson's to place her works of fiction, in the form of short stories rather than novels. Tillotson's was looking for this kind of writing to keep them competitive in the niche market for popular fiction, and scholars have argued that this was symptomatic of the commodification of fiction that was occurring in the 1890s as syndication agencies attempted to supply the demand for popular fiction, particularly in newspapers.[58] In the three years following her student days and up to and after her marriage, dozens of Robertson's short stories, dubbed "Storiettes" by Tillotson's, appeared in American magazines and newspapers, including *Harper's*, *Truth*, *Judge*, the *New York Recorder*, the *New York Evening Post*, *The [New York] Press*, and the

Philadelphia Times, as well as Canadian newspapers including the *Globe*, the *Mail*, and the *Collingwood Bulletin*.[59] The most common themes of her fiction pieces were romance, engagement, and marriage. This provides an excellent window through which one can assess what Robertson was thinking and how she presented New Woman ideas around the institution of marriage in her writing. Although some New Women held very radical views about the institution of marriage, Robertson's position was more moderate.[60] While she definitely tended towards the conservative end of the spectrum of views about marriage, there were New Woman elements, revealing once again that she was a transitional thinker between Victorian ideas and more modern ones.

Very often, Madge Robertson's stories on romance, such as "The Heart Knoweth," which opened this chapter, presented marriage as "problematic," giving a window into the woman's own views about the issues women faced in attempting to select a suitable mate. Chris Willis notes that the dilemma of how to find the right kind of man surfaced repeatedly in New Woman fiction.[61] In one of Robertson's short stories, entitled "The Illustration of the Orthopedic," a young woman found her true love in a man training to be a medical doctor (again, the autobiographical strains in Robertson's writing at this stage seem overt and irresistible). The young intern, who had difficulty in separating his emotions from his profession, gave a gift he had originally purchased for the heroine to a sick child instead; when his love heard about this selfless act of tenderness, she was not offended but firmly convinced they should be married.[62] Other female characters in Robertson's short stories also wrestled with the question of the woman's powerful role in deciding to accept or reject a proposal of marriage.[63] One of the most humorous of Robertson's short stories broached the question of whether or not a woman should keep secrets from her intended about previous love interests and experiences. In that example, the heroine revealed in confidence to her husband's friend that she had pressured the young man to propose to her but had always wondered if he was the right choice.[64]

Whether she was writing about careers, sports, or marriage Robertson adopted a witty style, making clever quips about well-known New Woman fiction, such as Grant Allen's novel *The Woman Who Did*.[65] At the same time, she was reflective, particularly when she wrote fiction and delved into the area of the "terra incognita" of the woman's own mind,[66] giving her characters some depth as she portrayed their perspectives on controversial questions. In her writing, Robertson was arguing for the normative nature of women pursuing careers, playing sports, and entering into marriage on their own terms. Yet, her writing was always intended for a popular audience, and so she was careful not to completely upset the status quo. Her use of humour underlined the fact that these ideas were still somewhat avant-garde: many of the women in her fictional cast of those discussing careers were not at all interested in working for pay; many of the women playing sports were not very athletic; and while an engaged woman might ponder her choice of suitors, she invariably ended up married.

When she wrote about marriage, Robertson freely offered her opinions about the reform of heterosexual relationships, although her views were somewhat ambiguous and sometimes contradictory. According to the cult of true womanhood, women were expected to be submissive to their husbands and even their suitors prior to marriage. Robertson's commentaries in the *Ladies Pictorial Weekly* suggest that while she did not completely support this notion, she still had a somewhat traditional conception of marriage. Unlike those who demonstrated an outright rejection of marriage, Robertson endorsed it. However, for her, like the majority of New Woman writers, marriage needed to be problematized. Within each of her articles on love and marriage, Robertson clearly articulated that women and men should form heterosexual unions and that these unions should ultimately lead to marriage.[67] At the same time, she strongly refuted the idea that women should be submissive to their husbands. She stressed the fact that women should have far more autonomy within heterosexual relationships than the cult of true womanhood dictated. This was a radical proposal for the time. Yet Robertson did not call for a complete overhaul of societal norms to advance her ideas. Instead, she called for women to work within their socially accepted roles to incite change. Robertson believed that women should become wives but work to create change within heterosexual relationships by asserting themselves within the union. This, she believed, was the only way for women to be truly happy within marriage.

Robertson also firmly expressed the belief that women's marital contentment hinged on the proper choice of a husband. She emphasized that a woman should be very selective when choosing her groom and she should not allow others to influence that decision, which was in itself a drastic break with Victorian norms.[68] Robertson was certain that if she could provide women with sound advice regarding how to choose a husband, they would no doubt make a wise, independent decision. In the June 4, 1892, article "Whom Not to Marry," Robertson counselled:

Never marry a man who had only his love for you to recommend him. It is very fascinating but it does not make the man. The most perfect man who did not love you should never be your husband. If the man is dishonorable to other men, or mean, or given to any vice, the time will come when you will either loathe him or sink to his level … Marriage is a solemn thing – a choice for life. Be careful in the choosing.[69]

Robertson ominously warned single women not to be duped by exaggerated male charm, lest they suffer the plight of the new bride who fell for a so-called "courteous man," then "bows her neck to the yoke when she notices how polite he is every place except at home."[70]

Once a woman chose the man she wanted to marry, Robertson believed that it was perfectly respectable for her to be the one to propose marriage. While she did not reject the institution of marriage, in a February 13, 1892, article entitled "Shall Women Propose," Robertson pushed for such a renegotiation of gender roles with regard to marriage proposals:

Some bachelor has been exciting himself on the question 'Shall Women Propose?' and I have been asked what I think about it. As to its expediency I cannot say … But I should imagine that it would be a very brave man who would refuse any lady who should do him such an honour. As to its advisability – that seems to me a matter of the lady's anxiety to get married. As to its propriety I fancy that in this, as in every other matter, each woman is a law unto herself … But seriously speaking … there are fewer matters needing reform than this.[71]

Afterwards, Robertson reassured her conservative readers that while some women might choose to propose to men, there was no need to worry about a complete overhaul of the social norm dictating that males should propose for "[t]he iron rod custom will never blossom into forgetfulness of male prerogatives […]."[72]

Within her editorial column that appeared directly beneath "Shall Women Propose," Robertson invited her readers to write to the *Ladies Pictorial Weekly* and share their opinions on the subject.[73] This may have been done simply to build a relationship with her readers. Considering that this article was only published in the second issue Robertson edited, however, it is highly probable that as a new editor, she used the opportunity to develop a deeper understanding of her readers' viewpoints, to determine whether they subscribed to Victorian norms or reformist New Woman ideals. If this was indeed the case, it is likely that readers responded positively to the notion of breaking certain heterosexual norms, for many subsequent articles focused on the subject.[74]

Robertson recognized that given society's emphasis on female submissiveness, women would also need guidance regarding how to maintain their autonomy within the marital relationship. She emphasized that women who were completely submissive to men would be terribly unhappy,[75] and proceeded to provide readers with ways that would allow them to push the boundaries within marriage and yet maintain the appearance of respectability. She astutely recognized that on the question of female submissiveness, it might be more strategic for women to use the ideals of female propriety to gain influence (and happiness) within marriage. In the April 9, 1892, article "Happy Wives," she insisted that "[t]here are few women who actually know how to control the worst of man's nature, and resort to the worst possible means to obtain this end. Wives, let me give you some kindly advice."[76] This advice included

> "[i]f he is away from you, do not follow him or pry into his habits; rest assured if he is in the wrong he knows it and likely tries to hide it from you. But if you, dear wife, find out then he is more likely not to care and to be more bold. If he is out late and comes home with an excuse, and you know he has spoken falsely, do not advise him of it, but say: 'Well dear, I am sorry but don't be so late next time.' If you make a row about it, the next time he will not only refuse to say where he has been, but go without sanction, while if you are patient his heart is full of remorse and he loves you the more ... a little indifference will draw him closer to home.[77]

Ending the article, Robertson noted that "[i]n time you can rid a man from his every bad habit and you will be much happier in the end."[78] The message put forth that women could actively influence their husbands' behaviour by exercising a certain degree of manipulation through indifference was subversive. While women would be able to appear as though they were maintaining female gender norms, they would actually be shifting the balance of power within marriage.

Another means of advocating marital reform within the *Ladies Pictorial Weekly* was to address husbands and the part they played in the submission of women. To begin with, Robertson asserted that contrary to popular opinion, husbands should be and remain emotionally invested in marriages rather than leaving all of the nurturing work to the woman without any reciprocation.[79] In her June 11, 1892, article, "Man's Love," Robertson undermined a commonly held stereotype by explaining that

> [a]lthough we have the dictum of Byron that "Man's love is of man's life a thing apart; 'tis woman's whole existence" we hold it to be but a poor and commonplace philosophy which teaches that man cannot love as truly and permanently as woman … In truth, the heart that has truly loved, whether it be feminine or masculine, seldom ceases to worship at the shrine of its pure, exalted devotion.[80]

As this passage demonstrates, Robertson dismissed too much emphasis on differences between men and women.

Instead, Robertson suggested ways that husbands could demonstrate their love and compassion for their overworked, under-appreciated wives. In her article "A Husband's Confession," Robertson traced the root of many marriage problems to the fact that some husbands "seem[ed] to have forgotten or purposely set aside" some of the "courtesies of life" they had shown their wives prior to marriage.[81] The article was supposedly written from the perspective of a male who believed that a lack of respect for wives led to a "lack of harmony and happiness in many homes."[82] Robertson called for a remedy to this problem by urging husbands and wives to maintain reciprocal respect for each other after they were married.

The article "Give the Wife a Vacation" took this notion even further, suggesting that husbands who respect their wives and the work they perform within the domestic sphere should arrange regular vacations for them. As Robertson reasoned,

> A man usually works eight, ten, or twelve hours a day, as the case may be; but when he is done he is done, the remainder of his time is a holiday … Is this the case with the wife? True she has not worked all day in the sun, but she has been very busy. Does her day's work end with his? Not at all. Cares follow her all over the house. The cooking, the baby to attend to, to-morrow's breakfast to look after … Can't the man arrange for a week's trip for his wife? [sic][83]

Whether men actually read these works in the *Ladies Pictorial Weekly* is unknown, but Robertson reveals a great deal about her personal circumstances at this stage, as she wrote from her vantage point as a playful, single, employed, university-educated young woman. One could easily argue that these relatively carefree years were one of the happiest times of her entire life. The witty and light-hearted nature of her writing appealed to a wide range of readers, and her writings tell a great deal about the ideas that she was entertaining around the changing roles of women when it came to careers, physical activities, and marriage relationships. Slightly subversive in her subtle suggestions about how women could exert more power over their lives and their relationships, she was still guarded enough not to completely challenge Victorian propriety. The ambiguity of her ideas was no doubt part of its appeal, as most of her published works brought a smile to the face of her readers either through the familiar debates she raised about education and employment for women, her cautiously progressive advice to housewives, or the charming yet often manipulative young women she created as characters in her short stories.

The playful period of Robertson's writing life came to an abrupt end in the spring of 1893 when her mother died. Returning from New York to Collingwood to help nurse her mother through the illness that claimed her life, Robertson put her own career interests on hold temporarily. The local newspaper reported Bethia Robertson's passing with great sympathy for her grieving family, and it is clear that her mother's death cast a long shadow over young Madge. In a rare instance of self-reflection written many years later, Robertson explained the impact of her mother's death in this short autobiographical sketch written in the third person:

> She spent a year in newspaper work in New York, writing short stories, humorous and sporting sketches, and children's stories for *Judge, Life, Puck, Leslie's Weekly, Truth, Vogue,* New York newspapers. But after the untimely death of her dearly loved mother, who had always been her inspiration, no further writing of this nature seemed possible.[84]

Within days after her mother's death, Madge Robertson celebrated her twenty-fifth birthday, and it seems that that significant milestone marked the end of her youth in more ways than one. It was the first time that she had experienced the death of anyone so close to her, but it was not the last time that death would mark a significant turning point in her life, as we shall see. Setting aside her writing career, her youthful pursuits, and her propensity to amuse others, seven months after her mother's death, Margaret Rose Robertson made a very serious decision and took the life-altering step of getting married and moving across the country to British Columbia.

Chapter Three

Playing Multiple Parts: Family, Society, and Sorrow

After writing so much about romance themes in her fiction it is not clear whether Madge Robertson, like the fictional new women she wrote about, initiated the proposal of marriage to her fiancé or not, but on December 14, 1893, the *Enterprise and Collingwood Messenger* recounted that

> [a] very pretty house wedding took place at the residence of Henry Robertson, Esq., Q.C., last Thursday afternoon, when his eldest daughter, Margaret Rose (Madge) was united in marriage to Alfred Tennyson Watt, M.D., of Victoria, B.C. The bride, who looked charming, carried a magnificent bouquet of white roses ... The knot was tied by the Rev. Dr. McCrae, of the Presbyterian church. The young couple left by the 4 o'clock train for New York, where the honeymoon will be spent.[1]

The newlyweds had known each other at least since their university days, and Madge had travelled to the west coast in 1892, presumably to visit the young doctor in the city where he had established a successful medical practice. Robertson wrote and published in instalments an account of her travels to the west, but there was no hint in those accounts that the purpose of her trip was to visit her varsity sweetheart.[2]

The twenty years that Madge Robertson Watt would spend in British Columbia from 1893 to 1913 represent a long and significant chapter in her life. Historian Jean Barman describes how British Columbia underwent a transformation during those same years from "a fragile settler society on the frontier of the western world [to become] a self-confident political and social entity."[3] In many ways Watt's personal experiences mirrored the development process that the province itself was undergoing, because as she and Alfred established their family life and public personae, they matured from twenty-five-year-old newly-weds to confident middle-aged professionals with a wide variety of public roles and responsibilities. For Madge Watt, these were her "coming of age" years, when she was simultaneously performing a variety of roles including wife, mother, writer, socialite, club woman, and advisor to government. In each of these roles, she not only drew upon her previous experiences, but also was shaped in ways that would uniquely prepare her for the challenges and adventures that she would face in the second half of her life.

Madge Robertson was not the first member of her family to see the west coast of Canada, nor was she the first to write about her experiences in travelling there. While Madge and Alfred were still at university, in 1888, her parents had also visited British Columbia as part of their transcontinental trip in conjunction with Henry's lodge activities. Her parents each published an account of their travels: Bethia in a newspaper, and Henry in a lodge publication. Though they could not have known at the time that their daughter would end up living there after her marriage, the Robertsons' impressions of Victoria are fascinating. Bethia described the city to her readers as "a quiet place, [that] has none of that restless activity so prevalent in western towns. The people seem so satisfied with their lot in life and content to take things easy."[4] She also took note of the wealth that was being generated from coal mining on Vancouver Island, mentioning the Dunsmuir family's business interests in particular, but of course she could not have predicted that several years later her own daughter would be socializing with those very people.[5] Mrs. Robertson recounted further that she and her husband "had a pleasant drive round the city and suburbs and saw lots of roses in bloom and many other flowers and some handsome residences. A stroll through the Chinese quarter and an inspection of their shops was very interesting."[6] Even with such a brief introduction to the city, her travel account highlighted the comfortable lifestyle of the elite, the wealth that could be accumulated there, and the interracial mix of the population. In a little more than five years' time, Bethia's daughter would be firmly installed as part of that city after her marriage, enjoying the very same aspects of the place that her mother had noted.

Henry Robertson's description of Victoria also highlighted things about the city that foreshadowed some aspects of his daughter's future life. He observed that in Victoria "most of the people are English – talking with an English accent, and living according to English customs.

In our hotel everybody was English from the proprietor down to the bellboy, except the chambermaids who were Chinamen."[7] Of course Robertson could not have known that just a few years later, the census records would reveal a Chinese labourer as part of his own daughter's household.[8] Nor could he possibly have known that her time living there would prepare her for the next chapter of her life, when she would relocate to England. Robertson noted that "if anybody wants to see an English town, and study English customs, and enjoy an English climate, without crossing the Atlantic, he need only go to Victoria, where he will find everything English except the politics, which are neither Liberal nor Conservative, but Victoria first!"[9]

Barman describes British Columbia in the first two decades of the twentieth century as "the most urban and the least urban province in Canada."[10] That description is intriguing because while Madge Watt revelled in the urban amenities she found in Victoria, it was there that she first cast herself as a rural woman and became active in organizing Women's Institutes. The fact that Watt lived out a mix of urban and rural experiences is due to the nature of the medical work that her husband took up, first in the city of Victoria, and from 1897 on, in the more rural setting of William Head, near Metchosin, BC, about thirty kilometres by land from the city itself. When the Watts lived there, on their property adjacent to the quarantine station, the place was somewhat isolated because there was no road access from their home to Victoria, and their travel was always by boat. Still, it was a trip that could easily be made in one day, and even after their move to William Head, the Watts were frequent visitors to Victoria. With such easy access to the amenities of the city, their experience of rural living would be scarcely recognizable to fellow British Columbians living in more remote resource-based communities.

Dr. Watt's medical expertise was welcomed in the rapidly expanding city, and his reputation was established quickly during his first few years there. Even before his marriage, the young doctor's name regularly appeared in the Victoria newspaper.[11] Concern about contagious diseases was heightened in Victoria at the end of the nineteenth century when the steady flow of international travellers continually put the city on alert for potential epidemics, testing its ability to cope with contagious diseases. As a result, the presence of medical practitioners like Watt was welcomed.[12] Alfred Watt was not the only medical practitioner in his family, nor the only one in Victoria; by the 1890s his father, Dr. Hugh Watt, who was previously the owner of a local newspaper in Meaford, Ontario, was both a medical doctor and a member of the BC provincial legislature.[13] Published reports of the discussions among elected officials demonstrate that the elder Dr. Watt was central to the policy discussions that dominated the provincial government's agenda, particularly on public health issues around quarantine and prevention of epidemics.[14] Having such a prominent father certainly must have helped the young doctor as he set up his practice and built his reputation in Victoria. Thrust into prominence because of his father's public life and proving himself to be a valuable addition to the local medical community in his own right, Alfred Watt was poised to do very well for himself as he welcomed his new bride to his adopted city.

When she arrived, Madge Watt entered fully into the society life of Victoria, and her cultural activities were numerous. She was a charter member of the University of Toronto's Alumni Association, and the Watts hosted the inaugural meetings for the planning of this group when the president of the University of Toronto came to Victoria in 1903.[15] The records of the Victoria chapter of the University Women's Club show that Watt was also a charter member of that club when it organized in July 1908.[16] She was the contact person and chief organizer for music testing that was conducted through the University of Toronto. She was also active in the local council of women, the Mothers' Club, the King's Daughters, and the women's press club. The Watts were regular guests at Government House for various functions, and even after they moved out to William Head, the couple made frequent visits to Victoria. News of their social activities regularly appeared in the social columns of the Victoria newspapers.

In the midst of her busy life as part of Victoria's elite, Madge Watt still maintained her literary interests on several fronts. In 1894–95 she was invited to give a series of lectures on literature to a group of young women at St. Ann's Academy in Victoria, where she spoke on a wide range of authors, including Woodsworth, Shelley, Browning, Milton, Tennyson, and others. The *Victoria Daily Times* followed her lectures closely, reporting on each one. Putting her own education to good use, she was clearly drawing on what she had learned in her courses at university, maybe even reworking some of the papers that she had read a few years earlier to the Modern Languages Club; in this and many other ways, Watt was a strong advocate of higher education for women. At the conclusion of the lecture series, she was quoted in the Victoria press as saying that "the cause of education ought to lie near the hearts of all good women."[17]

Meanwhile, although she would claim later in life that her mother's death had put an end to her light-hearted fictional writing, several more of her stories and contributions were published in New York magazines and papers, including *Truth* and *Harper's*, the last of these appearing in the summer of 1896.[18] Building on her previous reputation, she published these pieces under her maiden/pen name "Madge Robertson," and they offer proof that while she had moved on from her literary personae and her humorous creations, the products of her writing life were still enjoyed by a wide audience in the popular press. With a new name and a new identity as Mrs. Watt, however, it was possible for her to put distance between her more playful writing life in Toronto and New York and the public responsibilities she took on as part of her married life in British Columbia, while simultaneously combining the role of writer with those of wife, mother, and socialite.

From 1893 on, the Canadian government operated a quarantine station at William Head, BC, on Vancouver Island to inspect the passengers on ocean-going vessels arriving at the ports of Victoria and Vancouver.[19] That station was one of more than a dozen such facilities operated by the federal government from the nineteenth century well into the twentieth. Studying William Head, BC, as a place is fascinating. When I made a site visit to the former quarantine station, to explore the scene of Dr. Watt's work and the controversial end of his career, I had the rare privilege of being granted admission – rare because William Head is not a historic site that is open to the public. The former quarantine station is still a federal property, but it is now the site of the William Head Institution, a medium-security prison. Permitted to enter the facility, where I spent the day working in the on-site archives, I also toured the grounds to view the remains of the wharf where Dr. Watt greeted the arrival of ships destined for Victoria and Vancouver between 1897 and July 1913, to walk through the graveyard where he and his staff buried the victims who succumbed to their diseases, and to see many of the original quarantine buildings where Watt developed then state-of-the-art technologies for the disinfection of passengers and their baggage. Local historians around William Head are well aware of the history of the site, of course, and although the property's current use does not permit on-site restoration or commemoration, the local museum, housed in the Metchosin schoolhouse nearby, has artefacts and photographs from the quarantine station itself. A local history publication on the area's "pioneer families" includes a two-page entry about the Watts, but it concentrates more on the activities of Mrs. Watt than those of her husband.[20]

In January 1897, Dr. Alfred Watt was appointed supervisor of BC Quarantines, to be stationed at William Head.[21] Madge's husband was well-qualified for this position. After graduating from the University of Toronto in 1890, he practised medicine in BC, first for a number of months in Barkerville in the Cariboo District, and then in Victoria, where he became secretary to the Provincial Board of Health. By the time he accepted the appointment to William Head on Vancouver Island, his accomplishments included "inaugurat[ing] the first real public health work in this province [BC]. The Health Act was largely his work. Previously during the smallpox epidemic he had rendered good service."[22] Of course, it did not hurt that his father, also a medical doctor, was the MPP for the Cariboo District in the years leading up to his appointment.

William Head was a strategic location for the inspection of trans-pacific travellers entering Canada, and annual reports on the station, available from 1902 to 1914, show that during that twelve-year period, Dr. Watt was responsible for the inspection of more than 2,700 ships. However, the number of ships being inspected there was also declining; the all-time high was 442 ships in 1902, but from 1909 to 1914 the number fell to an annual average of 161 ships. While Watt served as inspector, during an average year he would detain only two ships after detecting contagious diseases on board.[23] The declining instances of ships being quarantined is a testament not just to a declining rate of traffic, but also to the fact that new measures were in place in ports around the world, requiring passengers to undergo mandatory vaccination; although smallpox continued to be the most common reason that Watt placed ships in quarantine, there was no major incident of smallpox outbreak or epidemic in Canada during the time that he served as the chief medical officer at William Head. The inspector's job was to identify individual cases of contagious diseases among arriving passengers, to administer vaccinations, and when he deemed it necessary, to impose quarantine as a preventative measure so that he could verify that no additional cases were likely to occur among fellow passengers of those who had manifested symptoms. The main priority of Watt and his staff was to be in a constant state of readiness so that as ships arrived, they could be inspected and either cleared to proceed to their port of entry or, in the case of an infectious disease being detected, be detained so that the ship's contents could be disinfected and its passengers and crew quarantined until all danger of new cases developing had passed.

During the first year of his new job, things went well for Dr. Watt. A press account in the fall of 1897 explained how "considerable improvements have been made at William Head, and the appliances and buildings are now in a better condition than ever before to handle a large number of passengers."[24] Taking pride in her husband's success, Madge Watt clipped this story from the newspaper and mailed it to her father back home in Collingwood so that he could read about his prominent son-in-law's accomplishments. "When Dr. Watt took charge," the paper reported,

> there was absolutely nothing in the shape of disinfecting appliances save a shed containing a chamber for super-heated steam. Baths were given in a common washtub and there was only one in the building, while the unfortunate bathers were compelled to dress in the open air.[25]

Henry Robertson included this clipping in the family scrapbook, acknowledging the importance of his son-in-law's work, not just in protecting individual passengers, but also as a public-health gatekeeper for Canada as a whole. Madge Watt shared this good report with her father, partly, perhaps, to illustrate the primitive conditions that she and Alfred had to overcome as they settled in to their new rural life, but also, no doubt, to underline the importance of the work that her husband was doing. "Dr. Watt has worked unceasingly to bring the station up to its present condition," the article declared, and because of him, "William Head quarantine station will be able to cope with any possible emergency. It will then be a pretty safe defense against any infectious diseases attacking us from the sea."[26]

The William Head quarantine station was lauded again five years later when Bernard McEvoy published his book, *From the Great Lakes to the Wide West: Impressions of a Tour between Toronto and the Pacific*, in which he highlighted not only the natural beauty of the country, but also the industrial and engineering developments that he noted along the way. Devoting almost an entire chapter to Watt's work at the quarantine station and the technological advances that he had introduced, McEvoy described him as "the right man in the right place," not only because the young doctor was sometimes called upon to perform the "athletic nautical feat" of boarding a ship in rough weather, but also because "as the governor of this little lonely settlement on the rocky coast he exercises manifold functions."[27] What really impressed McEvoy, however, were the advances that Watt was making in the science of disease prevention. He described the quarantine station in some detail, noting

> Down by the wharf ... things look very business-like and functionary. Here there are large sheds and very complete machinery for fumigating

and disinfecting. There is a sulphur apparatus by which brimstone fumes can be forced into a vessel's hold with great rapidity; a formaldehyde plant for producing another disinfecting gas, and a big steam disinfector for killing germs in clothes and bedding; also there is a bathing arrangement of great effectiveness, through which incoming Chinamen, nude and shivering, are always put.[28]

McEvoy was well-qualified to comment on the work that Watt was doing because he was "one of the first workers in steam sterilizing chambers and invented the first one used in Toronto."[29] It seems that McEvoy was something of a renaissance man, because while he had that science background, he was also a published poet and one who appreciated and followed with interest Madge's own writing and publications, describing her in his account of William Head as the "talented wife, well-known as a writer in New York magazines and newspapers."[30]

Madge and her husband had a heightened appreciation for global trends and events because of the time they spent at William Head. In Dr. Watt's annual reports to the government of Canada, he revealed his keen awareness of international developments and the impact they were having on his work. In answer to why he was detaining fewer and fewer ships as the years went by, Watt offered several explanations, including world-wide acceptance of the importance of vaccination, which meant that mandatory precautions were being taken at most major ports throughout the Orient. As a result, fewer cases of contagious diseases were being detected among passengers arriving in Canada. In 1905 he concluded that the $500 head tax imposed on Chinese immigrants to Canada "has prevented new arrivals entirely."[31] As well, effective January 1, 1905, ships arriving from San Francisco and ports north of there were exempt from inspection. Watt anticipated in 1907 that "work on the Panama Canal and the construction of a railway across Mexico from the Gulf to the Pacific ... [means] there will be a new point on the coast from which steamers will come to B.C. ports."[32] At the same time in 1907, he observed that world events such as the end to war between Japan and Russia had a direct impact on the number of ships arriving at BC ports. While some might have pitied the Watts for the degree of isolation they experienced at this outpost on Vancouver Island, it turns out that the doctor's work only served to heighten their exposure to and appreciation of global developments. Unbeknownst to her, this interest in world affairs was one thing that was shaping Madge Watt for her later international work.

When Dr. Watt accepted the position as inspector of quarantine, he uprooted his young family from their comfortable life in Victoria and relocated them to a more rural setting near Metchosin, BC. At that time, the Watt household included Alfred and Madge and their infant son, Henry Robertson Watt (nicknamed "Robin"), who was born in September 1896. Census records from 1901 and 1911 reveal some important details about the Watts' new life. For one thing, the job paid very well; when he was appointed in 1897 Watt was earning $2,500, commanding a salary that is equivalent to more than $320,000 in today's terms.[33] For a man who had not yet attained thirty years of age, that was an impressive earning level indeed; it meant that while they lived on a rural acreage near the quarantine station, complete with some prize sheep and ample space for gardens, the Watts could well afford to include hired help in their household. By the time of the 1901 census, they had a twenty-two-year-old Chinese labourer named Za Duok who assisted them with the farm work and did the cooking, a male lodger named Harold Anderson who was the assistant physician at the quarantine station, and a twenty-eight-year-old governess, Myrtle Winter, who helped with child care. By the time of the 1911 census, Dr. Watt's income had risen to $3,000, and their domestic helper was a twenty-one-year-old Chinese man named Juan Wah. A female lodger named Lee Cecilia Francis was also part of the household, and while it is not clear whether she was working as a caregiver, one suspects that she must have been, because the Watts had added another child to their household: Madge gave birth in December 1906 to a second son, Hugh, named for his paternal grandfather, but nicknamed "Sholto."[34]

Ten years seems a long time between babies in these early years of the century, and given the high rates of infant mortality, one might suspect that there were other births between these two boys. Indeed, for Madge's sister, Katie Robertson Arthur, who got married in Collingwood, Ontario, in 1900 and remained there for the rest of her life,[35] the childbearing years were punctuated with the deaths of three infant children, and the gravestones in the family burial plot in Collingwood reveal that sorrow was a regular visitor to the home of that young family.[36] For Madge and Alfred Watt, however, there is no trace of similar tragedy. No published record of births other than those of Robin and Sholto appeared in either the Victoria or Collingwood papers, and there are no Watt baby graves in the Ross Bay Cemetery in Victoria, the site of Alfred Watt's burial, nor in the Robertson family plot where Madge's nieces and nephews were interred in Collingwood. One possible explanation for this prolonged spacing between the children is that the Watts were practicing some method of birth control, which is plausible given Alfred's medical training. Whether by their choice or not, Madge and Alfred's family was completed with the birth of two sons, and it seems that they were spared the sorrow that was so common to other parents in this period, including members of their own extended family.

While it is difficult to know how the Watt household functioned in terms of daily responsibilities, we do have one glimpse into Madge Watt's views on raising boys in an 1892 opinion piece that appeared in the *Ladies Pictorial Weekly* while she was editor. With ideas that seem somewhat radical for the time, the article, entitled "Mother's Boy," suggested a certain fluidity of gender roles, as mothers were advised that

> it will not hurt your boys to learn to do many things pertaining to the domestic machinery of your home. They may be taught as easily as girls, and would be delighted to feel that their help was really needed and appreciated. Do not say 'What can a boy do?' for a boy can do any kind of house-work which a girl can, yes, he can learn to use a needle and thread just as easily. Do you not remember the trials you had in learning to sew, especially to use the thimble? Why not teach boys to sew on buttons, and mend torn garments as well as their sisters?[37]

Continuing with her instructions about how to prepare boys for adulthood, the author suggested that

> [a] boy who is careful not to bring in dirt on his boots, who puts papers and books where they belong, who always hangs up his hat, and who is looking out for places where he can help his mother, will make a better husband than the one who thinks his mother was made purposely to wait upon him.[38]

It is not entirely clear, of course whether Madge actually raised her boys this way or indeed whether these musings, written in the year before she got married, were actually describing her idea of an ideal son or an ideal husband. Either way, the notion that housework could be mastered by children of either sex suggests that Watt was quite progressive

in her ideas about parenting. One can only speculate whether her practices matched these ideas.

In the fall of 1896, just a few weeks after she gave birth for the first time,
and a short time before her husband assumed his new duties at William
Head, Madge Watt took up a new and rather demanding writing position as book reviewer for the *Victoria Daily Times* newspaper. Her book
review column, entitled "By Book Post," was a regular feature of the paper
for more than ten years, and her reviews ranged over a variety of titles,
including fiction, school textbooks, and Christmas gift-giving ideas. It
seems that she had an arrangement with several publishers in Toronto,
New York, and London, England, who sent her review copies of books,
and presumably paid her to comment upon them.[39] Having moved out
of the city to the countryside, it may be that Watt welcomed the work
because the reading and writing schedule would help to fill her days as
she adjusted to rural life away from the more familiar urban setting of
Victoria. Constance Lindsay Skinner's biographer noted that when that
Canadian writer turned to book reviewing, she did not do it for the money
since "book reviewing paid a pittance," but she "use[d] the genre for self-
promotion."[40] That explanation probably applies to Madge Watt as well;
given her husband's income, she certainly did not need the money, but
she loved to see her name in print, and now that she was a young mother
living in a rural setting, she might have welcomed this work to reassure
herself that she had not completely lost touch with the publishing world.

It is not surprising that during the late 1890s and after, several "New
Woman" novels crossed Watt's desk; Watt's reactions to these books
are interesting, particularly because of the New Woman tendencies that
had been so evident in her earlier writing career in Toronto and New
York. The first novel of this genre that Watt reviewed was Sarah Grand's
famous work, *The Beth Book*. She did not like the book very much, as her
review makes clear when she reported that it was a "jumbled, illogical,
but clever bit of work" and she felt that "[i]t would be unfair to con-
demn the book, since it is a work of such pretension and written with
moral intent. But it is unpleasant to read medical books unless one is a
doctor, even if disguised as novels." In judging the book's main character, Watt concluded that "Beth's cleverness saves her from being tire-
some. She is witty, if you like, but showing the poorest judgment in the
company she keeps."[41] Watt also gave a mixed review to another Sarah
Grand novel, *Babs the Impossible*. While she deemed Grand's writing
to be admirable (the story was "cleverly and satirically told"), she did
not condone the characters that Grand created.[42] Watt also read Ouida,

another well-known New Woman novelist, concluding that "even if Ouida is excessive, she is always picturesque."[43] One can conclude from these reviews that although she was not a great fan of New Woman novels, Watt did find some redeeming features in many of them.

There was, however, one New Woman novel that Watt found completely unacceptable. In 1898, the Robert Lewis Weed Publishing Company of New York released Mary Ives Todd's *The Heterodox Marriage of a New Woman*. Watt wrote a scathing review that is best expressed in her own words:

> Once in a while a thoroughly unworthy book comes through the mail. "The Heterodox Marriage of a New Woman" … has, so far as I can judge from a hasty skimming through, not a single redeeming feature. It is vulgar, pretentious, of no literary merit and with no good moral tendency. I shall not go so far as to say that it would ever have a bad influence, because no one will ever read it through.[44]

What would cause a progressively minded writer like Madge Robertson Watt to react so strongly against the work of a fellow New Woman author? Had married life and motherhood changed Madge Robertson's views so completely and given her a decidedly conservative turn of mind? In answering those questions, it is important to bear in mind that New Woman fiction was not without its implicit contradictions. Scholars of New Woman literature such as Angelique Richardson and Chris Willis have come to recognize that "New Women themselves did not always define their goals clearly: their fiction and prose-writing reveal contradictions and complexities which resist reductive, monolithic readings."[45] Yet while New Woman literature might defy categorization to some extent, Richardson and Willis maintain that "nevertheless, from the various competing definitions of the New Woman certain common features [do] emerge: her perceived newness, her autonomous self-definition and her determination to set her own agenda in developing an alternative vision of the future."[46] It is useful to approach Watt's book reviews with these characteristics and contradictions in mind. Certainly, as a married woman, her involvement in and promotion of higher education was still a firmly held conviction. Her fiction and sports writing continued with great success in New York, and in those publications there was no noticeable change in theme or tone during the years after her marriage, despite her own claim that she could never write in the same way again after her mother's death.

It was the marriage question alone, and specifically the suggestion of nontraditional marriage, that provided the one point of departure where Watt refused to entertain expressions of that institution that strayed too far outside her own views. The Mary Ives Todd novel that she reviewed in 1899 celebrated the marriage of a heroine that was performed outside the confines of Christian tradition; indeed, it was even outside the accepted legal practice of state-sanctioned civil ceremony. According to Watt's review, the heroine Rae and her fiancé Paul "marry themselves by each repeating part of the Quaker contract: 'They don't approve of church or state marriages.'"[47] And clearly, Mrs. Watt did not approve of their unconventional "ceremony" either. That expression of modernity was simply going too far for Watt, and her strong reaction was also reinforced because of the characters' political ideology. The heroine of the novel and her lover were deeply committed to socialist causes, intending to travel to Siberia to further the revolutionary movement.[48] Though she would be considered a "New Woman" herself, Madge Robertson Watt could not and would not accept a marital union that went that far outside the accepted boundaries of her Christian tradition and her views of proper monogamous heterosexual relations. Nor could Watt endorse an approach to reform that called for revolutionary overthrow of the ruling class, a class that she identified so closely with as a member of the educated elite in British Columbia at the turn of the century.

With a passion equal to that with which she had denounced *The Heterodox Marriage of a New Woman*, however, Watt applauded another book, *The Confessions of a Wife*, which she reviewed in her December 1902 column.[49] Watt simply adored this book. To quote her review: "The quality of the writing is of that same subtle sort that drives the plot and its elaborations far out of one's consciousness until the force of the story penetrates."[50] Having made clear her admiration for the writing, one might expect that Watt also admired the Victorian propriety and respectability of the book as its main virtue. Surprisingly, though, she found that part of the plot to be its greatest disappointment. Her review continued:

> The tale is of the most tragic. I think it is true that every reader will regard the re-union of husband and wife at the end as a distinct misfortune. It would have been so much more humanly and artistically pleasing if he had conveniently been killed by his charming morphine habit and had given way to the real hero of the book, Doctor Robert. There would have been general thanksgiving among the readers of this much-talked of book.[51]

It is that shocking recommendation of a different ending that catches the reader's attention. How is it that Madge Robertson, Mrs. Watt, the Presbyterian, leading society woman in Victoria, with her strong Christian world view could regard the "happy ending" of a reunited couple to be a "misfortune"? What she advocated instead was a romantic liaison between a married woman and a charming doctor (albeit made respectable by the death of the husband) rather than the propriety of a dutiful wife continuing to be trapped in a loveless marriage. As she put it herself,

> [t]he character of Marna, the wife, is too beautiful for me to profane it with words. Her self-confession in letters, written in the abandonment of joy and of sorrow is so sacred, so intimate, that the woman in all of us is roused by the cruel injustice of her life.[52]

Marna was clearly not leading the satisfying life that Madge Robertson had wished for New Women, who chose their partners carefully and negotiated the power relations within their marriages. That situation roused her (new) womanly instincts.

While it would be pretentious and even cruel to speculate too closely regarding possible autobiographical parallels, the fact that Watt wished for the death of this fictitious husband seems macabre in light of what would happen in her own marriage just a little more than ten years later. While there is not enough evidence to argue that the Watts had been living in a loveless marriage prior to her husband's death, Madge's tenderness and empathy for the fictional Marna is noteworthy. It seems that for Watt, more than ten years before she faced her own tragic turn of events, romance trumped tradition, and she noted with pathos the tragic ending of a fictional woman who dutifully lived out her life with a husband recovering from an addiction and mental illness. On the other hand, it is possible that Watt wrote that review with a deliberate over-statement of her sympathies for Marna, intending to amuse her readers. After all, there was no way she could have known what the future would hold for her, and she may well have been invoking her familiar use of humour. Compared to some of the New Woman novelists who were publishing highly controversial works at the time, Madge Robertson Watt adopted what Chris Willis has characterized as a "distinctly more light-hearted" tone in her writing, and as a writer for the commercial market, she was one of the authors who "by marketing the New Woman for mass consumption, … ensured her a prominent and lasting place in popular culture."[53]

One thing Watt did not embrace about New Woman thinking was its most radical aspects, particularly its rejection of the institutions of marriage and motherhood. Instead, she found a way to put her own writing career together with her marriage and her motherhood and to argue for reforms for women from a position of privilege as a member of the elite class in turn-of-the-century British Columbia. When it came to the question of marriage, Madge Watt stood in support of traditional marriage and in opposition to anything that contradicted her Christian world view. Watt's writing career (particularly the work she did as a book reviewer) serves to reinforce the interpretation that to a certain extent, the New Woman defies categorization and homogenization. Like the most interesting characters in a New Woman novel, Watt shared certain values in common with all new women, but at the same time, she remained complex enough to present certain contradictions that defy categorization. Her career supports the contention of Richardson and Willis that there is wisdom in an approach that "seeks to make a significant departure" from the homogenizing approach to the New Woman.[54] Because Watt was simultaneously occupying the role of writer, critic, society woman, and mother, it is not surprising that her life was riddled with complexities and contradictions.

Shortly after the birth of her second son in December 1906, Watt stopped writing her book-review column, presumably so that she could devote her attention to other things.[55] One of Watt's hobbies was her garden, and she was particularly renowned for her cultivation of roses. In May 1905, the *Victoria Daily Times* noted that "a splendid bouquet of red roses is on exhibition in the windows of the Tourist Association. The roses were raised in the open air on a vine cultivated by Mrs. A.T. Watt, of William Head, which has been in full bloom since the middle of April."[56] Watt also participated as an organizer for a 1910 flower show at the Empress Hotel as part of an annual fundraising event for the King's Daughters, one of her many club involvements.[57] The Watts also took numerous honours at the local fall fair in 1910, when Madge won prizes for her fruits, including loganberries, gooseberries, and raspberries; her preserves, including jams and bottled fruits; and her crafts of ribbon work and stencil work. Dr. Watt won prizes for the fruits from his trees, including pears, peaches, and nectarines.[58] Clearly, the Watts had adapted very well to rural living.

In January 1908, the same month that the Empress Hotel opened its doors in Victoria, the social page in the *Victoria Daily Times*, entitled "Over the Tea Table," reported that "Mrs. A.T. Watt, of William Head, is spending the winter months with Mrs. Cleland, 'Hawthorndene,' Pemberton road."[59] Pemberton Road was an enviable address, only a short distance from Government House. Mrs. Cleland was Annie Cleland, whose lawyer husband, Hugh M. Cleland, had passed away just a few years before. The Watts' connection with the Clelands can be traced back to the fact that Hugh Cleland also hailed from Collingwood, Ontario, and his father was active in municipal politics at the same time that Henry Robertson was seeking office. At first glance, the news of Watt spending the winter in the city might lead one to speculate about the state of the Watts' marriage or to conclude that Madge was a devoted companion to her recently bereaved friend, or to wonder if Madge was such a woman of leisure that she simply chose to be in the city to be closer to her beloved social circle. The real reason for her relocation, however, was a very serious one.

The short press account does not do justice to Annie Cleland because it turns out that she was a medical doctor who had graduated from Trinity College at the University of Toronto in 1892, though it is not clear whether she was practicing at the time that Watt spent the winter with her.[60] What is clear is that the two women were friends, and Watt chose to remain "in the city" because of her elder son's health problems. Few details about Robin Watt's condition were disclosed, but the same columnist reported several weeks later that Mrs. Watt had returned to William Head, "taking with her, her son Robin, who is now recovering from his serious illness."[61] One can only speculate whether the boy, who was almost twelve years old at the time, had contracted one of the diseases common to the travellers his father inspected (unlikely, because if that were the case, he would have been quarantined) or some other ailment. Whatever it was, the Watts decided that his condition warranted an extended stay in Victoria, and the fact that his mother could stay with a friend who was a doctor must have provided moral support at least and maybe direct medical care. One assumes that Watt's younger son, Sholto, who had marked his first birthday in December 1907, also spent this time in the city with his mother, but the newspaper was silent on that question.

Annie Cleland and Madge Watt worked together on a number of different projects, including the establishment of the Victoria branch of the University of Toronto Alumni Association.[62] In 1910 both of them appeared before the Royal Commission on Industrial Training and Technical Education to present briefs when the commissioners came to Victoria. Cleland spoke on behalf of the Local Council of Women, of which Watt was also a member, and in her presentation she highlighted the council's findings about the lack of opportunities for female workers to find vocational training in Victoria. In the city, whose population was 50,000 in 1910, the council estimated that between 3,000 and 4,000 women were working for pay, but opportunities for training were not adequate, and the brief called for a variety of solutions, reminding the commission that because "the skilled worker is one of the nation's most valuable assets, this training would be not only an individual, but a national asset."[63] Watt spoke to the commissioners about the situation that faced rural women on Vancouver Island, and her recommendation to the commission included expanded opportunities for rural women to profit from work such as beekeeping, herb production, and in particular, opportunities for women to receive training in the form of short courses that would benefit not just the women who already lived in rural BC, but also the immigrants who were constantly arriving from such places as India, China, Japan, and Australia. This is one of the earliest occasions when Watt cast herself into the authoritative role of spokesperson for rural women. Interestingly, it was also the first time she demonstrated an interest in women with international connections. In the next few years, she would lend her efforts heavily to the Women's Institutes, and it was this role that she used to shape her identity when she moved to England just a few years later. In many ways, her appearance before this commission marked her debut performance as self-declared expert on rural women:

> In her presentation, Watt waxed eloquent about rural living saying,
>   The ideal farm life is a beautiful one, – the soothing sounds of the country and the twittering birds, the children engaged in happy pastimes outside, the housewife filling the larder with apples for the winter, the home life around the country fires … [64]

Her concern, however, was that "the farm home is too often a house where they are living on canned foods. It is hoped that the Commission will remedy that condition."[65] The main remedy that Watt recommended to the commission was that the government of Canada should strengthen its support for the Women's Institutes because of the potential to work through these groups to effect change.

Women's Institutes were first organized in British Columbia in 1909 when the provincial government, in cooperation with the Farmers' Institutes in the province, invited Laura Rose, a lecturer from Ontario, to address groups of women about dairying, which was her area of expertise. Rose's lectures and organizing efforts met with great success, and the first branches of WI were established on Vancouver Island that fall. Among the communities that welcomed the WI was the one closest to Watt's home near the quarantine station, Metchosin. According to the Victoria press, the organizational meeting of the Metchosin WI was held on October 4, 1909, and Watt was elected as one of the directors of the branch.[66] Based on the model from Ontario where WI groups had been meeting since 1897, the monthly meetings of local branches became avenues for education, sociability, and activism for rural women.[67] It was a model that Watt strongly endorsed because she saw the potential in it to improve conditions of rural life for women. The BC groups caught on quickly; within one year, there were twenty-one branches in the province, with a membership of 590 women. Funding at the rate of fifty cents per member came from the Provincial Department of Agriculture with assistance from the Canadian government; the funds came at first through the Agricultural Assistance Act, and after 1913 through the Agricultural Instruction Act. These grants were created with the goal of enhancing rural life, thus resulting in "better and happier men and women."[68]

The Women's Institutes meant more to Watt than simply another good idea that should be supported and promoted. Seeing potential for helping rural women to improve the quality of their lives, she became so committed to the movement and what it might accomplish that she accepted an appointment to the British Columbia Women's Institutes Provincial Advisory Board in 1910 to act as an official promoter of Women's Institutes. Indeed, she devoted herself to performing the role of advocate for rural women and she brought to it her penchant for argument, her knack for effective expression, and her boundless energy. In this role, Watt worked with three other women representing different regions of the province to assist the provincial government in strategizing about how best to provide domestic-science education, access to health care, and various other kinds of support to rural women in their roles as homemakers and mothers. The advisory board met annually to set and review priorities for the promotion of the WI. Sometimes those promotion efforts meant that the board members themselves would travel throughout their districts, giving inspiration and practical advice to local women on how to create an Institute in their area.

The advisory board met for the first time on August 14 and 15, 1911, at the Parliament Buildings in Victoria. Mr. W.E. Scott, the deputy minister

of agriculture and the superintendent of Women's Institutes for BC, welcomed the four board members and "explained the reasons for the formation of the Board, and the need of expert advice on affairs coming under
his supervision which related especially to women."[69] He explained that
while the function of the board was an advisory one, "unless the[ir] suggestions should be contrary to the policy of the Government, the recommendations of the Board would be carried out by the Department."[70] At
that first meeting, Watt was chosen to serve as secretary to the advisory
board, a role she occupied for the next two years.

That small group of four women had a great deal of power over the
agenda of the WI movement, and together they decided the subjects
that should be covered by travelling lecturers who would visit the districts and offer domestic-science instruction. At their first meeting they
agreed together that a lecturer on cooking should be engaged, and that
young married women especially needed instruction in basic sewing
and dressmaking. Perhaps it was on the strength of her own experience
of country living over the preceding thirteen years that Watt accepted
to serve in this capacity and to cast herself as an expert on the needs
of rural women, but in her recommendations one can also see her continued insistence that women should be encouraged in their efforts to
make money from their rural work. One of Watt's resolutions that was
endorsed by the advisory board was that the Department of Agriculture should send experts to speak to rural women about gardening and
poultry keeping, and that these talks should make "special reference to
the commercial aspects for women."[71] That emphasis is reminiscent of
her much earlier writing, particularly her "By the Fireside" columns,
published in Toronto in the 1890s, where she waxed eloquent in making
her case on how and why women should pursue meaningful paid work.

Watt also insisted that rural women would enjoy and benefit from
books and literature:

> Mrs. Watt spoke of sending a dramatic speaker, who would give selections
> of good literature, and accompany the lecturer sent out from the Depart-
> ment. The members agreed that this would be a source of information and
> enjoyment, and it was resolved to take this up at some future occasion.[72]

One wonders if Watt pictured herself as a candidate for that role of
the dramatic speaker about literature; certainly it was the kind of talk
she would have been perfectly comfortable delivering. She was concerned that rural women did not have access to books and to current

publications in particular, and the advisory board agreed "[t]hat the Department [of Agriculture would] be asked to provide magazines and Books on Household Science, for the use of the Board, and for reference for Women's Institutes."[73] Here was further evidence of Watt's commitment to empowerment for women through meaningful education; because of her reputation as a book reviewer and literary critic, when she spoke about the need for good publications for rural women, the authorities listened.

In addition to paid work and good literature, a third element that Watt emphasized in her WI work was her insistence that women should be informed and involved in the political process. In the spring of 1911 she spoke to the Victoria branch of the British Columbia Political Equality League, where she gave an address entitled "Women's Institutes and Women's Suffrage." The newspaper notice before the event was in the form of an invitation, noting that "the meeting is open to the public and a large attendance is desired."[74] Unfortunately no record of the meeting survives, nor does the text that she delivered on that occasion. What seems clear, however, is that she had not lost her interest in women's issues and the question of advancing equality for women.

The kind of influence that Watt envisioned for women was very much in keeping with what historians have dubbed "maternal feminism," where women would extend their influence outside the home to shape their local communities through their nurturing efforts. In one of her 1910 talks, Watt gave advice to a community north of Victoria that was planning to create a local council of women. Her speech emphasized the idea of extending women's influence outside their homes, and what she proposed sounded very much like the things she hoped rural women would accomplish through the WI. At a bazaar in Ladysmith, British Columbia, Watt took as her subject the topic "Women as Citizens," and the local press reported that

> Mrs. Watt spoke of the uplifting influence which could be exerted by women in the ruling of the schools and beautifying the school grounds, in keeping the public streets clean and fresh, in serving as school trustees and in setting up a high moral standard for children and young people in amusements as well as in work.[75]

In a format mirroring that of a WI meeting, Watt's talk was followed by a lecturer on agriculture who spoke about how to preserve and sterilize milk, and "the most approved methods of keeping it pure and fresh."[76]

Combining talks that promoted the extension of women's influence with something as practical as the health concerns about pure milk was a format with which Watt felt completely comfortable because it was the familiar Women's Institute model. Perhaps it also reminded her of her days as editor of the *Ladies Pictorial Weekly* when she had printed household hints along with tips about female empowerment on the same page.

During this period from 1910 on, Watt was in the vanguard of several important movements on behalf of women. The popularity of Women's Institutes resulted in steady progress as the movement spread through British Columbia, growing from twenty-five branches and 974 members in 1911 to forty-seven branches and 2,857 members by the end of 1914.[77] Tireless in her efforts on behalf of so many causes, Watt was now regarded as a leader who was taking up a variety of path-breaking positions for women, including the honour of being one of the first women appointed to the senate of the new University of British Columbia in 1912.[78] Later that same year, Watt represented British Columbia at the International Dry Farming Congress held in Lethbridge, Alberta, on October 1912, having been named as a delegate by the WI advisory board. She then took the opportunity to continue her travels with her children, going east to Ontario to visit her brother-in-law and sister-in-law in Toronto, and her father and her sister in Collingwood. While she was in Ontario, her older child, Robin, became quite ill again, and Alfred made an unplanned trip to join the family as they sought treatment for their son's illness.

In the midst of this busy schedule of Madge Watt's comings and goings for professional and family commitments, work at the quarantine station had been continuing as usual with Dr. Watt and his staff performing regular upgrades to the facilities and maintaining the site in a constant state of readiness to receive quarantined passengers as necessary. In the spring of 1913, Alfred Watt quarantined a ship called the *Monteagle*, arriving from the Orient, because he identified two cases of smallpox on board.[79] That incident, which began as a familiar and routine procedure, quickly escalated into an extraordinary drama in the weeks following, culminating with a tragic personal crisis that would change Madge's busy but idyllic life forever.[80]

Upon arrival at William Head on March 30, 1913, the *Monteagle* had 379 people on board, including 290 Chinese passengers travelling in steerage and 46 first-class passengers, of whom 22 were men and 24 were women and children.[81] Dr. Watt explained that the two passengers with smallpox had both boarded the ship at Hong Kong and he suspected that "the infection presumably was from an exposure in one of the ports of Japan, possibly from an ambulant case among the stevedores." He reported that as a precaution, "all passengers have been landed also a number of the crew and the vessel which is undergoing disinfection [and] is upon completion to be released."[82] The fact that two cases of smallpox were found, one in a white passenger, and the other in a Chinese man, immediately points out the class and racial identities that were at the centre of this incident.

Anti-oriental attitudes were so widely accepted in British Columbia in 1913 that they were openly discussed in the press, and indeed, in the assumptions about the type of quarantine facilities that were required for the different races. The buildings on the grounds of the William Head quarantine station reflected those assumptions. One building was designated the Chinese quarters, another, the Japanese, and these were quite separate from the men's and women's quarters that were reserved for whites. One might predict then, that race played a large part in the 1913 incident. Those ethnic divisions were so widely accepted, however, that they hardly received comment during the inquiry. Instead, it was the alleged inadequacy of the facilities and services provided to the white, first-class passengers that proved to be the central concern. Clearly, there were uncontested assumptions at work here that white travellers were entitled to superior treatment because of their race and class.

In the case of the *Monteagle*, the ship itself was held for only a few days before it was released, manned by a small crew who were deemed to be immune to smallpox either because of their vaccinations or previous exposures. The ship, with its cargo of silk from the Orient, arrived in Vancouver, its original destination, on April 3. The passengers, who were detained at the quarantine station, settled in for a longer stay, and as they did so, the *Vancouver Sun* predicted that the unexpected interruption to the travellers' schedule would be only a small inconvenience because "Dr. Watt, the quarantine officer, is said to be a good entertainer and will provide every amusement possible for the enforced white guests, who will have the run of the station golf links and other forms of outdoor amusement provided."[83] As their stay dragged on for seventeen long days, however, discontent arose among several of the cabin passengers, and following an "indignation meeting" they formed a committee to take formal action to have their complaints heard.[84]

At one level, the protests that were being raised only seemed to be the self-centred complaints of a few unhappy first-class passengers who resented that their civil liberties were being curbed, but the consequences of their actions became extremely serious after they wrote a letter of protest to the Victoria *Daily Colonist* and to Martin Burrell, the Conservative minister of agriculture and Dr. Watt's supervisor. The complaints identified a variety of issues including housing, sanitation, and administration of the quarantine station. In response Dr. Watt expressed his frustration that the situation was escalating and countered that false claims had been published in the newspapers, which he felt were "both unfair to the Department and misleading to the public."[85]

The most vocal among the complainants was Dr. Judson Burpee Black, of Windsor, Nova Scotia, a past president of the Canadian Medical Association and a former Liberal member of parliament who had been defeated in the 1911 election.[86] Dr. Black and his wife found their stay at William Head particularly uncomfortable, understandable perhaps given that they were the oldest passengers aboard the *Monteagle* (Black was 71 years old, and his wife was 68), and that they were on the final leg of their journey, a trip that had taken them around the world. Wearied by the whole experience, Black did not hesitate to assert that he would use his political connections to gain the ear of Minister Burrell and have Watt censured. Meanwhile, Dr. Black made it clear when he spoke to the newspaper that "[m]y indictment is against Dr. A.T. Watt, superintendent of the quarantine station, and I accept responsibility for that indictment."[87] In fact, Black and a few other passengers took the complaints much further and made them far more personal against Watt than others were willing to do. Correspondence from other passengers to Minister Burrell suggests that while most of them agreed that the sleeping quarters allotted to first-class passengers were uncomfortably small, as experienced world travellers, they also acknowledged that the station was undergoing some upgrades at the time of their quarantine, and the conditions were not all that different from other quarantine facilities around the world. Because of this, they were quick to exonerate Dr. Watt from any undue blame for their inconvenience or discomfort in the episode. One passenger wrote a strong letter of support for Watt, telling Burrell that "the grounds of [the] complaint[s] against Dr. Watt [are] more personal than anything else ... Further I think that the so-called protest is more political than anything else, and it has been altogether too highly colored."[88]

Despite this kind of goodwill on the part of several other passengers who wrote similar letters, the call for a formal inquiry had already gone out, and it was answered with the establishment of a Royal Commission of Inquiry. Commissioner H.W.R. Moore, Esq., a Victoria lawyer, was appointed to head the investigation and report back to the minister of agriculture. Moore visited William Head quarantine station on May 20, 1913, to view the facilities, then presided at sessions of the commission held in Victoria and at William Head on subsequent dates in the coming weeks. Watt was called to testify to defend his management record and he was questioned about the detainees' complaints. In his answers Watt explained that when the quarantine period began, ongoing maintenance work was underway, but the initial problems were resolved within a day of the ship's arrival with the completion of the new septic system.[89]

Although Watt's testimony downplayed it all, the situation at the quarantine station was far from "business as usual" that spring and summer. While Madge Watt maintained her busy public life, her husband was facing a serious crisis that placed mounting pressure on him and spilled over into the Watts' personal lives. Alfred's troubles at work stemmed from issues that ran far deeper than questions of physical maintenance. During the course of the inquiry, personal accusations against the Watts were raised when Dr. Watt's assistant, Dr. Hunter, added fuel to the fire. During the year and a half when Hunter was employed to assist Watt, their relationship was constantly strained. The events in the spring of 1913 provided Hunter with the perfect opportunity to follow through on his complaints. Encouraged by the situation that was developing among some of the disgruntled *Monteagle* passengers, he tendered his resignation and waited for the commission to be formed to investigate. As the inquiry proceeded, it came to light that Hunter had previously complained to Ottawa about Watt and that he had been hoping all along to see an inquiry established to investigate his supervisor. Hunter's personal complaints about Watt included failure to train and inform his assistant, misuse of government property, and the lack of careful record keeping in financial accounts. The charge about misuse of government property was actually aimed at both Alfred and Madge Watt. The accusations centred on a boat acquired in 1905, which Dr. Watt had christened as *Madge*.[90] This steamer was the means that the Watts used to travel back and forth to Victoria and to bring supplies to the station, but Hunter resented the fact that, according to him, the Watts regarded it as their personal property. He also accused the Watts – both Alfred and Madge – of regularly taking supplies, including kitchen foodstuffs and feed for their own livestock, from the government storehouse without keeping record of repayment. Hunter intended these accusations, which the commission eventually concluded were unfounded, to call the Watts' integrity into question; the charges are prime examples of the mistrust that characterized Watt and Hunter's working relationship. In the final report of the inquiry, Commissioner Moore concluded that "in my opinion Dr. Hunter adopted a hot headed and unreasonable attitude. So far as he was concerned he seems to have done his best to make proper co-operation between himself and his superior officer difficult to the point of impossibility."[91]

As if that were not enough, the difficulties between Watt and Hunter were only one factor in a long list of things causing stress for Madge Watt and her husband in the spring of 1913. Their family life was also filled with troubles. Just a few months earlier, Dr. Watt had made that emergency trip to Ontario because of serious concerns over his son's health, joining Madge and the boys in Ontario and then travelling to Guelph, seeking treatment for what seems to have been a grave case of pneumonia. Dr. Watt left William Head in December 1912 and returned in early February, presumably leaving Hunter in charge during his absence. Other health problems were plaguing the extended family too, as Watt's brother was seriously ill in Toronto during that same period; Lorne Watt finally succumbed to his illness and died in mid-May 1913.[92] Dr. Watt was not even able attend his brother's funeral because it was held in Toronto on May 20, the very same day that Commissioner Moore arrived at William Head to do his first site visit of the facilities and to officially launch the Royal Commission of Inquiry. The Watt brothers had been very close (Lorne had served as Alfred's best man at his wedding twenty years earlier), and the emotional strain of Alfred's brother's death should not be underestimated.[93] These personal stressors were the backdrop to Watt's professional woes during that very difficult spring.

The commission of inquiry met several times at the quarantine station from mid-June to mid-July 1913, and Dr. Watt was represented by legal counsel in the person of his father-in-law, Henry Robertson. After the last formal session of the commission, Moore was left with the task of writing up his final report and in the course of doing so, he sought a point of clarification from Robertson, saying that he "would be glad to have the benefit of any observations that your client, Dr. Watt may care to make in this matter, when this letter and the reply will be attached to the record of the Commission." In his capacity as Watt's lawyer, Robertson replied on July 23, revealing that "Dr. Watt is not at all well and has been ordered by his medical advisors to have a complete rest."[94] It was the first clue indicating how much of a toll this stressful season was taking on Alfred's mental health.

Then things took a very unexpected turn: one week later, Dr. Watt was dead. The *Vancouver Sun* recounted events this way:

> Dr. Alfred A.T. Watt, superintendent of the William Head quarantine station, committed suicide while temporarily insane by throwing himself from a third-storey window in the St. Joseph's hospital [in Victoria] early Sunday morning. Dr. Watt had been worrying a good deal as a result of the enquiry into the conduct of affairs at the quarantine station ... His doctors thought it advisable to place him in the hospital for treatment, and he went in early last week and was being watched by two nurses in turn ... At five minutes to 5 o'clock he was still in a deep sleep to all appearances, and the nurse left the room to go across the corridor for some water. She was back within two minutes to find the bed empty and the window curtains disarranged. Dr. Watt was found below with his head crushed in and quite dead.[95]

Historian Susan Johnston concludes that in this period when the coroner declared a death to be a suicide, he "actively promoted a particular vision of British Columbia as a moral Anglo-Canadian society. Investigator and judge, the role of coroner required someone who could speak for the local community by deciding which deaths needed public explanation."[96] Dr. Watt's death obviously needed a public explanation, and for the coroner, there was the added dimension of explaining how a fellow medical practitioner came to this horrible end. The death certificate records that the "immediate or final determining cause of death" was "suicide – fracture of base of skull," while the "remote or earlier pathological or medical condition" was "melancholia."[97] According to historians John Weaver and David Wright, the tendency that emerged in the nineteenth century to link suicide to mental health "might well have represented a desire not to further punish families already suffering the pain and torment of the death of someone close to them."[98] In Watt's case, it is difficult to say whether the link to a mental health problem would have lessened the shame attached to his death or heightened it.

Because of the ongoing inquiry at the time of Watt's death, there was no way to keep this horrible news quiet; Madge's loss immediately became front-page news across the country. Her torment was complicated by the fact that public attention had already been fixed on her husband and Moore had not yet pronounced his final verdict about

Dr. Watt's guilt or innocence. In the eyes of Watt's critics, his death must have confirmed their suspicions, while his supporters must have concluded that Black and Hunter bore responsibility for pushing Watt to this unspeakable act.

Anne Nesbet has argued that after a suicide, "witnesses and analysts rush in to provide interpretation and theory,"[99] and so it was in this case. Almost immediately after this heart-wrenching event, the Victoria *Daily Colonist* was quick to point fingers at those who had driven Alfred Watt to his early grave. Partly out of sympathy for Madge and her boys, the editor of the Victoria *Daily Colonist* wanted to defend the well-known doctor and reaffirm his respectability in light of his tragic end. On July 29, 1913, the editorial page featured a glowing eulogy of Watt as a "public servant and guardian of public health" whose work, transportation-company officials and their passengers all agreed, was worthy of "sincere and hearty appreciation." Then, in solidarity with his grief-struck family, the editorialist let the accusations fly:

> There is no room at all for doubt that Dr. Watt died a victim of political persecution. That is a hard thing to say, but that the shattered condition of his nerves which was the direct cause of his death was due to the persecution to which he has of late been subjected is beyond question. Far be it from us to suggest that those responsible for the recent investigation anticipated any such tragic consequences; but the fact remains that a valuable officer has been lost to the public service, a valuable life has been lost to the community as a result of an investigation into baseless charges involving the integrity of one in whom a high sense of honour was combined with an unusual degree of sensitiveness.[100]

The editorialist went on to declare that the insubordination, criticism, and accusations levelled at Watt by members of his staff could clearly be traced to the worst aspects of political patronage at play due to "the change of administration in Ottawa."[101] That was a direct reference to the fact that Watt's assistant, Dr. Hunter, had been appointed by the new Conservative government, and that Watt had no power to fire him, even though he was ill-suited to the quarantine station post, lacking both experience and a willingness to learn from and submit to Watt as his superior.

That well-intentioned publicity must have added to the horror that Madge was experiencing as she struggled to come to grips with what had happened. The shock of her husband's death and the devastating psychological impact of that loss for herself and her boys are almost unimaginable. She steeled herself to what she had to do and arranged for the funeral and Alfred's final resting place at the Ross Bay Cemetery in Victoria. The next step was to resign from the work that she had been doing with the Women's Institutes and leave the province. She attended the September 1913 meeting of the advisory board to tender her resignation, but it seems that she left with some haste, understandably, and did not pass along any notes from that meeting.[102]

In the weeks following the funeral, Commissioner Moore filed his final report, clearing Dr. Watt's name by concluding that all of the charges against him were unfounded.[103] That must have been small consolation. The declaration of Alfred's innocence could not change Madge Watt's new reality: at the age of forty-five, she was a widow, and the wonderfully rich life she had been enjoying in BC was over. She had two sons – one a teenager, and the other a young schoolboy – looking to her for help in dealing with their own confusion and grief. Meanwhile, Madge had to deal with her own shock and sorrow, and figure out where she and her boys would go from there.

Sadly, Madge Watt's time in BC was bookended by two deaths: that of her mother in the months just before she arrived in the province, and that of her husband in the weeks just before her departure. In each case, the death marked the end to one set of roles for Watt, and the beginning of another. Just as her mother's death had brought her light-hearted writing career to an end with the launch of her new life as a married society woman, the death of her husband would also bring profound changes to Madge Watt's life and the roles she would occupy. This time, the changes had far-reaching consequences, as the second half of her life would be devoted to working with rural women and establishing a legacy of organizations that continue to touch the lives of countless women across the globe almost a century later. But no one could have predicted that impact when Madge Watt made arrangements to leave British Columbia in the fall of 1913; her more immediate goal was to get herself and her children out of the public eye and away from the setting that reminded all of them of what had just happened. They needed time to work through their private grief and make plans for a new beginning.

Chapter Four

Role Reversal: From Colonial Widow to Imperial War Hero

After her husband's death, Madge Watt found herself in circumstances that, perhaps for the first time in her life, she had not planned. As she emerged from mourning, she would meet her new circumstances head-on and embrace a whole new set of roles; this time she took on a role that, even more than before, made her a very public figure. During the next thirty-five years of her life she would spend most of her time travelling, sometimes based in Britain, at other times back in Canada and the United States, but also travelling internationally, doing the work that would establish her enduring reputation as an organizer of rural women worldwide. It was during World War One that Watt accomplished what was arguably some of her most important life's work: establishing the Women's Institute movement in the UK.

Madge Watt's World War One sojourn in the UK illustrates how her actions and decisions had a ripple effect in circles far beyond her own making. While this part of Watt's life is the story of one woman's wartime service to the Empire, it is much more than that. Madge Watt was a transnational figure, an individual whose transatlantic experiences were a product of particular circumstances and a specific context. Because of that wider context, her life and work are significant to historians interested in themes around the history of women and colonial and imperial relations. Sometimes what Watt encountered in Britain was familiar and recognizable to her as an English Canadian, and at other times, she was puzzled by the resistance that she encountered. Like other colonial women, Watt was experiencing what Adele Perry described as the contradictory ways of Empire.[1]

Historian Phillip Buckner has argued that for many English Canadians, the tug of the empire did not end with the emergence of nationhood after World War One. Instead, Buckner posits that those ties endured well into mid-century, lasting at least until the 1960s. The life of Madge Watt is part of that story about how and why English Canadians had such a "long goodbye" in their relationship with the British world. More specifically, studying Watt helps to shed light on other women's imperial involvements. Watt's outlook was typical of many other colonial women who "saw Canada as an integral part of a wider Empire."[2] When Watt transplanted the Women's Institutes from Canada to Britain, her actions were part of what was responsible for shaping "the opinions of ordinary English-speaking Canadians at the local level" and reinforcing the sentimental ties that existed in interwar Canada.[3] What Madge Watt accomplished during World War One was, in effect, an episode of reverse colonialism; she took the Canadian experience of creating Women's Institutes and carried the idea back to Britain.

Reconstructing the details of Watt's life in this period once again requires a great deal of detective work and splicing together fragmented sources. An obvious place to begin is the published commemorative histories of the Women's Institutes in both Britain and Canada. These sources must be used with caution because they tend to present Watt in mythic proportions, particularly the Canadian ones. For example, the book published on the occasion of the fiftieth anniversary of the WI in Ontario stated that the early WI organizers were "a sisterhood" of heroic women "carrying its gospel to many lands," and leaders like Watt were "women of rare genius, women of fine talents for organization, and capable of winning the confidence of other rural women of different countries."[4] Twenty-five years later, the next anniversary book claimed that "Mrs. Watt was brilliant, had a strong sense of duty, keen intuition, endless vitality, pertinacity and a strong will."[5] While these sources give a colourful mental picture of some of Watt's traits and leave no doubt that she was a remarkable person, they are tantalizingly scanty on the details of how and why she conducted her work and how she adapted to the challenges she faced at this time in her personal life.

More helpful are primary source materials such as the papers of the National Federation of Women's Institutes in England and Wales, housed in the Women's Library in London.[6] Other important pieces of Watt's story can be gleaned from the archival collection of the Federated Women's Institutes of Canada files held by Library and Archives Canada in Ottawa, Ontario. By supplementing these archival records with published sources, including government sessional papers, press clippings, and some examples of Watt's own speeches and writing in this period, one can retrace her steps. In that retracing, her own voice is often heard, and as a result, one has the rare opportunity to listen to her own rationale for how she did things and why she did them that way. Placing those self-representations into their context takes one beyond the glorified accounts so often presented in the commemorative works.

What emerges is a picture of Madge Watt, a colonial Canadian, newly widowed, visiting in Britain while she tried to figure out what to do with her life. She found some relief from the burden of her parenting responsibilities when she placed her boys in boarding schools (Robin, the older of the two, was enrolled at Sandhurst and saw active duty during the war); as a result, she had a newfound freedom to devote herself to other things. Watt threw herself into her work with an indefatigable zeal, keeping an incredible pace with her gruelling schedule of travel, speaking, and organizational work. Casting herself as rural expert because of the work she had done in British Columbia, she took her wartime service for the Empire very seriously, using her status as a loyal British subject and her colonial pragmatism to their fullest extent. The work she did in establishing the Women's Institutes throughout England and Wales during these war years is one of her most important achievements, and for it, she was seen a war hero and decorated as a Member of the Order of the British Empire. On the strength of that designation, she set her sights on playing an international role, as the next chapter reveals. Before any of that could happen though, the first step after her husband's death was to get away from William Head and from Victoria – as far away as possible.

Three months after Alfred Watt's death, Madge, Robin, and Sholto Watt boarded a passenger ship bound for England. The vessel they sailed on was the *Victorian*, a state-of-the-art turbine steamship owned by the Montreal-based Allan Line, which had made its maiden voyage a few years earlier.[7] Although Alfred Watt had $15,000 of life insurance coverage,[8] it is doubtful that Madge ever collected any of the money, given the circumstances surrounding his death. However, the passenger list of the ship reveals that Watt and her boys did travel in comfort as they were among approximately fifty first-class passengers, with almost 650 people on board.[9] It seems that Madge had wasted no time in arranging this travel after the final report of the commission was released on September 22, 1913. After packing their belongings at William Head, she and the boys travelled east by train, presumably spending some time with her father and her sister's family in Collingwood, Ontario, before making their way by train to Montreal for the transatlantic crossing. They departed on a Tuesday morning, October 21, 1913, the day after the Canadian Thanksgiving holiday, from Montreal, Quebec, and arrived in Liverpool one week later, on October 28.

The week-long journey across the Atlantic would have allowed at least some time for reflection.[10] Having lived for almost twenty years in the shadow of the quarantine station, Madge Watt was no stranger to international travel. This time, however, rather than being firmly installed on the shore to greet and mingle with world travellers, Madge herself was on a life-changing journey. As Cecilia Morgan points out in her study of transatlantic tourism in this period, travel aboard one of the Allan Line's steamships departing from Montreal was "eminently desirable," because vessels such as the *Victorian* were both large and commodious and one could be quite comfortable, provided the weather cooperated.[11] In her earlier life as a writer, Madge would have regarded the whole trip as a grand adventure, and she might have written about it happily to share the experience with her readers. This trip, though, was no "happy holiday"; and while it is clear that she did not intend to move to England permanently, the trip was a good chance for the grieving widow to get away and sort out her future.

Before leaving British Columbia, Watt had arranged to spend time in the company of a close family friend. Upon arrival in Liverpool, Canadian travellers typically stayed overnight in a hotel there before catching the morning train to London.[12] For Watt and her boys, the capital was only a temporary stop before taking another train south towards their final destination. It was not the hustle and bustle of London that beckoned these weary travellers, but a quiet country home in Sussex.

The woman who offered Madge Watt and her boys that place of retreat was Mrs. Josephine Godman, born in British Columbia and the daughter of the Rev. W.G.H. and Charlotte Ellison. Her Oxford-educated father was an adventurous pioneer who had served the church in India (where he met his wife, while she was serving with the YWCA in Bombay) before he was appointed naval chaplain at Esquimalt, BC. Later on, he became the parish priest at St. Mary's Anglican Church in Metchosin, the same community where Watt was a member of the local branch of the WI. When the Rev. Ellison ran into conflict with the local bishop, he left the church to operate a sawmill at Port Renfrew, British Columbia.[13] Born in 1890 in Esquimalt, BC, while her father was serving as chaplain, Watt's hostess Josephine was more than twenty years younger than she, but because of their many common connections in British Columbia, they were good friends nevertheless. In 1910 at age nineteen, Josephine had married Captain Frederick Tyrell Godman, a thirty-four-year-old British military man whom she met in Victoria when he was travelling on a world tour.[14] Just four years after her wedding, Godman was enjoying life at one of her in-laws' estates when she invited her grieving friend from BC to bring the children and come to her country home at Wivelsfield, in East Sussex.

The friendship between Josephine Godman and Madge Watt would become even stronger over the next few years as they lived and worked together to launch the Women's Institute movement in England, and they provided each other with moral support through the difficult personal circumstances of the war years. When the Watts arrived at Wivelsfield, it was Madge who was grieving and finding comfort in her friend's presence, but within four years the tables would be turned when Godman herself experienced a series of personal tragedies: her husband died as a prisoner of war during World War One, after which she gave birth to their second son, whom her husband would never meet; and then she lost her firstborn son to polio in 1918.[15] Through all those heartbreaking events, Watt and Godman remained dedicated to each other and to the work they shared. What Watt first envisioned as a temporary visit to recover from the shock of her husband's death stretched into a stay of almost six years because of the war.

The work that Watt took up during this period was the organization of Women's Institutes according to the model that she had been part of promoting in British Columbia. Like Watt herself, the WI movement traced its roots back to Ontario, Canada. The first Women's Institute in the world was organized in 1897 at Stoney Creek, Ontario.[16] Although she was not involved in those early meetings of the Ontario Women's Institutes, part of what had been keeping Watt so busy in BC just prior to her husband's death was her participation as an active member of and advisor to local Women's Institutes.[17] Across Canada the WI was generally agreed to serve a threefold purpose: to educate rural women in domestic science, to provide a forum for sociability among rural women, and to encourage rural women to be active in community organization.[18] Given the wide appeal of those three general purposes and the fact that Watt found herself installed in a comfortable country setting in England, she hoped to introduce the idea of Women's Institutes, a "made in Canada" concept of community organization for women, to rural Britain. It seemed to Watt that the generic ideas behind the WI should make the organization easy to transplant beyond the Canadian setting, but she would soon learn that selling her idea in rural England was no easy task. Historian Adele Perry has argued that "settlers occupied a strategic, curious, and contested place within the conduits of power that constituted the British World."[19] That was certainly true for Watt as a Canadian-born member of the Empire, settling in England and hoping to establish Canadian ways in the heart of the English countryside.

While it is beyond the scope of this book to give a full account of how the WI movement in Britain was founded, readers who are interested in that history can turn to a number of different published works for more background, including J.W. Robertson Scott, *The Story of the Women's Institute Movement in England and Wales and Scotland* (1925); Janet E. Courtney, *Countrywomen in Council: The English and Scottish Women's Institutes with Chapters on the Movement in the Dominions and on Townswomen's Guilds* (1933); Cicely McCall, *Women's Institutes* (1943); Inez Jenkins, *The History of the Women's Institute Movement of England and Wales* (1953); Simon Goodenough, *Jam and Jerusalem: A Pictorial History of Britain's Greatest Women's Movement* (1977); Piers Dudgeon, ed., *Village Voices: A Portrait of Change in England's Green and Pleasant Land, 1915–1990* (1989); Maggie Andrews, *The Acceptable Face of Feminism: The Women's Institute as a Social Movement* (1997); and Jane Robinson, *A Force to Be Reckoned with: A History of the Women's Institutes* (2011).[20] Andrews gives a thoughtful overview of the ways in which commemorative histories of the British WI movement provide "illuminating insight into dominant views of the organization at particular stages in its history" and how the writing of history serves political purposes in terms of constructing meanings and identities.[21] Clearly, the WI in the UK has a variety of meanings attached to its history. Watt explained that the value she saw in establishing these clubs for rural women throughout the UK was tied to the multifaceted purposes that the WI movement could serve, not the least of which was empowering women.

Despite all the potential that Watt saw in the WI movement, it was a hard sell to launch the idea in the UK, and although she spoke to a variety of audiences as a visiting lecturer in the first months after her arrival in England, her ideas were not well received. As Watt recalled,

My work had been with the Women's Institutes in British Columbia, and I felt that that organization might well be introduced into Great Britain. But unfortunately, perhaps for the first time in my life, I seemed to be the only person who thought so. I was asked to speak very often, and I think they liked the sound of my Canadian accent, and they were interested in what I was saying, but for a long while I made no headway. I spoke to London audiences quite often, and I spoke to large audiences of people, and I always spoke of the Canadian Women's Institutes. They said they might do for Canada, but they would not do for England.[22]

What was good for the colony was apparently not good for the mother country, or so Watt was told. Undaunted, Watt persevered with her strategy to stir up interest for the idea first in the capital city, because that was how she understood that British society operated: "Things start from London and radiate out into the country, and nothing can be started without first getting it going in London."[23] Pursuing that approach in the hope of gaining a hearing for her idea and attracting some leaders and resources for her cause, Watt recounted,

> I had to spend nearly a year battering at the doors of the people in London, talking to London audiences and introducing Women's Institutes to Boards of Agriculture. I also had to talk to educational bodies and to editors of rural papers and people interested in land problems, women who were training women, gardeners, heads of schools; everybody whom I thought might help me to get Women's Institutes in their village.[24]

Motivated by her feminist convictions, she observed that "the women of England were certainly not getting a fair show in life, and I wanted to do something to help them."[25] But the mother country was not accustomed to receiving help from one of her daughters, and Watt's colonial status was a hindrance to her work.

Despite what seemed to her to be a logical strategy and a laudable goal, Watt got nowhere with her plan, and to her great surprise, one of the biggest roadblocks came from an unlikely source – other women. Watt explained that

> in my innocence of mind I thought the wives of the Directors [of the AOS] would be interested in Women's Institutes, but after six months of vain endeavor, I found out that the wives were not likely to be interested, since they were not in the least in the Agricultural Society. Whatever their husbands might be doing, the wives neither cared nor knew anything about that particular branch. Most Canadian women know what their husbands are doing, but I found it was not so in England, and that was a blind alley that I had been following for six months.[26]

During this discouraging period, Watt's friendship with Godman became more important than ever. Describing their close bond, in very affectionate terms, she recalled,

> I could never have withstood the early discouragements of this work, or carried on the first experiments, had it not been for the constant sympathy, encouragement and active help of Mrs. Godman. Her home has been mine for these years of trial and of hope, and she has never failed me. She has never faltered in upholding the high ideals of Women's Institutes. Her sweet kindliness and entire sympathy with countrywomen have made her a beloved figure in the movement.[27]

One can imagine Watt venting her frustrations to Godman about the obstacles she was facing. Given their shared past, the two women no doubt made comparisons between the successes of the Canadian WI and its seemingly unstoppable progress, compared to the endless frustrations in England. What had worked for her in Canada was clearly not working in England. Back home in BC, Watt was used to having her voice heard among decision makers in the provincial capital and the newly established University of British Columbia. She had also enjoyed working very effectively through her network of well-connected women who, together with their husbands, had a pioneering spirit that made them keen to promote organizational development strategies as British Columbia continued its evolution from an outpost colony to a maturing provincial power. Given the fact that Victoria felt so British, Watt was surprised by the realization that her strategies for organizing rural women were not completely transferrable to England after all. The influence she had enjoyed back home in British Columbia was not translating into a similar status in her new setting.

Reflecting on why the proposal to establish WIs was slow to take hold, one British author mused that "often when a new idea is proffered to humanity, it is at first rejected; not because the idea is not good nor even acceptable, but because the time is not yet ripe."[28] The time would ripen with the outbreak of World War One, and the particular people and circumstances would finally align, but not when, where, or how Watt herself had expected.

During one of Watt's talks in London, the breakthrough that she was seeking finally came. Speaking to a group of Ontario Women's Institute members after the war had ended, she recounted that Earl Grey, who had served as Canadian governor general from 1904 to 1911, was chairing the 1914 meeting where she gave an address on cooperation and he endorsed what she was saying: "with that fine appreciation, which was his characteristic, he at once asked the audience to consider what I was saying, and see if something could not be done to start Women's Institutes in England."[29] In what Watt regarded as a stroke of good luck, "Mr. Nugent Harris heard me speak at that meeting, and made up his mind he would try and help me start Women's Institutes."[30] Harris was the general secretary of the Agricultural Organization Society (AOS), and his support carried weight, but even so, "he was the only enthusiast among them, but he was a good talker and he talked them into it."[31] On the strength of Harris's enthusiasm for her idea, Watt would finally begin to see some results because Harris had both the power and the networks of likeminded people who would help the fledgling WI movement to take root. Contrary to what Watt herself had expected, the support that Harris mustered did not emanate from London, and it was not women to whom Harris turned for support.

In what seems a rather unlikely setting, the first Women's Institute in England and Wales was established in North Wales, in a small village on the Isle of Anglesey with the claim to fame of having one of the longest place names in the world: Llanfairpwllgwyngyllgogerychwyrndrob-wllllantysiliogogogoch, (or Llanfairpwll for short), which means: "the Church of St. Mary, in a hollow of white hazel, near to a rapid whirlpool and to St. Tysilio's Church, and near to a red cave."[32] The story of why this small place, just across the Menai Strait from the city of Bangor, should have become the birthplace of the WI in the UK is well told in a book by Constance Davies, aptly titled *A Grain of Mustard Seed*.[33] Davies does a particularly good job of explaining the context in which Harris helped Watt to successfully establish the first Women's Institute, and at the same time, makes it clear that this historic achievement was not entirely the work of one person. As Davies explains,

> a good deal of constructive thinking had been going on in [North Wales] for many years, as consequent action proved. Before Mrs. Watt came, ... [others] had long been preparing the field. The soil at Llanfairpwll had been well and truly dug. Of the many seeds she scattered the one which dropped on this ground was the first to take root.[34]

Those who had "prepared the soil" included Nugent Harris, but also Colonel the Hon. R.S.G. Stapleton-Cotton, who lived in North Wales on the estate of his nephew, the fourth marquess of Anglesey, and was a great proponent of a number of rural causes, including the cooperative movement; he had had a variety of international experiences.[35]

The third individual who helped to pave the way for the acceptance of Watt's idea in North Wales was Sir Harry Reichel, the first principal of University College, Bangor, an educational institution which, under his leadership, "was the pioneer in agricultural studies at the university level."[36] According to Davies, it was Reichel's "keen perception of the good that would accrue from extending the benefits of education and social development to countrywomen" that led him to support Cotton and Harris's suggestion that "Mrs. Watt should be invited to address a meeting at the College on the 15th of June [1915]."[37]

The invitation to speak at University College of North Wales (now Bangor University) was indeed the breakthrough that Watt needed in order to launch the WI movement in the UK. After that strategic gathering where she addressed receptive listeners about how important the WI could be for rural women and for the country itself, she was invited to attend a meeting the following day, on June 16, 1915, in Llanfairpwll, where the decision was taken to form the first Women's Institute in England and Wales. According to a local press account, "A well-attended meeting, presided over by Col. Stapleton Cotton [sic], was held at Graig, by permission of Mrs. W.E. Jones, on Wednesday. The lecturer was Mrs. Watt, a lady from British Columbia, who gave an interesting account of the work done in that portion of the Empire, by means of the Women's Institute."[38] Interestingly, Watt's first real success came when her idea was recognized as an imperial proposal, something that had taken root with good effect elsewhere in the Empire. One wonders whether her audience in northern Wales felt that their situation was somehow parallel to that of other, more far-flung parts of the Empire, also somewhat distant from London. Whether it was geography or some other explanation, Watt's ideas resonated with her Welsh listeners.

The official founding meeting of that first local WI came a few months later, when Watt visited Llanfairpwll a second time in September 1915. By then she was being described as "Mrs. Watt, of the Women's Institutes of Canada, now with the Agricultural Organization Society," reflecting the fact that she was being paid by the AOS to do this organizational work. A record of her time spent in North Wales reveals that she visited other counties during the fall of 1915, attempting to establish WIs there as well. Now that she was on the payroll of the AOS, the report she wrote about this visit was, in part, an attempt to account for and justify the money that was paid to her for this work. In a published summary of her work, Watt recounted that she spent more than a month in North Wales that fall, between September 14 and October 18, during which time she

> acted in close touch with Colonel Cotton and Mr. Rupert Ellis of the North Wales Branch [of the AOS], and received kindly assistance from Mr. John Owen, of the Board of Agriculture. Meetings were arranged in Anglesey by Mrs. Cotton, near Criccieth by Mrs. Drage, near Glasfryn by Mrs. Williams Ellis, and near St. Asaph by Miss Williams-Wynn. Miss Wynn arranged four meetings with the assistance of local people and I made her home my headquarters in that part of the country. She took a great deal of trouble and she and her mother – Mrs. Williams-Wynn – deserve our gratitude for undertaking and carrying through what was quite a big piece of work. It was Colonel Cotton's plan that I should spend some time at Anglesey and he offered the hospitality of his home.[39]

Watt was very appreciative of the support she received from these enthusiastic individuals because, with their help, she had now established the kind of network of enthusiastic men and women of influence that allowed her to replicate the familiar pattern of organizational work she had done in British Columbia.

As she had also realized in Canada, Watt knew that one of the most pressing needs among the rural women of North Wales was for printed materials, and so she recommended "literature, and something more attractive and simpler perhaps in form than any we have at present should be prepared."[40] Her other priority was to establish rules for the new WIs, and she advised that "so far as the procedure and the conduct of the Institute is concerned, a modification of the rules of the British Columbia Institute would do."[41] She was confident that the Canadian documents would suffice as a working model because, she said, "these were prepared with great care by an unimpeachable authority and have not been altered since they were put in use some years ago."[42] The "authority" she spoke of was none other than Henry Robertson, her lawyer father, who was indeed an expert on organizational life.[43]

The developments in North Wales and her position with the AOS led to a turning point for Watt in her work, restoring her confidence as a WI organizer and giving her a familiar framework for her activities, very similar to her experience in BC. With her optimism restored because of the fact that three more WIs formed in North Wales before the end of the year 1915, the discouragement that had accompanied her since her arrival in England lifted. She credited this change in her personal outlook to the people who worked with her in Wales. Recalling their assistance, she said, "Their warm sympathy and practical and intelligent help was invaluable, and one realizes with gratitude that under the stimulus of their kindness I was able to push forward with energy and hopefulness."[44] With her hope and energy restored, Watt returned to her adopted home base in Sussex to concentrate on getting the WI movement established there.

The first success in that county came shortly after her return from Wales when, on November 9, 1915, Watt addressed the local War Agricultural Committee and the parish council at Singleton. Out of that meeting, two WIs were formed: Singleton and East Dean.[45] The following spring, together with her friend Josephine Godman, Watt hosted a meeting in March 1916 at Little Ote Hall, Godman's home in Wivelsfield. That initial meeting included a talk by Godman on goat keeping, demonstrations of "hay box cooking" and a bread mixer, a talk by Watt on the Women's Institutes, and the featured address, "Women on the Land," by a rather exotic guest, Princess Kropotkin of Russia, who was in exile and living near Brighton. At the conclusion of that meeting, there was general agreement to form a WI in Wivelsfield.

After these early days when the first English WIs were established, there was great momentum in the movement, and by the fall of 1917, there were 140 local Women's Institutes in operation. Rapid growth had happened with the Women's Institutes in Canada in the early years too, but only after the first branches were operational and a system of government funding was put in place through a grant known as the Agricultural Instruction Act.[46] In England, the pattern of growth was similar but even more dramatic than in Canada, because the English movement was tied to the urgency of increasing food production during the war years. As Maggie Andrews notes, "the number of Institutes went up from 187 in 1917 to 1,405 in 1919."[47] Obviously it was not humanly possible for one person to travel to so many locations in such a short length of time, speak to each group, assist in identifying suitable local leaders, and oversee the launch of each Institute, but Watt estimated that she had personally had a hand in establishing more than one hundred of those Institutes. According to Andrews, "significant in assisting in the ability to grow at such a rate was the decision to create Voluntary County Organizers (VCOs) who would operate at county level to help with the propaganda work and the formation and nurturing of new institutes."[48] The team of organizers fanning out across the English countryside made that impressive growth possible, yet Watt maintained the title of "chief organizer," a role of which she was very proud, because she could claim responsibility for all of these new groups even though she was not personally involved with every one of them.

A history of first WIs in England, entitled "Sussex, the cradle of the English WI," recounts how the movement took hold through the efforts of various individuals including Mrs. Watt, though it is clear that she did not work singlehandedly. As Anne Stamper puts it, "When it was obvious that WIs were going to thrive, the AOS set up a Women's Institute subcommittee to supervise the activity. Mrs. Nugent Harris became the Hon. Secretary [sic] and Lady Gertrude Denman from Balcombe in Sussex was appointed as permanent chairman."[49] Lady Denman was a brilliant choice for the role of chairperson: not only was she a titled woman with boundless energy who commanded great respect, but she also

> negotiated an arrangement whereby the formation of the WIs should be undertaken by the Food Production Department, [and] ... then became the responsibility of a National Federation of Women's Institutes – this meant that the WIs would lay down policy and make their own rules."[50]

Indeed, without Denman's personal endorsement and leadership acumen, it is doubtful whether the scheme would have enjoyed such phenomenal growth.

For Watt, who lacked Denman's influence and affluence, association with the AOS gave her the credibility she was missing; it also gave the WI a level of respectability because it was being led by a woman like Lady Denman. While the endorsement of the AOS was initially very important, there was an evolution to the organizational structure of the WIs over the next few years. As Stamper explains,

> the AOS had become concerned about the increasing work load and requested more funding from the Government in order to employ more paid organizers to help Mrs. Watt. The Treasury, considering that the WI was being expanded to the detriment of the genuine AOS work, refused further funds. Instead, they proposed that the administration of the WIs should be transferred to the recently formed Women's branch of the Board of Agriculture's Food Department (which had been set up to oversee the Women's Land Army).[51]

In the evolution of these administrative structures, there is no question that the context of wartime was a great impetus to encourage the creation of Women's Institutes. The enthusiasm with which women of all classes (but especially upper-class women) became involved is closely connected to the wartime urge to serve.

Reflecting on the work she did in Britain during her wartime sojourn there, Madge Watt explained to a Canadian journalist that she felt compelled to "do something" for the war effort when the conflict began in 1914. "Happening to be in England when the war broke out, Mrs. Watt felt she must do some war work, and wisely turned her thoughts to the subject she knows thoroughly: the development of practical knowledge amongst rural women."[52] Watt was committed to the ideas of liberal imperialism, and like countless others, she felt it was her duty to play her part and "come together in times of peril to defend the liberal institutions and values in which they all believed."[53] As a loyal colonial woman, it was simply the right thing to do, and she would make a significant contribution to what Katie Pickles has called "female imperialism."[54]

While there is no complete collection of Madge Watt's personal papers in any archive, from the scattered traces she left behind both in Canada and in Britain, one can begin to reconstruct her thoughts about wartime activities and educational schemes for women. In a series of point-form autobiographical notes in Library and Archives Canada in Ottawa, for example, Watt revealed something about her rationale for launching into WI work in England. She recalled that by the start of World War One, she had learned from

> Christopher Turner [a British diplomat] that the food supply would probably be [the] determining factor in war, that England had not more than three weeks supply of certain essentials in food in hand and if German submarine attacks threatened came off that we might be forced to make peace on their terms. [Watt] proposed to establish WIs to help increase food supply. [She] enlisted sympathy and help of friends to get meetings.[55]

Watt's self-confessed urge to "do some war work" and her strategy to "enlist sympathy and help of friends to get meetings," deserve further analysis. Clearly Watt did work through a series of personal networks, such as her close friendship with Josephine Godman. By working closely with such sympathetic women, particularly women of means, Watt's scheme for organizing rural women began to meet with success.

Historian Janet S.K. Watson, in her book *Fighting Different Wars: Experience, Memory, and the First World War in Britain,* differentiates between war work and war service, arguing that "work" denoted a blurring of traditional gender lines, such as women who worked in munitions factories or did heavy labour as part of the Women's Land Army. "Service," as Watson explains, "had a more genteel connotation, partly because it was temporary, only for the duration,"[56] and thus seemed less threatening to the social order of established gender roles. At the same time, "service" also tended to reinforce class standing. It seems that Watt's instinct was to "serve" in whatever way she could be most useful.

Watt was well aware of the class dynamics at work in Britain and she was told that the Canadian WI model, where women of various social standings mixed freely, would never be accepted in Britain. As Watt told the readers of *Saturday Night,*

> when it was suggested that the same sort of thing might be done in England there were a great many people who threw the proverbial cold water on the idea. It was excellent in Canada, and it might be copied in other countries, but not in England; conditions were altogether different, and even if applied the plans would have to be altered out of all recognition. But actual facts have proved these pessimists to be quite in the wrong. Canadian methods have been used here with no alteration, and wherever a Women's Institute has been set up it has been a success.[57]

It was not entirely accurate for Watt to claim that she implemented her Canadian methods with no alterations whatsoever. Her suggestions about establishing WIs were slow to find acceptance, and the great difference to which Watt's detractors referred was the rigid class structure that dominated the English countryside. As Watson explains,

> Perceptions of class position certainly played a crucial role in how different types of war work were viewed. Ideas about gender were also fundamental, and both criticism and support of war efforts were rooted in deeply held convictions about the preservation of a certain kind of social order.[58]

Watt's strategy to overcome this situation was not to ignore the class hierarchies, but to both blur and exploit them. Recognizing that she was not in Canada any more, Watt appealed to her listeners to set aside class differences and take a page from the colonial settler societies. When she travelled the English countryside promoting the creation of WI groups, observers remarked that "with her persuasive words, [Watt] dwells on the fact that the Women's Institute are for the mutual advantage of women of all classes meeting on the common ground of patriotism, and that any idea that they are 'for' any class is utterly false."[59] Yet, it seems that at the same time, Watt worked within the existing class hierarchy, "enlisting the help and sympathy of friends to get meetings," hoping to win over the upper-class women first and to present the WI to them as an opportunity to exercise social leadership. Watson contends that, in Britain, "aristocratic women, in particular, had a pre-war tradition of organizing voluntary effort and continued to play a role of social leadership during wartime."[60] Watt decided to approach the leading women in each village or community and enlist their help. She began with her own connections among the leading women of Sussex,[61] spending time to convince them of the value of the WI model, and presenting the idea as both an attractive way for the aristocratic women to serve, and at the same time, a venue for lower-class country women to be called into participation in the war effort without challenging their conservative world views about traditional gendered work. The WI seemed to be an ideal way for the "volunteering effort also [to] spread far down the social scale because most women in the Empire did not undertake paid work during the war."[62]

In her appeals to rural women, Watt recalled that she "spoke on how women could help in the war through Women's Institutes in increased production, better preservation, and management of food, in wider cooperation and in getting ready for reconstruction."[63] Asking country women of all classes to participate in food production and food preservation seemed to be an ideal English solution because while it preserved class privilege for the more well-to-do, it also preserved traditional gender roles for all by proposing that female work in the countryside could be put to patriotic ends. Historian Paul Ward has noted that many women in Britain found ways to make meaningful contributions to the war effort without leaving their traditional sphere of domestic work. "The majority of British women in the Great War," he argued,

> did not go into munitions factories or the auxiliary forces, or any other form of paid work. Many were too young or too old, or continued to be housewives and mothers. Many middle- and upper-class women did not face the economic imperative to work but chose to participate voluntarily in the war effort, and it is possible to examine their ideological motives for doing so.[64]

Madge Watt's reasons for serving were complex. First, as a Canadian visitor to Britain, with twenty years of experience living near Victoria, BC, arguably the most British of all Canadian cities, she felt a strong attachment to the Empire. Writing to acknowledge and thank the women who had cooperated with her in organizing and facilitating the spread of the Women's Institute movement, she said, "I am indeed deeply touched that a Canadian over here, such as I am, should receive such wonderful proofs as I do daily, in this the heart of the Empire, of English women's trust in and kindness towards her sisters from over the seas."[65] The rhetoric of the imperial tie served Watt very well in establishing her ties to the mother country, and her desire to "do something" when the war began.

Second, Watt was the mother of an enlisted soldier who was serving on the front lines. As the Canadian magazine *Saturday Night* reported in the spring of 1919, Mrs. Watt's "elder son (the younger is a school-boy) is Lieutenant 'Robin' Watt, who went from Sandhurst into the Yorkshire Regiment, has been wounded four times, has won the Military Cross and Bar, and is now ADC [aide-de-camp] to General Sir Arthur Currie, who commands the famous Canadian Corps."[66] As Phillip Buckner points out, Currie was one who stressed "that it was possible to be both 'thoroughly loyal to British institutions, to British traditions, and to the British Empire' and at the same time 'intensely Canadian.'"[67] With her son serving on the front lines, Madge Watt had built-in credibility among other women who had given up their men for the cause. A long and surprisingly detailed letter from Robin Watt to his mother, written in two parts, on July 1 and July 4, 1916, during the Battle of the Somme, was published in Watt's hometown newspaper in Collingwood, Ontario, where her proud father, Henry Robertson, followed the exploits of his daughter and his grandson (and namesake) with pride. In his letter to his mother, Robin Watt gave her some gruesome details about how he watched in horror as his men were rifled down, many of them dying before his very eyes. Most sobering for him as a platoon commander was the fact that three other commanders were shot dead within a few yards of emerging from their trenches. "Heaven knows how I got 100 yards without being touched," he told her, "perhaps good luck, but more probably your prayers, mother dear." [68] That haunting letter must have stirred her heart profoundly, and Watt used her own personal circumstances to establish an empathetic bond with women of various classes based on their common maternal experiences. What Watt shared with other women who offered their men to the cause of the war gave her a credibility factor, a form of emotional currency that other women immediately recognized as genuine.

Third, Watt was well-positioned through her friendships with women of wealth and stature to command resources for her cause and she felt it was her responsibility to use her influence for patriotic purposes and to encourage her wealthy acquaintances to do the same. For example, in 1918, when Watt taught the first Women's Institute School for Organizers in Sussex, a local couple who owned land, Mr. and Mrs. Bridge (she was the president of the Burgess Hill WI), loaned the use of their estate, "Wyberlye," as the venue for the three-week training course. Watt acknowledged women such as Mrs. Bridge, saying,

> I can never be grateful enough to these friends, who gave me just the encouragement and help I needed in the nicest possible way, and took off my shoulders what would have proved to me the hardest part of the work, namely, the details of the arrangements. Greatly to my surprise, and with what seemed to me extraordinary kindness, hospitality was offered in the homes of these ladies and their friends for all of those whom the Board of Agriculture should send to take this course; further than that, several of them offered to lend cars for transport during the course. Most delightful also a charming house with large rooms was offered as a place to hold the School.[69]

In contrast to the wives of the members of the Agricultural Organization Society, who disappointed Watt with their lack of interest in her cause, she eventually found important, tangible support from sympathetic countrywomen of means who offered to take care of local arrangements in a series of gestures that Watt genuinely appreciated. One can read that gratitude as deference to the women who supported her, but also as vindication against those who had doubted the early proposals she had made in London.

In addition to her imperialism, her maternal instincts, and her social connections, a fourth and final motivation for serving came out of Watt's personal experiences in rural Canada. Having spent twenty years in a rural part of Vancouver Island where she savoured the joys of rural living such as gardening, preserving, and socializing in her local WI branch, Watt became empathetic about the sense of isolation that countrywomen often experienced, and enthusiastic about the potential of combining information, affirmation, and opportunities for sociability. Watt told a Canadian journalist that she had "the greatest admiration for English village women." She was enthusiastic about her work among them, reporting that

> I have organized institutes in nearly a hundred villages and have found the women receptive and anything but lacking in intelligence, and they are keen to learn. It is quite unusual not to form an institute after holding a meeting, and I have found that the squires' wives and all the country people give eager and generous support.[70]

As a gifted public speaker, she had made presentations on numerous occasions, but looking back on her various activities during these years, Watt confessed, "the times I liked best in England were the times when I was actually speaking to the Institutes themselves."[71] No doubt it was partly the great admiration she garnered from local women, and the way that they accepted her folksy charm when she spoke that gave her such personal satisfaction. In part, however, her emphasis on small local gatherings of women was strategic. Explaining her success to an audience of WI organizers, she declared, "If you don't remember anything else I have said, please remember this: the whole thing that matters is that little tiny Institute in the little tiny village."[72]

Although Madge Watt seemed to be the ideal candidate to organize Women's Institutes in wartime Britain, the work was not easy. As journalist Mary McLeod Moore wrote in 1919,

> It was uphill work. Mrs. Watt had already offered her services to various organizations to assist with war work of the kind that appealed to her, but for over a year she ploughed a lonely furrow. After lecturing on every possible opportunity, and talking to those she hoped to interest, she at last convinced some of the persons of influence that village women could be so organized as to prove an important force to war service.[73]

For her leadership in the movement, Watt received the honour of being named a Member of the Order of the British Empire (MBE), a designation she proudly included after her name for the rest of her life.

In 1919 Watt wrote about what the WI movement had accomplished in the first four years of activity and her vision for the future of the British WI:

> Women's Institutes whilst carrying on war work were consolidating their position as rural centres of women's activities. They will be a permanent

factor in country life. Practically all their war activities are continuing and expanding, in some cases energy is translated into slightly different channels to suit the organization of peace. They have learned to work together for "Home and Country."[74]

After British women achieved the vote in 1920, the WI came to represent what Maggie Andrews called the "acceptable face of feminism."[75] For Watt, the rapid rise and expansion of these groups was evidence of their appropriateness for the British setting and she worked tirelessly to remind the membership and their leaders of the potential of their groups. Indeed, from the information that Watt provided it seemed clear that the WI was an institution with wide-reaching activities and enduring appeal. At every opportunity, she reminded both members and onlookers that the WI touched on many facets of life. In one of her publications, she included a list entitled "What the Women's Institutes Do," which was a 500-word treatise illustrating the long and impressive list of causes and activities that the WI took up.[76] The broad scope of the movement served to explain its wide appeal because it included everything from the educational and economic issues to social problems and health reforms. There was no question in Watt's mind that the WI would serve as a strategic way of rallying British women even after the war was over. Yet Watt was concerned that the very breadth of the movement might also prove to be a weakness.

With such an impressive list of involvements and achievements, the biggest challenge that WI organizers faced in the post-World War One years, according to Watt, was what she described as the impulse of some members to be "chiefly social." As the end of the war approached, the motivation to perform war work or war service was no longer going to provide a sustained raison d'être. In order to ensure the groups' longevity, Watt felt that it was crucial to continue the "serious" nature of the movement and to establish a certain level of professionalism, including businesslike training procedures for organizers so that the groups did not degenerate into simply a social venue. Having fought so hard to achieve recognition because of their war work, Watt was convinced that there was still great potential for the WI to empower women, but she feared that if they did not take themselves seriously, no one else would either. She explained the problem, saying,

We assume that Women's Institutes are simple little societies to which any one can belong, which can be run in any old way and which has [sic]

only to secure a government grant, pass a resolution against cigarettes, and hold a whist drive to be a successful Women's Institute. We start out to reform the world and very often we cannot conduct a meeting or even hold an Institute together.[77]

To accomplish the desired tone as a serious business operation, it seemed clear that new educational strategies were necessary in order to continue the kind of cross-class cooperation that had characterized the WI since its inception. The idea of working for peace and reconstruction became the new language that was invoked. Some of the wartime challenges of organizing British rural women lingered as WI organizers strategized about how to continue to overcome class differences among the women in the countryside.

Indeed, even before the war's end, Watt's vision for making a significant contribution to the British war effort had been realized. In her efforts to travel and organize WI branches across the English countryside, Watt was tireless. When she returned to Canada at the end of the war, a Montreal newspaper reported that "[t]here are now about 800 WI in England and Wales. There are eight regular organizers at work, and about forty voluntary county organizers under the Board of Agriculture, with Mrs. Watt as Chief Organizer."[78] With such rapid growth over a short period, the need to train additional organizers and leaders for the movement was evident. To meet this need, Watt proposed to hold a three-week training course in the spring of 1918, which she called a "Women's Institute School."

Quite a complete record of this "school for leaders" exists because Watt and her assistant published a book based on their experience of offering the training sessions. The training experience was strategically planned and executed, revealing Watt's knack for personal interactions with the women she taught and led. Well aware that the problem of class might prove to be a stumbling block for her proposal to transplant the Canadian model of WI to rural Britain, Watt was careful not to overlook this dynamic. In the report of the first training school for WI organizers held in Sussex, the problem of class was identified directly as a matter which "may be one of some danger to the welfare of certain Women's Institutes." Watt emphasized that organizers had to use their own powers of persuasion to attract people:

We *must* get at the cottage people by personal visits and ask them to come to the Women's Institute because there is going to be an economical cookery demonstration, and there may be a lot to find out at it; or, will they bring that beautiful sampler or bit of old needlework to an exhibition there will be next meeting? Or won't they come and help with a poultry and gardening scheme that is coming up? Cottage people are shy, and they are proud; they will not come by themselves in many instances, and unless they can be brought into the Institute early in its initiation they will not come at all.[79]

In Watt's plan, there would still be a role for elite women to play in using their influence to establish and promote the formation and continuation of WI branches throughout their counties, but at the same time women of the lower classes were especially welcomed. She shared strategies on this question with Nugent Harris, who delivered a lecture during the third week of the school on "The Psychology of Rural Audiences," in which he argued that class dynamics were a very real concern:

A rural audience's psychology is very much influenced by the personnel of those present. If there should happen to be a sprinkling, say 5 per cent of what is commonly called the upper classes from the locality, the influence of this 5 per cent will more than likely dominate the whole 'atmosphere' of the meeting, and create quite a foreign psychology of the 95 per cent. Domination by the 5 per cent is the cause of much of the non-success in organizing work in rural areas. This domination can be exercised powerfully without the 5 per cent ever opening its mouth.[80]

The widespread and rapid success of the WI movement across the British countryside is testimony to the fact that WI organizers managed to take Harris's and Watt's advice to heart, welcoming the material and moral support of the upper classes, yet ensuring that those of lower social standing felt at home in the meetings.

Using the resources at her disposal through her well-connected friends, Watt's strategy was to make certain that the training for WI workers was done in a setting that ensured the learners were comfortable – not only physically, but also at ease with one another socially. It seems that Watt had the knack of finding a very satisfying balance between formality and informality.[81] The training school had a definite structure because, after all, it was designed to bring uniformity to the WI movement as it expanded quickly in territory and in numbers. Yet Watt's folksy approach was evidently a very disarming and effective way to present the importance of uniform administrative structure. In a training session entitled "Electing and Instructing a new WI

Committee," she gave contradictory messages urging the organizers to be informal in their style of presentation, yet insistent on the formulaic structure of WI administration.

> You might try some such plan as this: make a little fun of red-tape, and work in naturally that although you personally do not worry much over rules, etc., still there are certain little formalities to be observed. ... Explain that no Institute stands alone, but is one of a group of sister Institutes; and just as the members of one family must all agree on certain things if they are going to work and live together happily, so we have had to work out a few things in common.[82]

With that light tone, Watt suggested that local difficulties and irregularities could be overcome. Concluding her session, however, the report reveals that "Mrs. Watt then dealt with 'Instruction of a Women's Institute Committee' and laid great stress on the important [sic] of being very thorough over this work."[83]

Watt's training strategy also concentrated on applied learning. She invoked demonstrations as one of the most practical methods of leadership training, advocating hands-on demonstrations and on-site training experiences where organizers-in-training attended local information meetings to observe the experienced organizers at work among the local women. During the three-week training course, her students learned through lectures and discussions, but also through site visits to a variety of WI meetings and activities. As Watt explained,

> I felt that the new organizers would require not only training and information, but being put absolutely on the right lines. I felt that they must learn from others as well as from me, that they must have practical demonstrations as well as lectures, that there must be ample time for discussions and questions and help, and that all of this should be given in an atmosphere impregnated with Institute work and ideals.[84]

In order to build in the practical elements, the daily schedule of the training sessions included afternoon outings to various destinations. As Watt explained, "The visits to local centres of women's activities in the afternoon were intended both to make a pleasant interest and also to show how these activities could be embodied in Institute work."[85] Some of these planned outings included visits to successful local WIs, intended as "object lessons" for the organizers, but they also included organizational meetings such as one at Upper Beeding in Sussex "to see Mrs. Watt start a Women's Institute and instruct the new committees."[86]

The fourth element of instruction that Watt built in to her training school and to her own work with local branches was the relational aspect. Madge Watt was lauded among British Women's Institute members because of her trademark personal touch: wherever she went, she managed to maintain grassroots connections to local groups. She achieved this by visiting the monthly meetings of established WIs, by mingling with the membership, and by observing the kinds of demonstration activities, speakers, and amusements that were part of existing WI meetings. These are the elements that she built into her training school as well. Always trying to strike a positive tone as she gave instruction, a close colleague described her as a skilled teacher: "Mrs. Watt has said to me, 'I never teach by fault-finding, but by bringing out and developing the good in people.' Surely this is the art of teaching."[87] Watt wrote about the intuitive nature of how she approached each audience when she was travelling to establish new WI branches:

> If I find the chairman unpopular I disassociate myself from him as amiably as I can; it is the audience I want. If you do not win your audience in the first five minutes you may not win them at all. You must get yourself in sympathy with your audience; a funny story will often do this. Remember you have gone there in order to get a Women's Institute out of that village, and will not likely succeed if they do not like the person who is speaking to them.[88]

With strategies in place to manoeuvre through the complexities of the class structures of the English countryside, to provide her students with a comfortable learning environment, to teach by demonstration rather than just lecture, and to establish cordial relations with her students and members, Madge Watt had one specific outcome in mind: to empower women. The kind of empowering that the WI offered to women was not radical or threatening to existing social structures; yet it seems to have had wide appeal. Even during her lifetime, Watt's supporters used the language of empowerment when speaking about her accomplishments. Explaining the benefits that women enjoyed through the WI training, one English woman invoked a North American metaphor of grand proportions to describe Watt's influence:

> In Mrs. Watt we have the master-mind. Through her the Women's Institute movement has become like the great Niagara in her Canadian

country, where, above the immense falls, the rapids running deeply amongst the high rocks, that seem to bar its passage, supply force to the numerous power stations through which illumination and warmth are conveyed to numberless homes. It is beautiful to think that England has heard of this splendid and far-reaching movement from her eldest daughter, Canada.[89]

Maggie Andrews, in her analysis of the WIs in Britain as "the acceptable face of feminism," observed that during the 1920s

[t]he NFWI [National Federation of Women's Institutes] perception of itself as an educational movement was open to two quite differing interpretations: either that of education as an instrument of bourgeois hegemony, the recipient of which was the ignorant rural housewife, or, alternatively education as empowering for the oppressed.[90]

In the life and work of Madge Watt one can see the ambiguity of those competing perceptions. It seems that Watt managed to handle both of these perceptions to full advantage and to straddle the implicit dualism of hegemony and empowerment without hesitation. While she was fully involved in the affairs of the National Federation's Executive Committee, chaired by Lady Denman and composed of many other titled women, Watt (perhaps more than any other member of the Executive Committee) maintained a close working relationship with local women in their communities. From the earliest days, she expressed a deep respect for the grassroots membership and worked tirelessly among them. As one observer commented about her in 1917,

Mrs. Watt, who has the utmost sympathy with and love for the poorer women of the rural districts speaks in high appreciation of the way in which they manage their homes and families on the small wages earned by laborers ... The institutes are giving the rural women the same chances as their town sister has had all along; they are giving her a new outlook, new openings, and, above all they are widening her interests and teaching her to "think Imperially."[91]

The WI, like the Imperial Order Daughters of the Empire, provided women of various means a mechanism to express their form of female imperialism.[92]

Because she was convinced that women who stayed at home tied to their domestic responsibilities could make a meaningful public contribution, Watt's vision of the WI embodies what Maggie Andrews has suggested about the potential of this movement to empower women. Lady Isabel Margesson characterized Watt's work this way:

> Mrs. Watt has patience as well as faith in the capacity of home-tied women to co-operate profitably with the State. She found in them a passionate patriotism partially wasted, because undirected and unorganized, and she has been able to direct that flow of patriotism into channels that will eventually change the face of the rural districts and discover a mine of ability, talent, and wealth in the women of the country.[93]

The 1918 training school scheme in Sussex was Watt's first and most widely publicized effort of educating WI workers, but her instructional efforts were not limited to that one format; she also regularly spoke directly to WI members at their local meetings. On those occasions, she delivered lectures to communicate her enthusiasm about the potential of rural women's organizations, and as she herself declared, addressing those local meetings was one of her fondest memories of the time she spent in England.

After the war ended, Watt was making plans to return to Canada when the June 1919 issue of the British Women's Institute journal *Home and Country* declared their affection for this colonial woman and her imperial contribution:

> Our members owe a debt of gratitude to Mrs. Watt who from over the seas brought the idea of Women's Institutes. She started our first Women's Institute ... in September 1915 ... When Mrs. Watt returns to Canada next month she will take a cordial greeting from our Institutes to the Pioneer Women's Institutes of her homeland as well as our heartiest wishes of goodwill for herself. Her name will be inseparably connected with the Women's Institutes in England and Wales.[94]

Watt would draw upon that goodwill and "inseparable connection" to catapult herself into her next role, as she would soon recast herself. Honoured by the British government with the title "Member of the British Empire," for the contribution she made in bringing the WI to England and Wales, Watt left England in mid-August 1919 and returned to Canada with almost a celebrity status. Arriving in

England six years earlier, she had been retreating from the media attention surrounding her husband's death and trying to adjust to her new reality as a middle-aged widow. Now, upon her return to Canada, she welcomed and used the media attention she received to leverage herself into her next role, that of international expert on rural women. She had succeeded in transplanting the idea of rural women's organizations from the colony to the mother country. Her next challenge would be to take that success further as she set her sights on a broader imperial project.

Chapter Five

On the World Stage: Forging International Networks

When Madge Watt left England in 1919, she was showered with fare-well gifts and tributes for the wartime contributions she had made to the Empire. She spent the next two years in Canada, during which time she was involved in the affairs of the newly created federation of Canadian Women's Institutes (Federated Women's Institutes of Canada, hereaf-ter FWIC). In 1921 Watt returned to England with an enlarged vision of what cooperation among rural women worldwide might mean. Her experiences after the war with Women's Institute groups in Canada and the various state extension efforts in the United States had con-vinced her that she had some larger, international role to play among rural women. Yet forging the networks and finding the right structures that would eventually lead to the creation of the Associated Country Women of the World (ACWW) took more time and effort than Watt had predicted. It required all of her attention to maintain a variety of con-tacts and opportunities to meet with others who shared her vision for the potential of international networks of women. She was convinced that her previous experiences, her passion for travel, and her personal alliances made her eminently qualified to lead women worldwide and she spent the next eight years trying a variety of schemes to make her vision a reality.

To situate Watt and her work with rural women's organizations in the context of other international organizations of women during the interwar years, the work of historian Leila J. Rupp is very useful. In her book, *Worlds of Women: The Making of an International Women's Movement*, Rupp traces the developments of the International Council of Women, the International Woman Suffrage Alliance (later the Inter-national Alliance of Women), and the Women's International League for Peace and Freedom.[1] The interwar years were a particularly rich period for women's organizations worldwide because in the context of heightened concerns over world peace, women took interest in various causes, buoyed up by recent successes in the fight for suffrage. For liberal feminists like those in Rupp's study, there was a shared idealism about the possibilities implicit in international collaboration. Although the idea of creating such a group specifically for rural women would prove to be a complicated undertaking, the effort was driven by individuals committed to imperial feminism and the internationalist ideal.

The class composition of international women's groups was a defining feature, and in this, rural women were no exception; participation was typically reserved for the more privileged.[2] While the mass membership might be drawn from across a wide spectrum, the active participants in international meetings can most aptly be described as "a gathering of the elite," as Rupp explains:

> Since members had to undertake lengthy and expensive travel to attend meetings, serve as officers, or participate in ongoing activities, only those with both the leisure and the independent means or with sufficient national or international stature to attract subsidies from organizations or individuals could take part.[3]

Clearly Madge Watt fell into that category of "the elite" because she devoted her time and energy towards a very active participation in these international gatherings. The grassroots membership of WIs composed of farm and village women in North America and Britain could only watch from the sidelines and try to imagine the experiences that Watt and her associates enjoyed as they recounted to the membership their exciting tales of luxurious international travel adventures and inspiring claims about the potential of an international coalition of rural women.

Watt, however, did not have great personal wealth, and money was continually a source of worry for her. Although she was very comfortable in the company of the elite because of the social circles she had moved in since her youth, she did not have access to the personal financial resources that were typical of other privileged clubwomen in the period.[4] One assumes that given Alfred's suicide, Madge Watt would not have been able to collect any life insurance benefits. Nor was her father's wealth available to her; according to a local history source, Henry Robertson, who passed away in 1923, had spent "his considerable wealth on an extravagant trip around the world" several years before his death.[5] Without those usual sources of financial security, Watt was constantly worried about money. Some of her activities were subsidized by governments or by the women's organizations themselves because of the reputation she had earned through her wartime service and because of her remarkable skills as a public speaker, but concern over funding, especially personal finance, was a constant pressure.

Though she could not see it herself, part of what slowed Watt's progress in realizing her goal of uniting rural women internationally was the fact that she was depending so heavily on her personal experiences being the link between various countries. That strategy proved to be both an asset and a liability. While she had travelled widely and enjoyed her contacts with rural groups in Britain, Canada, the United States, Germany, Scandinavia, Belgium, and Italy throughout the 1920s, she lacked the personal influence to actually realize her vision. As one of her acquaintances remarked, Watt "had neither prestige nor influence; neither money nor financial backing. She had no splendid presence."[6] Such a frank assessment would have deeply offended Watt because her perception of herself was quite the opposite. She thought she was the ideal person to translate the vision of international cooperation among rural women's groups into a reality, but in fact, she could never accomplish that alone.

When she first returned to Canada after the war, she regaled the press with accounts of her wartime work in the UK and welcomed the media attention that she received. Playing upon the notion that she had exported the Canadian idea of Women's Institutes to the mother country in an act of reverse colonialism, Watt emphasized that she had been particularly skillful in the way that she had packaged the concept of Women's Institutes for the British public. She told the Toronto *Globe* that "[w]e cut a great deal of red tape and did things on our own; we broke a lot of old traditions and preserved many others; we used the best of the old and introduced the best of the new."[7] The results were impressive, as the expansion of WIs across England and Wales attested; indeed, with more than a thousand Women's Institutes established in just four years' time, even the robust growth of the Canadian rural women's groups seemed meager by comparison.[8]

Also impressive was the fact that the movement in England and Wales managed to attract a wide variety of women, including what Watt called both "the highest and the humblest." The accent was clearly on "the highest" as she pointed out to the press that "the Queen is the real President of a real Women's Institute at Sandringham; the Duchess of Newcastle is another President; still others are Miss Elizabeth Robins, the playwright and novelist, and … Earl Grey's daughter, Lady Evelyn Gray."[9] Listing more than ten other prominent, titled women who were WI leaders, Watt clearly intended to impress her Canadian audience and establish her credibility because the movement she had launched held sway among some of the most elite women in the Empire. Watt used that cultural authority to elevate her own status and to leverage her ability to gain a hearing with WI sponsors and government officials across Canada. At the same time she was clearly attempting to capitalize on Canadians' imperial sentiment.

Another sign of Watt's impressive résumé of activities included the experiences she had enjoyed and the influence she had exerted beyond the UK. Recounting her most recent adventure just before her return to Canada, she explained how busy her travel schedule had been: "I worked in Belgium until August 13th and I left England on August 15th [1919]."[10] According to Watt, she had asked the British government to send her to Belgium to observe the rural women's organizations there, and she made a point of emphasizing the Canadian influences that were at work among rural women's organizations in Belgium. She explained that a few years earlier a party of Belgian delegates

> had visited Mr. Putnam [superintendent of the Ontario Women's Institutes] at the Parliament Buildings here [in Toronto], and I don't think anyone had visited them since. The visit was delayed by the Belgian Government until two weeks before I sailed, but the British Government said, 'We will send you nevertheless," and they sent me to Belgium and paid my expenses.[11]

Emphasizing the fact that she was sought out as an observer of rural women's clubs and that two different governments were involved in arranging and financing her travel, Watt wanted to offer further proof of the respect she commanded and the stature she enjoyed as an expert on rural women's organizations.

Watt capitalized on her new reputation as the founder of a highly popular and prestigious movement and she hoped to impress her Canadian audiences (particularly potential sponsors) with the fact that other governments sought her out and even paid her way to facilitate connections with other countries. Adding to that celebrity status was the fact that at the end of the war the British government recognized Watt by bestowing upon her the title Member of the Order of the British Empire

(MBE), a designation created in 1917 by King George V to honour civilians and military personnel for their wartime service to the Empire. The recognition was given to Watt because by bringing the WI to England and Wales during war, she was deemed to have made an important contribution to the war effort through her work in encouraging rural women to increase the food supply and take steps towards food conservation. The strategy was a simple one: WI members would plant "victory gardens," conserve food through careful household management, and store extra food by learning to can and make preserves. As a decorated war hero, Watt received preferential treatment from the British government; her transatlantic travel costs were paid, and she and her friend Josephine Godman sailed back to Canada together in early September 1919, although the patience of other travellers was tested while they waited for weeks and even months to gain a coveted spot for the postwar transatlantic crossing on one of the CPR ships.[12]

Once she arrived in Canada, Watt's strategy was to establish as many contacts as she could as quickly as possible across the country and to be recognized as an expert on rural women's affairs. On the day after she landed, a Toronto paper reported that she attended the Canadian National Exhibition in the company of several Women's Institute officers and the provincial superintendent of the WI. According to the Toronto press, "Mrs. Watt spent a large part of the day at the Exhibition, taking particular interest in the exhibits of the Department of Agriculture and the Provincial Board of Health."[13] From Toronto, she went north to visit her father and her sister in Collingwood, and then she embarked on a series of travels to solidify her networks with the WI across the country. As the *Globe* explained, "In October, Mrs. Watt expects to make some public speeches concerning her work and will after go West, speaking to the Alberta Government on her way through to British Columbia."[14]

Not only did she speak to WI conventions in Ontario, Quebec, and the Maritimes throughout the fall of 1919; she also took the opportunity to participate in the executive of the new national organization of Canadian Women's Institutes, the FWIC. When she took her place at the table with that group, it was a logical connection for her to make because it meant that she resumed the place she had occupied six years earlier, when she was busy with organizing WI branches in BC. Before she left for England, she had been part of the early talks about creating a federation to unite Canadian WIs from coast to coast. Now she was coming back to that group, but with the added prestige of her war work and her international travels to further enhance the contributions she could make.

Even though she had missed the founding meeting of the FWIC held in Winnipeg in February 1919,[15] six months before her return, Watt endorsed the federation because she had also been thinking about the potential for broader alliances among WIs. For example, when she led the training school for WI organizers in Sussex in 1918, her instructions to WI organizers reflected that broader outlook: "Make each member understand that when she joins a Women's Institute she becomes a member of a great rural sisterhood, not only here, but all over the Empire."[16] The opportunity to be involved in the new Canada-wide federation meant that Watt could observe how the fledgling federation operated and learn from that working example. She planned to take that experience and use it to bring groups together under one umbrella across the Empire and even beyond it. Working with the Canadian WIs, Watt observed how to create a federation from a group of pre-existing organizations with diverse constitutional and operational structures. Unlike the NFWI in England, where the London office oversaw individual Institutes organized within county federations, Canadian WIs operated with different practices, different functions, and even different names from province to province.[17] Despite those differences, Canadian rural women's groups still came together to forge a working federation. Being part of that process offered Watt a vision for an international entity where even national, linguistic, and cultural differences could be overcome. Just as it had been in wartime, the Canadian experience provided the model for Watt's next steps. Seeing how rural women in one of the dominions could cooperate so successfully made Watt imagine that what happened with the FWIC was possible elsewhere; she was convinced that rural women had more similarities than differences, no matter where they lived.

As the archival records of the Women's Institutes in Canada demonstrate, talks about forming a national organization for rural women had been going on for some time and the earliest of these predated Watt's departure for England. George Putnam, the superintendent of the Ontario WI from 1904 to 1934, kept up an active correspondence on the idea with Watt and others from 1912 onward. Those earlier discussions were interrupted by the war, yet those war years should not be understood merely as a stumbling block or a delay towards eventual federation. While the talks about national organization were stalled for a time, rural women across the country set about applying themselves to the task at hand – war work – and they emerged from those experiences with a sense of empowerment. Across Canada, women took up their tools to knit socks, sew pyjamas, and roll bandages for soldiers in cooperation with other national organizations such as the Canadian Red Cross. WI members also stepped in to increase food production: individually, as they carefully followed the rations imposed upon them in their own homes, and collectively, as they came together to preserve and ship fruits and other foods for overseas consumption. Here the members of the WI were in their element, because their expertise as homemakers was being turned to national and international causes.

Moreover, after years of campaigning for the vote for Canadian women, that right became a reality during the war under the terms of the Wartime Elections Act of 1917, when any woman who was directly related to an enlisted person was automatically granted the right to cast a ballot in the federal election that year. Some of the western provinces had already extended the provincial franchise to women earlier than 1917, and those provinces which had not yet done so quickly followed suit after the war. By 1922 women in every province of Canada except Quebec were eligible to vote. This marked an important step towards women's changing status in Canada and in public opinion generally; the newfound formal political involvement for women was a significant part of the context that factored into the creation of a national federation of Canadian WIs after the war.

Money was another factor. In 1913 the Canadian Conservative government had introduced the Agricultural Instruction Act, which committed $10 million over the coming ten years to programs and activities designed to assist and elevate the country's rural communities. Under the Act, each provincial Department of Agriculture was given a portion of the funds and directed to make allotments of the grant as it saw fit. Although the allocations differed from province to province, in every region at least some of the money went towards women's organizations and extension services; it supported travelling lecturers, underwrote the costs of club organizers, supplied printed materials, and funded various other activities and projects. It is safe to say, then, that rural women's activities in Canada were subsidized at least in part from the coffers of the national government.[18]

On the strength of wartime experiences, expanding political rights, and available funding, rural women's groups flourished across Canada. By 1919 there were almost 900 Women's Institute branches in Ontario alone, and Putnam told the delegates to a provincial conference that they were "an important section, the mother of organizations which have grown to large proportions and which are destined to play an important part in local and national affairs in the years to come."[19] In keeping with that sentiment, a national body – Federated Women's Institutes of Canada (FWIC) – was created as a result of a series of meetings held in Winnipeg in February that same year.[20] After just three days of meetings, the federation had been created, a name chosen, its constitution formulated, its officers elected, six standing committees formed, and ten important resolutions passed ranging from FWIC structure and finance to national legislation on prohibition and access for women to parliament. The group decided to hold biennial conventions of the federation, with executive meetings held between those conventions.[21]

When the FWIC met for the second time, in November 1919, Watt had already returned to Canada and was completing her busy itinerary of speaking engagements that fall. This time the meeting was held in Toronto, and Judge Emily Murphy, the president of the FWIC, welcomed Watt as the representative of the British Institutes, calling her presence at the gathering a "felicitous circumstance."[22] Watt was pleased to be recognized as the one who was the authority on the WI in Britain, and to bring greetings to the delegates on behalf of Her Majesty the Queen.[23] It was a busy meeting, spanning several days, and during the course of the sessions, Watt took on numerous responsibilities, including being named as an "unofficial" member of a newly constituted committee on the FWIC constitution, a member of a committee on an international constitution, and the convenor of a committee on Institute techniques and national events. Through the last committee, Watt hoped to implement a series of training workshops that would resemble the "schools for leaders" that she had introduced in the UK the year before. Her idea was to standardize WI procedures across the country, a rather strange goal for Canada given the differences that existed between the provinces and the variety of relationships that rural women's groups had with governments, agricultural colleges, and community organizations. Watt also secured for herself the assurance that she would "be welcome to use Provincial Headquarters of [the WI] Organization and their equipment as she might require in her Technique and Nat. Events Comm. [sic] work anywhere in Dominion."[24] With that kind of infrastructure at her disposal, she established her role as a key figure in the Canadian WI movement with access to clerical resources as needed.

Watt's main reason for participating in the FWIC meeting was to promote her idea of forging a formal link between the Canadian WI and the WIs in England and Wales. She spoke at length to the idea, as the minutes reveal:

> Mrs. Watt thought it advisable the definite plan of affiliation shd. come from Canada where Insts. had originated. The idea was that Gr. Brit. and Canada shd then draw up a Constn. and that any other country desiring to federate with us, shd. accept our Constn.[25]

That suggestion was revisited during a special session where the executive sought clarification on exactly what Watt was proposing for this international constitution. When pressed for details, it was clear that Watt did not have a definite proposal in mind, and she

> stated that her instructions were simply to co-operate with Canada. She wd. need the consent of the Nat. Fed. of England and Wales before taking any formal steps toward Federation. She could not exceed her powers. She however agreed that it would be advantageous if such a Fed. existed, but she held the view that this Fed. should exist in the Brit. Empire first.[26]

It is clear that Watt wanted this cooperation to take place, and while she saw herself playing the role of broker to make that happen, she needed to be careful to convince the Canadian WI that British women wanted this. At the same time, she wanted to be able to say to the British women that the initiative had come from Canada. In fact, it is not clear that at this stage anyone else shared Watt's vision or enthusiasm for the alliance.

At Emily Murphy's suggestion, the FWIC executive decided that they would "lay the whole matter of International Fed. before her [Great Britain] for consultation, asking her co-operation; and that we leave it with our own Executive to take in hand the consummation of that union."[27] That outcome was clearly worrisome to Watt, because after a motion passed to that effect, she reiterated that the Canadians needed to push for this to actually happen, restating her position that the initiative "should originate in Canada" and that to make sure this moved ahead, the FWIC should take the international constitution that she had laid before them, and refer it "to England for consideration."[28] Watt recognized that although imperial sentiment was strong in Canada, a formal union between the rural women's clubs of the dominion and the mother country was not likely to come about without someone steering the process and pushing towards its realization. In the years to come, she positioned herself to fill that brokering role.

Following the meetings in Toronto, Watt made her way to the west, steeling herself to return to BC for the first time since her husband's death in 1913. She arrived in Victoria, where she resumed her activity from six years before as a member of the Provincial Advisory Board on Women's Institutes. The chair of the advisory board had recently died, and when the group met to reorganize, Watt was elected to the chair's position because of her previous experience as a member of the board and "considering the service [she had] rendered in England."[29] It seems clear that Watt was not intending to make her return to British Columbia permanent, because the minutes record that "Mrs. Watt accepted in order to facilitate the business but on the distinct understanding that the position was only temporary."[30]

Although she occupied the position of chair for only ten months, Watt wasted no time in suggesting some significant changes to the structures that governed the WI in BC. Drawing on her experiences in England, she hoped to establish greater autonomy for the Provincial Advisory Board, freeing the group from having to answer to the provincial government.[31] As it turns out, however, Watt's real objection was only partly a constitutional one. The deeper issue was money, and the fact that one of her requests for funding had been denied. The question of how to finance her own travels in connection with Institute work was a recurring one; indeed, it would continually resurface, not only in her relationships with government sponsors, but also with her fellow executive members. According to the *Victoria Daily Times*,

> Mrs. Watt observed that under the present conditions the members of the Advisory Board were not allowed to visit the Institutes, no money being available for this purpose, so that it was impossible for the members of that Board to get into close touch with the Institute members.[32]

Yet Watt's experiences in England and Wales had shown that time spent with Institute members in their own locales was the one setting where her greatest powers of persuasion really shone. However, when she was invited to attend a conference of the Kootenay Women's Institutes, Dr. Warnock, the deputy minister of agriculture and superintendent of Women's Institutes for BC, denied her the opportunity to attend, claiming a lack of funds.[33]

The fact was that as the provincial government official charged with overseeing the WI in BC, Warnock did indeed have the responsibility to make decisions about the organization's budgets. When Watt suggested moving towards establishing greater autonomy from government control, she was actually advocating a model closer to that of the UK, but one sensible delegate cautioned that declaring independence might jeopardize any chance of receiving provincial grants to the WI in future. In response, Watt proposed that she was "in favour of the grant being administered by the Women's Institutes through … the Advisory Board, and that a budget should be rendered to the Government."[34] That model seemed perfectly sensible to Watt in light of the independence that English WIs enjoyed from government control, but given the conflicts that had ensued between Watt and Warnock, the chances of such a change being adopted by the deputy minister in BC seemed very remote indeed.

A few months later, at the next meeting of the advisory board, held in May 1921, the issue of independence from provincial control came to the table. It quickly became clear that Watt did not have support from the other members of the advisory board for her proposal to establish greater autonomy. Indeed, one member suggested that the board might "put a plebiscite to all the Institutes to ascertain how many … desired to dissociate themselves entirely from the Department, [but] that for her part there had been absolutely no dissatisfaction expressed by the Institutes in the Okanagan district."[35] The other board members quickly echoed that view, and were "unanimous in their opinion that there was no such desire on the part of the Institutes to draw out from departmental association or assistance."[36] Immediately after that discussion, E.D. Barrow, the minister of agriculture for BC, joined the meeting, and the minutes record that he "expressed an appreciation of the work done by the members and [the] good spirit prevailing. He regretted Mrs. Watt's departure, and expressed the wish that the stay [that she was planning in England] might not be long."[37] At the end of her short term as chair of the advisory board, it is clear that Watt's relationship with the provincial government was strained, and she learned that she would have to look elsewhere for the financial support she needed.

Around the same time Watt had tried to introduce another initiative in BC based on her wartime experiences in England; this also came to an unhappy ending. The idea was to have a "town Institute," a sort of "mother" Institute that would oversee the activities of local branches in the vicinity. Knowing that Victoria was the hub of activities for Vancouver Island, Watt and her friend Josephine Godman initiated a WI in that city, as they had done in so many "county towns" in England. The two friends divided their time between Godman's home in Esquimalt and Victoria, where they stayed with Watt's old friend, Annie Cleland. They used Cleland's prestigious address near Government House as their base when they mingled with other elite women in the society circles of Victoria, but they spent the majority of their time in the more rural setting of Esquimalt.[38] Establishing a WI branch in the city proved to be more difficult than they had imagined, especially because the women of Victoria resented Watt and Godman's attempts to control the affairs of the branch. Godman was named as president at the inaugural meeting of the Victoria Women's Institute on March 18, 1921, and although the branch met several times that spring with good attendance of up to forty women, the problem of finding a suitable, affordable meeting place was not easily resolved, and money was an ongoing problem for the group from its earliest meetings.

The minute books are not entirely clear on what other problems the branch encountered, but by the end of May, at a meeting of the executive when neither Watt nor Godman was present, the minute book records that the following motion was carried unanimously: "that Mrs. Godman's resignation be accepted with pleasure."[39] No details are given about why Godman had submitted her resignation, but clearly there was disagreement between her and the others. The minutes further record that "The Sec[retary] was instructed to point out to Mrs. Godman that any difficulty that may have arisen was no doubt do [sic] to the great difference between the English and the Canadian Institutes."[40] Exactly what those "great differences" were is unclear, but in previous meetings there had been discussion about the process of incorporating the Victoria Women's Institute; while many of the members thought it was a good idea, Watt disagreed. She advised the group not to incorporate (as all the other BC branches had done) because she argued that being an unincorporated group, they would have greater autonomy from the provincial government's control.[41] That position was the same one Watt had expressed a few months earlier during her conflict with Warnock over his decision not to fund her travels. There is no doubt that Godman would have supported Watt's position, and by removing her from the presidency, the Victoria WI members were sending a clear signal to the provincial authorities that they fully intended to remain firmly under the umbrella of provincial oversight.

At the same time, by asserting their preference for a "made-in-BC" model of WI governance, these Victoria women were sending another clear message: they would not bow to the English model that Watt and Godman were attempting to impose and they resented being treated as mere colonials. Clearly there was some dissonance between the experiences that Watt had had in England and the policies in effect there, and those she tried to implement in Victoria. When she attempted to transplant the English model back to British Columbia, local women resisted her efforts. It would not be the last time that Watt would encounter resistance to her attempts to impose her views upon a group; indeed that would become almost a defining feature in Watt's later years. Watt never spoke about this episode, but ironically, it seems that upon her return home to a colonial setting, she had stepped into the role of colonizer. In spite of this conflict, she continued to assert that no matter where she went, the similarities between women's groups were greater than their differences. Indeed, as her own best publicist, Watt continually minimized any resistance that she encountered.

Leaving the turmoil she had caused in Victoria behind her, Watt set her sights on returning to England, and began her travels eastward to spend some time with her father and her sister in Collingwood during the summer of 1921 before she sailed that fall. Conveniently, another meeting of the FWIC was taking place that June in Edmonton, and Watt planned her travels to coincide with that gathering. That meeting of the FWIC was a veritable "Who's Who" of prominent Canadian women reformers, including Judge Emily Murphy, also known as "Janey Canuck"; author and suffrage crusader Nellie McClung; Mrs. Sanford, president of the National Council of Women; Laura Rose Stephen, WI organizer and former professor of dairying at the Ontario Agricultural College, and Charlotte Whitton, social welfare advocate, later to become mayor of Ottawa. Murphy was ending her term as the first president of the FWIC, and she had arranged for the group to spend one evening at her home.[42] During the week-long gathering, Watt addressed the convention twice. On the first occasion, she gave a report of her visit to Belgium and recounted how impressed she was with the Cercles de Fermières groups there. In her talk, she pointed out that "she found the meetings usually occurring on Sundays, and she especially approved of the combination between Church and State in efforts to make the farmwomen efficient."[43]

In her second talk to the convention, Watt spoke in her role as the convenor of the FWIC Committee on Institute Technique, reporting that she had mapped out twelve instalments of a special magazine column instructing WI members on "plans for meetings, for methods of conducting enterprise, for finding what produces success, what failure and such like."[44] She admitted, however, that while several general articles dealing with WI work had appeared recently in the *Farmers' Advocate* and the *Western Women's Weekly*, her plans to have monthly instruction columns published in *Canadian Home Journal* had come to nothing. To explain the failure, she simply reported that she had been "under the impression that the space would be given," but when it was not, she was very "disappointed in the failure of this scheme."[45] However, even though she was resigning from her position as convenor of this committee, she assured the group that she had another plan in mind about how to circulate the material she had written and she "outlined the contents of her own work on The Principles and Practices of Women's Insts. [sic] and Kindred Rural Movements which will shortly be published."[46] That publication never appeared. It seems that Watt was no more successful at working out the logistics of how to get her publications completed than she had been at cooperating with the provincial authorities back in BC. Watt's failure to deliver on these basic organizational strategies were foreshadows of things to come.

The one thing that Watt did very successfully, however, was to cast vision and inspire audiences to imagine the potential of their organizations. Despite her lack of success in delivering any tangible results either in BC as part of the Provincial Advisory Board or with the FWIC in her role as convenor of Institute technique, Watt left the Edmonton meeting on a high note. The minutes record that

> [i]n giving up her office Mrs. Watt regretted the lack of appreciation of how big a thing the Women's Instit. [sic] really is. Finally she reaffirmed her belief that as long as we have faith in our movement there is nothing to prevent our being the greatest spiritual and educational force the Dominion of Canada has ever seen.[47]

Watt's faith in the WI movement knew no bounds. Indeed, she believed that not only could the WI be a great force for good in Canada, but if the various rural women's groups from across the Empire (and even beyond it) could join forces, there would be unimaginable benefits for women worldwide. The first step to realizing the worldwide outlook was to promote a formal affiliation between the dominion and the mother country, and that goal once again became her focus when she left Canada to return to England in October 1921.

The 1920s would prove to be a difficult decade for Watt as she worked to move forward with her agenda of bringing the country women of the world into a united body. Watt had built her reputation through her international travels, and she made a point of telling her Canadian audiences about her time in the UK and Europe. When she returned to England, she expected her audiences there to be fascinated by her travels and contacts in North America. However, her peers back in London were harder to impress, and Watt realized that she might be more successful with village women. Her first move was to re-establish and reinforce her credibility with the Women's Institutes in England and Wales after her two-year absence. Immediately upon her return to Britain in 1921, Watt announced that she was making herself available as a travelling lecturer. The monthly WI magazine published in London announced her return with enthusiasm:

> We are sure that all readers of HOME AND COUNTRY will be delighted to hear that Mrs. Alfred Watt, who first brought the Institute Movement to this country from Canada, and is again this year in England, hopes to be able to arrange through the County Federations lecture tours for Institutes.[48]

The announcement, entitled "Lecture Titles Proposed by Madge Watt for County Lectures, 1921," included a lengthy list of dozens of talks that Watt was prepared to give.[49] From that list, with titles such as "French Canadian and Belgian Cercles de Fermières," "The United Farm Women of North America," and "Canada's Proposals for International WI Organisation," it is clear that Watt was hoping to bring a different emphasis to the English and Welsh countryside during the postwar years. Clearly, her focus was upon enlarging the vision of local WI branches by informing them about developments she had observed while in North America and instilling in the membership a sense of the international possibilities for collaboration.

In order to establish her credibility as the one best suited to forge such international links, Watt needed to do more than simply regale her audiences with tales of how Canadian and American rural women organized themselves. She needed to convince British women that once again, the experiences of a colonial woman returning from Canada could be instructive on the other side of the Atlantic. She began by reminding the women of England and Wales about her role as the founder of the WI, hoping to give herself a level of imperial authority. Positioning herself strategically, Watt took several steps towards that end upon her return to England, but each one seemed fraught with its own set of problems.

The lecture series that Watt proposed, though it sounded innocuous enough, caused a great number of problems for the NFWI. First of all, Watt seemed to expect that the national office would be so delighted with her offer to lecture that they would manage the bookings for her speaking engagements. With more than a thousand Institutes potentially making individual requests, that was obviously going to entail a great deal of coordination and work, and therefore the London office made it clear that they would not be acting as Watt's agent. They suggested that county federations might collect local requests, and where sufficient interest was shown to create an itinerary, each county could book directly with Watt herself. The second issue that the NFWI was forced to clarify was finances. The NFWI emphasized that Watt was not employed by them and each local group who wanted to invite her to address them would have to bear the cost of paying her speaking fee (£1 1s. per lecture) and arranging her travel. Moreover, at Watt's request, the published announcement made it clear that "[a]s she is traveling a great deal, she is obliged to charge also first class traveling expenses, except in special circumstances."[50]

Arranging for Watt to remain at arm's length from the NFWI in her public speaking proved to be a double-edged sword, however. While it was true that she was not "officially" connected to the NFWI, in the eyes of the public she was clearly a Women's Institute spokesperson. Keeping the financial arrangements separate was obviously a prudent management strategy, but it meant that the London office had no real power over Watt's performances. The NFWI prided itself on strictly avoiding any discussion of politics or religion, but as a "free agent" Watt hit the lecture circuit, expressing her personal opinions about all manner of things. Because she also regularly reminded her audiences about her founding role in establishing the WI in England and Wales, it is understandable that a great deal of confusion arose about where the NFWI actually stood on some controversial issues of the day. The biggest problem came when Watt began to accept invitations to give lectures outside of local WI meetings, yet billed herself as the "founder of the Women's Institutes in England and Wales." On at least one occasion, her talk touched a nerve among Labour Party supporters, who interpreted her remarks as anti-Labour propaganda. Given the highly volatile political climate in England just months before the Labour Party first came to power in January 1924, that kind of negative attention was the last thing that the NFWI needed.

The issue had first been discussed at the NFWI meeting on January 10, 1922, but the controversy escalated further when the Labour Party threatened to organize an official campaign opposing the WI. Other highly charged political groups attempted to take advantage of the situation to make inroads for their causes. One example is the case of a feminist journal, *The Woman's Leader and Common Cause*, which encouraged readers with strong party loyalties and political agendas on the left that this was an opportune time to infiltrate the Women's Institutes in order to promote their causes.[51] In light of Watt's talks, this seemed to be a unique chance subversively to make inroads into the WI. The journal urged its readers to ignore what the Labour Party was saying about the WI being an "undesirable friend" because of its strong stance on remaining politically neutral, and to co-opt the local WI branches. Clearly, Watt was opening the door to all kinds of troubles for the NFWI. Some members of the NFWI executive concluded that Watt and her speaking tours were a big liability because she was blatantly ignoring the rule about remaining non-partisan and non-political.

The situation was urgent, and something needed to be done to offset the damage that Watt was causing. Accordingly, Lady Denman worked feverishly behind the scenes to quell opposition to the WI movement by meeting with Labour sympathizers to assure them that the WI was adamantly maintaining its neutral stance on all matters political. To put an end to the troubles Watt was causing, the NFWI executive took the unusual step of communicating with her by letter. The minutes of February 14, 1922, record that "Mrs. Watt had been written to and had been asked not to allow herself to be described as the Founder of Women's Institutes in England at any meeting that could be considered of a party political character."[52]

Watt responded to Denman's reprimand by capitalizing on it. Since the NFWI had raised the issue of her title as founder of the WI, she took the opportunity to solidify her status. She turned the request around, almost as if she was thanking the London executive for bringing up the question. It was something she had been meaning to ask for: official recognition as a permanent part of the organization. What she really wanted was to have her name on the letterhead of the NFWI stationery so that she could use her position to establish her legitimacy in negotiating with international rural women's groups. Without that official endorsement, she felt hampered in her efforts but she did not build her case using that argument. Instead, Watt explained that during her lectures to women's groups in the English countryside, a great deal of confusion had arisen. She reported that a great number of people were referring to her as the founder of Women's Institutes in Canada, which, of course, she was not. That honour was reserved for Adelaide Hoodless. She explained pedantically to the NFWI executive that people were saying that Lady Denman (the national president of the NFWI) was the founder of the English Institutes, which, of course, was not true either and she was certain that Lady Denman would want to clear up all this confusion. Watt wanted to reaffirm that she herself was the real founder of the movement in the UK, and she thought the best way to do that might be to have her name on the NFWI stationery.

The NFWI considered Watt's request at their meeting in mid-February 1922, and the minutes record that

> [a] long discussion had taken place and it had been finally AGREED that it was impossible to have Mrs. Watt's name printed on official stationery, as only names of officials authorized to sign letters appeared there, but it had been DECIDED to recommend the insertion in Home and Country after the list of officials, of the following words: 'Founder of the first Women's Institute [sic] in England and Wales, 1915, Mrs. Alfred Watt, MA, MBE.'[53]

This solution would please Watt because it would be an ongoing recognition of her significant role in the history of the British WIs. Yet the solution worked for the NFWI as well. Note how carefully the wording was chosen: by calling Watt "the founder of the first Women's Institute in England and Wales" (not "the founder of Women's Institutes"), the NFWI was subtly asserting that Watt was not solely responsible for the movement, and by placing the declaration in their own publication rather than on the official letterhead, they were limiting her influence.

A few months later, Watt was less pleased with the outcome of another request she was making. When three vacancies opened up on the NFWI Executive, she hoped to be named as a member so that she could participate fully in the affairs of the Women's Institutes and have a voice at the highest level of the organization. In the end, she was not chosen, and Lady Denman wrote to Watt to remind her that "there are so many interests and districts that feel they should be represented on that body."[54] As a consolation, Denman told Watt that she had been elected to a subcommittee on organizing local WI groups, explaining that "I think we all felt that on that Sub-Committee you would be able to advise us on Schools Organisation and that this would also give you the right to attend Organiser's Conferences."[55]

It was not what Watt had wanted, but at least it kept her in touch with the NFWI, and it did mean that her expertise for organizing local groups was being recognized. Indeed, as problems arose about various Institutes that were failing to conform to NFWI policy, the executive turned to Watt for help in persuading local women to comply. This mandate took Watt back to local Institutes, where she had done her very first work for the organization. Watt encouraged local leaders not to allow themselves to be so distracted by the social items on their agenda that they lost sight of their larger purpose. One particular case that is discussed in the minutes was the Institute work in Anglesey, Wales, where it is recorded that there was "a general disregard of the Rules, both in County Federation organisation and in the Institutes themselves. There had been a serious decline in membership and there were now very few working-class members in the Institutes."[56] When a WI staff member made a visit to try to correct the problem, there was resistance to that intervention, and although it was suggested that Watt might step in to resolve the problem, the executive voted instead to have Anglesey send representatives to the upcoming annual meeting of the NFWI, where they could be corrected by members of the NFWI executive. It was not possible to arrange that meeting, and in the end, since Watt was already planning to spend time in Anglesey, the NFWI asked that she should remind the WIs there to return to a focus on their original aims and purposes.[57]

Watt was very pleased to be recognized as an expert organizer of local groups and to have her name appear in *Home and Country* magazine as the founder.[58] Yet, just when she thought her influence was rising, she was about to face disappointment as she clashed again with the NFWI authorities in London. This time the conflict arose over an initiative Watt had in mind as the tenth anniversary of the founding of the Llanfairpwll Institute approached. Anticipating 1925 as a significant date, she pressed the NFWI to plan some official festivities around the upcoming anniversary and to make it a national celebration. She wrote a letter to the editor of *Home and Country* filled with suggestions about how to mark the upcoming occasion. "Dear editor," she wrote, envisioning what a grand occasion the celebrations might be, "May I call the attention of the Institute world to the fact that next year is the tenth year of Women's Institutes in Great Britain and the twelfth since I first mooted the subject of Institutes to English audiences?"[59] Emphasizing that the NFWI should capitalize on the appeal of history, Watt insisted that "[a]n Institute which is ignorant of our history and development is poor, when it might be rich in sentiment and tradition ... It is missing the inspiration of wider knowledge and of a broader outlook."[60]

Despite the grassroots support that Watt hoped to drum up for this initiative, the NFWI executive curtly dismissed the idea, because it was "agreed that the 10th anniversary was somewhat too early a date in the history of the movement to celebrate and it was DECIDED to explain to Mrs. Watt that for this reason the Committee did not feel able to fall in with her suggestion."[61] Evidently, British and Canadian ideas about what constituted a historic occasion were somewhat at odds, and as a colonial woman, Watt saw things differently than her counterparts on the London committee. Officially then, there was no national celebration, though *Home and Country* did devote an issue to a retrospective look at the progress of the movement over its first ten years. Watt's failure to persuade the NFWI executive about the worthiness of celebrating that anniversary was one more cause for disappointment.

At the same time, the Canadians were also losing confidence in Watt as their liaison on international questions. The minutes of the FWIC executive meeting held in Toronto in August 1924 record that there had been some frustration on the part of Canadian leaders in trying to communicate with Watt directly and through her, with organizations in other countries. Specifically, the problem was that Watt had been travelling in France, Italy, and Belgium; correspondence sent to her address in England was taking a very long time to reach her, and responses were not forthcoming. This had caused a problem for the FWIC when they made a request to the NFWI to mount an exhibit at the upcoming Canadian National Exhibition in Toronto. By the time the request reached the London office, it was too late to do anything about it. Details are not entirely clear about the other problems that had arisen, but there was correspondence from both the coordinator of the Cercles de Fermières in Belgium, and from a Miss Beale, a Country Women's Association organizer in Australia, who had hoped to make contact with the FWIC through Watt. The secretary to the FWIC was instructed to write to Beale "advising her that the proper authorities from whom to obtain information on [Canadian] Women's Institute matters is the FWIC."[62] The members of the Canadian executive agreed that the problems stemmed from Watt's failure to reply with the correct information and to do so in a timely manner. In light of these problems, the meeting agreed to "recommend that all communications between the FWIC and the Women's Institutes of other countries be conducted through their respective secretaries [rather than through Watt]."[63] The

144 A Great Rural Sisterhood

minutes further record that the Canadians were officially terminating Watt's role as their liaison with other countries; from now on, the FWIC would speak for itself rather than have Watt do so on their behalf. The carefully worded decision ended with this sentence:

> In closing our relationship with Mrs. Watt as our representative, we desire to express our keen sense of gratitude to Mrs. Watt for her services to our Canadian Women's Institutes in so ably presenting the high ideals which have animated our rural women "For Home and Country."[64]

In the fall of 1924, the London office received news of the FWIC's decision to sever their formal ties with Watt, and the November 11, 1924, minutes of the NFWI executive meeting record that "Canada further explained that Mrs. Alfred Watt was no longer acting as their international representative, and that all correspondence on international questions should theretofore in future go to the Canadian Federation Secretary."[65] Despite Watt's continued posturing as the one who could best broker the formation of an international organization for rural women, she could not control the fact that the national executives of the Canadian and English WI offices would now correspond directly with each other and she was not going to be part of the conversation. While Watt had plenty of enthusiasm for the idea of linking international partners together, as an individual with no staff or infrastructure at her disposal, she could not provide the kind of service that was necessary to facilitate timely communications between potential partners.

Losing influence with both the Canadian (FWIC) and the British (NFWI) executives was not a good sign for Watt, especially not when she saw herself as the one most suited to negotiate an international federation of WIs. However, Watt was not one to be easily discouraged, and in the 1920s there were several possible paths that might have led to the creation of an international grouping of rural women's organizations. Watt turned her attention to those other options. As historians have noted, "the decades between the world wars [were] a crucial and consolidating period of feminist international activism in diverse arenas around the world."[66] There were growing numbers of national and regional groups devoted to rural issues, and Watt attempted to maintain contact with all of them, reluctant to eliminate any possible partners. She was open to any possible configuration of cooperation, so long as her goal of solidifying the ties between rural women around the world would be realized. The initial idea, the one that Watt had been promoting during her time in Canada, was for Women's Institutes in Canada, England, Wales, and Scotland to come together to write a constitution that would provide for more countries to participate as the union grew. This idea appealed to Canadians especially, who recognized that such an initiative would protect their favoured status as the originator of Women's Institutes. Indeed, the FWIC felt such an affinity for all things British that they declared at one point in the early 1920s that the bond already existed and it was a mere formality to work out the details of the relationship. The English NFWI was quick to point out that no such entity existed, and could not exist until such time as a formal constitution was written and endorsed. Beginning in 1921 and for a few years following that, a great deal of energy was spent by both the FWIC and the NFWI to draft and redraft a workable constitution. That ongoing conversation was something that Watt had initiated, but neither the FWIC nor the NFWI felt completely comfortable with her as their spokesperson to broker a deal between them and others. As the exchanges continued between Canada and the NFWI, it became clear that Canada favoured a network of women's groups that was based on imperial ties. Somewhat surprisingly, this notion did not sit well with the NFWI executive in London, who insisted that "the only useful form of International Federation must be organised on an international, and not an imperial basis."[67]

In keeping with that call for a broader alliance, Watt turned her attention to building on the momentum that was emerging among European organizations that were hoping to create a forum for rural women in the spirit of interwar internationalism. There were a number of possibilities. The first of these was to affiliate with the International Congress of Agriculture, which was the favoured suggestion coming from Belgium and France. The idea was that this congress, which was already in operation, would create a women's section that would serve as the umbrella group to welcome other rural women's groups into their fold. Enthusiasm for this idea came from Belgium, where the most vocal advocate was Paul de Vuyst, the government official in charge of the Cercles de Fermières in Belgium. Watt had been Belgium in 1919 just before she returned to Canada and she agreed with her contacts there that an upcoming meeting of the International Congress of Agriculture to be held in Paris in May 1923 would be a good forum to consider constitutional models for the proposed international group for rural women. Watt was planning to attend the Paris meeting and she presented the idea with some enthusiasm to the NFWI executive. The problem with this suggestion, however, was that the Cercles des Fermières in Belgium and France found the model constitution proposed by Canada and England to be too limiting, and Canada and England found the French and Belgian model to be too loose. Obviously there was some distance to cover, but Watt maintained her enthusiastic relationship with the Belgian government, wanting to keep all the doors open.[68] Convinced that she had a central role to play in making that link, Watt's optimism was reinforced when she received two prestigious personal honours: France awarded her the Medaille d'or in 1923,[69] and the following year, Belgium proposed "to bestow upon her the Décoration Agricole de 1re Classe, which corresponds to the French Officier du Mérite Agricole."[70]

Another possibility for bringing about an international rural women's organization was to cooperate with a group called the Association of Rural Organizations, which was affiliated with the International Institute of Agriculture in Rome. In 1924 Watt personally attended a conference in Rome to explore this possibility.[71] For more than a year after Watt reported on her trip to Italy, it seemed that a closer relationship with this group might lead to the worldwide organization that Watt envisioned. However, by early 1926, the NFWI advised against pursuing this connection, because they perceived that the group was "too technically agricultural"[72] and would not be able to address the broad-ranging interests of groups like the WI and other rural women's organizations, devoted not only to "farm" women, but to all "country" women.

Among the options that existed to bring about an international federation of rural women's groups, the NFWI executive considered yet another possibility at their meeting in November 1926 when "the Secretary reported that she had seen a member of the League of Nations Union who was connected with the International Labour Office at Geneva, and thought that there was a possibility that the International Labour Office might assist in the formation of an International Federation if approached by NFWI."[73] Although the League of Nations was highly regarded during the interwar years, the suggestion for a close affiliation between the NFWI and Labour was an unlikely one. The minutes curtly record that "[a]fter discussion Lady Denman had moved and Miss Hadow had seconded 'That no further steps be taken in this matter for the present.'"[74]

Meanwhile, on the other side of the Atlantic, one more possibility presented itself through the International Commission for the Betterment of Rural Life; with a conference planned for Lansing, Michigan, in 1927. Watt's personal interest in this group emanated in part from her Belgian connections because that country was an active partner of the Americans in this initiative, and she welcomed the opportunity to attend the conference as a representative of the NFWI. The meeting took place in August 1927, and Watt combined her attendance at this event with a visit to her sister in Collingwood, Ontario, that same summer.[75] The Michigan meeting was bringing several groups together including "the International Organisation for the Embellishment of Rural Life [sic], the Annual Meeting of the American Country Life Association and Open Conferences on Rural Subjects for Men and Women Concerned with Rural Activities."[76] When Watt brought her report about this conference back to the NFWI in December 1927, she was reporting on yet another internationally minded group of people, and again, she was pleased to say that the participants shared her sentiments about the value of these international exchanges. The NFWI welcomed this report, but when Watt informed her British colleagues just over a year later that she had now received an invitation to the next meeting of the International Commission for the Betterment of Rural Life slated for Budapest in 1929, the NFWI cautioned her that this invitation would have to be regarded as "purely personal"[77] since they had not entered into any formal agreement to affiliate with the group. In other words, the NFWI would not be paying Watt's way if she chose to attend.

Keen to keep all the doors open, Watt came back to the NFWI again in February 1928 with what she thought was another promising possibility. She reported that she had "personal correspondence with the President of the Landwirthchafflicher Hausfrauenverine," a rural women's organization in Germany. Watt had taken the liberty of having some of the German materials translated into English for the benefit of the NFWI executive members so that they could consider establishing ties between the two countries.[78] It might have been due to the mounting tensions between England and Germany, or perhaps simply to keep from going off in too many directions, but the NFWI decided that it was too ambitious to try to simultaneously maintain involvement with all the various groups that Watt kept suggesting. For their part, the NFWI opted to be involved as a member of just one: the International Congress of Agriculture. After that decision, whenever Watt brought suggestions for other partnerships, the NFWI could say that their international ties were to the congress and no other. Given that position, the NFWI asked Watt to suggest to her German contacts that they might choose to explore membership with the International

Congress of Agriculture themselves if they wished to collaborate with rural women in the UK.

Watt hesitated to follow the NFWI in choosing just one of the many international possibilities before her. Watt's involvements with so many different international groups excited her, and in the spirit of cultivating interwar alliances, she decided to keep pursuing them all. Perhaps this was a sign of her open-mindedness, or perhaps it was an example of what one of Watt's contemporaries described as her inability to make a decision and stick to it.[79] Either way, Watt's rich networks led her to believe that she was uniquely positioned to broker the arrangements for a broad international federation of rural women's groups. Yet given her limited personal resources and her inability to persuade the NFWI to pursue the options she held out to them, she was unlikely to succeed at her bigger goal of uniting the various groups with whom she had contact.

Amidst the multiple possibilities for bringing an international group for rural women into existence, the NFWI heard about one more proposal, but this time Watt was not the one making the suggestion. This would prove to be the breakthrough that Watt needed, though at first, she failed to recognize its potential. Up to this point, the only international bodies that were under consideration, like the International Congress of Agriculture, which the NFWI had decided to join, were groups devoted to rural questions but without a specific focus on women. Watt's efforts had mainly focused on trying to convince those groups to create a separate division devoted to rural women's questions. This time, an offer came from an international *women*'s group, proposing to set up a division with a *rural* focus. The December 1927 minutes of the NFWI record that "Lady Aberdeen had submitted a draft scheme for forming within the International Council of Women a Federal International Section for national women's rural organisations."[80] The NFWI was not a constituent member of the International Council of Women, and despite the caveat that they would not need to join in order to take Lady Aberdeen up on this offer, they declined, citing the fact that their membership in the International Congress of Agriculture was their preferred option for international collaborations on rural matters.

Even though the NFWI had not accepted the original offer of the International Council of Women, Lady Aberdeen was still keen to do what she could to bring country women together into some larger grouping. Watt decided to break rank with the NFWI on this offer after she was introduced to Lady Aberdeen for the first time. According to

"The Straun," Robertson family home on Third Street, Collingwood. Collingwood Museum X 969.1.1.

Robertson family, circa 1875. Bethia Rose Robertson with her daughters, Margaret (Madge) Rose, born 1868 and Katherine (Katie) Leonora, born 1870. Courtesy of Helen Geissinger.

Collingwood Bicycle Club, 1893–94. Henry Robertson was a member and his daughter Katherine Robertson sometimes accompanied him on bicycle excursions. Collingwood Museum, X2009.15.1.

Collingwood Masonic Temple, Hurontario Street, Collingwood. Collingwood Museum, X970.470.1.

Henry Robertson, Masonic regalia, 1886. Collingwood Museum, 969.124.1.

Miss Madge Robertson, *Frank Leslie's Weekly*, January 19, 1893, p. 43. Library and Archives Canada.

Madge Robertson, editor of *Ladies Pictorial Weekly*, 1892. This photograph appeared on the editorial page for several issues in 1892 while Madge Robertson was editor of this magazine in Toronto in 1892. Library and Archives Canada.

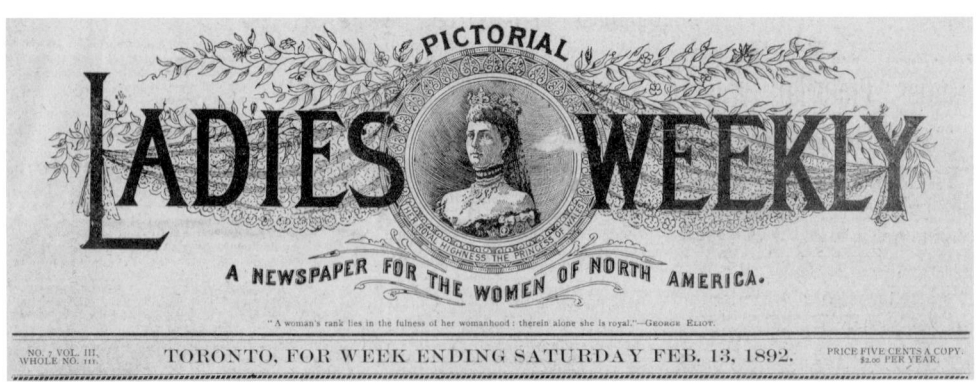

Ladies Pictorial Weekly masthead, February 13, 1892. Library and Archives Canada.

Quarantine station, William Head, British Columbia, [n.d.]. Library and Archives
Canada PA-126302.

Caretaker's quarters, quarantine station, William Head, British Columbia.
Library and Archives Canada PA-46454.

Watt Family, 1913. In the fall of 1913 Madge travelled to England with her sons, Henry Robertson ("Robin," born 1896) and Hugh ("Sholto," born 1906), to escape the publicity surrounding her husband's suicide. Courtesy of Helen Geissinger.

Llanfairpwll Women's Institute Hall, Llanfairpwll, Anglesey, Wales, 2008. Photograph by Robert Ambrose.

Llanfairpwll Women's Institute, First in Britain 1915 sign, 2008. Photograph by Robert Ambrose.

Left to right: Bethan Williams, Linda Ambrose, and Audrey Jones at Llanfairpwll Train Station, 2008. Photograph by Robert Ambrose.

"Lt. H.R. Watt, M.C. (late A.D.C. to G.O.C.)," Madge's older son, Robin, in his military uniform from World War One. Library and Archives Canada, PA-7977

Mrs. Alfred Watt, MA, MBE, circa 1918. Frontispiece in Mrs. Alfred Watt
and Miss Nest Lloyd, *The First Women's Institute School (Sussex 1918)*, Sussex
Federation of Women's Institutes, 1919.

Federated Women's Institutes of Canada executive, 1921. L. to R.: Mary MacIsaac, Laura Rose Stephen, Mrs. Todd, Isobel Noble, Mrs. Price, Mrs. Rogers, Mrs. [Alfred "Madge"] Watt, Emily Murphy, Mrs. Cameron, Eliza Campbell, Mrs. [David] Watt, Mrs. Beaubier, Edmonton, Alberta 1921. Photograph by McDermid Studio. Library and Archives Canada, PA-139660.

Meeting of the Federated Women's Institutes of Canada, University of Alberta, Edmonton, Alberta, June 23, 1921. Photograph by McDermid Studio. Library and Archives Canada, PA-136751.

Mrs. Alfred Watt at the 1933 Founding Meeting of ACWW in Stockholm. Frontispiece in Mrs. Neve Scarborough, *History of the Associated Country Women of the World and Its Member Societies,* London: Rydal Press, 1953.

Madge Watt, pencil sketch by Robin Watt, 1934. The Women's Library, London School of Economics, London, UK.

Mrs. Alfred Watt addressing the London conference of ACWW in 1939. The Grey Roots Archival Collection, WI F20–1-164–1.

Lady Albemarle (left) greets Mrs. Alfred Watt while attending the 1947 ACWW conference in Amsterdam. The Women's Library, London School of Economics, London, UK.

Mrs. Alfred Watt, circa 1948. This photograph was published posthumously in January 1949 in *Home and Country* announcing Watt's death in November 1948. The Women's Library, London School of Economics, London, UK.

"Mrs. Alfred Watt Birthplace." This Collingwood, Ontario, house was actually built in 1935, more than 65 years after Madge Robertson's birth. The Grey Roots Archival Collection, WI F14–1-113–2.

one account, "Mrs. Watt was at first diffident," but "Lady Aberdeen was very enthusiastic, and finally persuaded Mrs. Watt to attend."[81] The International Council of Women's proposal that came out of their 1927 meeting in Geneva was to hold a meeting in London in 1929 with representatives of rural women's organizations from as many different countries as possible. Up until that point, Watt had depended on her own personal travel adventures to collect accounts of what rural women from around the world were doing and communicate them as widely as she could. Bringing women from all those places together for a face-to-face meeting was not something that Watt had proposed, probably because she knew she did not have the personal resources or influence to make it possible. As president of the International Council of Women, Lady Aberdeen was more than able to do so.

Beginning on April 30, 1929, representatives from twenty-three countries met together for four days in London, England, at Lady Aberdeen's invitation under the auspices of the International Council of Women. The participating countries included Australia, Canada, Ceylon, Czechoslovakia, Denmark, England and Wales, Estonia, Finland, France, India, Ireland, Italy, Netherlands, New Zealand, Norway, Poland, Rumania, Scotland, South Africa, Sweden, the United States of America, and Yugoslavia.[82] With women from so many diverse backgrounds participating, the meeting followed a very simple format in which every member present spoke, describing what her own association of rural women was doing.[83] That kind of storytelling caused a sense of shared excitement, and Dorothy Drage, who attended as a representative from Wales, recounts that "we realized that a great moral and spiritual urge towards co-operation and good fellowship had arisen spontaneously among women in different parts of the world, quite independently of each other."[84] The simplicity of the format and the spontaneity of the occasion appealed to Watt, particularly after she had spent many long years trying unsuccessfully to encourage some kind of organization, only to be met with roadblocks over questions of constitutions, structures, and politics. The inspiration she found among these two dozen storytellers was precisely the kind of energy that always fuelled her enthusiasm: women, speaking out of their own experience, were finding that they had much in common. From that meeting, a new entity was formed that was known as "The Liaison Committee of Rural Women's Organizations." This committee was actually a subcommittee of the International Council of Women, and it was the forerunner of what would come to be called "The Associated Country Women of the World."[85] There were still details to be worked out, but with Lady Aberdeen's endorsement all of the necessary support, resources, and infrastructure became available to clear the way and set the stage for international rural women to meet again in Vienna the following year. After that 1930 meeting, the Liaison Committee found its own head-quarters in London and began to make plans about financing ongoing efforts. Watt was installed as the head of the new organization, a role she was very pleased to fill.

Very much in step with the interwar optimism of the day, Watt hoped that her efforts to unite the world's country women could go some dis-tance to promoting world peace. Watt asked rural women to imagine the difference that they could make in world affairs and she used one of her reports to remind her readers that although the publication they were holding in their hands was printed "in a time of trouble," even so

> it may cheer our readers to know that there are some people who are not at one another's throats, who are doing as they would be done by in inter-national connection. Would not our troubles be less if others realized as we do how sensitive and how potent are the links of friendship; and that the life of a farm woman in Estonia may be intimately bound up with that of one in Manitoba? If we make efforts to help in individual difficulties, personal and national, shall we not thereby serve the general good?[86]

That kind of rhetoric was idealistic to be sure, yet it resonated with those who hoped that another world war could be averted. In suggest-ing to women that their small gestures of friendship could be extended on a larger scale to avert a pending global conflict, Watt's idealism was premised on her determination that the differences among rural women should be minimized and their common values magnified. In her opin-ion, one of the most important functions that the new group would perform was simply to share information among women about what was happening in other parts of the world. To that end, she was eager to publish reports from the various countries, and to step into her presi-dential role as head and international spokesperson for rural women.

Watt's dream for a separate, independent international organization for rural women was finally fulfilled in 1933 at the meeting in Stock-holm when the International Council of Women's four-year old Liaison Committee on Rural Women's Organizations became an independent entity, the Associated Country Women of the World (ACWW).[87] One of Watt's associates described the outcome of that meeting as "reaping the benefit of sharing the arrangements made for the International Council of Women."[88] On that occasion the ACWW emerged with "a new name, a constitution of our own" to take its place on the world stage as "a free and independent body under the leadership of Mrs. Watt as President and Chairman."[89] Because the rural delegates could enjoy the benefits of gathering as part of the International Council's meeting, they did not have to be concerned about the details of local arrangements and instead could devote their time to working out the structure of their new organization. When discussion arose about what to call themselves, the name "Associated Country Women of the World" was deemed a "brilliant idea" because "it embodied just the idea that Mrs. Watt most desired, the idea of association without federation."[90] A famous photograph of that historic meeting records that after agreeing upon that new name, it was written across a blackboard in four different languages: English, German, French, and Swiss. As Dorothy Drage recalls, "Thus constituted and christened, we were, as Lady Aberdeen expressed it, launched upon the world."[91] For Watt, this was the "goal for which she had been working for twenty years."[92]

When it came time to write up a framework for the new organization, Watt was said to be "apprehensive about the harm too many rules might do,"[93] probably because over the previous ten years she had seen how difficult it was to find common ground when such variety existed among the world's rural women's groups. As a result, the original ACWW constitution, a concise two-page document, listed only three objectives:

   a) To promote and maintain friendly and helpful relations between the country women's and homemakers' associations of all nations, and to give any possible help in their development.

   b) To further the common interests of these organizations, in the economic, social and cultural spheres, while avoiding political and sectarian questions of a controversial nature.

   c) To encourage the formation of organizations, working for such common interests in countries where this need has not already been met.[94]

The ACWW, very much a product of its times, was a quintessential example of the interwar internationalist ideal.[95] The group's official history highlights the importance of its triennial conventions for helping to accomplish these objectives because in the early years, at each meeting, "personal friendships have been made and cemented, views exchanged between women of many nations, knowledge and experience pooled. For many people, a foreign country has suddenly ceased to be 'foreign.'"[96]

As part of the commitment to encourage these friendships and the exchange of information, the decision was taken at the Stockholm conference to publish a monthly ACWW magazine. *The Countrywoman* would act as a means of disseminating literature and information that was pouring in to the London office from around the world, providing another means of "promoting and maintaining friendly and helpful relations" among its readers. Each year since 1929, the group had produced a substantial annual volume called *What the Country Women of the World Are Doing*; the third volume was more than 200 pages in length. The format was simple: each of the ACWW's constituent societies submitted a brief report about rural women's activities in their province, state, or country, and readers could enjoy browsing through the book, noting the common interests of rural women around the world. Sales of the first three volumes proved to be very strong (the 1930 volume sold 3,000 copies),[97] and Watt reasoned that a monthly ACWW journal was bound to be every bit as popular. Indeed, she expected that sales of *The Countrywoman* would be a major source of revenue for the organization. Based on her previous experience as the editor of a woman's magazine, Watt thought she knew a lot about the world of publishing. However, her experience was forty years out of date, and her work with the Toronto-based *Ladies Pictorial Weekly* was hardly comparable to editing and financing an international publication. While a monthly journal for the ACWW sounded like a great idea, it was not financially viable. Finding advertisers to support the publication proved to be very difficult, and while purchasing the annual volume had appeal for the membership, no adequate number of monthly subscribers for the magazine ever materialized. In short, "costs were high and sales were comparatively low."[98] Yet Watt was convinced that she knew what she was doing "and since Mrs. Watt could not grasp hard financial facts, and would not be advised by others if the advice was not to her liking, debts increased."[99]

The problem of financing ACWW publications was only the first of several money problems that would face the young organization. According to the constitution, no set membership fee was dictated for the constituent organizations that joined; each group was free "to contribute annually ... as they shall themselves determine," and life memberships were offered to individuals for a one-time fee of only £10, while others would give an annual subscription of £1.[100] That arrangement did not provide an adequate or predictable source of income, and finances continued to cause disagreements among the ACWW executive for several years. Indeed, it would be almost ten years before a reasonable degree of financial stability was achieved, and that was in spite of Watt, not because of her.

The credit for getting the organization's finances in order belongs to Elsie Zimmern, who, along with Lady Aberdeen and Watt, is considered a co-founder of the ACWW.[101] Involved from the very beginning as the ACWW's honorary secretary, Zimmern had previously worked as the general secretary of the International Council of Women, and it was Lady Aberdeen who recruited her and first introduced Zimmern to Watt in 1928. While Watt enjoyed the "limelight and the stimulus of an audience,"[102] Zimmern preferred to work quietly in the background. They were an unlikely pair, but their mannerisms and abilities were both necessary for the ACWW to launch well and to continue strong. Scarborough recounts that

> Miss Zimmern had never heard of Mrs. Watt until the Marchioness united the pair of them in a kind of marriage of convenience which lasted until Mrs. Watt retired ... in 1947. From the results which they achieved, the "marriage" must be regarded as an unqualified success, but it would be useless to pretend that it was completely harmonious![103]

Conflict between Zimmern and Watt most often revolved around money issues, with Zimmern, the more practical of the two, constantly trying to keep Watt's grandiose spending in check.

When it came time to think about the next triennial conference, the ACWW executive was delighted that the Americans, headed by Grace Frysinger, of the United States Department of Agriculture, agreed to make local arrangements to welcome the ACWW to Washington, DC, in June 1936. Frysinger, who had been encouraging American involvement in the ACWW for the past six years,[104] requested funding for the event from the Finance Department of the United States government, "with the gratifying result that the Treasury agreed to allow her £2,000 ($10,000 USD) for the expenses of the Conference."[105] This was extremely good news for the young organization, and with that generous injection of finances, concerns about money were temporarily set aside as Watt and her travelling companions made the transatlantic crossing from England to New York. They sailed on the North German Lloyd steamer, *Bremen*, so that Scandinavian and German members were able to board the ship at Hamburg.[106] The crossing was a very comfortable one, although Watt kept her committee members busy with meetings. "When we got on board," Dorothy Drage, the ACWW vice-president from Wales, recalled, "we found bouquets and flowers awaiting us in our cabins. Mrs. Watt had daily meetings on board with her officers and committees to prepare our minds for the coming fray."[107] According to Drage, Watt was nervous about making sure that all the details of the upcoming meeting would go well, and as a result, she was relentless in the schedule she kept, and expected her fellow executive members to keep it too. While other delegates enjoyed some sightseeing in New York, "Mrs. Watt's whole being was full of apprehensive anxiety about the Conference, so several of us caught an early train for Washington, having only seen the wonderful panoramic view of New York as we sailed up the harbour."[108] Once they had arrived in Washington, the pace did not lessen, and while other delegates were treated to a visit to Mount Vernon, Drage described how she and two other members of the executive "were Mrs. Watt's slaves, and unable to go."[109]

There was plenty to be nervous about, given the fragile state of world peace in 1936. In anticipation of the meeting, Watt had written a memorandum "to all delegates and visitors attending the Washington Conference" to remind the women that the second objective of the ACWW constitution was very clear on the point "that 'political and sectarian questions of a controversial character' must be avoided."[110] She wanted to be clear that this principle was a far-sweeping one and that the "Executive Committee interprets this clause to apply within the scope of our association and more particularly to the Conference period, [as well as] ... all public and private speech."[111] With the mounting tensions that characterized international relations during the interwar years, it is not surprising that Watt was going out of her way to reiterate this position. She was convinced that the ACWW had the potential to help preserve what was good about country living, promote maternal values among women, and protect world peace, but participants in the ACWW needed to be reminded that any differences they might have on issues such as international affairs, specifically the League of Nations, should be left unspoken.

After the executive had arrived in Washington, DC, they were joined by delegates representing twenty-two nations who came for this historic meeting. It was only the third meeting of the fledgling organization since the 1929 gathering in London; this was the first meeting outside of Europe and the first time the attendance had topped 300 women. Indeed, the attendance swelled as thousands of rural women from across North America travelled to join the official delegates and share in the excitement of such an auspicious gathering. The convention quickly garnered media attention: the *New York Times*, for example, ran daily coverage of the proceedings, reporting that while the original projection for registration was 200 delegates, by mid-week 7,300 women had registered.[112] President Franklin Delano Roosevelt addressed the delegates and gave his personal blessing to their meeting,[113] suggesting that "as a result of this friendly meeting, the farm life of every nation is bound to march forward with increasing efficiency and increasingly high standards."[114] The list of other dignitaries who addressed the gathering reads like a veritable who's who of American public figures, including the First Lady Eleanor Roosevelt, U.S. Secretary of Agriculture Henry A. Wallace, U.S. Secretary of State Cordell Hull, and feminist peace activist Carrie Chapman Catt. Each of the speakers was careful to frame their remarks around the assumption that this audience of rural women had particular roles to play on the world stage during the troubling times of the 1930s.

According to the *New York Times*, when conference attendees were welcomed to a presidential reception, there was nothing in the appearance of the delegates that gave away the fact that they were rural. Indeed, the journalist reported that

> [n]othing in the festive array of women at the opening meeting or at the garden party afterwards identified their fashions as distinct from urban ideals. Against the cool green stretches of the White House lawn the pastel shades of fluttery chiffon and organdies, foulards and taffetas formed a kaleidoscope of color.[115]

Apparently this gathering looked like any other group of club women. However, there were other telling signs that indicated the thousands of women who flocked to the White House lawn were not all equals. The conference venue for the meetings was the elegant and historic Willard Hotel, and the same *New York Times* journalist observed,

> There is a noticeable dearth of delegates around the swankier hotels. The smaller hostelries, the rooming houses, and the tourist camp near the highway bridge, adjoining the speedway, were thronged with women. One party of sixty from New York State made the trip in three large buses. They brought a number of roomy tents which have been pitched in the tourist camp.[116]

The women who crowded into those buses and campsites had likely never experienced the luxuries of transatlantic travel to which Watt and her colleagues had grown accustomed.

Before the conference began, one journalist erroneously assumed that the delegates who would be participating were "farm women" from around the world. Kathleen McLaughlin wrote, "Farm women of many countries will participate. Fifty of them arrived on Thursday on the Bremen [sic] from Europe, including Mrs. Alfred Watt of Vancouver Island, Canada."[117] Watt, however, could hardly be described as a farm woman, nor could her travelling companions. According to the principal of the Ontario Agricultural College, who offered dormitory accommodation in Guelph, Ontario, to the disgruntled travellers during a Canadian tour they took following the Washington conference, "I was asked to receive fifty-eight farm women, whereas you brought fifty-eight elderly aristocrats, not one of whom looks like she had ever milked a cow in her life."[118] The group refused to remain on the campus for more than one night, choosing instead to travel on to Toronto to find more comfortable lodging. Watt's travelling companions seemed much more at home later that week when they spent their final night in Canada at the Château Frontenac in Quebec City.[119] The fifty-eight European delegates were not "honest-to-goodness farm women"[120] as their North American hosts had expected them to be, but rather women who had the private means or the public connections to fund their travel. They were prime examples of the women Rupp identified as likely participants in international organizations: leisured women of means with international status.[121]

The women who made the transatlantic crossing with Watt were the power brokers of the ACWW.[122] Although more than 7,000 women attended the Washington Conference, only about 200 had voting privileges at the meetings. A heated discussion ensued during the election of ACWW executive members to represent various geographic areas. A member of the American Farm Bureau Federation raised the question of "how many of those nominated as Vice Presidents were actually farm women."[123] In defence of the nominees, it was explained that "on going through the list it was found that every one of them was intimately connected with the rural life of her district."[124] Discussion ensued about whether the ACWW was restricted to "farm" women, and the conclusion was that the association "was broad enough to include 'all country women.'"[125] As the election of the various officers unfolded, Grace Frysinger, an employee of the United States Department of Agriculture and the Extension Service, was nominated to represent North America, but she asked that her name be withdrawn because "she felt that not a professional but a rural woman should be elected."[126] As the minutes curtly record, however, she was overruled and her name remained on the list. Apparently the *New York Times* reporter was not the only one who grappled with the question of what it actually meant to be a "rural" woman. For the majority of the ACWW's voting delegates, the distinguishing feature of a country woman was not that she worked in agriculture directly, nor even that she lived in a community of a certain size, but rather "[i]t is a question of whether you are country-minded or not."[127] By that definition, Grace Frysinger, a professional home economist employed by the United States government, apparently qualified as a rural woman.[128]

Watt concurred with this more ephemeral notion of rurality. When she made comments based upon her experiences in England, she expressed the issue this way: "The question is how are these people to be used to develop a better countryside and to be made to become a part of country life?"[129] For Watt, "being rural" evidently demanded some investment in the social life and concerns of the community, measured by one's involvement therein. Henry A. Wallace, the U.S. secretary of agriculture, reinforced Watt's romantic notions about rural living when he embraced the rural idyll theme in his address to the conference. He argued that "[f]rom the farm woman comes the breath of life to our cities, now that our cities over the entire western world are no longer producing enough children to maintain themselves."[130] Indeed, Wallace linked rurality and farm women to the preservation of civilization. His ideas about rural living have been described as "practical idealism," and it is clear that he subscribed to the gender stereotypes that were not really applicable in the case of working farm women. He put them on a proverbial pedestal, and in doing so, he actually minimized their economic contributions to farm life.[131] The social representation of rurality as idyllic may have served to reinforce the hegemony of rural women of leisure (like the club women who were enjoying the comfortable amenities of the Willard Hotel), but it did little to address the realities of working farm women (like those who had arrived by bus and pitched their tents in the nearby campground). By declaring that "the farm mother's true function" was to "inspire the members of her family to appreciate the beauty of day-to-day living and the joy of a future rich in possibilities,"[132] Wallace was denying rural women's economic contributions to farm life and making their role a merely inspirational one.[133] Wallace's rhetoric was very attractive to Watt. Just as she had waxed eloquent in her speech at a FWIC conference several years earlier, telling the delegates there that the WI could be "the greatest spiritual and educational force the Dominion of Canada has ever seen," now she had the U.S. secretary of agriculture telling ACWW members the same thing, except that according to Wallace, the impact would be felt not just in one country or on one continent, but around the world.

After the conference officially ended, Watt arranged to take the visiting delegates from Europe and the UK on a tour of historic sites pertinent to Ontario Women's Institute history. En route to southern Ontario, the group stopped at Cornell University in Ithaca, New York, where Watt had some personal connections with faculty members, including Dr. Ruby Green Smith from the College of Home Economics.[134] After leaving the Cornell campus, the delegates were treated to an elaborate ceremony that took place at the Peace Bridge between Buffalo, NY, and Fort Erie, Ontario, on June 16, 1936. That event was a significant opportunity to reinforce the timely topics of internationalism and peace initiatives. One of the delegates described the day this way:

> After a marvelous lunch [at Buffalo], we greatly enjoyed the crossing of the Peace Bridge. A plaque had been placed there and a New Zealand delegate unveiled it, with much speechifying about the goodwill between the Stars and Stripes and the Union Jack. One flag was flying at one end and the other, to our great joy, at the other end of the bridge.[135]

The "speechifying" was intended to emphasize to the international delegates that Canada and the United States enjoyed a long, undefended border, and other countries would do well to emulate that peaceful coexistence.

Watt's own remarks on that occasion reveal her idealism about what the ACWW could accomplish. Referring to the fact that the ACWW was composed of representatives from "nearly 100 free and independent large organizations of rural women of the five continents of the world," she spoke eloquently about what internationalism could inspire:

> Our societies, working each in their own countries, are laying the foundation of a better social order. They are raising the status of the country homemaker. They are giving to the world the greatest example of spiritual and practical cooperation that has ever been known in the history of mankind.[136]

For Watt, this was one of the highlights of her career as world president, because she felt that she was taking part in an object lesson; she saw herself, like the bridge, as a link between her country of origin and the American neighbours to the south. She also believed that in the presence of representatives from every continent, she was proclaiming that the organization she was leading had the power to demonstrate "that world friendliness and good will need not wait upon political or national development." In her view, "no one could be unmoved by this poignant and momentous ceremony,"[137] and no one could mistake that Watt herself was the obvious person to lead it forward.

From the Peace Bridge, the delegation made its way to Stoney Creek, Ontario, where they were greeted by some members of that very first Women's Institute in the world, some of whom had personal connections to Adelaide Hoodless, the founder of the Canadian movement in 1897. They also saw Niagara Falls and the Ontario Agricultural College at Guelph, where they were scheduled to stay in dormitory accommodations. Preferring the comfort of the Canadian Pacific hotels, they cut their visit short and arranged instead to stay at the Royal York Hotel in Toronto, before proceeding on to Montreal, where they said their good-byes to Mrs. Watt and departed on June 27 aboard the *Duchess of Atholl* to sail to Liverpool, arriving eight days later, on July 4, 1936.[138] For those weary travellers, their North American visit had been a very full six weeks of discussions and events that reinforced their commitment to the internationalist ideal.

Before the Washington conference ended, there had been several heated back-room discussions about finances with the American organizers of the conference on one side, and Watt and the committee members from London on the other. At issue was who should control the proceeds that came from two sources: delegates' fees and visitors' fees. Apparently Watt expected all of the money generated by the conference to flow directly back to the London office, whereas the Americans were adamant that they should control those monies until all the outstanding conference expenses were covered, especially the visitors' fees (which were generated from the thousands of North American women who had made the trek to Washington in such large and unexpected numbers). That position seemed reasonable to all except Watt.

At one particularly heated meeting where this issue of money was on the table, both Grace Frysinger, the American chief organizer, and Watt became very stubborn in defending their opposing views. With the help of a mediator in the person of Dr. Ruby Green Smith of Cornell

University, they came to a reasonable compromise, and according to another member of the ACWW executive, "Miss Frysinger dried her eyes and Mrs. Watt started being a human being again and stopped being a statue."[139] The solution was that the Americans would control the visitors' fees (the bulk of the funds, since each overseas delegate had paid £80 to attend the conference),[140] until they had settled all the outstanding conference expenses, and then they would send along the balance of the money to the London office. According to Drage, this still represented a substantial amount, with £600 coming into the ACWW treasury as a result.

Buoyed up by the great success of the Washington conference, feeling proud to have hosted such a great gathering, and inspired by the speakers who had reinforced her idealism about the potential of international exchanges among rural women, Watt embarked on the biggest travel adventure of her lifetime: a world tour. World tours were very much in vogue during the interwar years. Two examples suffice to illustrate that fact. First, the Imperial Order Daughters of the Empire planned and executed the English Schoolgirl Tour in 1928 for twenty-five young women from elite English public schools to tour across Canada in conjunction with the Society for the Oversea Settlement of British Women.[141] Second, in 1930 Lady Aberdeen made plans to set up a tour for a group of American women to travel to various European countries to learn about rural women's activities after attending the meeting of the International Council of Women in Vienna.[142] The difference with Watt's world tour was that rather than taking a delegation with her, she proposed to go on her own. The idea was that she would visit rural women in each country, distribute literature about the ACWW and encourage the women to become part of the new international network. Watt saw this as part of her role, to fulfil the objectives of the ACWW constitution by "promoting and maintaining friendly and helpful relations" between various rural groups, and "to encourage the formation of organizations working for such common interests in countries where this need has not already been met."[143]

This explains why Watt had been so stubborn with Frysinger about the money issue: she needed the funds to finance her trip. At the same time, she wanted to expand the ACWW magazine, *The Countrywoman*, because she remained convinced that it could be a money-making venture for the organization. In the end, she had to submit to the will of the London committee when they insisted that half of the funds coming to the London office from the Washington conference should be squirreled away for maintenance.[144] This left Watt with the sum of £300 towards the cost of her travels. According to her own logic, even if she overspent, she could justify it because she was convinced that reports of her trip would provide fascinating content for later publication in *The Countrywoman*, and enthusiastic readers would respond by joining the organization, thus boosting membership revenues. Or so she hoped.

After saying her farewells to the entourage of ACWW delegates in Montreal on the night before they sailed, she spent the next six weeks with her sister in Collingwood making preparations for her own travel. Then, on August 19, 1936, Watt departed for her six-month tour. Her itinerary included destinations in the South Pacific and the Middle East, including Hawaii, Samoa, New Zealand, Australia, Ceylon (now Sri Lanka), Egypt, and Palestine.[145]

She travelled with a personal assistant, Elizabeth Smart, who kept a diary of the trip with almost daily entries. Smart was a young Canadian (21 years old at the time of their travels), who would later become an internationally acclaimed author for her classic book *By Grand Central Station I Sat Down and Wept*. Her parents, Russell (a well-known lawyer in Ottawa) and Louise Smart, were friends of Watt's. The Smart papers in Library and Archives Canada include a great deal of personal correspondence between Watt and Louise Smart, as well as Louise Smart's letters to Elizabeth, some of which contain references to the time Watt spent with the Smart family.[146] The Smarts moved in elite circles, both in Canada where they socialized with civil servants and diplomats and enjoyed a family cottage next door to Prime Minister Mackenzie King at Kingsmere; and in London, England, where they sent their daughter to study music and art. By the time she travelled with Watt in 1936, Elizabeth had been dating the grandson of Lady Aberdeen, Lord John Pentland.[147] Though she was young, Smart was already well-travelled; she had studied in London, England, visited Germany and Sweden in 1933, and sailed with her father from Montreal to Sweden and Norway in 1935. Clearly she knew what to expect from travel by train and luxury steamship; she had already experienced the transatlantic crossing between Canada and England several times.

Smart's diaries give a more personal insight into Watt's personality than any other source, although the fact that Watt and Smart had endless conflicts should be read carefully, given the great differences between the two women. These unlikely travel companions were, after all, two generations apart and very different in temperament. Like an overprotective grandparent, Watt sometimes reprimanded her young assistant on a variety of issues, including her personal deportment, her need for more physical activity, and her choice of reading materials. For example, when Watt discovered that Smart was reading D.H. Lawrence's *Lady Chatterley's Lover*, she confronted her, asking, "Isn't that book banned in England? ... It must be pretty disgusting if England won't allow it. They're awfully lenient about literature ... I think it's perfectly disgusting to want to read a book my country won't allow." Smart mused to her diary,

> I did not reply. I could not. Why tell her I did not even know it was banned. That several "Oxford people" had been a bit scornful [of me] because I had not read it. That I bought it because I thought it was something I should read? That anyway I don't care one way or any other what my country read? That it was good. Great ... And also I said, "Goodness! Can't you form your own opinion?" She looked glum and aggrieved. I hurried back to read it after lunch.[148]

Smart's frankness in the diary entries reveals a side of Watt that other sources only hinted at: her stubbornness and difficult moods. At one particularly low point in the relationship, Smart struggled with what she called "evil thoughts" about Watt, calling her "'a cross old woman'" who was prone to "snobbery and overbearing and insistent pride in personal distinction. And pettiness and sulkiness and aggrieved-ness."[149] The bitter tone of that entry makes one realize that perhaps Watt was not the only "sulky" personality involved here, but with more than forty-five years between their ages, it is not surprising that they might annoy one another from time to time.

Smart reveals another part of Watt's life that no other source records: her health challenges. In 1936, Watt was 68 years old, and Smart describes the fact that she had some trouble walking. When they went out for dinner one evening, the diarist revealed, "We walked home. You know our waddle."[150] On another occasion, Smart recorded that when they walked together, Watt reminded her young travelling companion, "[D]on't go too fast I can't you know."[151] Apparently Watt also had some trouble with her eyes, which caused her a great deal of discomfort and motivated her to seek medical attention while they were in New Zealand. Smart recorded that once during a meeting of country women, "Mrs. Watt's eye began to get terribly painful and she sat at a table with her forehead in her hands," and later "she went off again to the Dr."[152] While Smart could be sympathetic on such occasions, sometimes she thought Watt's physical ailments were mostly psychosomatic, making her very demanding and unpleasant without good reason. "I can't be sorry when she pretends to be sick – *she's so sorry for herself.*"[153] Smart recounted one such episode in great detail, explaining that she had torn herself away from watching a lovely sunset on the ship's deck in the company of some young men to tend to her elderly boss:

> I went down to see if Mrs. Watt wanted anything. She wanted me to come to bed so that if she was sick in the night I would be there. She was ill all day with terrible pains. She thought she was going to die. I didn't. She looked cross and discontented and sorry for herself. I was sorry too, but not worried. She was like a hurt and hungry bear – she was in pain and had to sit in uncomfortable positions all day. It was only gas. She thought it might be her heart. She was cross that other people weren't more concerned. I did everything I could. I went to bed even though the sun was still streaking the sky, even though we were stopping to see a candlelit abbey.[154]

It is impossible to know whether Watt insisted on having Smart go to bed earlier that night for the sake of her own health problems, or whether this was Watt's not-so-subtle attempt to be motherly and remove Elizabeth from the company of those star-struck young men.

Smart admitted that sometimes the conflicts she had with Watt were also partly of her own making: "I *am* selfish ... There have been days ... when I have been so far from sympathetic with her that I have come near to hating her."[155] At the same time, Smart explained to herself that part of the problem just came from being in such close quarters for such a long time: "It is living, night and day, month in month out, with her. If I did utterly sympathize with her, I should *be* her."[156] Sometimes she felt sorry for Watt, recognizing that "[s]he is old. She needs someone. She is poor and tired and disappointed. It should be good for me to try and supply all the things she needs. When I undertook this enormous task I thought I could put love into her life."[157]

Some of Smart's accounts about spending time with Watt were steeped in pathos, particularly when they were in Victoria, and Watt became somewhat disoriented as they walked from the Empress Hotel where they were staying to what Smart described as "the once-familiar-to-her but now not clearly remembered street, to a restaurant she once knew."[158] On such occasions, Smart was capable of showing genuine compassion for Watt, especially when she got glimpses of the difficult things that had happened to her in connection with Alfred Watt's death. When they were leaving BC in the fall of 1936, Watt had arranged for them to travel by train through Seattle to San Francisco rather than departing by ship from Vancouver or Victoria; this would have necessitated passing by William Head, where the Watts had lived near the quarantine station at the time of the suicide twenty-three years earlier. Watt explained to Smart, "I never go near the house, you know, because that was the scene of all my husband's tragedy. I just couldn't."[159] Another time Smart overheard a private conversation that Watt was having with someone they met during their travels. She was explaining some of the circumstances around her husband's death, and Smart heard some details she had not known before about the professional pressures Dr. Watt was dealing with around the commission of the inquiry at the quarantine station. Smart processed this new information in her diary, musing that she thought she was beginning

> to understand at last what has puzzled me so long about Mrs. Watt – her rather embitteredness. The shock she got about herself when she was widowed was too much. She must have been through some bitter and terrible things – all the same, there is that weakness in her that made disappointment make her "bittah" instead of "bettah." I do wish, I do hope I will understand her better, I will find out everything in truth and completeness. Otherwise I am a poor selfish unobservant creature, not fit for my opportunities.[160]

As an aspiring writer, there is no doubt that Smart was an insightful observer of character, but in Watt she had definitely found a complex case study. "How can I expect to make a Hamlet," she asked herself, "when I can't even analyse a Watt?"[161] It is not clear from the diary whether Smart actually knew that Alfred Watt's death was a suicide; had she known that, she might have had even greater insight into and empathy for her travelling companion's haunting memories.

Smart's more sympathetic observations meant that sometimes she did manage to catch glimpses of the personal magnetism that Watt so often displayed, especially when she was performing at her best before a crowd as the inspiring speaker and leader that she could be. Indeed, Smart's diaries perceptively capture both sides of Watt: the difficult, snobbish, demanding elderly woman, who was sometimes even mean-spirited, and at the same time, this intriguing individual who rose above those character weaknesses, health challenges, and past experiences to be dynamic, inspirational, and sometimes, in Smart's estimation, even "delightful" and "light-hearted." Smart tried to help Watt in her role as a leader, on one occasion discreetly pointing out to her that she needed to pose for one of her admirers. When they were being observed by a WI member unbeknownst to Watt, Smart whispered

> "That lady's one of your institute women," and she was waving anyway. They waved excitedly and the woman made the children wave and they waved with both hands and the lady brought a handkerchief and waved and waved. She was very excited. Mrs. Watt was pleased.[162]

Despite their differences, Smart did have a respect for Watt and her abilities. Indeed, after a brief meeting with Watt's sister, Smart rather unkindly described Katie Robertson Arthur as a "grey-haired almost toothless old lady [so heavy that she looked like she was] big with child. I was shocked."[163] But that unflattering description led Smart to make the following observations:

> She was Mrs. Watt's sister who's been sick. She has some of Mrs. Watt's little characteristics but none of her fire. It's queer to see similar sisters one of whom has something of the divine fire. One that took and one that didn't. So what is the thing that makes one person unimportant like Mrs. Watt's sister, buried like millions, unknown, unenterprising, unambitious, and another important, so like her, yet with something added?[164]

Admiring Watt's easy manner when speaking to a group of women in northern Ontario, Smart wrote that "[s]he spoke about the hard beginning of The Associated Country Women of the World and peace. It was quite inspiring and stimulating."[165] A few days later in Vancouver, Smart recorded that "Mrs. Watt's speech was delightful … Human and absorbing. She ends by saying, 'I had a grand ending all ready but I can't remember it,' and sits down. They loved that."[166] No doubt that folksy conclusion to her talks was strategic, something meant to endear Watt to her audiences, just as she had instructed WI organizers in Sussex to do, almost twenty years before, when she told them to avoid undue formality when trying to win over rural audiences.[167]

When she returned from her travels Watt arranged to publish accounts of her trip for the enjoyment of the ACWW's constituent members. The Ontario WI magazine's report of her adventures in the spring of 1937 recounted a trip that most readers could never imagine themselves taking. The editor explained that Mrs. Watt had "added more adventure to her already colourful career. During the course of her world tour, she flew over the Tasmanian Ocean ..." But in addition to her adventures as a tourist, the account also revealed that Watt had been a tireless worker. During the fall of 1936 she had apparently "addressed 70 organizations in New Zealand and twice that number in Australia, sometimes traveling by the most modern equipment and at other times going back to such ancient methods of locomotion as the camel."[168] If this account about the number of meetings Watt conducted is accurate, then during December 1936 while she was in Australia she kept a very full, almost frantic, pace with several meetings and speaking engagements each day. Perhaps that demanding schedule explains why Smart's diary entries are so sporadic for that month. This provides quite a different picture of Watt from the one painted by Smart in her diaries. To keep such a demanding pace of work, she could hardly have been the hypochondriac that Smart sometimes made her out to be; on the other hand, if that was an accurate recounting of the schedule she was keeping, no wonder she sometimes gave in to bouts of tiredness.

As their trip was nearing an end, Smart recorded that she felt some sympathy for Watt because "she is going home to an upset office and unions and she will have to make rows" and "she had an unsatisfactory letter from Sholto [her son] saying he hadn't found a suitable house and that Joan White, the ACWW secretary, had been sent to Geneva. I *felt* so for her, but there wasn't much I could do."[169] The pressures of leading a complex organization like the ACWW were immense. Despite the exhausting schedule that Watt endured during her tour, her efforts were not enough to offset the problems that surfaced again upon her return, including money problems.

As the ACWW world president, Watt was returning to some challenging realities in London, and the biggest task before her was that of planning and executing the next triennial conference of the ACWW, scheduled to take place in that city during the summer of 1939. With memories of the very successful Washington conference in the not-so-distant past, Watt hoped to repeat the success of that gathering and she set out to plan on the same scale as the Americans had done. If she could manage a repeat performance, it would be confirmation that the international work she was doing was important, and not only in her own estimation. Of course this was not something she worked at single-handedly. There was an entire committee, the London Hospitality Committee, devoted to the logistics of welcoming the international delegates and visitors.

While the conference organizers worked out details for venues, speakers, and accommodations, Watt eagerly worked behind the scenes to try to boost the number of delegates. Just two months prior to the conference date, Watt became aware that only twelve women from Canada had declared their intentions of coming to the conference. Taking matters into her own hands, she took a copy of the preliminary program with her and went to see His Excellency The Honourable Vincent Massey, the Canadian high commissioner in London, to ask him to do what he could to ensure that Canada would be well represented. She told him that as many as fifty Australian delegates were expected, and she asked Massey to write to Ottawa to ask the government to sponsor some more Canadians to come. Massey acquiesced, writing to J.G. Gardiner, the Canadian minister of agriculture, saying, "Mrs. Watt tells me that she has already written to the Prime Minister, whom she knows personally, on the subject of Canadian representation. I hope you will not regard it as inappropriate on my part to bring this matter to your attention. I hope that you may find it worthy of sympathetic consideration."[170] Gardiner replied that the Canadian Women's Institutes were under provincial jurisdiction and because no request had come from any of the staff of his ministry to attend, he could not be of any help.

A few months earlier Watt had written directly to Prime Minister Mackenzie King, reminding him that Canadian women had a long history with the Women's Institute movement, and ending her letter with a personal plea that it would mean a great deal to her if there was a sizeable delegation from Canada. She asked King to consider "[i]s it not also worth something that a Canadian woman has been chosen to preside over this coming great gathering, and that she would be supported by a large delegation of her fellow country women?"[171] Whether King realized that she was referring to herself with that plea, is not clear. There is no record of whether or not she received a reply to her letter.

Another of Watt's big hurdles in planning the conference was the reluctance of the NFWI's executive committee to lend her their support. The NFWI had come into the ACWW somewhat late, only becoming a constituent member in 1935. The ACWW triennial meeting was planned to coincide with the NFWI's 1939 annual meeting in London so that some resources could be shared and members travelling to one event could participate in the other as well. The NFWI's hesitations with assisting Watt were twofold. First, they had maintained their involvement with the International Congress of Agriculture and they did not want to act in haste to leave that association for the one that Watt had helped to found through the auspices of the International Council of Women. In addition, the NFWI was hesitant to give their full support to one of Watt's schemes, because they were familiar with her previous grandiose plans and they were not convinced that her projections were realistic. There was a good chance that the event would not break even, let alone make a profit. Understandably, the NFWI was very cautious because past experience had taught them that though she could be inspirational, Watt's idealism made her a risky business partner.

The preliminary program that Watt had shown to the high commissioner outlined an ambitious program that would run in London from May 30 to June 10, 1939, and then be followed by a series of events in various counties outside the capital the following week. The first two days of meetings were planned for the Central Hall Westminster, with most of the remaining sessions to be held at the Friends House, Euston Road. The grand finale of the conference would be a special service for the delegates at Canterbury Cathedral on the final Saturday. There were to be a series of entertainments, tours and dinners to round out the ten-day event. It was a huge undertaking, and Watt had every reason to worry about whether the attendance would be high enough to cover the costs of putting it on.

As it turned out, the concerns about money were well-founded. While the ACWW meetings were deemed to be a success in many ways ("Socially the conference was a great success," the official history declared),[172] the conference debt was staggering. The next financial statement of the ACWW after the London conference showed a shortfall in the 1939–40 budget of £1,050, an amount recorded as the "extra total required on the General and *The Countrywoman* Account to balance."[173] It was a stark contrast to the large surplus of £600 that had been generated by the Washington conference just three years earlier. Some of that shortfall came from the costs of hosting the conference in London, with an attendance much lower than Watt had hoped; English women from the countryside did not flock to London by the thousands as the North Americans had done at Washington. In addition, there is no doubt that the debt also reflected outstanding expenses that Watt had incurred on her world tour.

The final source of money problems was Watt's persistent blind devotion to the idea that her beloved magazine would be the solution to the ACWW's financial problems. To everyone else on the ACWW executive it was clear that the magazine was "costing far more than it brought in."[174] When a session was arranged to talk about that very problem, Watt would not allow the discussion to deviate from the question of how to increase circulation, refusing to consider that perhaps there were ways to find economies by scaling back the publication to a smaller size (each issue was twenty-four pages long) or by publishing it less frequently. According to Dorothy Drage, Watt made things very difficult because she took the question of the journal "very much at heart … and was convinced [it] would make the ACWW completely solvent."[175]

None of these money troubles or challenges to Watt's leadership was evident to the general delegates attending the London conference. Instead, they saw a carefully staged series of events rolling out, steeped in the inspirational optimism that was Watt's trademark. In her presidential address, she was her usual dynamic self. One published report in the fall 1939 issue recounted that

> Mrs. Watt struck a note of optimism and progress in her presidential address. Membership and new societies had increased since the Washington conference, horizons had widened, respect and tolerance for others were more and more recognized, and country women of the world were seeking that leadership and education which will make them more intelligent homemakers and citizens. World friendship had increased through the Association as thousands of local organizations, institutes and home bureaus had communicated with similar bodies in other countries.[176]

As inspirational as that all sounded, just a few weeks later it would ring quite hollow in the ears of delegates who faced the new reality of a world once again at war. Mrs. Watt's rhetoric about "women interested in world affairs [being] a factor, and a new one, everywhere making for peace,"[177] must have sounded very empty indeed as the women of the world prepared themselves once again to send their men to war. The leader of the ACWW was still saying all the right things, but this time her rhetoric seemed less convincing.

Chapter Six

Sidelined by War: Waning Influence, Denial, and Death

With the whirlwind of activity surrounding the London conference behind her, Watt set her sights on returning to Canada to rest and to visit with family members. To honour her hard work on the ACWW conference and to acknowledge the contributions that Watt had made to the English Institutes as a member of the Executive Committee, the NFWI planned a luncheon in her honour before she departed, inviting all the members of the Executive Committee and its subcommittees, informing them of the event. "As you are probably aware," Frances Farrer, the NFWI secretary, wrote, "Mrs. Watt resigned from the Executive Committee at the end of the electoral year, 1938/39, thus having completed fourteen years consecutive service. The Executive Committee is arranging a luncheon in her honour ... on Wednesday, July 12th ... It is hoped very much that you will be able to come."[1] There seemed to be unanimous agreement that it was time to laud Watt's efforts and accomplishments, and the July 1939 issue of *Home and Country* did just that, invoking two British allusions to honour the founder of the English WIs and the ACWW. In the first, the writer contrasted Watt with King Alfred the Great, saying she was "not in the least like [him]" because while he "pondered how to save England from the Danes while he let the cakes burn, Mrs. Watt would have drawn up a defence scheme with one hand, and pulled out the cakes (nicely browned) from the oven with the other."[2] In the second allusion, the writer praised Watt effusively, suggesting that she might be compared to Christopher Wren, whose famous epitaph in St. Paul's Cathedral says, "If you seek his memorial – look around you." Those attending the London joint conference of the NFWI and ACWW were exhorted that they might say the same about Watt. As the architect of these expansive women's

organizations, the writer suggested that credit was due to "the eloquent, indomitable white haired lady who has been the voice and the
hands of the Women's Institutes in the remotest corners of the earth."[3]
These generous accolades must have been a source of great joy to Watt
as she reflected on her career in organizing rural women over more
than twenty-five years. However, the fact that she was described as the
"white-haired lady" was a reminder that Watt was well advanced in
years and her influence was declining.

With war looming on the horizon, international women's organizations were about to face new challenges as they grappled with how
to continue their operations and what would happen at war's end.
Indeed, Rupp asserts that for international women's groups in general,
World War Two "nearly severed the international connections," and
after the war, "transnational interactions jumped out of the well-worn
transatlantic tracks."[4] The ACWW was certainly not immune from
that pattern, and at the heart of it was the question of Watt's continuing involvement, which proved to be particularly complicated for the
organization. In large part, these complications arose because Watt
refused to concede that her age, leadership style, and wartime location
were hindrances to the ACWW's ongoing operations. Instead, Watt
held to her unwavering conviction that internationalism depended
on personal connections and she insisted that she was uniquely qualified to lead because of her vast international experiences. In fact, her
reticence to share the task of directing the ACWW was largely born
of stubbornness and her continuing need to leverage her position as
world president into a means of supporting herself financially. Watt's
folksy, grassroots approach to leadership, where she would personally address large gatherings of women, seeking to inspire them by
recounting her personal encounters, was quickly becoming stale and
outdated, yet Watt was among the last to realize that her influence was
waning. If anything, a second war seemed to revive her sense of self-
importance and lead her to assume that once again, she had an essential role to play in service to the empire, to the allied forces, and to rural
women worldwide. However, she was not prepared for what leadership of an international organization would entail going forward into
the postwar era.

Although Watt's plans after the summer of 1939 were not clearly
spelled out, the NFWI's luncheon in her honour definitely marked the
end of an era for her. In the August edition of *Home and Country* Watt
expressed her gratitude for the support she had received in hosting the

recent ACWW conference in London. "Perhaps I may add a word of personal thanks," she wrote,

> I do trust you will let me say "thank you" from the bottom of my heart to England and the English for what they have done this month, and very specially to Women's Institute members. Our [ACWW] Conference gave them a chance for a great gesture, and the gesture was made generously and with deep feeling, as from one set of human beings to another. We believe that there will result lasting benefit to international relationship[s], and that many anxious women from overseas have been comforted because they found sisterhood and affectionate welcome in England.[5]

No one, not even Watt, could have imagined how important those long-distance links were about to become. Shortly after her return to Canada, Britain declared war on Germany, and the world was plunged into a six-year conflict during which Watt found she was unable to return to England to observe her beloved WIs or to give direct leadership to the ACWW.

Watt returned home to Canada and remained in North America for the duration of the war for a variety of reasons. First of all, her only sister, Katie Robertson Arthur, was seriously ill, and Madge needed to spend time with her family in Ontario. When Watt had departed for her world tour in 1936, Katie had already been sick for some time, and she eventually died in the spring of 1945.[6] But family troubles provide only part of the explanation for why Watt did not return to England; wartime security was another. Although transatlantic crossings were still possible during the war, such travel was greatly curtailed because of the risk involved, and London was hardly a safe destination, given the bombing raids. Watt's home away from home in England had always been with Josephine Godman at Little Ote Hall in Wivelsfield, Sussex, but Godman no longer occupied that property and she spent the war years working in London. Without her friend's country house to return to, Watt really had no place to go to in England.[7] Furthermore, Watt simply could not afford to return. Finances were a constant concern for her as she divided her time in Canada between various addresses; she sometimes received mail in Collingwood at her sister's home, and because her sons were living in Montreal, she also had an address there. Other times she made her base at the Château Laurier Hotel in Ottawa, financed by the Department of Agriculture because of her work with the WI, or the Empress Hotel in Victoria, where she depended on the hospitality of friends, including the

Smart family.[8] From these various locations, Watt travelled a great deal and looked for government funding to pay her way. Indeed, her financial insecurity helps to explain why she so stubbornly refused to step down from her leadership role in the ACWW. She used the title of world president to argue that she still had a role to play, despite her advanced age, and she was tireless in lobbying the Canadian government to provide funds to support her travel itineraries.

Meanwhile, back in London, the ACWW carried on even after war was declared in September 1939. The association was saddled with that heavy debt from the London conference, and as the war heated up the suggestion was made that perhaps activities should be suspended for the duration. Certainly many normal activities were curtailed because travel to and even communication with some European countries was simply not possible. Yet in spite of the odds against them, the leadership of the ACWW in London was determined to soldier on. Much of the credit for that perseverance belongs to the ACWW's honorary secretary Elsie Zimmern, who refused to be defeated by the war. According to the official history of the organization, Zimmern never missed a day at work during the entire war, although the office itself was downsized both in terms of staff and physical space. Her wartime leadership is legendary among ACWW members, both for her sheer tenacity and for her financial acumen.[9]

By June 1941 Zimmern was happy to announce that the post-conference debt was all but eradicated.[10] Her schemes for eliminating the debt included trimming the office staff down to a skeleton crew of only two people and some creative fundraising ideas. At the same time, income from a membership fund called "Pennies for Friendship" began to arrive. This scheme encouraged members worldwide to collect their pennies (or their country's equivalent, smallest coin) and send in the proceeds. These small amounts quickly multiplied into impressive sums and expanded the donor base significantly. With limited events to finance, the ACWW soon found itself on the firmest financial footing it had ever known. As Scarborough commented in her history of the ACWW, "It sounds like a miracle; and, indeed, it was a miracle of hard work, self-sacrifice and magnificent co-operation."[11]

The wartime story of the ACWW is not, however, an entirely happy one, nor was it conflict-free. The fact that Watt found herself in North America for the duration of the war was a source of frustration to her. While Watt's absence gave Zimmern a chance to demonstrate her leadership and management skills, the great physical distance between the two women only served to reinforce their very different ideas about what was best for the ACWW and its future. It is well known in ACWW circles that Watt tried unsuccessfully to bring the ACWW office to America, and her failure to do so was clearly a loss of power for Watt and a victory for Zimmern and her vision of what the ACWW could be and how it might go forward in the postwar period. The story of Watt's failed attempt to relocate the ACWW office deserves telling in some detail because it has rarely been depicted from the North American perspective nor has it been described within the context of Watt's other activities during the war.

Moreover, examining the war years of ACWW history with Watt's personal experiences at the centre, one is struck by the fact that she was struggling to carve out exactly what role she would occupy; the question revolved around what form her leadership of the movement would take and how she could exert her influence. Unlike earlier episodes of her life, however, this time it would be a story of decline and defeat. Despite her best efforts to reaffirm the importance of her leadership among rural women's organizations, her distance from London became increasingly significant, not only in a literal sense, but more importantly in terms of the power that Watt was able to wield within her beloved organization. In part this was due to her increasing age, but the wedge that came between her and her colleagues in the ACWW was largely of her own making as she stubbornly sought to reaffirm her control. Unsuccessful in her attempts to establish the legacy she was hoping for, her overbearing personality meant that she made a lot of enemies instead.

Even before she left London in July 1939, Watt was already busy making plans for how she would spend her time in Canada. At the London conference, she spoke with Mrs. H. McGregor from Penticton, BC, president of the Federated Women's Institutes of Canada, about how Watt might play a role in the upcoming biennial conference of the FWIC to be held that October in Edmonton, Alberta. As part of the planning, Watt asked McGregor to approach the Canadian government on her behalf about financing travel to the conference. Using Watt's title as the president of the ACWW and billing her as an expert on international rural women's experiences, McGregor wrote to James Gardiner, Canadian minister of agriculture.[12] Gardiner replied in early August to say that he was "recommending that a grant of $200 be paid to the Federated Women's Institutes towards meeting Mrs. Watt's traveling expenses."[13] That recommendation marked the beginning of a long relationship between Watt and Gardiner that would last throughout the war years.

In September 1939 Watt strategized further about how she could put her expertise to use on behalf of the Canadian government. Her whole scheme was eerily reminiscent of the first war, only in that case Watt found herself in England, middle-aged, newly widowed, and in need of money; now she was home in Canada, more than seventy years of age, and still in need of money. With some sense of déjà vu, Watt wrote to Gardiner in early September, saying, "It seems plain that the Food Supply will be of vital importance. I am meeting the Ontario Women's Institute representative tomorrow at Toronto, as I met the Quebec Convention two weeks ago ... about the probable part which will be taken by the Women's Institute of those two provinces at least."[14] The strategy was exactly that which Watt had employed twenty-five years earlier in convincing the British authorities that WI branches could be central to increasing the food supply. Now she was positioning herself as the person most qualified to coordinate the work of Canadian WI branches to do the same thing for this war.

A briefing note for Gardiner prepared by his staff was one of the earliest indicators of how persistent Watt could be in pursuing the minister's support for her work:

> Mrs. Watt called yesterday to try and arrange for a chat with you. She told me that she has many offers to address women's meetings and also to make some radio addresses and would like to get your views on things so that she might follow them in her addresses. This is the woman who originated the Women's Institutes etc. throughout the world and who headed agricultural work for women in England during the last war. She spent last year touring Germany and other European countries and is well versed on what they have been doing for agriculture.[15]

Watt followed up that request for "a chat" with a written proposal. Outlining how she could lend service to the Department of Agriculture, she listed the titles of a series of talks she was prepared to give, set out the need for coordination of efforts among provincially run WI groups, and then finished off her memo with a section about herself. Fully persuaded that her past experiences were precisely what the Canadian government required, she boldly outlined what she called her "special qualifications for this work":

> Knowledge from personal experience of organizing country women's work in relation to National Service throughout the Dominion and

colonies of the Empire, in America, British Isles, Baltic States, Scandinavian countries, France, Germany, Italy and other European countries.

Life-long study of rural economics and rural sociology.

Was chief organizer of women's part in food production for British Board of Agriculture during Great War, considered of greatest importance by Government, £10,000 a year being voted for this purpose. I was awarded Order British Empire, and the Belgian Order of Agricultural Merit and the French Order of Merit, for this service.

Possession of the confidence and liking of the whole membership of the Women's Institutes in Canada, who have shown themselves ready to be guided by me.[16]

Though she was clearly overestimating her potential influence, Watt's self-aggrandizing claims can also be read as evidence of her commitment to internationalism built on the strength of personal contacts.

In her continuing correspondence with the minister, Watt was unrelenting in her pursuit of his endorsement for her work, and more importantly, his funding. One month after the initial grant was approved to cover her expenses to travel to Edmonton in October 1939, Watt began to campaign for an expanded role for herself, reasoning that "[a]s you are already sending me to Edmonton would it not be a simple beginning to send me to other big meetings to deliver at least the urgent part of your messages to country women?" In her postscript to that letter, she wrote, "In my mail today I had 14 invitations to speak at big meetings some from British Columbia where, as you know food production goes on all the year."[17] In making her case, Watt pointed out the urgency of communicating to rural women that they had a unique role to play in the war effort, different from women in towns and cities. In what she called "a rough memorandum ... not really a plan," Watt argued that "[i]f the country woman takes on work townswomen can do she will be unable to cope with the vital work which she alone can do in the rural home and community." In Watt's opinion, rural women could make their best contributions by "increased production in the smaller lines of agriculture, dairying, poultry, small stock bees, gardening," and by keeping "informed and up to date in government requirements, in all matters relating to the food supply."[18] Watt also saw rural women playing a central part in keeping up morale by "the checking of false rumours" because "country women with their frequent meetings together, their neighbourly attitude and their sense of solidarity of the rural population," were uniquely positioned. To seal her argument about why she should be hired to help facilitate all this, Watt added, "I find that women cooperate more readily in rural communities and that appeals to them are rarely disregarded."[19]

Watt's arguments about why country women should be a particular target for the minister of agriculture proved convincing. Gardiner agreed to finance her public speaking tour throughout the fall of 1939, and after she left Edmonton in early October, she gave speeches in Manitoba, Saskatchewan, and British Columbia. For Watt, who had long been accustomed to touring and public speaking, travelling by rail, staying at CPR hotels, including the Empress in Victoria, Hotel Vancouver, and the Château Laurier in Ottawa, it was a demanding but comfortable and satisfying agenda. The terms of her employment were that she should be paid $5 per day plus expenses.[20]

While Watt clearly enjoyed her work as an inspirational public speaker, her itinerary was not problem-free. Complications arose early in 1940 when it became evident that the funding she had enjoyed during the fall of 1939 was not going to be extended. With her funding base gone, Watt tried desperately to capture the attention of the Liberal government and to urge Gardiner and his deputy minister Dr. G.S.H. Barton to do everything they could to reverse the decision of the Treasury Board on her case. Her Liberal funders were otherwise preoccupied on the election trail during February and March 1940, but Watt continued to plead with them that her work was essential to the war effort, and perhaps even to their own political futures. Reasoning that the rural voters would not understand if she had to cancel previously scheduled visits to WI groups in British Columbia, Watt enlisted the help of other British Columbians to petition Gardiner. First, she asked the FWIC president, Mrs. McGregor, to write on her behalf once again, this time using a regional argument about isolation to try to convince Gardiner's deputy minister that he should put the resources into funding Watt's lectures. McGregor wrote, "[W]e sincerely trust we may be permitted to have her [Watt] return. B.C. is unfortunately so far from available Dominion lecturers we deem it a privilege to have been given this opportunity."[21] When the funds were not immediately forthcoming and WI meetings "in the interior of BC, Okanagan and Kootenay" were about to be cancelled, McGregor followed up with a second letter to Barton making her disappointment clear. "Regret very much this has happened particularly in view of work Mrs. Watt did for England in Conservation and Preservation during the last war. If plans could be reconsidered am sure the ultimate value would more than compensate for expenditures."[22]

A second round of lobbying came from Ian Alistair MacKenzie, MP for Vancouver Centre and minister of pensions and national health, who wrote to Gardiner arguing that Watt was doing good work in British Columbia and that her services should be continued. If that was not possible, then MacKenzie requested that at the very least, Watt should be repaid her "out of pocket expenses for the engagements she fulfilled after her services had been terminated." He reasoned further that "it was necessary for these engagements to be made ahead of time and that, if Mrs. Watt had not fulfilled them, it would have caused considerable hard feeling."[23] The Liberals could not afford to cause such disappointment among BC voters, particularly not during the election campaign, and Mackenzie and Gardiner both knew it.

Watt herself wrote to Gardiner arguing that cancelling the meetings was politically dangerous. "The Deputy Minister here considers that [cancelling] would be calamitous. Your friends here think the same, especially just now. I cannot myself think of anything more calculated to cause dissatisfaction."[24] Watt continued to urge Gardiner to find the money to fund her lectures, arguing that by funding her, he actually was gaining political favour for himself with rural women voters:

> If the meetings are cancelled now, our women will certainly consider that they have been let down. As you know, women will not be affected by remote political considerations. But they will be stirred by simple things like neglect of soldiers' welfare, which they can visualize. There is all the more need for the re-assurance [that] someone they like and trust can give them.[25]

Convinced that she was the right person to do that job, Watt pleaded with Gardiner to give her financial support because she was quite sure that there was no one else with her international experience and stellar record of service from the last war. To make that point very clear, she included a newspaper clipping from the London (England) *Daily Sketch* outlining the work of Women's Institutes in that country. She told Gardiner that he might find it instructive to see "how the [UK] Ministry of Agriculture uses Women's Institutes."[26] While it is obvious that Watt needed the money to carry on her work, her appeals to Gardiner were almost a form of political blackmail. Convinced that her knowledge was invaluable to the government of Canada, and that she had insights that would help the Liberal Party win the current election, Watt wrote to Gardiner revealing her mixed motives. Admitting that without continued funding she was "certainly in a quandary personally" and that she was "very anxious to see you if you can spare a few minutes today," she appealed to Gardiner's political instincts, saying, "Aside from my personal problems, I have had special opportunities of noting the reactions of women in the present situation, and I should be able, I think, to give you some helpful information."[27]

Though he could not release the funds during the election campaign, just a few days after the Liberal victory on March 26, 1940, Gardiner did grant Watt's wishes, when he approved the extension of Watt's services for a six-month period, retroactive to January 1, 1940. Again, her terms of employment were that she should be paid $5 per day plus expenses.[28] Gardiner's rationale for continuing Watt's employment was that

[t]here are still a number of Institutes in British Columbia which have requested Mrs. Watt to visit them and other requests have been received from various parts of Canada. It also seems desirable that Mrs. Watt visit both Quebec and the Maritime Provinces and, since the cost of Mrs. Watt's services to the Department is very small, it is felt that a further extension of her period of appointment for an additional three months [sic] is desirable.[29]

Indeed, it seems clear that Gardiner was getting his money's worth from Mrs. Watt. The political benefits were numerous, and Watt proved to be a tireless worker.[30]

Watt continued to follow Gardiner's political career closely. In the summer of 1940, Prime Minister Mackenzie King appointed Gardiner to serve as minister of national war services, and at the same time asked him to retain the agriculture portfolio.[31] In his new role, Gardiner travelled to England in 1940 and upon his return that fall he addressed the nation by radio to speak about England's domestic war efforts. Watt wrote to congratulate her benefactor for making what she called a "magnificent speech." An experienced speaker herself, she enthused, "I do think that every word you uttered will be taken to heart. The speeches were at once vigorous & insightful which is not so easy to achieve."[32] After that flattery, Watt went on to reveal that she had remained in Ottawa in hopes of having a personal meeting with Gardiner because based on her travels from Prince Rupert to the Gaspé, she had "a number of things I should like to tell you and particularly suggestions to make for the practical working out of your plans in relation now to agriculture & women's services. I know you will find some useful ideas in my reports."[33]

In addition to giving Gardiner some of her ideas, she hoped to hear more of his ideas so that she could incorporate them into the future speeches she had promised to give in the United States. "My next meeting is in Baltimore," she explained, "with members of the American Farm Bureau Federation (42 states) & the next to the New York Agricultural Society, & next to Cornell University. Besides that a great deal of broadcasting is to be arranged. I have just given a world broadcast from USA."[34] Watt was spending increasing amounts of time in the United States, and although that work was outside the scope of what Gardiner was funding her to do, she wanted to explain to him how important these cross-border connections were, not only for her, but also for Gardiner himself and for Canada. Telling him about that work, she recounted that, "My visit coincided with the Russian attack upon Finland and at times it was almost impossible for me to speak. But everyone present was deeply moved."[35]

Watt's sense of Canadian-American and Anglo-American relations came through as she advised the minister on the kind of "propaganda to America" that would be well received in the United States as the Americans maintained their neutral stance. She explained her approach, saying,

> I was able to show that American sympathy for the Allies could be at once directed to Canada, that co-operation in Agriculture would be helpful, that helping Canada especially just now, was doing war service. As they were well disposed that way, it seemed best to emphasize this. In other words, to cash in on the friendly feeling towards Canada, which is greater than for England."[36]

Watt's advice to the minister of agriculture provides a fascinating glimpse into her sense of self and the role she perceived that she was playing on the world stage. Her recommendations to Gardiner, which she suggested he should pass along to the government of Canada, about how to get along with the Americans is fascinating. It is clear that when she was speaking to American audiences, she knew that she needed to present herself as a Canadian with international experience, not as a British subject who spoke on behalf of the Empire.

Gardiner and Watt shared their unbridled enthusiasm for the Empire and both of them were popular figures and effective speakers.[37] Indeed, they shared a sense of duty to fight on behalf of the Empire, and they shared the conviction that agriculture had a major role to play in strategizing for victory. Watt advised Gardiner about the kind of rhetoric that would carry weight with Americans if Canada hoped to persuade her reluctant neighbour to join the Allied forces, and she reported to Gardiner that the American audiences she encountered were very discriminating. Inexperienced lecturers should not be sent to them because, in her view, they were "too experienced with spell-binders to be impressed," and she recommended that "no professional propagandists should be used, but only those already trusted for one reason or another."[38] In other words, she was recommending entertaining, experienced, and engaging speakers such as herself.

It is difficult to judge how seriously Gardiner took Watt's advice and whether he ever brought any of her suggestions forward in meetings of King's war cabinet. It is clear, however, that at least one source was advising Gardiner not to take her seriously. In an unsigned memo to Gardiner dated June 11, 1941, the author offered him a very different perspective about the value of Watt's contributions. Whoever wrote the memo wanted the minister of agriculture to realize that Watt's public speaking was not respected by everyone and that much of what she was proposing was completely outdated. After hearing Watt speak at the 1939 FWIC convention in Edmonton, the writer cautioned Gardiner that

> I heard considerable criticism of the wartime advice which Mrs. Alfred Watt gave to the rural women on that occasion. The leaders of women's work in several of the provinces felt that it was impractical and savoured of 1914 rather than 1939. In deference to her past accomplishments as president of the Associated Country Women of the World, and also in consideration of her age, Mrs. Watt has been cordially received in several of the provinces by the directors of women's work. I know however, from speaking to them personally, that some at least are not anxious to arrange further work for her with the rural women.[39]

Urging Gardiner to think very carefully about whom he was endorsing and funding, the writer reiterated that Watt was not a good choice to speak on behalf of the government, not only because her ideas were ones she was recycling from twenty-five years earlier, but also because her long absences from Canada meant that her understanding of Canadian women's organizations was not as accurate as she believed it to be.[40] Gardiner's advisor was trying to warn him that Watt, the self-proclaimed expert on rural women, was clinging to ideas and making suggestions that were both outdated and out of touch with the wartime reality of Canadian women's groups. This might serve to explain why Watt often found it so difficult to arrange meetings with the minister; perhaps his tardiness in responding to her requests for meetings and additional funds was only partly due to his busy schedule.

Unaware that such opinions about her were being offered to Gardiner, Watt remained an eager informant for him, and there is no question that she saw herself as playing an indispensable role as a government strategist. The fact that she was doing this as a woman in her seventies makes her work all the more fascinating. It is reasonable to assume that the deference that audiences were showing to Watt was simply out of respect for her age and her impressive world travels. One thing is striking about the letters Watt wrote to Gardiner: her networking efforts seem always to have been one-sided conversations. In her letters Watt regularly reported to Gardiner about her speaking engagements, specifically how well received she and her ideas were, but rarely, if ever, did she offer any new ideas she had gathered from her travels. Indeed, she perceived herself very much as the expert, who told other people what to do to make contributions to the war and how they might mobilize rural women, but she did not report back with new information. Indeed, it seems that Watt travelled to speak, but not to listen. Her failure to listen was about to cause her one of the biggest disappointments of her career.

It is important to remember that while Watt was doing this work under the auspices of the Canadian government, she still held the title of president of the ACWW. The outbreak of the war brought about special challenges to that organization, and Watt faced one of the biggest controversies of her leadership: the proposed relocation of the central office of the ACWW away from London for the duration of the war. Before the end of September 1939 she was already looking for a North American solution to the problem of how the ACWW could best carry on during the war. In a letter that Watt circulated to "the Heads of the Constituent Societies Belonging to the ACWW in America" she explained the problem and her proposed solution:

> I have heard from England, from Mrs. Drage, senior Vice President of the ACWW … of the extreme difficulty of carrying on the Central Office. She thinks it will be impossible to do so or to publish the journal. It seems to me that it would solve many of the difficulties if the Association were carried on in America for the war period.[41]

Watt went on to explain that her letter was intended to canvass the American constituent societies of the ACWW, and she urged the recipients, "If you consider that the American Societies would welcome this idea, or the one with which you are closely connected, please let me know."[42] Watt assured her correspondents that staffing the new headquarters would not be a problem: "As I shall be in this country and America for some time to come, it is likely that I can devote much of my time to office and other work." Moreover, while the letter was intended to solicit offers of accommodation for the ACWW to relocate to America, Watt was quite certain that she spoke not only for herself, but also international colleagues when she said, "It would indeed be not only a pleasure for me personally to have such an invitation extended but I feel sure it would be an immense relief to the Vice Presidents of the Association."[43] To demonstrate that she had thought through the issues arising from relocation, she attached a document to the letter entitled "Points to Consider Regarding Transfer of ACWW Central Office to USA."[44] In that document, she discussed both constitutional and practical points that would have to be considered, both in England and in America, revealing her dream that "it might well be that the Central Office, if in America, would become a real meeting place for farm women from USA and Canada and for visitors from other lands."[45]

Within two weeks after sending her letter, Watt received the invitation she was hoping for. It came from one of the contacts she had made as a result of the 1936 ACWW conference in Washington. On November 8, 1939, Flora Rose, a professor of home economics at Cornell University, wrote to Watt to say that she and several colleagues were "all agreed that we would like to extend to you an invitation to establish temporary international headquarters for this association at Cornell."[46] In making the offer, Professor Rose wrote on behalf of herself and her colleague Ruby Green Smith of the College of Home Economics, as well as the Cornell University president, and the dean of the New York State Colleges of Agriculture and Home Economics. Rose emphasized the fact that Cornell had an established reputation for internationalism, both in its student body, which represented over forty-two countries, and among its faculty members and alumni. As Rose explained,

[M]any Cornellians are in the diplomatic service the world around and members of the University staff have traveled widely. It seems to us, therefore, in keeping with this spirit of internationalism for the University to offer hospitality to the Associated Country Women of the World during this time when its office is to be transferred temporarily from London.[47]

Rose went on to explain that the space being offered was that of the New York Home Demonstration Agents, whose offices were in close proximity to those of the State Federation of Home Bureaus, a group that had the distinction of being the first to have joined the ACWW as a constituent society.[48]

The Cornell offer seemed to be the ideal solution, and Watt was quick to respond. Within ten days of Rose's original letter, Watt wrote back expressing her delight with the offer. She seemed certain that the process of realizing the transfer would be quick and problem-free as she outlined the next steps: "I am transmitting the invitation at once to the senior Vice President of the ACWW Mrs. Drage, with the request that she transmit it at once to our Societies either direct or through their representatives in London and asking for replies by cable."[49] She indicated that because she had already polled the Canadian Women's Institute groups in every province and received their approval for the hypothetical move, she was convinced that there would be unanimous worldwide support for the idea. When Flora Rose received Watt's eager reply, she shared it with her colleague Ruby Green Smith, who wrote a quick note back to Rose that spoke volumes about how much this offer meant to Watt. In Smith's view, "Mrs. Watt's pleasure in this invitation is touched with pathos, but it is the happiest letter of hers I've seen since the war started."[50] While Smith felt that Watt's eager reply was almost pathetic, it was only a foreshadowing of what would emerge in the coming weeks and months as Watt's enthusiastic plans for the relocation quickly turned against her and she lost hold of the last remnants of her power to direct the course of her beloved ACWW. The very thing that made Watt the happiest she had been since the war began would ultimately prove to be her greatest disappointment.

While Watt waited for her overseas colleagues to reply with their endorsement of the Cornell plan, she wasted no time in moving forward with the process of working out the details. At the end of November 1939, she spent four days in Syracuse, New York, attending the convention of the New York State Federation of Farm and Home Bureaus, and as she reported to James Gardiner, "During the Conventions, I spoke four times, three long speeches, gave two broadcasts, was interviewed by ten different papers, was entertained at two dinners and three luncheons given for me, had a number of consultations with farm women leaders and attended some of the Committee meetings. So it was not uneventful."[51] Watt continued with her report, explaining that her networking efforts outside of the formal sessions were important as well, "[b]ut the conversations and discussions between meetings were what I relied upon to win sympathy. These were almost continuous."[52] Her report gives a glimpse into the indefatigable pace that Watt set for herself during conferences.

One of the speeches that she delivered in Syracuse was entitled "What the proposed transfer of the Associated Country Women of the World to the United States will mean,"[53] in which she outlined her proposal to move the ACWW office to Cornell and provided her rationale for that course of action. Her speech brought together some of the ideas she had been proposing that fall, and she explained that her preoccupation over the past few weeks had been trying to figure out how the ACWW "could profitably be moved out of England to this side of the water for the war period." She was pleased to announce,

> To the everlasting glory of the New York State Home Bureaus and the Directors of Cornell University and the New York Extension Service, these bodies have come to the rescue of the Association and an invitation has resulted to house the ACWW at Cornell University for the time. With this invitation has come the offer of practical help in services such as rent, heat, light, etc., and of cooperation of staff and demonstration agents which make the whole offer both possible and practical.[54]

With all those details in hand, Watt's mind was made up. In her view, the Cornell offer was a perfect solution to her problem of being separated from the headquarters of the organization she had helped to found. Therefore, she revealed, "I have accepted this offer provided our officers and our constituent societies agree to its acceptance." Watt was very confident that those conditions would be easy to meet because, as she explained, "I had secured before the formal offer was made, the opinion of the Canadian Women's Institutes and from the Atlantic to the Pacific there was but one opinion, namely that if Cornell University should extend an offer every effort should be made to get it accepted."[55]

Watt had put a great deal of thought into the logistics of the move. In her own mind, she had already made some major decisions about staffing and financing the new office. She explained that "only the files necessary for carrying on [would] be brought from England with probably one person who understands them to remain in charge, the expense of transport to be borne by the ACWW. This would be the first expense – the salary of such a person." Evidently, she already had the person selected, though whether she had consulted with that individual is unclear. "One of our staff, who has worked a good deal in the office and also in journalism in New York, might be the logical person and her participation would make it possible to continue "The Countrywoman," [the ACWW magazine] probably in some abbreviated form." Watt had also thought beyond the problem of staffing to the question of decision making. She had determined that

> a new executive committee would have to be appointed which would be done by the societies naming representatives, and it is thought that many nationals at Cornell University would be suited to represent societies of country women of different lands. The officers of the association would remain as they are now, and as the Honorary President, the President, and one Vice-President are now on this side of the water, they would normally act in the same capacity.[56]

Speaking as though the deal were already done, Watt concluded her outline of the planned relocation, saying, "by this invitation Cornell, and the New York Home Bureaus, especially, have placed me in their debt forever, a debt which can never be repaid by me but for which I am confident repayment will come from the hearts of country women the world over."[57] In fact, many country women had something very different in their hearts; they were not excited by the scheme that Watt had drawn up in collusion with her friends at Cornell, nor were they were inclined to endorse the actions of a president who acted without consulting them.

If Watt had been setting out to start a brand-new organization, then these plans might have been very impressive indeed. But of course she was not starting from nothing, and she was by no means the only one responsible for giving leadership and direction to the ACWW. She had proceeded with her detailed planning as though she were the only one with any responsibility for or opinion about the organization. Indeed, one might even say she had proceeded as though she personified the ACWW. Finding herself an office space at Cornell and strategizing about how she might get some office "help" seemed to be the extent of her concern. The fact that she had gone this far without consulting her colleagues in London was not only inconsiderate, it was also offensive. Ironically, at the helm of an organization that existed to foster international cooperation among rural women, Watt's greatest failure was her refusal to consult with others. Even Dorothy Drage, who had originally suggested to Watt that a move to

America might be the best strategy, had changed her mind once she learned the opinion of the constituent societies. As she recounted,

> At first it seemed to some of us that this arrangement [with Cornell] might be advisable, but naturally we had to ask the societies for their opinion. Their replies were almost unanimously against the offer. We were in London; the ACWW funds were in English currency; and the societies felt more secure with us in London than anywhere else.[58]

For Drage and everyone but Watt, it seems, the course of action was clear: ACWW should stay put in London.[59] But Watt did not see it that way, and so she forged ahead, creating more offence as she went along.

The offence became even greater when Watt turned to the question of finance. Money sense had never been Watt's forte, and in the first ten years of the organization, she had been more of a financial liability to the ACWW than an asset. One can only imagine, then, how her advice about financing the move to the United States was received back in England. Claiming that "the raising of funds in England and elsewhere to carry on our association has largely fallen to me, and I do not feel that I can carry that particular burden much longer," she explained that "this consideration of finance must be noted."[60] No doubt her colleagues in London were delighted that she thought finances should be considered and noted, because in their view, she had never paid much attention to money before this. Her plan was to finance the move and the operations without any help beyond North America. She proposed that the annual fees of the constituent societies should come directly to her and she assumed that "we may take it for granted that most of the money required for our prosecution of this work will have to be found in this country and countries outside Europe."[61] Watt explained that she "was of the opinion at first that a considerable sum would be required, but the offer of Cornell University has made a great deal of difference."[62] The logic of not imposing on countries that were at war seemed to be a gracious gesture, but in fact it excluded Watt's English colleagues from contributing funds or controlling the money. Left with the large debt that the ACWW London office was shouldering at the outset of the war, the thought that all the North American membership dues would not be forthcoming for the duration of the war was totally unacceptable in their eyes.

Watt's next suggestion about money must have seemed all too familiar to her English colleagues. She suggested that one need not have all the money in hand before starting the venture, because she agreed with a suggestion that she said several North American members had made to her that "once a good thing is started, money which could not be collected beforehand will undoubtedly come in as required."[63] That pattern had proven to be Watt's downfall before, and the London office must have shuddered to think about the debts that Watt might incur when she was half a world away and out from under their close surveillance. Watt confessed that she would rather have the money in hand before beginning the venture of moving offices, but she indicated she would be ready to proceed if she at least had "assurance before we start" that the money was promised.[64]

Not only were Watt's calculations about financing amiss, but her assumptions about how her English counterparts would receive her proposal were far from accurate. She assumed that "there would be great relief to those who so freely, and yet so anxiously, have been responsible for this work in England … if arrangements can be made, they will, I am sure, be most grateful."[65] Gratitude is not what the English members, staff, and executive committee members felt. Indeed, they were alarmed that Watt was proceeding with such a detailed plan, communicating it widely, and trying to garner support in North America without any consultation with London. As it turns out, Elsie Zimmern, a co-founder of the ACWW with Watt, was not anxious to give up the London office and operations, and she was not grateful that Watt was trying to assume single-handed control of the organization. In fact, Zimmern had a much more realistic picture of ACWW finances than Watt did, and while Watt was proposing how to raise funds to start a new centre of operations at Cornell, Zimmern was still trying to eliminate the outstanding debt that had resulted from the London conference, Watt's travels, and the failed publishing ventures.

Watt's other rationale for moving the office to America was her conviction that the ACWW should be operating from a neutral country, and in 1939, the United States of America fulfilled that criterion. Again, she misread the feeling of the international membership when she assumed that "taking the association as a whole, there will be more confidence in many countries in our international activities if these are conducted from a neutral country. It is probable that communications can be more readily maintained than from a combatant country."[66] While there was some agreement in principle with the idea of operating from a neutral country, the membership actually wanted to explore one of the Scandinavian countries rather than look as far away as North America.[67]

Finally, invoking the idea that change is good, Watt reasoned that a change of venue, especially of an international body, would inspire confidence as being evidence of its sincere internationalism. "It is all to the good if we can show that our internationalism does not entail our home being always in the same place. The moral effect of the move cannot fail to be good."[68] But once again, Watt's confidence was misplaced. Indeed, what the ACWW needed during the trying war years was not a new vantage point, but a secure foundation. While her arguments for moving might have made sense as a good-will gesture to assure members that the ACWW was flexible, the women of Europe reasoned that war was not a time for flexibility as much as it was for security. When the association's constituent members were polled, the vast majority indicated that they wished the ACWW to stay put in London and to soldier on from there for the duration of the war.[69]

What Watt did not know was that while she travelled and lectured about the advantages of the Cornell offer, a whole series of discussions were going on without her participation. Watt made the argument that relocating to an American headquarters would not be very disruptive because "the officers of the Association would remain as they are now, and as the Honorary President, the President, and one Vice-President are now on this side of the water, they would normally act in the same capacity."[70] The three officers that she referred to were Lady Susan Tweedsmuir (honorary president), who was married to the Canadian governor general, Watt herself as president, and Grace Frysinger (vice-president, America). What she failed to indicate however, was that she had not consulted with the other two officers to be sure that they were in full agreement with her about the move to Cornell. Meanwhile, some high-level discussions were going on in the background involving an exchange of letters between Tweedsmuir and the American First Lady, Eleanor Roosevelt. Just one week after Watt's initial letter of response to Cornell, on November 25, 1939, Tweedsmuir wrote to Roosevelt suggesting that "[i]f you could give it your interest and your support it would, of course, make the whole difference."[71]

While Roosevelt might have had influence over the American rural women's groups, she had little influence over the other constituent societies, especially those in Europe and beyond. Roosevelt, looking for direction on how to reply to Tweedsmuir, had her staff refer the letter to Flora Rose of Cornell University for her advice on how she should respond. Rose replied to Roosevelt suggesting, "I do not believe you would be making a mistake to state to the group you believe in our disinterestedness in asking them," or in other words, that there was no ulterior motive in Cornell extending the invitation to the ACWW. Roosevelt, who consulted widely on how she should respond, decided rather to follow the advice she received from another source which suggested that "it would be wiser to wait until the recommendations of the member groups from all over the world are reviewed by the executive committee and the member organizations are notified as to the result."[72] Roosevelt's advisor went further, saying that the First Lady should delay her endorsement of the move because until the constituent societies from around the world had spoken, "it would seem to be unethical for any step to be taken in the United States [to support the move]."[73] The one giving this advice to Eleanor Roosevelt was none other than Grace Frysinger, the American vice-president of the ACWW. Therefore, while Watt seemed confident that she, Tweedsmuir, and Frysinger could provide the ACWW with the leadership necessary from this side of the Atlantic, this correspondence reveals that the three of them were quite divided.

Although Watt was sure that polling the worldwide membership was simply a formality, Flora Rose received a very different message from the ACWW office in London. In a letter dated December 13, 1939, the Executive Committee wrote to explain why they had decided not to accept the Cornell offer. In the letter, Lady Eleanor Cole of South Africa cited two main reasons for declining the invitation. First, she explained,

> the changing situation made it undesirable to add to the confusion by moving the ACWW centre at this juncture. Representatives of the European countries present made it clear that they felt we should lose touch with them if the office was out of Europe and so far away as America. They felt the move would inevitably cause an interruption to the work of the ACWW, just when continuity was most wanted, and when connecting links were none too strong, and in no position to stand a jar.[74]

The second reason that Cole cited was that of finance. She explained that "generous as we feel your offer to be, we did not really see how it would make a big difference, anyhow in the first year's working. What we gained in one way we felt we should lose in others."[75] What Cole referred to here was Watt's scheme of redirecting the North American membership fees towards financing the Cornell move. That would, of course, represent lost revenues for the London office as they tried to pay down the outstanding debt. Cole's letter was gracious as she repeated how grateful the ACWW was to Cornell for the offer and then added, "I hope most of our friends in the USA will feel we have made a right decision, if we can find the means to carry on. We should all like to feel that the door you opened to us is not locked, and should the need arise later, we might yet seek your hospitality and shelter from the storm."[76]

When Watt realized that this decision to turn down the Cornell offer had been taken without her knowledge, she was incensed. She wrote to Rose herself, expressing her shock. "I am very much surprised to receive a cable from the Associated Country Women of the World saying that the Executive Committee had declined your kind invitation."[77] The purpose of Watt's letter to Rose was to say that the decision was not final and that she hoped that Rose would keep the offer open. Watt explained that in her view, the Executive Committee did not have the power to make this decision. "As I know that the Constituent Societies have not had your offer as yet I am taking the stand that they and they alone can decide."[78] Certain that the membership was behind her, even if her executive was not, Watt held out for a different outcome. She told Rose that she had "sent a letter to London by Air mail ordering it to be sent to all Societies by Air Mail."[79] But it was too late for Watt to give orders because what she did not know was that "by December, thirty-six replies [from Constituent Societies] had been received, and of these twenty-four were unhesitatingly in favour of the office remaining in England."[80] Evidently, the membership was backing the Executive Committee in London, and Watt was left holding on to empty hope that the plans she had orchestrated would somehow still prevail.

Watt's defeat on the proposal to relocate the office of the ACWW represented a shift in her ability to achieve her objectives. The personal influence she counted as her greatest asset was clearly waning as she had been virtually cut out of the decision-making process. The official history of the ACWW written in 1953 described it this way:

> The decision must have come as a great shock to Mrs. Watt, as crippling, temporarily, as the loss of a limb. She found herself cut off from the executive of the organization into which she had poured her vast energy and drive, and her genius for persuasion. Very naturally, she cried out, in pain and in anger. The decision had the appearance, to her, of an unnecessary and a possibly fatal amputation. She was convinced that if the office were to remain in England, it would surely die.[81]

As it became clear that she could not lead the ACWW from the other side of the Atlantic, Watt retained her role as president of the ACWW but reluctantly relinquished the role of chairman of the Executive Committee. A memo to the ACWW constituent societies explained the situation this way:

> when it was known that Mrs. Watt was not proposing to return to England, it was considered advisable to make a permanent arrangement, so that the office staff could have someone in authority with whom they could be in constant touch. It was considered that the acting chairman should be resident in London, fully conversant with all aspects of the work of the ACWW, and able to give some time to the work of the Association. The obvious person to fulfill all these conditions was Miss Zimmern, who was consequently appointed by the Executive Committee on May 9th, 1940.[82]

The Executive Committee welcomed that development and immediately endorsed Elsie Zimmern in her new role as acting chairman. While Watt's removal from running the day-to-day affairs of the ACWW must have been disappointing to her, it was obvious to everyone else that it was the right thing to do. Despite the fact that the membership had clearly expressed their view that the ACWW office should remain in London, Watt still retained her title as world president. In that role, she went ahead and accepted Cornell's offer to provide her with personal office space and she began using it to write letters and communicate with the North American rural women's organizations. The existence of two ACWW offices was evidently causing a great deal of confusion, and therefore Zimmern and the Executive Committee took steps late in the summer of 1940 to clarify the situation by writing a letter to Flora Rose at Cornell. Zimmern explained that she wanted "to be sure that it was realized in the USA that the ACWW could only have one executive office and that that office could only be the one under the control of the Executive Committee, the body responsible between Conferences for carrying on the business of the association."[83]

With that letter, the conflict between Zimmern and Watt escalated even more. In the same letter Zimmern expressed, in somewhat condescending terms, her gratitude to Rose for providing a space for Watt where she could feel useful:

> We now hear from Mrs. Watt that you have most generously placed a room at her disposal for her private use as an office and want to thank

you most warmly for this mark of understanding and sympathy. It will make all the difference to Mrs. Watt to have a place where she can leave her papers and write her letters. We cannot imagine a more delightful spot for the purpose.[84]

Meanwhile, when Watt found out that Zimmern had written to Rose without her knowledge, she was both angry and embarrassed. After learning about the letter, Watt wrote directly to Rose herself, saying, "I wish to ask you to accept my apology for being the cause of your receipt of this letter." If that had been the end of Watt's letter, it might have brought about a gracious conclusion to the whole matter; but that was not the case, because Watt went on to vent her anger. "I hope you will realize," she told Rose, "that the ACWW executive is not very representative at present or closely in touch with our societies. Miss Zimmeran [sic] is practically in entire control … As I had not written the committee they are not in possession of the facts, and I have directed that these be laid before the next meeting."[85] Watt's "apology" continued, not by asking forgiveness for her own part in causing the confusion, but by explaining indignantly that she had personally reprimanded Zimmern for writing the letter at all. "I have written her," Watt huffed, "that when she addresses the administrative head of a great college and an international president, and indeed the bulk of the members in America, she can at least assume that we know the difference between executive and administrative work and the duties of a president."[86] Ironically, it is not entirely clear that Watt understood the differences herself, except that the new arrangement left her free from committee meetings and free to operate quite independently, almost as a one-woman force, as the North American voice of the ACWW.

Watt did cherish her title as president of the ACWW, and in that capacity, she channeled her undiminished energies into more lectures and more letters. Writing from her office space at Cornell, Watt did not have access to any stationery supplies from the London office, and so she created her own. Her correspondence during 1940 appeared with this typewritten letterhead at the top of each letter: "The Associated Country Women of the World, From the Personal Office of the President, Room 259, Martha Van Rensselaer Hall, Cornell University, Ithaca, New York, USA." From that office, she wrote a year-end message of eight pages to be broadcast to the membership of the ACWW in December 1940 that she herself described as "disjointed" and "chatty." In many ways her message to the membership contained glimpses of a younger

Madge, writing up various tidbits of information, hoping to inspire her listeners as she had done many years earlier with her journalism.

The text of the broadcast gives many glimpses into Watt's psyche as a seventy-two-year-old woman. She was clearly thriving on the travel and lecture circuit, enjoying the international correspondence and contacts she had through her travels and her letters. And she was enjoying life's simple pleasures – a letter from her daughter-in-law in England ("She writes to cheer me up, I who am safe! ... Don't worry we are alright and will soon be all together again."); a conversation with her sister about the beauty of their mother's trousseau blankets ("We both thought that blankets which were milled seventy years ago must have been well made"); and fond memories of a friend in Sussex writing about gardens and cookery ("She was the first organizer I trained in England and herself formed 400 Women's Institutes which is a record").[87]

At the same time, throughout the broadcast, Watt made frequent references to faith, thus showing a softer and more vulnerable side of her personality. While she could be the feisty, argumentative Watt who battled with the London office or the calculating, strategizing Watt who manoeuvred her way into the good graces of Ottawa politicians, she could also be a charming "chatty" correspondent when she communicated with the ACWW membership at large. In a section of her broadcast subtitled "Religious Revival," Watt included an excerpt from a letter she had received from "an older lady, in a luxurious country home" in England who wrote, "I just want you to know that we are all calm and humbly confident and that our faith in God cannot be shaken. We may have to go in the darkness but we can put our hand into the hand of God and all will be well."[88] Another English friend wrote to her, saying, "We have complete confidence knowing that God is behind us as he has shown His hand plainly twice, once at Dunkirk, the other in the storm over the invasion barges."[89] Confessing that she did worry about friends and family in England, Watt admitted that "my anxiety about those in the office is very great." But she also went on to say that she took comfort from her faith and the encouragement of friends, such as one who "not only writes me comforting letters when my soul is in travail, but she sends me little poems and sayings, and often hymns and verses of scripture which she feels particularly appropriate to the problems I have on hand."[90]

Indeed, by the following summer, Watt seemed to have put the relocation controversy behind her, as though she had simply decided to continue undaunted with the opportunities at hand. She attended the biennial convention of the FWIC in Fredericton, New Brunswick, in June 1941, and according to a report in *Chatelaine* magazine, the FWIC had debated the merits of whether or not to even hold their convention during wartime, but decided to proceed with the meetings, in part "to take advantage of the leadership of Mrs. Alfred Watt, M.B.E., president of the Associated Country Women of the World, now in Canada, and who admittedly knows more about Women's Institute purposes and practices than any other woman in the world."[91] Such accolades published in the leading national women's magazine in Canada must have been a great consolation to Watt in light of her recent defeats. Her reputation as the world's leading international authority on rural women was still intact, at least in Canada, and Watt took advantage of the respect she was offered to ask for the FWIC's support for her next venture: a regional conference of the ACWW.

Having conceded that she was not running the official head office of ACWW from North America, Watt was nevertheless determined that she would still use her reputation and influence to play a leadership role by hosting an ACWW conference, albeit on a smaller, more regional scale than the usual grand triennial meetings. The plans were already in the works before the FWIC convention in Fredericton, but on that occasion, Watt asked for and received the blessing of the FWIC for her event. *Chatelaine* reported that the FWIC delegates "decided to be the official hostess of a Western Hemisphere regional conference of the Associated Country Women of the World, called to meet in Ottawa, in September [1941], by the International president, Mrs. Watt."[92] The report went on to explain that

> the theme of this conference will be 'Women's Part in the Defense [sic] of the Western Hemisphere.' It is expected that it will be attended by country women leaders from United States, the South American republics, ACWW war refugees now living on this hemisphere, as well as outstanding women experts to lead the round-table discussions pertaining to the theme.[93]

The conference did proceed as Watt had hoped, from September 3–10, 1941, with a wide variety of hosts and participants covering a vast array of topics, including Food Problems and Agriculture; Natural Resources; Services for the Consumer; Nutrition and National Security; Organized Effort of Women in National Service; Democracy; Racial Problems; and Reconstruction Today and Tomorrow. Watt found cooperation for hosting the event from the Federated Women's Institutes of Canada, the

Hadassah of Canada, the Local Council of Women at Ottawa, and the Federated Women's Institutes of Ontario and Quebec. Canadian, American, and international presenters shared the stage, with representatives from McGill University, the Associated Farm Women U.S.A., the U.S. Forest Service, the Consumer Divisions of U.S.A. and Canada, the Office of Civilian Supply, Price Administration U.S.A., the New York Home Bureaus, the director of nutrition services U.S.A., Cornell University, the food consultant to secretary of war U.S.A., the chief inspector of catering, Canadian Defence Department, Garden Clubs of America, the New York Extension Service, the minister of national war services, Canada, Canadian MP Agnes Macphail, and a variety of representatives from Women's Institutes of six different provinces in Canada.

The stated conference theme proved to be yet another divisive issue between ACWW leaders on the two sides of the Atlantic. While Watt insisted that the theme was to be "Women's Part in the *Defence* of the Western Hemisphere," her associates in the London office were disturbed that such militaristic language was being invoked. Their suggestion was to change the word *defence* to *development*, but Watt would not hear of it.[94] This was more than a petty disagreement over semantics. For Watt, it was a question of establishing the important role that rural women could play in the war effort, both to give women a sense of their importance to the war effort and to give government officials a reason to fund rural women's groups and individuals, such as Watt herself, from the war coffers. For the executive officers of the ACWW in the London office, however, neutrality at all costs was a high principle, even while bombs were exploding over London. Scarborough recounts that "[i]t is a remarkable fact that, looking through the boxes and files full of reports, letters and minutes which make up the material from which the history is constructed, you would not find one word about war or defence or aggression in any national or partisan sense." In her view, "the Central Office remained as impartial, pacific and constructive as a Quaker meeting."[95] However the correspondence that was exchanged between Watt and the London office was anything but peaceful. Reminiscent of the squabble over the Cornell relocation offer, Scarborough reports that

> [c]ables crossed the Atlantic as fast as in 1939 ... there was, however, no possible chance of reaching an understanding. *Defence* remained the theme. Talks bristled with angry references to Hitler and his brigands, to bullies, temper tantrums, and manifestations of aggressive, cruel, tyrannical, morbid personalities.[96]

That tone is not surprising given the fact that the conference found major funding from the Canadian minister of agriculture, who had just completed a term as minister of national war services. Moreover, one of the conference keynote speakers was H.R.H. Princess Juliana of the Netherlands, who had taken refuge in Canada. There was no way that the conference organizers or personnel were prepared to soft-peddle their stance that an all-out war effort was the only appropriate position. Unhappy with that decision, but realizing there would be no change in the wording of the conference theme, "the [ACWW] Central Office bowed its head and covered its ears."[97]

At the close of the conference, Watt acknowledged all of the participants by sending them a personal gift of potpourri that she had made herself. She sent a note with each sachet, explaining that

> [t]his potpourri contains: rose leaves from the bouquet sent to me by Gen. de Gaulle in thanks for our message to French Country Women; Rose-leaves from the garden of Carrie Chapman Catt; Cedar sprays from Kingsmere, Ottawa; Bitter-sweet from the Laurentian hills; Pepper seeds from Long Island, N.Y.; Bay-leaves from the Florida home of Mrs. Arlie Hopkins; Lavender flowers from Surrey, England, ... and my love. M.R. Watt.[98]

Watt's gift served to reinforce the significance that she placed on her personal experiences and contacts since all of the potpourri ingredients were items that she had personally gathered in the course of her travels. Sentimental and unique, Watt's gift symbolized the extent of her personal investment in her networks with high-profile individuals. It was also characteristic of the emotional bonds that frequently formed between participants in international work.[99]

Watt also wrote a friendly letter of thanks to Gardiner for his part in the conference and to tell him about some of the outcomes. "We are all most grateful for your participation in the proceedings," she told him.

> Not only did it add to our knowledge but it was inspiring to have a Minister of the Crown so ready to listen to others & yet keep his stated point; and we shall not forget how sympathetically you forge us all into your scheme of things. Thank you very much indeed.[100]

Watt told Gardiner how happy she was about the impact of the conference and the publicity it had received. "I am delighted with the completion of the Conference. The results have begun already. There are requests for arranging meetings along the border. The newspapers in USA are carrying reports given by returning delegates. Every mail brings congratulations even from Utah way!"[101] Watt went on to explain that after the conference they had decided to keep the organizing committee intact because they wanted to use it "as a further channel of communications" for cross-border cooperation, a sort of "coordinating committee of American and Canadian women for their defence problems." She assured the minister that "when there are developments, I will let you know at once."[102] Gardiner's response to Watt is difficult to judge, though he did write to acknowledge her gift, thanking her for the "little sack of leaves, representative of so many different countries."[103]

One of the developments that arose from the conference was that the proceedings were published under the auspices of the Canadian Department of Agriculture.[104] The booklet was to be circulated widely; indeed Watt assured Gardiner that the expense of printing it would be rewarded when she told him that the report would enjoy worldwide circulation. "I know you realize the most important contributions to the place of women in agriculture in wartime, were made at this conference. I know that other countries will appreciate this fact when they see the report."[105] Watt may have wanted to use the report to demonstrate to the ACWW constituent societies that she was still very much the active president of the organization, and that although England and the European countries were too embroiled in the war to take action she was providing leadership among the women of North America. Moreover, while the central office in London insisted on maintaining their pacifist principles, Watt was unabashedly declaring that the rural women of North American were proud to be playing their part to help win the war for the Allies.

When Watt channeled her considerable energies into the war effort, her tireless enthusiasm translated into some impressive and concrete contributions beyond the conference itself. Two examples serve to illustrate this success. First, an article in the *New York Times* in January 1941 described a project known as American Seeds for British Soil, and explained that Watt had first promoted the project in a talk she gave to women of the American Farm Bureau at their annual convention in December 1940.[106] The idea was that North American women would send vegetable seeds to England to help ensure an adequate food supply. According to ACWW sources, "[T]he seed distribution was showing excellent results in blockaded Britain and elsewhere. Large quantities had been sent from USA and Canada for use in European countries."[107] The first shipment of seeds, sent in February 1941, was estimated to be approximately two tons, and the Americans inquired about seed varieties that might be required for autumn sowing so that a second consignment could be prepared and dispatched.[108]

While the scale of North American generosity demonstrated in this operation was impressive, it did create problems on the receiving end. When the NFWI requested assistance from the British Ministry of Agriculture with the cost of distribution of the seeds, they were informed that no funds were available for that purpose. The central office of NFWI distributed the seeds to county federations, who in turn distributed them to local women through their WI branches. The counties and local institutes were expected to refund the cost of the distribution to the NFWI office. This arrangement led to countless problems, delays, and mix-ups. Some women complained of receiving the wrong type of seeds, others reported that the seeds arrived too late for planting, and others recounted their frustrations with the local arrangements.[109] Despite these logistical problems, the popularity of the seed shipment program reinforces the fact that Watt's inspirational leadership did motivate countless women to pitch in on the war effort. It was yet another way for women to express their personal commitment to internationalism through gestures of friendship and support.

A second initiative that bore the mark of Watt's persuasive speaking ability was her promotion of a program called the Letter Friends scheme. Beginning under the auspices of the NFWI in England and Wales, the idea was to encourage women to make international bonds on a personal level by signing up for an overseas pen pal. Although Watt was not personally responsible for running the program (it was first the offices of the NFWI, and later the ACWW, who dealt with the clerical logistics of matching women up with those from other countries), she did remain a dogged supporter of the concept. Speaking about the value of broadening their outlook and making links through this kind of personal correspondence, Watt saw these exchanges as a way to offer individual rural women a taste of what she herself relished in her own international travels. It was the personal contacts that she felt were most important for building and solidifying ties between women, and Watt was convinced that these small links would translate into larger bonds of internationalism between countries. The importance Watt placed on this kind of initiative was completely in step with the spirit of internationalism that Rupp observed when she said, "[T]o make a devoted friend from another nation represented one small victory for internationalism."[110] The scope of the program was very impressive. At the 1946 annual meeting of the ACWW, it was reported that "3,420 applications had been received, and 1,169 had already been put in touch with pen-friends. By midsummer 1946, there were in all about 20,000 country folk who were corresponding."[111] Results like those were a source of immense satisfaction for Watt because as the titular head of the ACWW organization, she could claim such results as her own, even though she was not the one doing the work on the frontlines.

As the war dragged on, Watt continued her relentless appeals to James Gardiner for funding and other forms of support. Her correspondence to him reveals that she was working on a book manuscript, hoping that the minister of agriculture would give his endorsement for her work by writing the foreword. Gardiner experienced two personal tragedies during the war years: his son died at Dieppe in 1942; and two years later, his grief-stricken wife committed suicide. Watt's requests for Gardiner's endorsement continued throughout this period until the spring of 1944, when she acknowledged with gratitude that her request for the foreword had been fulfilled. Gardiner had actually passed the writing task on to one of his staff members, and there is no evidence that Watt ever completed the book; if the manuscript was written, there is no trace of its publication.[112] Nevertheless, Watt's sense of her own importance was not diminished. She continued to offer her services to Gardiner's deputy minister, questioning who else could supply him with the kind of intelligence that she possessed because of her previous international work. In 1944 Watt wrote to Barton to return some materials she had borrowed from him for the preparation of her book. In her handwritten note accompanying the materials, she wrote,

> I am still available if you need me. I cannot but feel that my special experience in rural economics and sociology would be helpful – not to mention my knowledge of world conditions. I am wondering who is giving for instance information about the help that could be given by rural women organized in France Italy Belgium Holland and even Germany as I could![113]

Barton patiently replied, marvelling at the fact that Watt was so persistent in presenting herself as an expert in international affairs. The tone of his reply, however, indicates that he was trying to make Watt realize that new developments were unfolding, and that given her advanced age, she might not be equipped to deal with the rapidly changing international realities:

I see you are still as keen as ever to be in harness. There are so many developments pending at present that one has difficulty in knowing just what
form they are likely to take ... Just what provision may be made for the
service of women in the liberated countries I do not know at present. I am
not aware of any provision for this type of activity under UNRRA but, of
course, this organization has hardly begun to function pending the transfer of responsibility from the military priorities."[114]

Undaunted and indefatigable, Watt wrote back to Barton again in the
spring of 1945 to ask for financial help to attend the FWIC conference
in Victoria in June that year. In making her request, she revealed her
disapproval of the trend she observed of rural homemakers as consumers, not producers.[115] This is one of the clearest indications that Watt was
completely out of touch with the direction that consumer trends would
take at the end of the war and that she hoped to reverse it. The main
point of her letter, though, was to ask for financial help because, as she
explained, "I am anxious to attend this conference and to speak and
take part in discussions, but I find it difficult to manage financially."[116]
Barton replied to her request for funds to say that he could not help
her.[117] Clearly, the time for her to give advice to the officials in Ottawa
or to exert influence over the affairs of rural women had passed.

Watt's influence in ACWW circles was also waning. At the end of the
war the decision was taken to hold an ACWW convention in Amsterdam in 1947, the first since the 1939 London meeting.[118] Watt made her
arrangements to be part of that reunion, and the trip would be the last
overseas visit of her lifetime. She planned to use that occasion to inform
the ACWW delegates of her intention to resign the presidency (finally!),
and she wrote a letter explaining that her reasons for stepping down
were "not for reasons of health, or incapacity, or lack of interest, but
solely because I believe it would be in the best interests of our Society."[119]

Though she denied it, there is little doubt that age was a consideration in her decision; after all, she would mark her eightieth birthday
the following year. Despite her advanced age, upon her arrival in England around the time of the Amsterdam meeting, she offered to take up
the same feverish schedule of travelling and lecturing that had been
so familiar to her more than thirty years earlier. The July 1947 issue of
Home and Country published by the NFWI announced,

Mrs. Alfred Watt, M.B.E., founder of the Institutes in England and Wales,
is to be in England during the next six months and will be very pleased

to speak at W.I. meetings and gatherings and to meet old friends in the movement. Her subjects for talks include "The Canadian W.I.s Today and Yesterday," "U.S.A. Extension Service for Rural Women," and "The Associated Country Women of the World."[120]

Of course, Watt soon realized that she simply could not keep up the same pace that she had enjoyed in previous decades, and she issued a statement apologizing for the fact, saying, "I very much regret that I was unable to accept so very many of the kind invitations to speak at Institute gatherings, chiefly through lack of time. I also regret that I cannot accept any more at present."[121]

But there was more to Watt's resignation than age. The chief reason why she stepped down was realization on her part that the ACWW organization had become more complicated than she could ever have predicted. "Her cry, whether in her letters, her speeches or in her private conversations, was always the same: 'Keep the organization simple!' [But] in a world hideously complicated by war, it is almost impossible to keep anything simple."[122] Early in 1947, the ACWW had been granted "Consultative Status (Certificate B) under Article 71 of the Charter" of the United Nations.[123] Exactly what that new status would entail remained to be seen, but it was clear to everyone, even Watt herself, that she would not have a role going forward. Dorothy Drage described the conference this way: "For me, Amsterdam was a somewhat sad conference as Mrs. Watt's retirement meant the end of an era."[124]

Indeed, the era of Watt's involvement with the ACWW was over. Reflecting on that fact, Watt remarked that despite her limitations, she was very pleased that she had been able to make the trip. Speaking about her travels, and particularly the time she spent in England and Wales on that last visit, she said, "When I could go to meetings I had a very happy time."[125] What made her most happy, it seems, were the tributes that were paid to her by WI women. "The welcome clapping as I entered the door always warmed my heart and I went forward with my head in the air! Then the kind appreciation of my services, so often over-estimated, expressed in such glowing terms, still further swelled my pride so that I fear I shall never be modest about myself again."[126]

Of course, modesty had never been one of Watt's defining features, and that fact was particularly evident during the war years when she had constantly reiterated her own importance. From the moment she arrived back in Canada in 1939 she was both literally and figuratively distanced from the operations of the ACWW, yet Watt still insisted on being recognized as a key leader. In her correspondence with civil servants in Canada she presented herself as one who could provide government officials with strategic advice and insight into the international situation of rural women. Other sources reveal, however, that Watt was not as highly regarded nor as indispensable as she thought. Indeed, when she lost her bid to relocate the ACWW offices to America, it was a sign that she had also lost control of the affairs of the organization. While she busied herself with wartime activities in North America that inspired women to collect seeds and write letters to international pen pals, her colleagues in the London office worked to successfully regain financial stability and to position the ACWW to assume consultative status to the United Nations; something Watt had never envisioned. When she called for a return to earlier ways and the need to simplify the organization, it was clear that she was out of step with the future direction of the body she had worked so hard to create. As Rupp asserts, internationalism in the postwar era was expanding beyond the patterns that were familiar,[127] and Watt, who was very much a product of the past, would find it impossible to understand or appreciate the changes that were coming. While she continued to regard herself as the one most suited to give leadership to the ACWW, her real influence had waned considerably, and she was relegated to the position of figurehead. Her own advanced age and the complexities of the postwar world meant that this time, Watt would be unable to recast herself into a leading role. As the Amsterdam conference so clearly illustrated, the organization she helped to found had outgrown her. When she resigned the presidency in 1947, it was clear even to Watt herself that she no longer held the power or the influence that she had imagined.

In one of her last statements to the membership of the English and Welsh WIs in 1947, Watt said, "This is only *au revoir* as I cannot bear to think I may not come again."[128] But she would not travel again. Approaching eighty years of age when she returned to Canada from her Amsterdam trip in 1947, Watt was not in good health, yet she tried to maintain her independence as long as she could. At first she returned to the west coast, to enjoy Victoria with its familiar surroundings and amenable climate. In the summer of 1948, Watt's health took a turn for the worse and she was afflicted with a severe case of influenza-like symptoms. Her son Sholto wrote to the NFWI office in July 1948 explaining that he had just returned to Montreal after flying to visit his mother in Victoria. He was pleased to report that doctors expected her to make a full recovery and he was making plans for her to spend time at his home in Montreal that fall. He wrote to her friends at the NFWI office at his mother's request because, as he told them, "She particularly wanted me to let you know that the Women's Institutes are always very much in her heart. It is a great joy to her to read of their progress and to know that the movement is going well."[129]

Happily, after having endured three months of illness, Watt's health began to improve in early September 1948 after she moved to Montreal to be closer to her sons, and she enjoyed one of the highlights of her final days when the Canadian Women's Institutes presented an honorary life membership to her.[130] In making that presentation, some of the historical facts of Watt's life were erroneously construed, and while they might not seem like serious mistakes, it was typical of the kind of licence that would be taken with her story, as WI commemorations have invented traditions about her by "a process of selection that is both conscious and unconscious and arises from a wide variety of motivations and circumstances."[131] In September 1948, Mrs. A.C. Macmillan, president of the FWIC, and Mrs. A.E. Abercrombie, director of publicity of the FWIC met Watt in Montreal to have lunch with her at the Mount Royal Hotel. After the meal, "at Mrs. Watt's request they repaired to her son's apartment where she was staying, and there, Mrs. Macmillan presented the Life-Membership."[132] Always appreciative when her accomplishments were recognized, this quiet little ceremony was one that would have pleased Watt very much. In making the presentation, Watt's admirers outlined her lifetime service in the WI movement and captured several aspects of Watt's life that would continue to be repeated in WI circles for years to come. The citation read:

> We find from the records, that your interest in rural women has extended over a long period of time. When, nearly half a century ago, you went as a bride to William Head, B.C., you soon joined the Women's Institute Branch at Metchosin, a farming community nearby, and later encouraged the BCWI women to organize provincially. In 1913, on the death of your husband, Dr. Watt, you took your two small sons to England to live, and there set to work organizing Women's Institutes throughout the land. Today there are more than 6000 Institute branches in England and Wales and the numbers are increasing, and are being recognized as carrying much weight in public affairs.[133]

When Watt first moved to BC in 1893 (almost 55 years before this presentation was made), she lived in Victoria, not William Head. Moreover, her involvement with the WI did not begin "soon after her arrival"; it was a full sixteen years after she arrived that the first WI in BC began in

1909. Finally, although the citation claimed that Watt moved to England in 1913 with her "two *small* sons," Robin Watt was seventeen years of age and would soon enlist in the army.

During the time she spent in Montreal, Watt maintained regular correspondence with Frances Farrer, secretary to the NFWI, who had written to send the good wishes of the NFWI executive for her speedy recuperation. Watt appreciated the gesture and replied with affection, "Dear Fanny, This is just to thank you for your kindly thought of me during my illness and to say that I am at last beginning to get better. Your cable certainly gave me a turn for the better when I was having very depressing days."[134] As part of that ongoing exchange, it is clear that Watt took pleasure in thinking about her connections to the WI and ACWW in London. Watt told Farrer that she was still unable to write very much but she promised "as soon as I feel fit I will send a message, partly of thanks, to the English Women's Institutes, which I hope you can find space to publish."[135] Farrer assured Watt in late September that "when you are well enough to send a message we shall be delighted to publish this in Home and Country."[136] Happy to oblige, Watt set to work on preparing some remarks for the New Year's issue of 1949 to greet the WI membership. In her reflections, she wrote about how proud she had been to see the strength of the WI when she had visited in 1947 in connection with her trip to Amsterdam. She was impressed with the organizational aspects of the movement, and the fact that WI had "become a part of the national life and structure." On a more personal note she expressed to Farrer that she had been "deeply touched" by the welcome she had received on her visit to England. She told her friend that she was

> more than ever thankful that I had chosen the Women's Institutes for my life work. I can never tell what it has all meant to me. Indeed I have received much more than I have given … May I thank from my heart all those of you who made my last stay in England of dear and sweet remembrance.[137]

Unfortunately Watt's message could only be published posthumously. It was her son Sholto who broke the sad news to the NFWI office in London in a telegram written on November 30, 1948, where he simply stated,

> Deeply regret to inform you my mother Mrs. Alfred Watt died suddenly heart attack today stop She spent last three months with me happy and

apparently recovering from serious summer illness stop She spoke often and lovingly of Women's Institutes of United Kingdom and was preparing New Year message of warm good wishes stop She found her greatest happiness in her Institute work and I can state that her prayers always included all members of the movement whom she considered sisters and friends.[138]

Arrangements for the funeral and memorial service were shared by Sholto and his brother Robin, who decided on a simple service and interment in Montreal.

At the same time, the Watt brothers requested that the NFWI might want to arrange for a memorial service in London so that their mother's WI associates and colleagues in the UK could gather to honour her memory. In a telegram to the NFWI president on December 1, Sholto reported that his mother had been "buried quietly in Montreal" and that there also would be a memorial service in Victoria. Then he asked, "Could you arrange memorial ceremony London for mothers many dear friends stop If difficult please inform me and I will ask Canada House undertake it stop But believe Women's Institutes much nearer mothers heart."[139] That seemingly simple request actually did prove to be difficult and it led to no small degree of controversy and complication. Claiming that the NFWI could not be responsible for hosting such a gathering, the national Executive Committee declined to make the arrangements.

Even so, a service was held on December 14, presumably arranged, as Sholto alternatively suggested, through Canada House. Though the NFWI declined to organize the gathering, their office did help to promote it by sending a letter to all the county secretaries of the Institutes throughout the country, announcing, "A memorial Service will be held at St. Martin-in-the-Fields, Trafalgar Square, London, at 12 noon on Tuesday, December 14th. Mrs. Watt's relations hope very much that Women's Institute members will attend. Notices of the Service will appear in 'The Times' and 'The Daily Telegraph.'"[140] A report of that service also appeared in the next issue of *Home and Country* providing details of the event for those who had been unable to attend.[141]

The NFWI's decision not to take on the arrangements for their founder's memorial service is puzzling. At a meeting of the NFWI executive held two days after the memorial service, Lady Albemarle, NFWI chairman, "reported that Mr. [Sholto] Watt had asked the NFWI to sponsor a Memorial Service but it had been explained to him that it would not be possible for the NFWI to do this."[142] The minutes of that meeting do not elaborate on precisely why it was "not possible to do this," but the rationale became clearer just a few weeks later. The minutes of the February 1949 meeting of the executive reveal that the NFWI had received a letter from some WI members "deprecating the fact that the National Federation Exec Comm had not accepted the responsibility of arranging a Memorial Service for Mrs. Alfred Watt, and expressing disappointment that such short notice had been given of the service."[143] Exactly who lodged that complaint is not clear, but in response to it, "[t]he secretary was asked in the reply to repeat that Exec considered it would have been an infringement of our non-sectarian rule to arrange the service, and to stress the responsibility felt by the Exec Comm for the correct interpretation of our rules."[144]

Evidently, "following the rule" of promoting only non-sectarian activities, the NFWI executive felt it could not organize a Christian church service even if that occasion was in honour of the movement's own founder. The question about whether or not to participate in religious events did arise with some regularity for the NFWI when branch secretaries frequently wrote to the WI headquarters to ask whether or not it would be appropriate for their local WI to attend Thanksgiving services at a church for example, or whether the local WI might participate in fundraising drives for local church renovations. Whenever the issue arose, the national executive consistently took a very conservative stance, always saying no to such inquiries and citing the principle of remaining non-sectarian. The occasion of Watt's memorial service was a real test of this conviction, but consistent with their previous position, the NFWI Executive Committee again interpreted the non-sectarian "rule" as a binding one to which no exception should be made, not even on the occasion of their own founder's death and memorial service.

Still, there might have been more at stake than a simple adherence to a principle. The fact that Watt had alienated herself from many of her English colleagues was no secret. In the official announcement of Watt's death and memorial service that was published in the January 1949 issue of *Home and Country*, the description of Watt's leadership style was far from flattering. For example, one paragraph read, "There was something of the autocrat about Mrs. Watt; she was so sure that *her* way was the best that she had a tendency to override the wishes of her committee, convinced that at heart they really agreed with her, whatever opinions they might have expressed."[145] It seems odd that such a frank description of Watt's difficult personality was chosen for inclusion in a memorial tribute. Evidently when the time came to deliberate about whether or not to organize a memorial service for Watt, the members of the Executive Committee refused to be bullied into acting against their wishes as Watt had frequently convinced people to do during her lifetime. Decision makers cited their adherence to the principle of non-sectarianism, but for those who had frequently lost battles against Watt's iron will in the past, there must have been some sense of vindication in the logic of their official refusal to organize the memorial service.

It would be misleading however, to conclude that Watt was not respected or appreciated by NFWI leaders. At the next annual general meeting held at the Royal Albert Hall in London in June 1949, the chairman acknowledged Watt's role among rural women both internationally and in Britain itself. Beginning with the larger picture, delegates were reminded that

> Country Women all over the world have sustained a loss during this year by the death of Mrs. Watt, a loss which is felt personally by many people in many lands. This courageous, dynamic woman, by the clearness of her vision and her untiring persistent work, succeeded during her life's span not only in inspiring many national associations of country women, but in uniting them in one great international movement.[146]

The chairman also noted that the ACWW had recently been granted consultative status by the United Nations, meaning that "owing to Mrs. Watt's farsightedness the voice of country women is heard to the counsels of the nations for the first time in world history."[147] At the same time, the NFWI leadership also acknowledged the contribution that Watt brought to British rural women specifically. After recounting her international achievements, she continued,

> But to us here today she stood in a nearer and dearer relationship. It was she who brought to us from Canada a gift which has been an incalculable enrichment to our national life, and which … has done more for the countryside than any other single factor during this century – she brought us the idea of Women's Institutes; and it is for this above all else that we pay tribute to her today.[148]

How to pay adequate tribute to Watt was a question that arose frequently during NFWI business meetings for the next few years, and these discussions deserve some historical analysis. With the initial controversy about organizing the memorial service behind them, the next item up for debate was the question of how Watt's contribution to the British WI and the ACWW should be commemorated. At the January 1949 meeting of the International Sub-Committee of the NFWI, members observed a moment of silence in honour of Watt, but they referred the matter of creating a suitable memorial to the Executive Committee.[149] The following month, the Executive Committee considered a letter from Dyserth WI suggesting a memorial for Watt, but curiously, the minutes record that "it was finally agreed that no general appeal [for donations] should be made."[150] Again, this decision not to establish a memorial fund to mark Watt's memory seems odd. Why would the organization not want to ask friends and colleagues to make donations to a memorial fund in honour of their founder? That suggestion stands in stark contrast with the responses they made to the deaths of other key figures in the WI movement where special funds quickly were established to mark the fondness and honour attributed to women such as Lady Denman, Grace Hadow, and Elsie Zimmern.[151]

Even though it had been almost ten years since Watt had been actively involved in the day-to-day affairs of the ACWW and longer still since she had worked closely with the Executive Committee of the NFWI, it quickly became apparent that the decision makers underestimated the esteem that British women held for Watt. The controversy that arose about the commemoration once again reinforces the fact that Watt was estranged from some of the powerful decision makers by the time of her death. Indeed, local WI groups and county federations made several suggestions to the NFWI about what they might arrange to commemorate and honour their founder. One particularly popular idea was to create a facility in London to accommodate women travellers who needed short-term lodgings; and not surprisingly, the recommendation came from WI members outside of London. The idea to create such a facility had been on the table for more than two years at the time of Watt's death,[152] but the idea of a hostel was revived again after Watt's death when several women wrote in to say that they thought that such a facility would be a very fitting memorial to Watt, who had worked so tirelessly to establish branches across the country and who had served for such a long time as a member of the Executive Committee of the NFWI, faithfully attending meetings in London.[153]

In fact, though, the postwar complications of finding a suitable location for a hostel in London and then financing, staffing, and maintaining such a facility were not something that the NFWI wanted to manage. Indeed, by the late 1940s, the attentions of the organization were directed elsewhere because of the NFWI's recent acquisition of a property eight miles south of Oxford that would become Denman College, a short-term residential adult-education facility for WI members. In her history of the college, Anne Stamper described the property and the timing that led the NFWI to purchase it:

> [In] November 1945 they found Marcham Park in the village of Marcham near Abingdon … It had come on the market de-requisitioned from the Air Ministry, and was a late Georgian mansion in a hundred acres of parkland. There were a small lake and two cottages and a large walled kitchen garden and it seemed to meet all the requirements.[154]

The purchase price of £16,000 was, of course, only the first expense of many because extensive renovations would be required before the property and its facilities could be suitably modified for the WI's use. Accordingly, the NFWI set the goal of raising £60,000, and understandably, this capital campaign demanded the organization's full attention in the coming years.[155]

Given the financial burden of raising money for Denman College, the NFWI was being particularly conservative in its fiscal matters at the time of Watt's death, which serves to explain the decision not to launch a separate and competing appeal for a memorial fund. With the newly acquired property, it was logical that the NFWI might find some suitable way to honour Watt as part of that site. They reasoned that branch members from all over the country would come to the new facility to take courses on a variety of topics, and given Watt's attention to training and educating rural women, Denman seemed to be a very appropriate place to honour her memory. Yet even after the decision was taken to include some memorial to Watt at Denman, the NFWI remained very cautious about how best to do this. They were not convinced that any significant amount of money would come in as a tribute to Watt, and therefore they settled on a modest project that would not jeopardize the solvency of the NFWI or the new college. On the Marcham Park property, there was a walkway lined with lime trees, and in February 1949, it was decided that Watt could be suitably memorialized by "naming the new avenue at Denman College after her."[156] Given that the landscape planning was already underway, the London committee determined this was a good solution to their problem of what to do in Watt's memory and how to finance it in case the donations did not materialize. As part of the rejuvenation of the Denman College grounds, the plan was to cut the existing lime trees down because of their age and sell the wood for profit. Wood from lime trees had a significant market value because of its specialized use in the creation of musical instruments, and the proceeds from that sale would cover the purchase of young lime trees to replant the walkway. In other words, there was no financial risk involved.

With that plan all worked out, the NFWI reversed its earlier decision not to publish an appeal for memorial funds, and the following announcement appeared in the *Home and Country* in June 1949: "Institutes are reminded of the Fund which has been opened to provide a memorial to the late Mrs. Watt. The memorial will take the form of an avenue of Lime Trees at Denman College. Contributions should be sent to this office marked 'Watt Memorial.'"[157] In response, donations poured in to the London office from virtually every county across England, with the contributions, totalling more than £439. That sum clearly exceeded committee members' expectations. In death, as in life, Watt enjoyed greater popularity among the grassroots membership than she did among the committee members in London. The grounds committee of Denman arranged for the sale of the wood, which netted £370. This meant that with more than £800 in hand, the NFWI was well placed to finance the planting of new trees at a total cost of only £300. The remaining funds earmarked for the Watt memorial were used to enhance the pathway between the two rows of trees and to make improvements to the herb garden.[158] Almost sixty years later, the lime tree walk still stands as a tribute to Watt's memory, although in 2008 it was not clearly marked as such.[159]

Plans for a second memorial to Watt at Denman College were put in motion when, in the fall of 1949, the NFWI executive asked Watt's sons if they could provide a good portrait of their mother that would hang in the college as a tribute to her role as the founder of the British Women's Institutes.[160] The brothers consulted one another, and several weeks later, Sholto Watt replied to apologize for and explain the brothers' delay in responding:

My brother and I have been looking around for something suitable of mother, and we think the best thing is for Robin to work over one of his sketches. He has started on that and says he thinks he will have a good likeness. I am afraid there is a little delay as Robin was away in Toronto.

However, we think this will be better than a photograph. We shall be very happy to think that it will be on the walls at Denman College.[161]

Madge Watt would no doubt have been very pleased to know that her accomplished artist son had agreed to create this new portrait and that it would hang in a place of honour at Denman College. Writing to Farrer when he was completing the painting a few weeks later, Robin Watt gave his suggestions about framing and revealed the creative licence he had taken in producing this likeness of his mother.

I would suggest a putty coloured frame with a little gold showing through: nothing too dark or too strong in colour as the portrait is of necessity rather tentative, unfortunately I never did a recent portrait of her, but perhaps it is just as well as she was rather haggard towards the end, and I prefer to remember her as she was in her bustling prime![162]

The portrait was completed in the spring of 1950, and in early June, Farrer wrote to Robin Watt advising him that the portrait had arrived safely and had been shipped to Denman College for installation. Some mystery surrounds this portrait because at the time of writing, it is was not hanging at Denman College, and efforts to locate its whereabouts did not turn up any portrait in storage either.[163]

The third and perhaps most significant opportunity to commemorate Watt in Britain arose in 1952 when Fanny Farrer took on the task of writing a biographical entry about her for the *Dictionary of National Biography*.[164] When she corresponded with Watt's sons during the process of completing the task, Sholto replied to Farrer to thank her for writing the entry and he concluded his letter by saying that his mother "would have been so very proud to be included in the national reference work."[165] In that same letter he also gave some insight about his mother that might help to explain why Madge Watt's relationships with her British colleagues were not always problem-free. Sholto explained that his mother "deeply loved England, even if perhaps she never fully understood it."[166] While it is not clear what Sholto meant by the remark about his mother's lack of understanding about England, it seems clear that given her difficult personality, her son was ready to concede that she herself might have been part of the problem.

Meanwhile, Watt's Canadian colleagues made their own plans for commemorating her life. Several projects launched simultaneously.

The first was a fund to which "each member of the Women's Institutes and Homemakers' Clubs across Canada is to be asked to donate 10c ... the interest from which is to be used to send a representative to the Triennial of ACWW."[167] The second tribute came from the Quebec Women's Institute in the form of a scholarship in Watt's memory.[168] Given the importance that Watt placed on travelling to the international meetings and to higher education for women, these two memorials were particularly apt. The third tribute was designed to mark the international scope of Watt's work, and her dedication to the cause of world peace through establishing ties of friendship between various countries. Rural women from both Canada and the United States worked together to create a plot in Watt's memory within the International Peace Garden on the border between the two countries.[169] The International Peace Garden is a 2,339-acre botanical garden located between Manitoba and North Dakota, approximately 70 miles south of Brandon, Manitoba, and 106 miles northeast of Minot, North Dakota.[170] By July 1952, the FWIC was pleased to report that a memorial cairn and bird bath were to be placed in the FWIC plot of the peace garden in honour of Watt,[171] and by the following year, it was established that each provincial organization of rural women throughout Canada was expected to donate towards the Peace Garden Project.[172] The installation was completed in time for a dedication service to take place as part of the FWIC biennial meeting held in Winnipeg in June 1955.[173]

The speech on the occasion of this dedication shows that in North America, there was a definite tone of celebration about the fact that Watt occupied the place of a hero in the eyes of her Canadian admirers. Mrs. Stella Gummow, superintendent of the BC Women's Institutes, "who had known Mrs. Watt well," spoke in her honour, claiming that throughout

> her whole lifetime she labored in the cause of peace through understanding. Her life work was to bring the women of the world together to understand and know each other, to break down barriers of suspicion and distrust and to work together. She was a great leader, a woman with vision and courage, who saw the need of a united organization of countrywomen and who was able to bring this dream to fruition.[174]

Such a public occasion of celebration and dedication is, of course, a time for eulogizing, but it is significant to note that the more difficult aspects of Watt's personal leadership style and the conflicts that attended her years of service to the WI and ACWW were not mentioned at all in the North American commemoration. These competing versions of how Watt conducted herself reinforce the fact that WI and ACWW workers on the two sides of the Atlantic experienced very different personae where Watt was concerned. In British circles, she was the difficult, even autocratic leader, whose relationships with co-workers were often strained. But on Canadian soil and in North American circles, she was regarded differently – as the one who almost single-handedly worked ·to establish her personal vision of a worldwide association for rural women.

Putting Watt at the centre of the creation of the ACWW made it seem like she was the sole driving force behind the movement, and this was understandably offensive to English women who worked behind the scenes to keep the organization on a stable financial footing when Watt's dreams and plans (not to mention her extravagant international travels) threatened the very survival and continuation of the organization. Elsie Zimmern, who is credited with saving the ACWW from financial ruin during the war years, was gracious in her reminiscences of Watt, when she commented on her "force and drive." Zimmern recalled about Watt that

> we learnt to appreciate her boundless energy and persistence, which never let her take "no" for an answer. She carried us along by the force of her personality, she insisted on starting an endowment fund when we had barely enough to pay our way on publishing a sixteen-page "Country-woman" which was to make our association independent of other sources of income. Mrs. Watt travelled widely for ACWW; ... It can be truly said that Mrs. Watt made the initials ACWW well known in many countries, and during the war she valiantly kept the flag flying in Canada and the United States.[175]

What Zimmern discreetly avoided doing in her comments was to make any mention of how much strain Watt's enthusiasm and travels put on the other ACWW executive members, and especially Zimmern herself as she worked to re-establish solvency for the ACWW in the wake of Watt's world tour in 1936–7, her unrealistic predictions about the ACWW journal, and the unmet expenses after the 1939 London conference.

When Zimmern died in April 1967 at the age of 91, opinions about her were more unanimous and more positive. One tribute to Zimmern celebrated that "[s]he broke down the grand ideas emanating from Mrs.

Watt's brilliant vision and genius and translated them into a working pattern." Characterized by thoroughness and humility, to Zimmern, "nothing was too unimportant for her to deal with. Completely calm and unflustered, whether Mrs. Watt was agitating or the typists in a flap or bombs falling during the war, Miss Zimmern tenaciously dealt with the matter in hand."[176] When she passed away, the ACWW moved quickly to establish the Elsie Zimmern Memorial Fund in her honour, with money to be raised by ACWW members, and "the interest from the invested capital to be used for training in organization and leadership." According to one of her close associates, a fund geared to leadership training was a very appropriate way to honour Zimmern because "she could train people better than anyone I know and she organized and ran the Liaison Committee and its office in London on a shoe string in the first tentative years of ACWW."[177]

The contrasting ways that Watt and Zimmern were memorialized speak volumes about their different personalities and the contributions they were perceived to have made to the ACWW. While it is clear that Watt was the public speaker who loved to perform before crowds and share her boundless enthusiasm for the international organization, it was Zimmern who quietly held things together at the London office, bringing a more pragmatic approach to the fledgling ACWW. How their two very different contributions and personalities were memorialized presents a most interesting case study of biography and the performed self. Watt won accolades from crowds of women while Zimmern built relationships one on one. Both women were committed to the internationalist ideal, but they acted out that commitment in very different ways. Canadians celebrated Watt's achievements abroad because her successes were a point of national pride, in step with Canada's postwar rise to middle-power status on the world stage.

Interpreting the Significance of Madge Watt

In 2007 Parks Canada designated Madge Watt as a person of national historic significance, citing the fact that she was a "key driving force in the foundation of the Associated Country Women of the World (ACWW) in 1933, first president from 1933 to 1947."[1] The application requesting this designation came from a group of BC Women's Institute members, and after historians at Parks Canada completed background research, it was determined that Watt was indeed worthy of this prestigious designation. With that decision, Watt joined an elite group of just over seventy Canadian women who have been so designated; in her case, her work was recognized in the category of "building social and community life/community organizations/education and social well being."[2] At the time of writing no plaque had yet been installed, although the Parks Canada website did indicate that a plaque was proposed to be erected in Metchosin, BC, where Watt had lived for almost twenty years before she moved to England in 1913.

Writing about historical heroes, Alan Gordon has argued that such figures are "historical constructs,"[3] meaning that the interpretations of their lives are mutable, due to shifting representations and the changing context of those who ascribe the meanings. Gordon explored Jacques Cartier and found that over time Cartier's significance was broadened from "discoverer of Quebec" to "the discovery of Canada" to align with changing political perceptions and sensibilities.[4] In another example of this same phenomenon, Norman Knowles studied the Ontario Loyalists and observed that "in the pluralistic Ontario of the late twentieth century, the Loyalists were reinvented as the nation's first refugees and the founders of multiculturalism."[5] Knowles concluded that the monuments that were erected to honour the Loyalists "rarely sought to commemorate an objective past" but rather "they celebrated a version of the past that reflected the values, attitudes, and objectives of their promoters. Aimed at a wide audience, monuments had a didactic role in communicating traditions and beliefs from generation to generation ..."[6] The point here is not to draw parallels between Madge Watt and Cartier or Watt and the Loyalists, but rather to consider the questions of how to understand the historical representations that have been made about her.

As the preceding chapters have demonstrated, Watt occupied an astonishing variety of roles throughout her lifetime, manifesting what biographical theorists call "multiple selves," and therefore, it is not surprising that details about Watt's life and significance are not easily reconstructed. How she should be remembered is subject to the problem of contested representations. Many questions arise in connection with the task of interpreting Watt's life, including whose version of that life should be the "official" one, which part or parts of her life should be highlighted, and what value, significance, and meaning should be attached to her involvements and achievements. Depending on which sources are considered and which individuals are consulted, the answers vary. Those whose knowledge of Watt comes through association with the Women's Institutes and ACWW are, for the most part, unaware of her university life and her subsequent writing career. Those whose chief interests are the history of higher education for women and/or Canadian literary history are usually surprised to learn of Watt's influence later in life through her close association with rural women's organizations. Any one of these phases of her life seems to stand alone as a story in and of itself and might lead to different conclusions about her historic significance.

The competing interpretations of Watt's life reflect the dynamic nature of historical interpretation and provide evidence of Watt's "usefulness," both for historians of women and for participants in rural women's organizations. There are three Canadian sites dedicated to her memory (not counting the proposed Metchosin plaque) and each one of them illustrates the perplexing problems that arise about how to preserve the memory of Madge Watt and how to interpret her achievements. The first is a historic plaque that is located in Collingwood, Ontario, where Madge Robertson Watt was born in 1868. The second is a cairn located in Fort Erie, Ontario, near the international Peace Bridge where, as president of the ACWW, Watt welcomed international delegates to Canada following the 1936 triennial meeting in Washington.

At that site Watt herself unveiled a plaque celebrating the tradition of peaceful relations between Canada and the United States. The third is Watt's gravesite at Mount Royal Cemetery in Montreal, the city where she had been staying at the time of her death. Each one of these three sites has been subject to reinterpretation and refurbishment since its original installation, and the tales of those changing perspectives and restoration efforts shed important light on the question of how Watt has been and should be commemorated and the meanings attached to her life by rural women's organizations. Considering each one of the three markers of Watt's life is instructive for understanding more about the woman herself and about the historical process of interpreting her. Thus, we turn to the plaque, the cairn, and the gravesite.[7]

In 1957, when enthusiasm for the new historical marking program in Ontario was still gaining in popularity, local WI women from Watt's hometown lobbied for the creation of a historic plaque to mark Watt's historical significance. Public historian Paul Litt has written about the process and the problems associated with fixing interpretations and attributing social meaning to places, people, and events by using historical markers.[8] The story of the plaque that was erected to commemorate Watt in her hometown makes a wonderful case study for the interpretive problems that Litt raised in that article because the marker has been removed, recast, reinterpreted, and reinstalled. Members from two different Women's Institute groups in Collingwood, Ontario, each wrote to the Archaeological and Historic Sites Board of Ontario (AHSBO). First, the Georgian Women's Institute, which claimed that Watt had been a member of their group,[9] asked "for some information concerning the erection of a plaque on a house here were [sic] a very famous lady was born."[10] Meanwhile, the Mrs. Alfred Watt Memorial Institute explained in their letter, written just three weeks later, that they had "a personal interest in this plaque as our Institute is named in her memory."[11]

At a meeting on June 24, 1957, the AHSBO approved in principle the request for a plaque, thanks in part to one board member in particular, Mrs. J.R. Futcher, who had served as president of the Federated Women's Institutes of Ontario (FWIO) from 1947 to 50.[12] Futcher was the kind of advocate that Litt referred to when he observed that the board included members of the public who "were being accommodated politically by the sites board apparatus," and who represented various interest groups including "women's organizations, business, and various religious denominations."[13] Yet the fact that these women succeeded in lobbying for a plaque devoted to a female subject was a rare accomplishment, because Litt estimates that even twenty years later, only about 5.1 percent of Ontario's historical plaques were devoted to women's history themes.

In order to prepare the text for the plaque, the AHSBO asked the Collingwood WI members to assist them by providing historical facts and details from local sources about Watt and her work. Specifically, the AHSBO wanted to know about

> the exact period during which she lived in the Collingwood house, when she entered the Women's Institutes, what offices she held, the exact con- nection between the Women's Institutes of Canada and The Associated Countrywomen of the World and so on. Incidentally, when was the house in question built and would the owner be in favour of a plaque on the property?[14]

These were very important questions indeed, and Women's Institutes across Ontario have taken particular interest in local history, so mem- bers were happy to comply with the AHSBO request for content.[15] Only later on would it become clear that rather than trusting local research, a more thorough investigation of those questions should have been undertaken.

The text of the plaque, created by the AHSBO, was approved by the Georgian WI who wanted to include the fact that Watt had been a mem- ber of the Georgian branch, but the AHSBO patiently explained that space was limited, and so that kind of information had to be left off.[16] Convinced of Watt's historic significance and satisfied by the infor- mation provided to them, the AHSBO proceeded with the creation of the plaque and made plans for its installation. The text that all parties agreed to was:

ASSOCIATED COUNTRY WOMEN OF THE WORLD

> The first Women's Institute was organized in 1897 by Mrs. Adelaide Hood- less and a group of rural women at Stoney Creek, Ontario, with the aim of home and self improvement. This movement grew rapidly throughout Canada, and in 1914, Mrs. Alfred Watt (1867–1948), who was born in this house, carried the idea to England whence it spread to many other coun- tries. In 1933, at a meeting in Stockholm, Sweden, rural women's organiza- tions throughout the world united to form the Associated Country Women of the World. Elected its first president, Mrs. Watt served until 1947.[17]

The plaque, on the front lawn of the house at 63 Maple Street, was unveiled in the summer of 1958 as part of the town's centennial celebrations while many local dignitaries and WI members were on hand to witness the event. Norman Knowles has observed that historical monuments provide "a sense of rootedness and tradition at a time when urban growth and change raised serious questions about future community stability."[18] For the town of Collingwood and local WI women, it was a proud day.

A few years later, several significant errors in the text were discovered, revealing that the AHSBO's initial questions about sources and proof should have been more thoroughly investigated. First, while the plaque at 63 Maple Street declared that Watt "was born in this house," that turned out to be false. The matter came to light when, with the excitement of Canada's centennial celebrations in the air, the Federated Women's Institutes of Ontario purchased the Maple Street property in 1967, with the idea of creating a historic site where WI members from across the country and around the world could visit Watt's birthplace. Elsie Bell, a WI member who had made some of the initial inquiries ten years before about how to get a plaque created and installed, was the first to inform the AHSBO about the error. Now serving as a provincial board member for the WI, she explained that the Federated Women's Institutes of Ontario "had purchased the property with the idea of making this house an historic site. When we searched back to the date of the house it was built in 1935 and Mrs. Watt wasn't born in the existing house. So we just couldn't have the house as historic."[19]

Hoping to redeem the situation, Bell suggested that the plaque might be corrected. "Would it be much of a job," she wondered, "to have the words 'this house' removed from the plaque and the word 'Collingwood' engraved where the other words are?" At the same time, she suggested that a relocation of the plaque might be in order. "We feel this plaque would be seen by many more Women's Institute members if it were moved to the grounds of the Collingwood Museum as it serves no purpose where it is now because the house is a new one where the plaque is."[20] While the Robertson family had lived at that street address when Madge was born there in 1868, the existing house was clearly not the original one.

When the FWIO purchased the property in good faith, they made an honest yet serious mistake, but it was not the only mistake associated with this plaque. In the text of the plaque, Watt's birth date was erroneously engraved as 1867, when in fact she was born in 1868. A further problem was associated with the date 1914, when Watt allegedly "carried the idea to England." In fact, Watt arrived in England in 1913, after the death of her husband, and the first WI in the UK was established in Wales (not England), in 1915, not 1914. However it was the location of the plaque and date of the house's construction that tipped the balance in favour of removing the plaque. Still, no immediate action was taken until the summer of 1978, when the new owner of the house hired a lawyer to deal with the AHSBO on the matter of removing the plaque from her property. Beyond the nuisance of having tourist and women's groups traipsing across her lawn for photo opportunities at the site of the plaque and taking unauthorized pictures of her house, the property owner's complaint centred on the fact that the plaque should never have been erected there in the first place. The lawyer, in researching the case, spoke to people with some expertise in local history to confirm the error of location. He reported, that he had learned from the "head of the Museum Board that Mrs. Watt was not, in fact, born in the house in question. Thank you for your co-operation in this matter."[21]

The errors on the plaque and the need to remove it were an embarrassment to both the AHSBO and the local advocates who had first suggested its creation. Local members of the WI were concerned about the fate of the plaque, and made inquiries about whether it might be displayed in the museum anyway, as evidence of the importance of Mrs. Watt, the Women's Institutes, and Collingwood's place in the movement's history. As Litt explains, the disposal of old plaques, particularly those found to contain errors of fact, is usually done discreetly, and so the request to retrieve the discarded plaque, let alone to display it anew, had little chance of coming to pass.[22]

Local WI women were persistent in their campaign for a replacement plaque, and in the spring of 1990, Collingwood's *Enterprise Bulletin* newspaper published a photograph of three women smiling proudly beside the new and improved plaque, including Watt's niece, Bethia Elliott; Tracy Marsh, the director/curator of the Collingwood Museum who gave the new plaque a home on the museum grounds; and Donna Lowe, the president of the local WI branch. The fact that it was only three women who were featured with the plaque indicated that this was not such a momentous occasion as the 1958 installation had been. Correcting an error more than thirty years after the fact was an important thing to do, but not an occasion that drew politicians and clergymen as the original occasion had done. The novelty of the plaque program was past, and the AHSBO had been absorbed in 1974 by a new provincial government agency, the Ontario Heritage Foundation (OHF).[23] Moreover, by then the Women's Institute movement had also passed its height of popularity.

The text of the new plaque was a further indicator of changing times and changing interpretations around Mrs. Watt and the ACWW. The new text read:

> A non-political international women's organization, the Associated Country Women of the World was formed largely through the efforts of Margaret Watt, a Collingwood native. Mrs. Watt was a member of the Women's Institute, a Canadian association devoted to the concerns of rural women, and she introduced the organization to Great Britain during World War I to help in work to counteract food shortages. With the expansion of the Women's Institute movement to Commonwealth and European countries after the war, Mrs. Watt began to advocate the establishment of an international alliance. Finally in 1933 in Stockholm, Sweden rural women's organizations including the Women's Institute united to form the Associated Country Women of the World. Mrs. Watt, by then a Member of the British Empire, was elected the body's first president.[24]

This second version of the plaque contained significant revisions from the first one. To avoid the controversy about the Watts' home on Maple Street, there was no mention of the birthplace except to say that Watt was "a Collingwood native." Neither was any date given for Watt's birth, an omission that deftly side-stepped the problem of resolving the differences between official records and other local sources. Similarly, by describing the creation of the WI in Great Britain as an event that occurred during World War I, the plaque avoided the controversy of pinning down the exact date of the creation of the British WI, along with the problems and setbacks that occurred in the process. By changing the wording from "England" to "Great Britain," the new plaque more accurately reflected that the first WI in the UK was created in Wales, not England. This new version reflected the fact that while the ACWW brought together existing rural women's organizations, Watt had not spread the WI movement around the world single-handedly. By simply stating that Watt served as the first president of the ACWW, and not saying how long she stayed in that role, the new plaque discreetly avoided the issue of Watt clinging to power throughout World War Two and the controversy she caused in the last years of her presidency.

Two other significant aspects of the new plaque reveal the context in which it was created. First, the new plaque was bilingual, reflecting the Ontario government's new language policies. Although Watt knew French from her university days, she never worked in French among the WI of Ontario, British Columbia, or Great Britain. She did attend meetings in Europe (Belgium and France) where the proceedings were in French, but though translating the plaque's text into French was a priority for provincial government, it certainly was not for the local women who had advocated for the new version to be created. Second, the new text was a sign of the times in the way that it referred to Watt. The first time she is mentioned in the text, she is referred to as "Margaret Watt," and subsequently as "Mrs. Watt." This was a point of controversy during the drafting of the text because WI members insisted that she should be called "Mrs. Alfred Watt," the name that she used in all her formal correspondence and the name with which rural women around the world were familiar. However, including the husband's name to refer to such a prominent woman did not seem right to the OHF researchers who drafted the text. "Referring to … Mrs. Alfred Watt will increasingly be considered an anachronism," one of them mused, and therefore, "My own inclination is to drop the Mrs. altogether and certainly the Alfred." In deference to the WI members, researchers conceded that although the use of "Mrs." "will increasingly be seen as a peculiarity [it] will nevertheless accurately represent the mores of the period."[25] Dropping the formality of "Mrs." was not acceptable to WI members, who explained that "[w]e recognize the modern usage, by the media, of surnames only for women, but considering the times in which Mrs. Watt lived, and the respect given to her accomplishments, our members feel that the words 'she' or 'Mrs. Watt' should replace the word 'Watt' in three places where it is used."[26] The historians who worked on the file compromised; for them it was clear that writing history was a political act, and as Alan Gordon has argued, professional historians must be cognizant of the fact that "their interpretation of the past, and more precisely their methods, reflect the common sense of their own times."[27]

Despite the conflict over how Watt should be addressed, one thing is clear from the files of the Ontario Heritage Foundation researchers: this time the content of the plaque was thoroughly and professionally researched. Although the text increased only from 95 to 129 words, the research to substantiate the claims involved an in-depth search of archival materials at the Archives of Ontario, the provincial archives of British Columbia, the national archives of Canada in Ottawa, the

1871 Census, and the Office of the Registrar General of Ontario, none of which had been done in 1958. Though the installation of the second plaque in 1990 attracted less attention from politicians and dignitaries than the original one had, this revised version was certainly more historically accurate and it was informed by the sensibilities that had been aroused by the emergence of women's history during the last quarter of the twentieth century. In many ways, the saga of the ACWW plaque captures the themes that have been ongoing in the practice of women's history, particularly the attempt to balance historical professionalism with local enthusiasm.[28]

A second controversial historical marker deals with Watt's role as ACWW president and involves a complicated story of another plaque and its unveiling, subsequent removal, disappearance, recovery, and reinstallation. Readers will recall that on the occasion of the 1936 ACWW conference at Washington, DC, Watt had welcomed a group of international delegates to southern Ontario so that they could tour some of the significant sites of WI history before their departure for England. Given the interwar tensions that were dominating international concerns at the time, it seemed appropriate to Watt and the organizers of the event to take the opportunity to celebrate the peaceful relations between Canada and the United States symbolized by the long, undefended border between the two countries. The plan was to install on the Peace Bridge between Fort Erie, Ontario, and Buffalo, New York, a plaque marking the historic occasion of the visit of these rural women as ambassadors of peace, with Watt, as world president, proudly presiding over the event.

Having received the endorsement of the appropriate officials, a ceremony was set for June 16, 1936. In fact, due to the hasty planning, the actual plaque could not be manufactured or installed in time, and so rather than an "unveiling," a replica was used in the ceremony, and it was "presented" rather than unveiled. The ceremony took place on the bridge at its centre point, the international boundary line, to symbolize the harmonious relationship between the two countries. Traffic was halted to allow for the formalities, something that had only happened once before, in the 1920s.[29] Keynote speakers representing both countries addressed the delegation, celebrating the peaceful relations between the two countries, expressing the sentiment that "what has been achieved on this continent between the United States and Canada can well be exemplified to other parts of the world."[30] Newspaper reporters on both sides of the border attended and photographed the historic occasion. The text on the temporary plaque read as follows:

"Pilgrimage of friendship. Plaque commemorating the crossing of the Associated Country Women of the World from American to Canada June 16, 1936." After the ceremony, the international delegation of women continued on their tour through southern Ontario, before proceeding to Quebec for their return trip across the Atlantic.

Meanwhile, preparations were underway to manufacture and install the permanent plaque on the Peace Bridge, and a second ceremony was held on July 29, 1936, when it was unveiled in its permanent home on the centre parapet of the bridge. Again, dignitaries attended from both countries, though of course the overseas visitors who had been there in June could not be present on this occasion. This new plaque had been revised in its design in order to fit into the available space on the bridge, and even more importantly, the text was significantly different. It read:

A pilgrimage of friendship. This plaque marks the crossing from the United States of America into the Dominion of Canada of a delegation from the Associated Country Women of the World and is dedicated to the rural women of this continent and entrusted to their perpetual care. Peace Bridge June 16, 1936.[31]

Although no one present at the unveiling could have known it at the time, there was a deep irony in the statement that the plaque was "entrusted to the perpetual care" of the rural women of North America, because sometime later the plaque disappeared, much to the embarrassment of local rural women, specifically WI members.

The plaque has since been recovered and reinstalled, but the story of how the lost was found is an interesting episode of careful research and tenacious detective work on the part of two women: Bev Jewson, a WI member and local historian from Fort Erie, and Marion Egerter, who served as public relations officer for the Niagara District and Hamilton Area of the WI from the late 1990s to early 2000s.[32] At some point, probably between 1954 and the early 1960s, the plaque was removed from the bridge, presumably so that maintenance work could be completed.[33] In the late 1990s, after conducting historical research in newspaper accounts about the 1936 ceremonies and the two versions of the plaque, Egerter contacted authorities from the Buffalo and Fort Erie Peace Bridge Authority (PBA) and the Niagara Parks Commission (NPC) to ask about the plaque's removal. Because neither the PBA nor the NPC had any record of the plaque's removal, Egerter launched a public appeal by writing letters to the editors of local newspapers on both sides of the border during the spring of 2000 in order to ask for the public's help in locating the plaque. A reporter for the *Niagara Falls Review* became intrigued by the mystery of the disappearing plaque, and when he wrote an article, complete with a photograph of a recreation of the plaque, in early April 2000, the plaque was recovered within two weeks.

How the plaque was returned is almost as mysterious as its original disappearance. In an email message to the provincial president of the Ontario WI, Egerter's account of the plaque's return simply began, "Hallelujah! We found it!"[34] She went on to recount that "someone has quietly returned the ACWW plaque anonymously (so far) to the Fort Erie home of Bev Jewson, who found it leaning against the wall of her porch after returning from a few days vacation on April 19." That version of events belies the efforts that Egerter and others made over several months through their careful library research, countless visits to historical society events and offices, and persistent hounding of government and municipal authorities. While Egerter's historical curiosity about where the plaque went and who returned it was not fully satisfied, the plaque was back in the hands of rural women, and the next obvious question was what they should do with it. Realistic enough to realize that the plaque would not be reinstalled on the bridge itself, they began to explore other possibilities. One thing that made the plaque's recovery particularly timely was the fact that WI members in Canada were making plans to host the twenty-third triennial convention of the ACWW in Hamilton in 2001. This was a very special occasion because the ACWW had met on North American soil only four times since the Washington meetings in 1936: twice in Canada and twice in the US.[35] In a series of email exchanges in 2000 with the president of the FWIO, Egerter wrote:

> What now? Should I inquire about re-installing the plaque near the Peace Bridge – e.g. along the nearby walking trail. And we could have a 2001 re-enactment of the event there. Apparently the plaque is very heavy so I guess we wouldn't want to tote it to Hamilton [ACWW meeting 2001]. I know we can't put it on the centre of the Peace Bridge again. Whom do we involve in the planning?[36]

After a series of inquiries and negotiations, the plaque found a new home in Mather Arch Park, Fort Erie, Ontario, near the base of the Peace Bridge. The plaque was re-installed, this time in a garden, attached to a large stone monument that also bears an additional, smaller plaque explaining the significance of the original one.[37] The explanatory plaque, endorsed by the Niagara Parks Commission, bears this text:

> Mrs. Alfred (Madge) Watt, MBE, MA, co-founder and first president of the Associated Country Women of the World (ACWW) dedicated this plaque to the rural women of this continent in a ceremony at the centre of the Peace Bridge on June 16, 1936. It was organized by representatives of the New York State Federation of Home Bureaus and the Federated Women's Institutes of Canada on the occasion of the 1936 Washington, DC Conference of the ACWW.
>
> With the cooperation of the Niagara Parks Commission, this plaque was re-dedicated during the 23rd Triennial Conference of the ACWW in Hamilton, Ontario in June of 2001.

After all the drama that had unfolded in locating the original plaque and negotiating a new home for it, it seemed fitting that the rededication ceremony should incorporate Egerter's suggestion of some kind of dramatic re-enactment based on the 1936 ceremony. With the research she had done in her efforts to recover the missing plaque, Egerter seemed well placed to create such a dramatic piece, and so she wrote a script for a presentation to be performed in Mather Arch Park on the afternoon of June 19, 2001, as part of the ACWW's Hamilton meeting. The final script however, was not at all about re-enacting the 1936 Peace Bridge ceremony. Instead it was about offering a revisionist interpretation of Watt's life and her deserved place in the history of the ACWW. Inviting local WI members to attend the ceremony, Egerter described the play briefly and explained that her rationale for creating it was an "attempt to pay some long-overdue homage to this outstanding Canadian who dedicated her life to the ideal of the sisterhood of women."[38] In further communication with the author, Egerter explained that she wanted to use the occasion of the international visitors' presence to question some of the accepted version of ACWW history and to expose some of the controversy about how Watt's role has been perceived and depicted. In a four-page letter she outlined the rationale behind the script and concluded,

> As you can see I have left out more than I put in about my personal views of the unfairness of Madge's undeserved obscurity. I felt that many in my intended audience would resent a negative presentation so have kept my references as subtle as possible for the negatives, and have attempted to keep the descriptions positive.[39]

Egerter's play included some history (gleaned mostly from existing ACWW publications) and a great deal of creative licence. In an attempt to depict some of Watt's mentors and associates, Egerter created eight characters in addition to Watt herself, including a narrator; Watt's mother, Bethia Robertson; Adelaide Hoodless; Josephine Godman; Emily Murphy; Lady Aberdeen; Miss Zimmern; and Watt's sister, Katherine Robertson Arthur. Particularly with her interpretation of Watt's mother and sister, there is little historical evidence to support the play. Indeed, in her attempt to highlight the positive, feminist influence that Bethia Robertson had upon her daughter, Egerter took great creative licence. Bethia Robertson died in 1893, four years before the first WI was created in Ontario, and therefore she never did promote the WI idea to her daughter or to anyone else. Despite the historical inaccuracies though, Egerter's attempt to explore the mother-daughter relationship among the Robertson women was an important line of inquiry. As we saw in chapter one, Bethia probably did influence Madge towards a life of activism, but because she passed away when her daughter was only twenty-five years old, that influence was short-lived and it did not include any promotion of causes to support rural women. Certainly Mrs. Robertson could not have foreseen the very public roles that her daughter would play in WI and ACWW circles since these organizations only came into existence after her death.

Similar musings might apply to the creative licence that Egerter exercised in writing about how the other characters thought about Watt too, but the important thing is that after conducting her research, Egerter identified the seeming "lack of acknowledgement" for Watt's role in history. In correspondence with the author, she wondered about the implicit biases in existing accounts of ACWW history. What is of interest to historians of biography and of public history is how the seemingly simple act of dedicating a historical plaque is so closely tied to the process of interpretation in history. As Litt observes, "it is not realistic to expect the general public to be sophisticated enough to regard plaques as artifacts and interpret their texts as tracts for past times. Historians are trained to do this, but the average citizen tends to take anything cast in metal and bearing an official coat-of-arms as the gospel truth."[40] It is clear that as a WI historian, Egerter consciously set out to defend Madge Watt as a Canadian hero and, as Gordon argues, "historical heroes do not assume their place of importance by the strength of rational discourse, but by the power of emotion and symbolism."[41] Egerter's emotional defence of Watt was based on a perceived injustice about how other sources depicted her. It was important to Egerter, on the occasion of Canada hosting the 2001 ACWW meeting that Watt's contribution should be emphasized and the Canadian roots of the organization highlighted.

Although it is not as complicated as the stories of the plaque at Collingwood or the Peace Bridge monument, the site of Watt's grave is also somewhat curious, and it provides a third example of how meanings are affixed to historical markers to communicate particular cultural messages. As the obituaries made clear when Madge Watt died in November 1948, she was interred at the Mount Royal Cemetery in Montreal. While this seems logical given that she was with her sons in Montreal at the time of her death, at the same time there were two other, more obvious locations where Watt might have been buried. The first was in the Ross Bay Cemetery in Victoria where her husband, Dr. Alfred Tennyson Watt, was buried in 1913. It is customary for married couples to be buried together, and given that Madge Watt never remarried after the death of her husband in 1913, it seems odd that she was not buried there. Perhaps the trauma of Alfred Watt's premature death by suicide meant that Watt had requested not to be buried there, but she certainly did return to Victoria on numerous occasions after that tragic incident, and her ties to British Columbia were strong enough that her sons arranged for a memorial service to be held there. It might also be that the Watt brothers discreetly decided not to reopen painful memories or remind the Canadian public about their father's suicide by drawing attention to that gravesite at the time of their mother's death.

Another possible burial site would have been the Robertson family plot in the Presbyterian Cemetery just outside of Collingwood, Ontario. This is the gravesite for Watt's parents, her infant siblings, and her sister Katherine Robertson Arthur and her family. Certainly at the time of Watt's death in 1948 there was still space at this site because several members of the extended family have been buried there since that time. Watt maintained ties with her home town throughout her life, and it presumably would have been a viable option for her to be buried there with other members of her extended family.

Despite those options, Watt's sons decided to bury their mother in Montreal. Given the expense and inconvenience of making an alternate arrangement, it was not an unreasonable decision. Very little attention was paid to Watt's final resting place until Canadian WI members began to prepare for the 1997 centennial celebrations of the Women's Institutes. Brainstorming about possible tours that might be of interest to Canadian and international delegates who would be touring on that occasion, WI members turned their attention to sites that might be of interest to their visitors. The obvious list included Stoney Creek, Ontario, near Hamilton where the first WI was organized, the Adelaide Hunter Hoodless Homestead, a museum owned and maintained by the FWIC, and the plaque about Watt as founder of the ACWW located in Collingwood, Ontario. But when the suggestion arose about visits to Madge Watt's gravesite, there were questions about the exact location and condition of her grave marker. When FWIC members began to explore the possibility of adding the Mount Royal Cemetery to the list of sites of interest, they were surprised to learn that the grave was virtually unmarked. The simplicity of Watt's gravestone belied the fact that she had had such an illustrious career, first as a writer, and later as an organizer of rural women. Indeed, there was really nothing at the grave to indicate that she had been such a public figure.

Surprised to learn about this, members of the FWIC and the Quebec Women's Institute determined to rectify the situation. In anticipation of the 1997 celebrations to be held in Hamilton, Ontario, the time seemed right to create what they deemed a more "appropriate" marker for Watt's grave, and the FWIC took up the task of restoring Watt's gravesite as a project to mark the WI centennial in Canada. The result of their efforts was a bronze plaque for the gravestone that made clear the international role that Watt played in establishing and leading the ACWW. The grave marker bears the logo of the ACWW, and the text reads:

> Madge (Mrs. Alfred) Watt MBE MA
> Born Margaret Rose Robertson
> 1868–1948
> In Collingwood, Ontario
> Founding Member, First President
> Associated Country Women of the World
> Erected by Women's Institute Members
> 1997 – Centennial Year of Women's Institutes[42]

While Robin and Sholto Watt had recognized how important their mother's work with rural women had been to her, they did not choose to mark her grave with reference to that work. Why they did not do so is unknown, and because the sources are silent on these questions, one can only speculate. What is significant here is how Canadian WI members rallied behind their shared disapproval of the marker chosen by Watt's family and decided to replace it with something that seemed to them to be a more fitting tribute. Because Watt's two sons both died in 1964, and neither of them had any children, there were no immediate family members to consult about the proposed change to the gravesite and no one to explain why the original grave marker was so modest in its design. By insisting that Watt should be commemorated at her grave as the founding president of the ACWW, the women who worked on this project were appropriating the right to interpret and ascribe meaning to Watt's life. To them, the obscurity of the original grave marker seemed inappropriate and even disrespectful to the woman whose memory they wished to honour. By placing the ACWW logo on her grave, Canadian WI members defined for perpetuity the contribution that Watt made to this international rural women's organization, and by extension, they established a permanent indicator of the centrality of Canada's contribution to the group. This marker serves to solidify the interpretation that despite other versions of the ACWW history that list Watt as one of three co-founders, for visitors to this gravesite, Watt's (and by extension, Canada's) status within the organization was elevated and commemorated as central.

Each of the three examples, the Collingwood plaque, the Fort Erie cairn, and the Montreal grave, illustrates how the revisions, representations, and reconstructions of Watt's history reflect as much about the times in which the changes were made and the people behind those changes, as they do about Madge Watt herself. In each of the three cases, members of the WI were adamant that the original markers should either be resurrected or revised and replaced. In Collingwood, a plaque that was originally installed in the spirit of "great woman" history had been removed because of factual errors, and WI members pressed for the promise of a replacement to be fulfilled. In Fort Erie, a plaque that had originally been installed to symbolize interwar peaceful relations between two countries was lost and then recovered, and the obvious thing to do was to reinstall it somewhere so it could be displayed for all to see. WI members took the occasion of the reinstallation as an opportunity to dramatize Watt's life and demonstrate to visitors that a Canadian held a place of prominence in the movement's history. In Montreal, the humble gravestone placed by Watt's family seemed inappropriate to WI members almost fifty years later who wanted to take their visitors to see Watt's final resting place. To correct the situation, the FWIC decided to erect a permanent fixture and inscribe it with text that would attach meaning to Watt's life by making it clear that she was the Canadian who was central to the founding of an important international organization for rural women.

In all three instances, a sense of duty spurred the women to take action, but in each case there were other motivating factors at work that must be understood in the context of rural women's organizations as well. By the 1990s, the WI in Canada was in serious decline given its plummeting membership numbers: in Ontario, for example, the number of active branches declined from more than 900 in 1993 to less than 800 just three years later.[43] Despite those negative trends some important historic occasions were approaching, namely celebrating of the 1997 WI centennial, and hosting the 2001 triennial ACWW conference. The urge to identify and mark significant historic sites connected with that movement was in part, motivated by these occasions. Commemoration and celebration of the movement's past greatness were definitely in the air. So too, was the urge to mark with permanence the fact that it was a *Canadian* woman who had accomplished so much for the international movement. Moreover, for members of both the WI and the ACWW, the erection of permanent historical markers was a way to ensure the permanence and importance of their movement. Threatened by rapid social change and declining attention to rural issues, the women of the Canadian WI and ACWW were insisting that their groups were an enduring part of Canada's past, and that they, like the plaque, the cairn, and the gravestone, were here to stay, despite indicators to the contrary such as an aging membership suggesting that the movement was in decline.

By marking significant sites and occasions in rural women's history and by showing the world what an important role Canadian women have played these markers commemorating Watt provide examples of historical reconstructions that "served the needs of the present."[44] One of the most pressing needs for rural women's organizations at the turn of the twenty-first century in Canada was to reinforce their legacy for the past and carve out a future role for themselves. For that purpose, Madge Watt fit the bill. As Gordon has argued, using a heroic figure from the past who "can be presented also as a timeless individual, can be a powerful tool of social cohesion."[45]

Beyond the reasons that members of rural women's organizations found to commemorate Madge Watt, the story of her life is important to the wider historical community. When Watt is considered in the larger context of women's experiences in the late nineteenth and early

twentieth centuries, her life serves as a launching point to explore a
new era for women in Canada. For example, she was one of the first
women in Canada to enjoy the privilege of a university education. As
part of the story of women's struggle for the right to postsecondary
co-educational opportunities in Canada, it is helpful to trace what
happened to these pioneering women after their schooling ended. As
a student and young career woman, Madge Robertson was an out-
spoken advocate for women's rights to co-education and paid work.
Raised by prosperous, civically minded parents, her father with his
deep ties to fraternal organizations and her mother deeply devoted
to church missionary work, Madge understood the power of organizational life tied to respectability and rooted in imperialist sentiment. Ideologically, Watt reflected the thinking of the so-called New
Woman, who insisted on an enlarged place for women in the public sphere as well as shifts in the accepted notions about women in
their private relations with men. Watt represents a transitional figure
because she embraced many new ideas, insisting that women should
be educated, have the right to work for pay, and to be equal partners
in setting the terms of their romantic relationships. Yet, as progressive as those ideas were, Watt also clung to conventional assumptions
about Christian marriage when she gave up her career as a single-
woman journalist and editor in New York and Toronto and opted for
a traditional marriage. Her husband enjoyed a highly paid government appointment as a medical doctor and civil servant in British
Columbia, and therefore the marriage placed Watt into social circles
where she and her peers brought professional leadership and social
influence to that colonial setting. In her privileged life on rural Vancouver Island, Watt was drawn to the prestige she enjoyed as part
of Victoria's small but influential elite society. At the same time, she
recognized the challenges that existed for women who experienced
the isolation of country living. While she raised her two sons, she
exerted her influence through the auspices of the provincial government when she took on a leadership role in promoting the establishment of Women's Institutes to address the needs of rural women. In
the early twentieth century just before women gained formal political rights in Canada, Watt is an example of a liberal feminist who
believed that by working within state initiatives like the provincially
sponsored Women's Institutes, she had the power to improve the
lives of local rural women through her leadership in an organization
that was specifically tailored to their needs.

When Watt's personal circumstances took a shocking and unpredictable turn in 1913 with her husband's suicide, she was thrust into new circumstances as a widow without financial security. That agonizing family tragedy explains why Watt was transplanted from British Columbia to England as she took refuge in the home of her friend in the English countryside to work through her grief. It was from that setting that she performed her legendary war work in the UK by establishing Women's Institutes in Wales and England. While it was common for imperially minded Canadians to support the British war effort, it was rare for a Canadian idea to be successfully transplanted to Britain. After some initial difficulties, Watt's suggestion to establish Women's Institutes took firm root in the mother country, becoming such a highly popular phenomenon that within a few years, the number of Women's Institutes there vastly outnumbered the Canadian branches. This act of reverse colonialism provides an important part of the story of transnational women's organizations, and it provides a unique chapter in the history of imperialism in Canada. The experiences and contributions of this one colonial woman offer historians the opportunity to explore questions raised by Philip Buckner and others around imperialism's enduring attraction for English-Canadians in the first half of the twentieth century. Because Watt is best known for her work with Women's Institutes and related groups, her biography also gives insight into transnational women's organizations during the first wave women's movement as an expression of female imperialism; in this case, providing a rural parallel to studies such as Katie Pickles's treatment of the Imperial Order Daughters of the Empire.[46]

At the same time, Watt's role in founding the Associated Country Women of the World is a noteworthy achievement that offers scope for exploring the workings of international women's organizations in the interwar years. Historian Leila J. Rupp's important book, *Worlds of Women: The Making of an International Women's Movement* raises awareness among women's historians of "transnational women's organizations to tell the story of women's struggle to construct a feminist international collective identity."[47] The life of Madge Watt is part of that story, but her emphasis on the concerns of international *rural* women adds an important dimension to the existing histories. The ACWW still exists and, eight decades after its founding, it continues to enjoy consultative status with the United Nations. At ACWW triennial conferences in the twenty-first century, one can listen to debates and resolutions that capture the attention of delegates from seventy different countries around the world as they speak for rural women worldwide on issues that range from sustainable food production to trafficking in girls and women. Watt's role in envisioning and bringing into existence a group for rural women is highly significant for the history of such organizations, even though she personally could not have foreseen the extent of the causes and issues that the group would take up. Although the members of Women's Institutes and the Associated Country Women of the World know and acknowledge the role that Watt played in their histories, her work deserves to be more broadly known and appreciated as an example of the transnational initiatives that were so typical of women's groups in the first half of the twentieth century, but in this case, with a focus on rural women.

Another significant reason to consider Madge Robertson Watt and her work is because of what her life can tell us about women and imperialism in an era of transition. As a colonial woman from Canada, her accomplishments are an exception to the usual pattern. In her case, her work was an act of reverse colonialism. Moreover, her dream of envisioning the potential of an international group for rural women gives insight into the accomplishments of one woman's influence. Watt was typical of her period for her emphasis on transnational cooperation. She is an example of the kinds of public roles that well-educated, well-connected women could play in the first decades of the twentieth century, when the internationalist ideal was so widely shared. Watt's story is the story of how one woman's life and work typify the transnational ties that united women in the first half of the twentieth century. Her life, her work, and the groups she was instrumental in establishing were precursors to an era of global pursuits. To look at this one life is to look at the question of women's transnational involvements. Watt embodied those trends. Her tireless vision for a worldwide association of rural women was driven by the force of her personality. She enjoyed the excitement of international travel and she loved to see her own name in print, both for the personal gratification she took from that, but also for the impact her writing could have on others. She took immense personal satisfaction in knowing that what she wrote engaged other people and caused them to dream about the potential of women uniting worldwide around their rural experiences.

Watt travelled widely in an era when global travel was becoming more common but was still a luxury enjoyed mostly by the world's elite. While she hoped to encourage networks of women that transcended national borders, unlike other club women of the era who had more personal and family resources at their disposal, Watt struggled to finance her travels and her initiatives. Though she was very independently minded, she was by no means self-sufficient. In achieving her goals, Watt made some enemies as well as friends, at least partly because of her propensity to claim credit primarily for herself, but there is no question that she could not have achieved what she did without well-connected networks of women behind her. As a result, she relied heavily on friends and acquaintances like Annie Cleland in Victoria, Josephine Godman in Sussex, Dorothy Drage in Wales, Lady Denman in London, Lady Aberdeen in Geneva and Stockholm, and Flora Rose in Ithaca, New York, to provide the infrastructure for her schemes to be accomplished by providing accommodation for her and making their own wider networks available to her.

In addition to the support she enjoyed from such women, Watt constantly positioned herself to persuade government officials that they should lend financial support to her ideas and her travels. While this model worked for her with varying degrees of success for more than three decades from 1915 through to the end of World War Two, it became increasingly difficult for her to persuade officials that her ideas were still just as relevant in the 1940s as they had been in the 1910s. Watt seems not to have entertained the thought that her ideas might become less relevant and her role might be diminished as she reached old age. On the contrary, she remained tireless in her efforts at self-promotion because she honestly believed that her personal experiences were invaluable to the authorities and unmatched by her contemporaries. She came to believe that she was the ultimate world authority on rural women's issues, and she remained firmly committed to that perception even as it became increasingly obvious to her colleagues in the WI and the ACWW that she was sometimes more of a liability than an asset.

Despite Watt's difficult personality and apparent lack of self-awareness as she aged, the fact remains that she and her life work matter to the history of rural women's organizations. Her significance lies beyond the "great woman" model of history; that is, beyond simple commemoration as the founder of the British WI and the co-founder of the ACWW. Her life story provides an example of one who worked in the interwar context of international women's organizations to promote awareness of world issues among women, and in her case, rural women at the grassroots level. Driven by her interwar ideals about internationalism, she was most effective when she stood to address audiences of rural women and inspire them with her charismatic and folksy public speaking. She took the most personal satisfaction from directly address-ing groups of women and sharing with them her vision of international sisterhood. She was a gifted communicator, and with her inspirational speaking and writing, she became a key figure to introduce rural women across the globe to the idea of transnational cooperation – what she called "a great rural sisterhood."[48]

Notes

Introduction: Framing the Life of Madge Robertson Watt

1 Jean Robinson, *Three Women of B.C. and the A.C.W.W.* (Sooke, BC: Shirley Women's Institute Historical Research Group, 1990), 32.
2 For more information on the Associated Countrywomen of the World (ACWW), see their website: www.acww.org.uk.
3 The designation came about at the urging of the British Columbia Women's Institute, who made a submission in 2005 calling for this designation to be granted. Email correspondence to the author from Dianne Dodd, Historian, National Historic Sites Directorate, Parks Canada, September 27, 2005.
4 Robinson, *Three Women of B.C.*, 32.
5 Frances Farrer, "Watt, Margaret Rose (1868–1948)," in *Dictionary of National Biography 1941–1950,* ed. L.G. Wickham Legg and E.T. Williams (Oxford: Oxford University Press, 1959), 931.
6 Phillip Buckner and R. Douglas Francis, eds., *Rediscovering the British World* (Calgary: University of Calgary Press, 2005), 17.
7 Phillip Buckner, "The Long Goodbye: English Canadians and the British World," in *Rediscovering the British World,* ed. Buckner and Francis, 181–208.
8 Katie Pickles, *Female Imperialism and National Identity: Imperial Order Daughters of the Empire* (Manchester and New York: Manchester University Press, 2002), 58, 176–7.
9 Adele Perry, "Interlocuting Empire: Colonial Womanhood, Settler Identity, and Frances Herring," in *Rediscovering the British World*, ed. Buckner and Francis, 160.
10 Ibid.

11 Donald Wright, "Reflections on Donald Creighton and the Appeal of Biography," *Journal of Historical Biography* 1, 1 (Spring 2007): 14–26; David D. Anderson, "Another Biography? For God's Sake, Why?" *The Georgia Review* 35, 2 (1981): 401–6; John A. Garraty, "How to Write a Biography," *The South Atlantic Quarterly* 55, 1 (1956): 73–86; Dianne Hallman, "Introduction to Special Issues on Biography," *Ontario History* 84, 4 (December 1992): 257–61; Thomas O. Hoover, Marion White McPherson, and John A. Popplestone, "Documentation, a Difference between Gossip and History," *Manuscripts* 26, 3 (1974): 184–9; Glen Jeansonne, "Personality, Biography, and Psychobiography," *Biography* 14, 3 (1991): 243–55; Glen Jeansonne, "Teaching a Course in Writing Biography," *Perspectives* 26, 1 (1988): 13–15; J.R. Mallory, "Biography, History and Social Sciences in Canada: Different Questions, Different Answers," *Journal of Canadian Studies* 15, 4 (Winter 1981): 125–8; Luisa Passerini, "Transforming Biography: From the Claim of Objectivity to Intersubjective Plurality," *Rethinking History* 4,3 (2000): 413–16.

12 Carolyn Heilbrun, *Writing a Woman's Life* (New York and London: W.W. Norton & Co., 1988).

13 For more on feminist approaches to biography, see Elaine Sargent Apthorp, "Speaking of Silence: Willa Cather and the 'Problem' of Feminist Biography," *Women's Studies* 18, 1 (1990): 1–11; Bell Gale Chevigny, "Daughters Writing: Toward a Theory of Women's Biography," *Feminist Studies* 9, 1 (Spring 1983): 79–102; Gail Grant, "That Was a Woman's Satisfaction: The Significance of Life History for Woman-Centered Research," *Canadian Oral History Association* 11 (1991): 29–38; Jacquelyn Dowd Hall, "Second Thoughts: On Writing a Feminist Biography," *Feminist Studies* 13, 1 (Spring 1987): 19–37; Elizabeth Lennox Keyser, "Woman in the Twentieth Century: Margaret Fuller and Feminist Biography," *Biography* 11, 4 (1988): 283–302; George A. Kizer, "Ralph W. Tyler – A Living Legend: Problems of Biography," *Vitae Scholasticae* 7, 1 (1988): 19–29; Andrée Lévesque, "Réflexion sur la biographie historique en l'an 2000," *Revue d'Histoire de l'Amérique Française* 54, 1 (2001): 95–102; Mary Niles Maack, "'No Philosophy Carries So Much Conviction as the Personal Life': Mary Wright Plummer as an Independent Woman," *The Library Quarterly* 70, 1 (January 2000): 1–46; Suzanne Morton, "Faire le saut: la biographie peut-elle être de l'histoire sociale?" *Revue d'Histoire de l'Amérique Francaise* 54, 1 (2001): 103–9; Patricia E. Prestwich, Review of *The New Biography: Performing Femininity in Nineteenth Century France*, by Jo Burr Margadant, *Histoire Sociale* 34, 67 (May 2001): 230–2; Nancy Pagh, "Our Emily: A Review Essay," *BC Studies* 114 (Summer 1997): 89–91; Nell

Irvin Painter, "Review Essays: Writing Biographies of Women," *Journal of Women's History* 9, 2 (Summer 1997): 154–63; Adele Perry, "Writing Women into British Columbia History," *BC Studies* 122 (Summer 1999): 85–8; Carolyn Steedman, "Difficult Stories: Feminist Auto/Biography," *Gender & History* 7, 2 (1995): 321–6; Steven Weiland, "Biography, Rhetoric, and Intellectual Careers: Writing the Life of Hannah Arendt," *Biography* 22, 3 (Summer 1999): 370–98; Emmy Stark Zitter, "Making Herself Born: Ghost Writing and Willa Cather's Developing Autobiography," *Biography* 19, 3 (1995): 282–301.

14 Elisabeth Griffith, *In Her Own Right: The Life of Elizabeth Cady Stanton* (New York: Oxford University Press, 1984).

15 Barbara Tuchman, "Biography as a Prism of History," in *Telling Lives: The Biographer's Art*, ed. Marc Pachter (Washington, DC: New Republic Books and National Portrait Gallery, 1979), 132. See also Yvan Lamonde, "Problèmes et plaisirs de la biographie," *Revue d'histoire de l'Amérique française* 54, 1 (Été 2000): 89–94; Lévesque, "Réflexion sur la biographie historique en l'an 2000"; and Morton, "Faire le saut: la biographie peut-elle être de l'histoire sociale?".

16 Cecilia Morgan, "'Of Slender Frame and Delicate Appearance': The Placing of Laura Secord in the Narratives of Canadian Loyalist History," *Journal of the Canadian Historical Association* 5 (1994): 195–212.

17 Norman Knowles, *Inventing the Loyalists: The Ontario Loyalist Tradition and the Creation of Usable Pasts* (Toronto: University of Toronto Press, 1997); Alan Gordon, *The Hero and the Historians: Historiography and the Uses of Jacques Cartier* (Vancouver: University of British Columbia, 2010).

18 Jo Burr Margadant, "Introduction: Constructing Selves in Historical Perspective," in *The New Biography: Performing Femininity in Nineteenth-Century France*, ed. Jo Burr Margadant (Berkeley, Los Angeles & London: University of California Press, 2000), 7.

19 Judith Butler, "Performative Acts and Gender Constitution: An Essay in Phenomenology and Feminist Theory," in *Performing Feminisms: Feminist Critical Theory and Theatre*, ed. Sue-Ellen Case (Baltimore and London: The Johns Hopkins University Press, 1990): 270–82.

20 Carol J. Dennison, "Housekeepers of the Community: The British Columbia Women's Institutes, 1909–1946," in *Knowledge for the People: The Struggle for Adult Learning in English-speaking Canada, 1828–1973*, ed. Michael R. Welton (Toronto: OISE Press, 1987): 52–72; Catherine C. Cole and Judy Larmour, *Many and Remarkable: The Story of the Alberta Women's*

Institutes (Edmonton: Alberta Women's Institutes, 1997); Georgina Taylor, "Shall I Drown Myself Now or Later? The Isolation of Rural Women in Saskatchewan and Their Participation in the Homemakers' Clubs, the Farm Movement and the Co-operative Commonwealth Federation, 1910–1967," in *Women, Isolation and Bonding: The Ecology of Gender*, ed. Kathleen Storrie (Toronto: Methuen, 1987): 79–100; Naomi Black and Gail Cuthbert Brandt, "Il en faut un peu: Farm Women and Feminism in Quebec and France Since 1945," *Journal of the Canadian Historical Association*, NS 1 (1990): 73–96; Yolande Cohen, *Femmes de parole: L'historie des cercles de fermieres du Quebec, 1915–1990* (Quebec: Le Jour, 1990); Margaret C. Kechnie, *Organizing Rural Women: The Federated Women's Institutes of Ontario, 1897–1919* (Montreal and Kingston: McGill-Queen's University Press, 2004); Linda M. Ambrose, *For Home and Country: The Centennial History of the Women's Institutes in Ontario, 1897–1997* (Erin, Ontario: Boston Mills Press, 1996); Linda M. Ambrose and Margaret Kechnie, "Social Control or Social Feminism: Two Views of the Ontario Women's Institutes," *Agricultural History* 73, 2 (Spring 1999): 222–37; Linda M. Ambrose, "'What Are the Good of Those Meetings Anyway?': Explaining the Early Popularity of the Ontario Women's Institutes," *Ontario History* LXXXVII, 1 (Spring 1995): 1–19.

21 Ruby Heap, "From the Science of Housekeeping to the Science of Nutrition: Pioneers in Canadian Nutrition and Dietetics at the University of Toronto's Faculty of Household Science, 1900–1950," in *Challenging Professions: Historical and Contemporary Perspectives on Women's Professional Work*, ed. Elizabeth Smyth et al. (Toronto: University of Toronto Press, 1999): 141–70.

22 Monda Halpern, *And on That Farm He Had a Wife: Ontario Farm Women and Feminism, 1900–1940*, (Montreal: McGill-Queen's University Press, 2001); and Louise Carbert, *Agrarian Feminism: The Politics of Ontario Farm Women* (Toronto: University of Toronto Press, 1995).

23 Maggie Andrews, *The Acceptable Face of Feminism: The Women's Institute as a Social Movement* (London: Lawrence & Wishart, 1997).

24 Sholto Watt, ed., *What the Country Women of the World Are Doing* (London: The Liaison Committee of Rural Women's and Homemakers' Organisations, 1932).

25 Dorothy Schwieder, *75 Years of Service: Cooperative Extension in Iowa* (Ames, Iowa: Iowa State University Press, 1993); Mary Neth, *Preserving the Family Farm: Women, Community and the Foundations of Agribusiness in the Midwest, 1900–1940* (Baltimore: Johns Hopkins University Press, 1995); Deborah Fink, *Agrarian Women: Wives and Mothers in Rural Nebraska,*

1880–1940 (Chapel Hill: University of North Carolina Press, 1992); Debra Reid, "Rural African Americans, Gender Roles, and Progressive Reform in Texas," paper presented to the Rural Women's Studies Association Meeting, Minneapolis, Minnesota, June 2000.

26 Deborah K. Stiles, "Rural Women, Underdevelopment, Health Knowledge, and Modernity: Women and Family Farms as Part of a Broader Context of Change," in *Perspektive Žena u Obiteljskoj Poljoprivredi I Ruralnom Razvoju / Women Perspectives in Family Farming*, ed. Anita Silvana Ilak Persuric (Porec, Croatia: The Institute for Agriculture and Tourism, 2003), 130–5; and D. Stiles, C. Rangel, J. MacLaughlin, L. Sanderson, and K. MacNeil, "Rurality, Gender, and Leisure: Experiences of Young Rural Women in a Nova Scotia Community," *Journal of Rural Community Psychology* E10(2) (2007). Available: https://www.marshall.edu/jrcp/ARCHIVES/V10%20N2/stiles.pdf (accessed July 29, 2014).

27 See the collection of student papers from the course "Rural Cultures, Rural Women," taught by Kate Hunter at Victoria University of Wellington: Emma Dee and Tanya Granich, eds., *Rural Women in the Colonial Context: Women as Workers and Homemakers in Rural New Zealand, Australia and North America in the Late Nineteenth and Early Twentieth Centuries*, Rural Studies Research Occasional Papers No 1 (Wellington, New Zealand: History Department, Victoria University of Wellington, 2000); Margreet van der Burg, *'Geen tweede boer'. Gender, landbouwmodernisering en onderwijs aan plattelandsvrouwen in Nederland, 1863–1968* ('No second farmer'. Gender, Agricultural Modernisation and Education for Rural Women in the Netherlands), (Hilversum: Uitgererij Verloren, 2002); Elizabeth Teather and Margaret-Ann Franklin, eds., *Country Women at the Crossroads: Perspectives on the Lives of Rural Australian Women in the 1990s* (Amidale, NSW: University of New England Press, 1994).

28 Leila J. Rupp, *Worlds of Women: The Making of an International Women's Movement* (Princeton: Princeton University Press, 1997), 3; see also Rupp's "Challenging Imperialism in International Women's Organizations, 1888–1945," *National Women's Studies Association Journal* 8, 1 (1996): 8–27; "Constructing Internationalism: The Case of Transnational Women's Organizations, 1888–1945," *American Historical Review* 99, 5 (December 1994): 1571–1600; and Christine Bolt, *Sisterhood Questioned? Race, Class and Internationalism in the American and British Women's Movements, c. 1880s–1970s* (London: Routledge, 2004).

29 Julia Bush, "Edwardian Ladies and the 'Race' Dimensions of British Imperialism," *Women's Studies International Forum* 21, 3 (1998): 277–89;

Angela Woollacott, "Inventing Commonwealth and Pan-Pacific Feminisms: Australian Women's Internationalist Activism in the 1920s–30s," *Gender & History* 10, 3 (1998): 425–48; Mrinalini Sinha, Donna J. Guy, and Angela Woollacott, "Introduction: Why Feminisms and Internationalism?" *Gender & History* 10, 3 (1998): 345–57; Leila J. Rupp, "Feminisms and Internationalism: A View from the Centre," *Gender & History* 10, 3 (1998): 535–8.

30 Mrs. Alfred Watt and Miss Nest Lloyd, *The First Women's Institute School (Sussex 1918)* (Sussex Federation of Women's Institutes, 1919), 45.

1. Formative Years: Family Influences and University Life

1 Jo Burr Margadant, *The New Biography: Performing Femininity in Nineteenth-Century France* (Berkeley: University of California Press, 2000), 9.

2 A. Miles, *The 'Chicago of the North': Anecdotes from Collingwood's Past* (Collingwood: Town of Collingwood, 2004), 33.

3 Collingwood Board of Trade, *Annual Report of the Collingwood Board of Trade for 1893*, 43.

4 Miles, *Chicago of the North*, 70. The date of Robertson's arrival in Collingwood is disputed. Although Miles claims that he came to the town in 1861 after his graduation from the University of Toronto, other sources indicate that he was involved with civic affairs in the town as early as 1856. See, for example, Collingwood Public Library, Genealogy Room, Family Histories, Box P–S, file: Robertson, Henry. Q.C., "Record of Offices Held on Public Library Board by Henry Robertson, Esq. K.C., 1856–1908."

5 Ibid., 70.

6 Collingwood Public Library, Local History Collection, *Annual Report of the Collingwood Board of Trade for 1893*, 51. Brief histories and some photographs of several homes in the same neighbourhood as the Robertson house are featured in Laurel Lane-Moore, *Collingwood: Historic Homes and Buildings* (Collingwood: Blue Mountain Foundation for the Arts, 1989).

7 Collingwood Public Library, Genealogy Room, Family Histories, Box P–S, file: Robertson, Henry. Q.C., "Notes on the Life of Henry Robertson, QC 1840–1923."

8 Collingwood Public Library, Cemeteries, Town of Collingwood [Index]. Section 3: Presbyterian Cemetery, Collingwood Ontario. Grave markers in the Robertson family plot record the exact ages of the Robertsons' two

male babies: "Frederic ROBERTSON died September 15, 1872. Aged
2 months 16 days"; and Henry ROBERTSON died August 5, 1878. Aged
8 months 27 days." This trend toward infant mortality was repeated
again in the next generation when Katie and her husband, Dr. J.R. Arthur,
lost three of their five children in infancy. Those babies are also buried
in the family plot just outside Collingwood: Isobel Robertson ARTHUR,
June 21, 1901–August 29, 1901; Frederic Housten Robins ARTHUR,
July 10, 1902 –August 11, 1903; ARTHUR infant November 5, 1908.

9 Katherine Robertson followed in her mother's footsteps through her
church involvements. Katie remained in Collingwood her whole life,
eventually marrying a prominent young physician, Dr. J.R. Arthur.

10 Collingwood Public Library, Local History Collection, *Gazetteer and
Directory of the County of Simcoe, 1872–1873*, 84.

11 B. Arp, ed., *Reflections: Collingwood, an Historical Anthology* (Collingwood:
Town of Collingwood, 1983), 83.

12 It is not clear exactly when Robertson received the designation of Queen's
Counsel. Although one biographical source claims that he received
the designation in 1890, another claims the honour was bestowed in
1891. Both of these are found in the same file at the Collingwood Public
Library, Genealogy Room, Family Histories, Box P–S, file: Robertson,
Henry. Q.C.

13 *Enterprise Messenger*, November 21, 1901, 8.

14 "Death of Hy. Robertson, K.C.," *Collingwood Enterprise*, September 20,
1923, 1.

15 Collingwood Public Library, Local History Collection, *The Annual Report
of the Collingwood Board of Trade for 1893*, 59–60. In 1896, the library
became a "free" library. See Collingwood Public Library, Genealogy
Room, Family Histories, Box P–S, file: Robertson, Henry. Q.C. "Record
of Offices Held on Public Library Board by Henry Robertson Esqu, K.C.
1856–1908."

16 Ibid.

17 Collingwood Museum, Untitled Scrapbook [Henry Robertson] (Hereafter
cited as Collingwood Museum, Robertson Scrapbook), 176, records that
Henry Robertson was: 1864 Elected Councillor for West Ward; 1865
Defeated by one vote in West Ward; 1866 Elected by acclamation for West
Ward; 1867 Defeated for Reeve by John Hogg by 51 majority (9–39); 1872
Defeated for Deputy Reeve by C. Cameron 45 majority; 1876 Defeated
for Deputy Reeve by C. Cameron 72 majority; 1877 Elected Councillor
for West Ward; 1878 Defeated by 3 in West Ward; 1881 Elected Deputy
Reeve by 154 majority (HR 267, Michael Brennan 113, Hal Telfer, 83);

1882 Elected Deputy Reeve by acclamation; 1883 Defeated for Dep'y [sic] Reeve by Andw. [sic] Lockerbie by 78 maj.; 1889 Defeated for Mayor by A Lockerbie by 103 maj; 1890 Elected 2nd Dep'y Reeve by acclamation; 1891 Elected 2nd Dep'y Reeve by 121 maj over H. Evison; 1892 Elected 2nd Dep'y Reeve by acclamation; 1893 Elected 2nd Dep'y Reeve by acclamation; 1894 Elected 2nd Dep'y Reeve by acclamation; 1895 Retired; 1868 to 1874 Member of Collegiate Institute Board; 1873 & 1874 Chairman of Collegiate Institute Board; 1877 & 1878 Chairman of Public School Board; 1897 Appointed to Public Library Board; 1898 to 1904 Chairman of Public Library Board. Robertson's election to the 1864 town council is confirmed in Collingwood Museum, Accession Number X972.119.1, *1887 Jubilee History of the Town of Collingwood*, 9.

18 "Mayoralty 1889," *Enterprise and Collingwood Messenger*, January 3, 1889, 1. Robertson had declared his candidacy on December 10, 1888, approximately three weeks after he returned from his trip to the Pacific, to attend the Grand Lodge meeting of the IOOF.

19 "Municipal Elections: Lockerbie's Great Victory," *Enterprise and Collingwood Messenger*, January 10, 1889, 1.

20 Collingwood Museum, Accession Number X972.119.1, *1887 Jubilee History of the Town of Collingwood*, 18.

21 Ibid., 18–19.

22 *Enterprise and Collingwood Messenger*, July 22, 1886, 3.

23 Henry Robertson, *A Digest of Masonic Jurisprudence, Especially Applicable to Canadian Lodges; Together with an Essay on the Duties and Powers of District Deputy Grand Masters; A Code of Procedures for Masonic Trials, and A Valuable Collection of Forms for the Use of Lodges and Members of the Ancient and Honorable Fraternity of Free and Accepted Masons.* Second Edition. (Toronto: Hunter, Rose and Company, 1889).

24 Mary Ann Clawson, *Constructing Brotherhood: Class, Gender and Fraternalism* (Princeton: Princeton University Press, 1989), 95.

25 *Toronto Empire*, reprinted in *Enterprise and Collingwood Messenger*, December 19, 1889, 8.

26 Ibid., 8.

27 Lynn Dumenil, *Freemasonry and American Culture 1880–1930* (Princeton: Princeton University Press, 1984), 81.

28 Ibid., 83. Mary Ann Clawson concurs when she states that "American fraternalism was primarily a force for social order." Mary Ann Clawson, *Constructing Brotherhood: Class, Gender and Fraternalism* (Princeton: Princeton University Press, 1989), 264.

29 Dumenil, *Freemasonry*, 84.

30 Ibid., 88.
31 Ibid., 100.
32 Ibid., 111.
33 *1887 Jubilee History of the Town of Collingwood*, 18–19.
34 Lane-Moore, *Collingwood: Historic Homes and Buildings*, 75.
35 *Collingwood Bulletin*, October 23, 1890, cited by Miles, *The 'Chicago of the North'*, 71.
36 Ibid., 19.
37 Roger Burt, "Freemasonry and Business Networking during the Victorian Period," *Economic History Review* LVI, 4 (2003), 660.
38 Ibid., 680.
39 Clifford Putney, "Service over Secrecy: How Lodge-Style Fraternalism Yielded Popularity to Men's Service Clubs," *Journal of Popular Culture* 27, 1 (1993), 183. See also Dumenil, *Freemasonry*, 25; Jessica Harland-Jacobs, "'Hands Across the Sea': The Masonic Network, British Imperialism, and the North Atlantic World," *Geographical Review* 89, 2 (April 1999), 241–2; and Mark C. Carnes, *Secret Ritual and Manhood in Victorian America* (New Haven and London: Yale University Press, 1989), 14.
40 Collingwood Public Library, Cemeteries, Town of Collingwood [index], Section 3: Presbyterian Cemetery, Collingwood, Ontario, 308 – Robertson, Henry.
41 Dumenil, *Freemasonry*, 50.
42 Ibid., 51.
43 Harland-Jacobs, "'Hands Across the Sea,'" 239.
44 Ibid., 242–4. Buckner, "The Long Goodbye," 203.
45 See chapter 4, on the founding of the British WI. On Canadian Masons and World War One, see Harland-Jacobs, "'Hands Across the Sea,'" 249.
46 Dumenil, *Freemasonry*, 9.
47 Harland-Jacobs, "'Hands Across the Sea,'" 251.
48 Leila J. Rupp, *Worlds of Women: The Making of an International Women's Movement* (Princeton: Princeton University Press, 1997), 183–4.
49 Dumenil, *Freemasonry*, 17.
50 "Death's Heavy Hand," *Enterprise and Collingwood Messenger*, May 18, 1893, 1.
51 Patricia R. Hill, *The World Their Household: The American Woman's Foreign Mission Movement and Cultural Transformation, 1870–1920* (Ann Arbor: University of Michigan Press, 1985), 77.
52 Ibid., 54–5.
53 Ibid., 59.
54 Ibid., 60.

55 Wendy Mitchinson, "Canadian Women and Church Missionary Societies," *Atlantis* 2, 2 Part II (Spring 1977): 57–75.

56 It is not clear where these columns appeared in print, but press clippings of them are located in the Collingwood Museum, Robertson Scrapbook, "A Lady's Notes of a Trip to the Pacific: Mrs. Robertson in Santa Fe," 11. The Robertsons left Collingwood on September 5, travelling by train and arrived in Los Angeles on September 17. They returned home one month later on October 17, 1888. Bethia's published account takes up seven pages of the family scrapbook.

57 Mrs. Alfred Watt and Miss Nest Lloyd, *The First Women's Institute School (Sussex 1918)* (Sussex Federation of Women's Institutes, 1919), 139.

58 *Enterprise and Collingwood Messenger*, May 18, 1893, 1.

59 Presbyterian Church in Canada Archives, *18th Annual Report Women's Foreign Missionary Society, 1893–94* (Toronto: Press of the Canada Presbyterian, 1894).

60 On the term "Mother in Israel," see Jean Miller Schmidt, *Grace Sufficient: A History of Women in American Methodism 1760–1939* (Nashville: Abingdon Press, 1999), 51–2, 75; Marilyn Whiteley, *Canadian Methodist Women, 1766–1925: Marys, Marthas, Mothers in Israel* (Waterloo: Wilfrid Laurier Press, 2005), 3, 245; Catherine A. Brekus, *Strangers and Pilgrims: Female Preaching in America, 1740–1845* (Chapel Hill: University of North Carolina Press, 1998), 152; and Debora M. Valenze, *Prophetic Sons and Daughters: Female Preaching and Popular Religion in Industrial England* (Princeton: Princeton University Press, 1985), 35–6.

61 Mitchinson, "Canadian Women and Church Missionary Societies," 64.

62 Library and Archives Canada, MG 28 I 316, vol. 8, file 14, Mrs. Alfred Watt, President, "The Future of the ACWW, 1939," 4.

63 Ibid.

64 Ruth Compton Brouwer, *New Women for God: Canadian Presbyterian Women and India Missions, 1876–1914* (Toronto: University of Toronto Press, 1990), 42.

65 Mitchinson, "Canadian Women and Church Missionary Societies," 60–1.

66 Ibid., 73.

67 Ibid.

68 Ibid., 72–3.

69 Ibid., 63.

70 This table was compiled by Stephanie McPherson, from material housed in The Presbyterian Church in Canada Archives. The WFMS annual reports, 1885–92, include presbyterial reports with statistics from each local auxiliary. These statistics are taken from each of the annual reports

of the Barrie Presbyterial Society. The Presbyterian Church in Canada Archives, 10th to 17th Annual Reports, WFMS (Toronto: Presbyterian Printing and Publishing Company, 1886–93).

71 This table was compiled by Stephanie McPherson, from material housed in The Presbyterian Church in Canada Archives. The WFMS annual reports, 1885–92, include presbyterial reports with statistics from each local auxiliary. These statistics are taken from each of the annual reports of the Barrie Presbyterial Society. The Presbyterian Church in Canada Archives, 12th to 17th Annual Reports, WFMS (Toronto: Presbyterian Printing and Publishing Company, 1887–93).

72 Mitchinson, "Canadian Women and Church Missionary Societies," 63.

73 Madge Robertson, "Editorial," *The Ladies Pictorial Weekly*, May 14, 1892, 2.

74 Ibid.

75 Madge Robertson, "Visitors in the Sanctum," *Ladies Pictorial Weekly*, May 21, 1892, 2.

76 Hill, *The World Their Household*, 89.

77 Charles M. Levi, *Comings and Goings: University Students in Canadian Society, 1854–1973* (Montreal and Kingston: McGill-Queen's University Press, 2003), 54–70.

78 *Varsity*, vol. VIII, 5, November 26, 1887, 56.

79 *Enterprise and Collingwood Messenger,* June 6, 1889, 8.

80 Sara Z. Burke, "'Being Unlike Man': Challenges to Co-education at the University of Toronto, 1884–1909," *Ontario History* XCIII, 1 (Spring 2001), 18.

81 Ibid., 11.

82 Ibid.

83 Sara Z. Burke, "New Women and Old Romans: Co-education and the University of Toronto, 1884–1895," *Canadian Historical Review* 80, 2 (June 1999), 241.

84 Jo LaPierre, "The Academic Life of Canadian Coeds, 1880–1900," *Historical Studies in Education/Revue d'histoire de l'Éducation* 2, 2 (Fall/ automne 1990), 225–46.

85 Collingwood Museum, Robertson Scrapbook 19. The press clipping is taken from a publication entitled *Life*, though the citation is not complete.

86 *Varsity*, vol. VIII, 22, June 12, 1888, 267.

87 Levi, *Comings and Goings*, 3–14.

88 *Varsity*, vol. VII, 19, March 26, 1887, 230. The first presentation of the paper was reported in *Varsity*, vol. VI, 13, February 13, 1886, 156.

89 *Varsity*, vol. VI, 13, February 13, 1886, 153.

90 *Varsity*, vol. VII, 13, February 12, 1887, 158.

91 Nile Erie Enevist, "The Biglow Papers in Nineteenth-Century England," *New England Quarterly* 26, 2 (June 1953): 219–36; and Arthur Voss, "Backgrounds of Lowell's Satire in 'The Biglow Papers,'" *New England Quarterly*, 23, 1 (March 1950): 47–64.

92 *Varsity*, vol. VIII, 3, November 12, 1887.

93 *Varsity*, vol. IX, 3, November 17, 1888.

94 *Varsity*, vol. VII, 21, April 9, 1887, 258.

95 See, for example, "The Modern Languages Course," *Varsity*, vol. V, 23, April 4, 1885, 260; "Modern Language Memorial," *Varsity*, vol. VII, 21, April 9, 1887, 261; "Recent Changes in the Arts Curriculum," *Varsity*, vol. VIII, 6, December 3, 1887; "The Modern Languages Department," *Varsity*, vol. IX, 4, November 24, 1888; and "On the Study of Modern Languages," *Varsity*, vol. IX, 14, March 2, 1889.

96 *Varsity*, vol. VI, 16, March 6, 1886, 188.

97 Collingwood Museum, Robertson Scrapbook, 17: Greta, "Drama," *Saturday Night*, February 16, 1889.

98 Greta, "The Higher Education," *Varsity*, vol. IX, 8, January 19, 1889, 1.

99 Ibid.

100 Old Roman, "The Higher Education Again," *Varsity*, vol. IX, 1, November 3, 1888, 1.

101 *Varsity*, vol. IX, 8, January 19, 1889, 65–6.

102 *Varsity*, vol. VIII, 1, October 29, 1887. The Senkler brothers were Alfred Watt's teammates on the varsity rugby team, and it is possible that Watt was also among the "Varsity men" who went along to cheer for the team.

103 Sara Burke includes photographic evidence of female students attending a football game in 1909, (though it is not clear whether the game in that case was at home or away) and she concludes that this was evidence that women "quickly settled themselves into undergraduate life, and by 1909 they were displaying a new confidence on campus." See Burke, "Being Unlike Men," 12.

104 Reports of Watt's games include Varsity vs. McGill, *Varsity*, November 20, 1886; Varsity vs. Ottawa College, October 29, 1887; Varsity vs. McGill November 12, 1887; Toronto Football Club vs. Varsity, November 19, 1887; Toronto vs. Varsity November 10, 1888. During the 1887 season, the Varsity Rugby Club's record was six wins out of seven matches, and during the 1888 season, out of six matches, the record was 4 wins, 1 draw, and 1 loss. *Varsity*, December 10, 1887, and December 8, 1888.

105 *Varsity*, vol. VII, 10 January 1887, 121; *Varsity*, vol. IX, 2, November 10 1888, 15.

106 *Collingwood Bulletin*, June 12, 1890.

107 Martin I. Friedland, *The University of Toronto: A History* (Toronto: University of Toronto Press, 2002), 175–6.
108 *Varsity*, cited in Friedland, 176.
109 *Varsity*, vol. VII, 7, December 10, 1887, 77. Details about the revised regulations surrounding graduate work at the University of Toronto can be found in public documents: Ontario, *The Revised Statutes of Ontario, 1897*, Legislature of Ontario, volume II, (Toronto: L.K. Cameron, Law Printer to the Queen's Most Excellent Majesty, 1897): Chapter 298, 3466–79.

2. Scripting the New Woman: Writer and Editor

1 Madge Robertson, "The Heart Knoweth," *Globe*, July 11, 1891, 5–6.
2 Ibid.
3 Ibid.
4 Locating these publications was no small feat. There is no central repository of Robertson's writing, and it was only through painstaking searches of newspapers, journals, archives, and databases, as well as the lucky find of her father's personal scrapbook, that I was able to amass the collection I now have gathered. To date, I have collected more than one hundred of her publications, not counting the book-review columns which she wrote during her years in BC.
5 Jean Barman, *Constance Lindsay Skinner: Writing on the Frontier* (Toronto: University of Toronto Press, 2002), 58.
6 Collingwood Museum, Untitled Scrapbook [Henry Robertson], 39: press clipping from *The Week*, January 29, 1892. Hereafter cited as Collingwood Museum, Robertson Scrapbook.
7 Margaret Beetham, *A Magazine of Her Own? Domesticity and Desire in the Woman's Magazine, 1800–1914* (London and New York: Routledge, 1996), 129.
8 Collingwood Museum, Robertson Scrapbook, 39: "Gone to New York," unidentified press clipping, January 1893.
9 For information about the colourful life of Frank Leslie and the Frank Leslie publishing empire, see Budd L. Gambee, *Frank Leslie and His Illustrated Newspaper, 1855–1860* (Ann Arbor: University of Michigan Press, 1964), and Madeleine B. Stern, *Purple Passage: The Life of Mrs. Frank Leslie* (Norman: University of Oklahoma, 1953).
10 Cited in Elizabeth Ammons, *Conflicting Stories: American Women Writers at the Turn into the Twentieth Century* (New York: Oxford University Press, 1991), 7.
11 Examples of New Woman novelists include Grant Allen, Sarah Grand, George Egerton, and Ouida, among others.

12 Clarence Karr, *Authors and Audiences: Popular Canadian Fiction in the Early Twentieth Century* (Montreal and Kingston: McGill-Queen's University Press, 2000), 220.

13 Talia Schaffer, "'Nothing by Foolscap and Ink': Inventing the New Woman," in *The New Woman in Fiction and Fact: Fin-de-siècle Feminisms*, ed. Angelique Richardson and Chris Willis (London: Palgrave, 2001), 49.

14 Hugh Stutfield, cited in Chris Willis, "Heaven Defend Me from Political or Highly-Educated Women!: Packaging the New Woman for Mass Consumption," in *The New Woman in Fiction and Fact*, eds. Richardson and Willis, 53.

15 Lyn Pykett, *The 'Improper' Feminine: The Women's Sensation Novel and the New Woman Writing* (London and New York: Routledge, 1992), 144.

16 Circulation rates appeared regularly in various issues of the *Ladies Pictorial Weekly*: May 14, 1892, 317; May 21, 1892, 333; May 28, 1892, 351; June 11, 1892, 384; June 18, 1892, 399; June 25, 1892, 416.

17 Beetham, 130.

18 Cynthia Wright, "'Feminine Trifles of Vast Importance': Writing Gender into the History of Consumption," in *Gender Conflicts: New Essays in Women's History*, eds. Franca Iacovetta and Mariana Valverde (Toronto: University of Toronto Press, 1992), 231–4.

19 Karr, *Authors and Audiences*, ix.

20 "Let Us Live," *Ladies Pictorial Weekly*, February 13, 1892, 5.

21 Ibid.

22 Ann L. Ardis, "Organizing Women: New Woman Writers, New Woman Readers, and Movement Feminism," in *Victorian Women Writers and the Woman Question*, ed. Nicola Diane Thompson, (Cambridge: Cambridge University Press, 1999) 198.

23 *Ladies Pictorial Weekly*, February 6, 1892– June 25, 1892.

24 Ibid.

25 Ibid.

26 *Ladies Pictorial Weekly*, April 30, 1892.

27 "Keeping Pots and Pans Clean," *Ladies Pictorial Weekly*, February 6, 1892, 10; "How to Select Wall-Paper That Is Cheerful and Effective," *Ladies Pictorial Weekly*, February 13, 1892, 10; "Saving Work," *Ladies Pictorial Weekly*, March 12, 1892, 10; "Horrors of Dishwashing," *Ladies Pictorial Weekly*, April 2, 1892, 218; "Floral Bedrooms," *Ladies Pictorial Weekly*, May 14, 1892, 316.

28 "What to Try," *Ladies Pictorial Weekly*, February 6, 1892, 10; "Home Hints," *Ladies Pictorial Weekly*, April 2, 1892, 218; "Useful Household Suggestions," *Ladies Pictorial Weekly*, May 28, 1892, 348.

29 "Useful Household Suggestions," *Ladies Pictorial Weekly*, May 28, 1892, 10.

30 *Ladies Pictorial Weekly*, March 19, 1892, 188.

31 "Mother," *Ladies Pictorial Weekly*, March 12, 1892, 11; "Fighting the Wolf with Buttonholes," *Ladies Pictorial Weekly*, April 9, 1892, 237.

32 "Teach Your Children Self-Reliance," *Ladies Pictorial Weekly*, February 13, 1892, 14.

33 Ibid.

34 Ibid.

35 "Woman – A Bird's Eye View," *Ladies Pictorial Weekly*, March 19, 1892, 177.

36 Ibid.

37 Ibid.

38 "Women of the South," *Ladies Pictorial Weekly*, February 6, 1892, 5.

39 Ibid.

40 Ibid.

41 "Brown Bros. Co. Want Advertisements," *Ladies Pictorial Weekly*, February 13, 1892, 15; March 12, 1892, 14; March 26, 1892, 205; April 2, 1892, 221; April 9, 1892, 237; April 16, 1892, 254; April 23, 1892, 270; April 30, 1892, 286; May 7, 1892, 302; May 14, 1892, 319; June 4, 1892, 366; June 18, 1892, 397; June 25, 1892, 413.

42 Platt-Owen Want Advertisements," *Ladies Pictorial Weekly*, June 18, 1892, 398, and June 25, 1892, 414, and *"House and Home* Want Advertisements," *Ladies Pictorial Weekly*, March 12, 1892, 14; April 16, 1892, 256; April 23, 1892, 271; April 30, 1892, 287; May 7, 1892, 302; May 14, 1892, 318; May 21, 1892, 333; May 28, 1892, 349; June 4,1892, 368; June 11, 1892, 384; June 18, 1892, 400.

43 "Platt-Owen Advertisement," *Ladies Pictorial Weekly*, June 18, 1892, 389.

44 Chris Willis, "'Heaven Defend Me From Political or Highly-Educated Women!': Packaging the New Woman for Mass Consumption," in *The New Woman in Fiction and in Fact*, eds. Richardson and Willis, 53.

45 Barman, *Constance Lindsay Skinner*, 10, citing Sandra Gilbert and Susan Gubar, eds., *No Man's Land: The Place of the Woman Writer in the Twentieth Century*, vol. 1, *The War of the Words* (New Haven: Yale University Press, 1988), xiv.

46 Ann Heilmann, cited in Lyn Pykett, "Portraits of the Artist as a Young Woman: Representations of the Female Artist in the New Woman Fiction of the 1890s," in *Victorian Writers and the Woman Question*, ed. Thompson, 135.

47 Hilary Fraser and R.S. White, eds. "Introduction," *Constructing Gender: Feminism and Literary Studies* (Perth: University of Western Australia Press, 1994), xviii, cited in Barman, *Constance Lindsay Skinner*, 10.

48 *Saturday Night*, January 25, 1890, 7; June 10, 1890, 3.
49 For a discussion of the autobiographical nature of new woman fiction, see "Writing Women: Writing Woman" in Lyn Pykett, *The 'Improper' Feminine: The Women's Sensation Novel and the New Woman Writing* (London and New York: Routledge, 1992), 177–91.
50 Collingwood Museum, Robertson Scrapbook, 45: Madge Robertson, "By the Fireside," *Globe*, January 28, 1893, 6.
51 Ibid.
52 Ibid.
53 See Marjory L. Lang, *Women Who Made the News: Female Journalists in Canada, 1880–1945* (Montreal and Kingston: McGill-Queen's University Press, 1999); Anne Innis Dagg, *The Feminine Gaze: A Canadian Compendium of Non-Fiction Women Authors and Their Books* (Waterloo: Wilfrid Laurier Press, 2001); Barman, *Constance Lindsay Skinner*, 33–58.
54 Madge Robertson, "By the Fireside," *Globe*, January 21, 1893, 6.
55 Graham Law, "Tillotson's," in *Serializing Fiction in the Victorian Press* (Basingstoke: Palgrave, 2000), 64–92.
56 Jenni Calder, *Women and Marriage in Victorian Fiction* (London: Thames and Hudson, 1976), 163.
57 Willis, "'Heaven Defend Me,'" 55.
58 Law, "Tillotson's," in *Serializing Fiction*, 91.
59 See Collingwood Museum, Robertson Scrapbook, *passim*.
60 Pykett, *The 'Improper' Feminine*, 144.
61 Willis, "'Heaven Defend Me,'" 57.
62 Madge Robertson, "The Illustration of the Orthopedic," *Truth*, December 7, 1895, vol. xiv, 451, 12–13.
63 Collingwood Museum, Robertson Scrapbook, 39: Madge Robertson, "Poor Ainsley," *Globe*, December 24, 1892, 1; and "A Fine Sense of Humor," *Truth*, May 18, 1895, vol. xiv, 422, 6.
64 Madge Robertson, "The Delicate Question Which?" *Truth*, June 6, 1896, vol. xv, 477, 10–11; see also Collingwood Museum, Robertson Scrapbook, 127.
65 Originally published in 1895, the novel was reprinted on the centennial of its release. Grant Allen, *The Woman Who Did* (Oxford, New York: Oxford University Press, 1995). Robertson made reference to the "new woman" in her 1896 story "The Delicate Question Which?" mentioned above.
66 Kate McCullogh, "Mapping the 'Terra Incognita' of Woman: George Egerton's *Keynotes* (1893) and New Woman Fiction," in *The New Nineteenth Century: Feminist Readings of Underread Victorian Fiction*, ed.

Barbara Leah Harman and Susan Meyer (New York: Garland, 1996), 205–24.

67   "Don't Be a Bachelor," *Ladies Pictorial Weekly*, June 11, 1892, 381.

68   As Beth Light and Joy Parr suggest, "[t]he choice of a husband was not a young woman's alone." Because of the economic and social ramifications of marriage on entire families, "parents exercised as much control as possible over a young woman's transition from maiden to wife." Beth Light and Joy Parr, *Canadian Women on the Move, 1867–1920* (Toronto: New Hogtown Press, 1983), 110.

69   "Whom Not to Marry," *Ladies Pictorial Weekly*, June 4, 1892, 358.

70   "Courteous Men," *Ladies Pictorial Weekly*, March 19, 1892, 181.

71   "Shall Women Propose," *Ladies Pictorial Weekly*, February 13, 1892, 2.

72   Ibid.

73   "Visitors to the Sanctum," *Ladies Pictorial Weekly*, February 13, 1892, 2.

74   Karr, *Authors and Audiences*, 205–8

75   Ibid., 3.

76   "Happy Wives," *Ladies Pictorial Weekly*, April 9, 1892, 237.

77   Ibid.

78   Ibid.

79   Ramsay Cook and Wendy Mitchinson, eds., *The Proper Sphere: Woman's Place in Canadian Society* (Toronto: Oxford University Press, 1976), 225.

80   "Man's Love," *Ladies Pictorial Weekly*, June 11, 1892, 381.

81   "A Husband's Confession," *Ladies Pictorial Weekly*, March 26, 1892, 198.

82   Ibid.

83   "Give the Wife a Vacation," *Ladies Pictorial Weekly*, March 19, 1892, 189.

84   Watt and Lloyd, *The First Women's Institute School*, 139.

3. Playing Multiple Parts: Family, Society, and Sorrow

1   "Wedded," *Enterprise and Collingwood Messenger*, December 14, 1893, 1.

2   "Afloat in Georgian Bay," *Globe*, September 24, 1892, 6.

3   Jean Barman, *The West Beyond the West: A History of British Columbia*, revised edition (Toronto: University of Toronto Press, 1996), 129.

4   Collingwood Museum, Untitled Scrapbook [Henry Robertson], (hereafter cited as Robertson Scrapbook) "A Lady's Notes of a Trip to the Pacific," 14, column 1–2.

5   On Dunsmuir's interests in coal mining, see Barman, *The West Beyond the West*, 120–2. The Victoria newspaper reveals that the Watts attended a dance hosted by Mrs. James Dunsmuir on June 30, 1905. See *Victoria Daily Times*, July 3, 1905, 8.

6 Collingwood Museum, Robertson Scrapbook, "A Lady's Notes of a Trip to the Pacific," 14.

7 Collingwood Museum, Robertson Scrapbook, "A Roundabout Ride by Henry Robertson," 7. Henry Robertson's accounts of the trip to the Pacific, like those of his wife, were serialized. They were published in the periodical of the IOOF, *The Oddfellow*. The clippings in the family scrapbook do not give complete citation information about the dates on which these columns appeared.

8 Library and Archives Canada (hereafter cited as LAC), *Census of Canada, 1901*, RG31, microfilm reels T-6428 to T-6556. Year: *1901*; Census Place: *Metchosin, Victoria, British Columbia*. Page 2, Family No: 17; and *Census of Canada 1911*. Ottawa, LAC. Microfilm reels T-20326 to T-20460; Year: *1911*; Census Place: *Metchosin, Nanaimo, British Columbia*. Page 3, Family No: 26 (accessed November 24, 2009, at ancestry.com).

9 Collingwood Museum, Robertson Scrapbook, "A Roundabout Ride by Henry Robertson," 7.

10 Barman, *The West Beyond the West*, 194.

11 "Declared to be Suicide," *Daily Colonist*, October 12, 1892, 5; "Strongly Condemned: Sir M.B. Begbie's Opinion of the Treatment of Smallpox by the Victoria Authorities," *Daily Colonist*, October 27, 1892, 3; *Daily Colonist*, May 5, 1893, 5.

12 "The Smallpox Cases at Victoria," *Globe*, July 12, 1892, 1.

13 Meaford Public Library, Meaford, Ontario, Frank Harding Local History Collection, file 13M: Newspapers, typescript. Between 1868 and 1876, Alfred Watt's father, Hugh Watt, lived in Meaford, Ontario, in Grey County, approximately thirty kilometres (about eighteen miles) from Madge Robertson's hometown of Collingwood. Before Hugh Watt became a medical doctor, he owned and edited a newspaper in Meaford. "The first newspaper published in Meaford was the *Meaford Monitor and St. Vincent, Euphrasia and Collingwood [Townships] Journal*. It was founded by Hugh H. Watt, Editor and Proprietor. First issue was Thursday, June 4, 1868 ... About 1876 Watt lost interest [in the publishing business] and went to Toronto to study medicine ... the paper was edited by A.H. Watson until 1879 when he assumed full control when Watt graduated and went to B.C. to practice [medicine]."

14 See Naomi Miller, "Hugh Watt: Physician and Politician," *British Columbia Historical News* 37, 1 (Winter 2003): 18–21. On January 31, 1893, the *Daily Colonist* published one of Dr. Hugh Watt's speeches in the BC legislature in which he "advocated for an isolation facility at William Head. Low [sic] and behold, his son Alfred became Doctor in Charge for the first twenty years of its operation." Miller, 19.

15 *Victoria Daily Times*, September 15, 1903, 6; September 18, 1903, 8.

16 University of Victoria Archives, McPherson Library, University Women's Club, Victoria Branch, 1908–1993, AR 175, box 7, file 7.1, p. 4, 5, 13; and box 8, file 8.10, p. 1, 5, and 7.

17 Collingwood Museum, Robertson Scrapbook, 55: Press clipping from *Victoria Daily Times*, February 1895. On education as a nation-building tool in British Columbia, see Barman, *The West Beyond the West*, 130; Jean Barman, *Sojourning Sisters: The Lives and Letters of Jessie and Annie McQueen* (Toronto: University of Toronto Press, 2003).

18 The last two publications, both published in June 1896, appear to be "The Two-O'Clock Train," *Harper's*, June 1896, 160; and "The Delicate Question Which?" *Truth*, June 6, 1896, 10–11.

19 Geoffrey W. Burns, *A History of William Head* (William Head: William Head Institution, 1982), 14–16. See also Victoria *Daily Colonist*, January 7, 1893, 6, where it was reported that "[t]he B.C. Board of Trade moved at their [January 6, 1893] meeting that a quarantine station be placed at either Albert or William Head to screen steamers and passengers."

20 Elizabeth Gordon, "Dr. and Mrs. Alfred Watt," in *Footprints: Pioneer Families of the Metchosin District Southern Vancouver Island 1851–1900*, ed. Marion I. Helgesen (Metchosin: Metchosin School Museum Society, 1983), 245–6.

21 "Dr. A.T. Watt Killed by Fall," *Daily Colonist*, July 29, 1913, 1.

22 Ibid.

23 These statistics are drawn from the annual reports of Dr. A.T. Watt, Superintendent of BC Quarantines, BC Provincial Archives, microfilm reel B-8648 GR 2005; Canada. Department of Public Health William Head Quarantine Station, 1902–1956 [Reports of the Division of Quarantine – British Columbia, 1897–1956]. For more detail on the operation of the quarantine station at William Head, see Linda M. Ambrose, "Quarantine in Question: The 1913 Investigation at William Head, B.C." *Canadian Bulletin of Medical History/Bulletin canadien d'histoire de la medicine* 22, 1 (2005): 139–54.

24 "Doing Good Work," *Victoria Daily Times*, September 1, 1897, np. This clipping is included in the Collingwood Museum, Robertson Scrapbook, 127.

25 Ibid.

26 Ibid.

27 Bernard McEvoy, *From the Great Lakes to the Wide West: Impressions of a Tour between Toronto and the Pacific* (Toronto: William Briggs, 1902), 201.

28 Ibid., 202–3.

29 Madge Robertson, "By Book Post," *Victoria Daily Times*, April 4, 1903, 12.
30 McEvoy, *From the Great Lakes to the Wide West*, 204. See Watt's review of McEvoy's earlier book of poetry, *Away from Newspaperdom and Other Poems* (Toronto: G.N. Morang, 1897), in her column, "By Book Post," *Victoria Daily Times*, September 15, 1897, 6.
31 BC Archives, microfilm B 8648 GR 2005, Canada, Department of Public Health, William Head Quarantine Station, 1902–1958, A.T. Watt, Superintendent of BC Quarantines to the Minister of Agriculture, October 31, 1905.
32 Ibid. See also A.T. Watt, Superintendent of BC Quarantines to the Minister of Agriculture, April 1, 1907.
33 When Watt first took the job in 1897, he was paid $2,500 per year. Microfiche copy of 16 books, "The Civil Service List of Canada," 1885–1900 (all as of 1st July), CIHM 46477-46492, fiche 1–3 in each year. http:// search.ancestry.ca/ (accessed November 24, 2009). A $2,500 salary in 1897 is equivalent to $321,616.54 in 2008 dollars. See Samuel H. Williamson, "Six Ways to Compute the Relative Value of a U.S. Dollar Amount, 1790 to Present," MeasuringWorth, 2009. URL http://www.measuringworth .com/uscompare/. My thanks to Andrew Smith for suggesting these conversion tools.
34 LAC, *Census of Canada, 1901*, RG31, microfilm reels T-6428 to T-6556, Year: *1901*; Census Place: *Metchosin, Victoria, British Columbia.*, Page 2, Family No: 17; and LAC, *Census of Canada 1911*, microfilm reels T-20326 to T-20460; Year: *1911*; Census Place: *Metchosin, Nanaimo, British Columbia.* Page 3, Family No: 26 (accessed November 24, 2009 at ancestry.com).
35 News of Watt's travel to attend her sister's wedding appeared in the local papers: *Victoria Daily Times*, June 6, 1900, 8, and June 8, 1900, 3, 5; "Arthur-Robertson Nuptials," *Enterprise Messenger*, May 31, 1900, 8; and "Arthur-Robertson," *Collingwood Bulletin*, June 1, 1900, 1.
36 Collingwood Public Library, Cemeteries, Town of Collingwood [index], Section 3: Presbyterian Cemetery, Collingwood, Ontario, 308 – Robertson, Henry. Listed in this index are three of the Arthurs' children who died as infants: Isobel Robertson Arthur, June 21, 1901 – August 29, 1901; Frederic Housten Robins Arthur, July 10, 1902 – August 11, 1903; and Arthur, Infant, November 5, 1908. Katie and her husband had two other children who survived: Noel Robins Arthur and Bethia Rose (Arthur) Elliott. Bethia Elliott died at the age of 94 in 1997, and she was predeceased by her brother. *Collingwood Enterprise Bulletin*, November 12, 1997, B7.
37 "Mother's Boy," *Ladies Pictorial Weekly*, June 18, 1892, 2.
38 Ibid.

39 Linda M. Ambrose and Kristin Hall, "A New Woman in Print and Practice: The Canadian Literary Career of Madge Robertson Watt, 1890–1907," *History of Intellectual Culture* 7, 1 (2007): 1–19. Available online: http://www.ucalgary.ca/hic ISSN 1492-7810.

40 Barman, *Constance Lindsay Skinner: Writing on the Frontier* (Toronto: University of Toronto Press, 2002), 157–8.

41 Madge Robertson, "By Book Post," *Victoria Daily Times*, March 11, 1898.

42 Madge Robertson, "By Book Post," *Victoria Daily Times*, June 27, 1901.

43 Madge Robertson, "By Book Post," *Victoria Daily Times*, May 25, 1900.

44 Madge Robertson, "By Book Post," *Victoria Daily Times*, January 23, 1899.

45 Richardson and Willis, *The New Woman in Fiction and Fact*, 12.

46 Ibid.

47 Madge Robertson, "By Book Post," *Victoria Daily Times*, January 23, 1899; Mary Ives Todd, *The Heterodox Marriage of a New Woman* (New York: Robert Lewis Weed Company Publishers, 1898), 182–3.

48 Madge Robertson, "By Book Post," *Victoria Daily Times*, January 23, 1899.

49 Mary Adams, *The Confessions of a Wife* (Toronto: Copp Clark, 1902); Madge Robertson, "By Book Post," *Victoria Daily Times*, Saturday December 27, 1902, 12.

50 Ibid.

51 Ibid.

52 Ibid.

53 Willis, 54, 64.

54 Richardson and Willis, *The New Woman in Fiction and Fact*, 31.

55 In the fall of 1905, Watt donated fifty "volumes of selected literature" to the Victoria public library. According to the newspaper account, "the books cover a wide range of subjects and are duly appreciated." *Victoria Daily Times*, September 15, 1905, 6

56 *Victoria Daily Times*, May 5, 1905, 6.

57 *Victoria Daily Times*, April 15, 1910, 7, 12.

58 *Victoria Daily Times*, September 27, 1910, 5.

59 "Over the Tea Table," *Victoria Daily Times*, January 18, 1908, 6.

60 Annie Cleland and Madge Watt were both charter members of the University Women's Club of Victoria when it first organized in 1908. University of Victoria Archives, McPherson Library, University Women's Club, Victoria Branch, 1908–1993. AR 175, box 7, file 7.1, p. 4, 5, 13; and box 8, file 8.10, p. 1, 5, and 7.

61 "Over the Tea Table," *Victoria Daily Times*, February 29, 1908, 8.

62 The Watts were very involved in the Victoria chapter of the University of Toronto Alumni Association, hosting a gathering in the fall of 1903 to

meet President Louden, and standing for office in the association. Madge was elected as secretary-treasurer, and Alfred as councillor. *Victoria Daily Times*, September 15, 1903, 6, and September 18, 1903, 8. The Clelands were a part of this circle of friends. Hugh Mackenzie Cleland died on November 4, 1903, just a few weeks after the alumni chapter in Victoria was established. *Daily Colonist*, November 5, 1903, 3.

63 Canada, Royal Commission on Industrial Training and Technical Education, *Report of the Commissioners*, Ottawa, 1913, 2349. Although this report was not published until 1913, Cleland and Watt appeared before the commission in December 1910. See "Views of Many Citizens Heard: Royal Commission Ends Its Sitting," *Victoria Daily Times*, December 6, 1910, 4.

64 Canada, Royal Commission on Industrial Training and Technical Education, *Report of the Commissioners*, Ottawa, 1913, 2352.

65 Ibid.

66 *Victoria Daily Times*, October 8, 1909, 3.

67 On the Ontario Women's Institutes, see Linda M. Ambrose, *For Home and Country: The Centennial History of the Women's Institutes in Ontario, 1897–1997* (Erin, Ontario: Boston Mills Press, 1996); and "'What Are the Good of Those Meetings Anyway?': Explaining the Early Popularity of the Ontario Women's Institutes," *Ontario History* LXXXVII, 1 (Spring 1995), 1–19.

68 Canada, Royal Commission on Industrial Training and Technical Education, *Report of the Commissioners*, Ottawa, 1913, 2353. On the Agricultural Instruction Act, see Linda M. Ambrose, "'Better and Happier Men and Women': The Agricultural Instruction Act, 1913–1924," *Historical Studies in Education/Revue d'histoire de l'éducation* 16, 2 (2004), 257–85.

69 BC Archives, microfilm reel A1660, Women's Institute, Advisory Board of Women's Institutes of British Columbia, Minutes and Papers, 1911–1932, "Minutes of Meeting of Advisory Board of Women's Institutes," August 14 and 15, 1911, 1.

70 Ibid., 2.

71 Ibid., 9.

72 Ibid., 1.

73 Ibid., 2.

74 *Victoria Daily Times*, Tuesday, April 11, 1911, 8.

75 *Victoria Daily Times*, Friday April 29, 1910, 9.

76 Ibid.

77 BC Archives microfilm reel A1660, Women's Institute, Advisory Board of Women's Institutes of British Columbia, Minutes and Papers, 1911–1932, "Notes on Women's Institutes in B.C.," 1.

78 *Victoria Daily Times*, August 10, 1912, 5; and August 24, 1912, 10.
79 The annual records of the quarantine station show that during the period from April 1, 1913, to March 31, 1914, the *Monteagle* was the only ship that was quarantined.
80 For a full account of this episode of quarantine history, see Linda M. Ambrose, "Quarantine in Question: The 1913 Investigation at William Head, B.C." *Canadian Bulletin of Medical History/Bulletin canadien d'histoire de la medicine* 22, 1 (2005), 139–54.
81 BC Archives, microfilm reel B 7927 GR 1739 Canada, Immigration Branch, Ships' Passenger Lists, 1905–1919. R.M.S. *Monteagle*. The following ports of embarkation and dates of sailing in 1913 are listed as part of the voyage: Hong Kong, 8th March; Shanghai 10th March; Kobe 14th March; Yokohama 16th March, Bound for Vancouver.
82 BC Archives, microfilm reel B 8648 GR 2005, Canada, Department of Public Health, William Head Quarantine Station, 1902–1956, Reports of the Division of Quarantine – British Columbia, 1897–1956, Dr. A.T. Watt, Superintendent of B.C. Quarantines, to the Minister of Agriculture, Ottawa, March 31, 1913.
83 "Liner Arrives Here with Half Her Crew," *Vancouver Sun*, April 3, 1913, 5; "William Head Depot Grows Like Mushroom: Six Hundred and Fifty Passengers on *Monteagle* Form Quite a Townful," *Vancouver Sun*, April 2, 1913, 7.
84 LAC, RG 17, vol. 1190, correspondence 228392, file 228852 Messrs Heberdeen, McCarrison, Grahame, Bromhead, and Cohn to the Editor, *Daily Colonist*, Victoria, BC., April 9, 1913.
85 LAC, RG 17, vol. 1190, correspondence 232194, file 228852, A.T. Watt to Messrs. Heberdeen, McCarrison, Grahame, Bromhead and Cohn, April 12, 1913.
86 "Black, Judson Burpee," http://www.parl.gc.ca/parlinfo/Files/Parliamentarian.aspx?Item=1b637cfa-e603-4e85-9454-14ead2cf59eb&Language=E (accessed July 29, 2014).
87 "Quarantine Station Conditions Cause of Serious Indictments by Passengers of *Monteagle*," *Vancouver Sun*, April 17, 1913, 1.
88 LAC, RG 17, vol. 1190, correspondence 232194, file 228852, R.S. Kinney to Hon. Martin Burrell, Minister of Agriculture, Ottawa, April 19, 1913. See also BC Archives, microfilm reel B 7927, GR 1739, Canada, Immigration Branch, Ships' Passenger Lists, 1905–1919.
89 The state of the quarantine station's septic system was a central issue during the inquiry. LAC, RG 17, vol. 1190, file 228852, H.R.W. Moore, "Report of the Commissioner in the Matter of the Investigation of the

Quarantine Station at William Head, B. C.," September 22, 1913, 8–16; and LAC, RG 17, vol. 1190, file: Transcript of Royal Commission 244492, 12–13, 22–3, 33–7, 85–6, 104–8.

90 *Victoria Daily Times,* June 27, 1905, 2; See also BC Archives, microfilm reel B 8648 GR 2005, Canada. Department of Public Health, William Head Quarantine Station, 1902–1956, for Watt's Annual Report 1905–1907, 37.

91 LAC, RG 17, vol. 1190, file 232194, H.R.W. Moore, "Report of the Commissioner In the Matter of the Investigation of the Quarantine Station at William Head, B.C.," September 22, 1913, 5.

92 "Toronto Loses a Well-Known Citizen: Mr. Hubert Lorne Watt, Treasurer of Canada Life Assurance Co. Passes Away," *Victoria Daily Times,* May 23, 1913, 22; Archives of Ontario, MS 935 reel 183, Death Registration # 003730 1913 Herbert [sic] Lorne Watt. Date of death May 15, 1913. Cause of death listed as "Cirrhosis of liver non-alcoholic; pulmonary tubercular lesions." My thanks to Rosemary Ambrose for locating this death registration through the Latter Day Saints Family History Centre.

93 Among the items collected during the inquiry, one personal item is preserved: a bookmark with an excerpt from Tennyson's poem, "In Memoriam" that seems to have captured Alfred Watt's feelings for his brother very effectively. The quotation reads, "To my dear Brother, 'But thou and I are one in kind/ As moulded like in nature's mint/ And hill and wood and field did print./ The same sweet forms in either mind/ At one dear knee we proffer'd vows/ One lesson from one book we learn'd/ Ere childhood's flaxen ringlet turn'd/ To black and brown on kindred brows.'" LAC, RG 17, vol. 1190, file 228852.

94 LAC, RG 17, vol. 1190, file 228852, H.B. Robertson letter to H.W.R. Moore, "Re: Quarantine Investigation," July 23, 1913.

95 "Well-known Doctor Escapes from Nurse and Jumps to Death," *Vancouver Sun,* July 29, 1913, 1.

96 Susan J. Johnston, "Twice Slain: Sex-Trade Workers and Suicide in British Columbia, 1870–1920," *Journal of the Canadian Historical Association/Revue de la Société historique du Canada* 5, 1 (1994): 149.

97 British Columbia, Division of Vital Statistics, Volume 028, Death Registrations 010284 to 011002, Death certificate of Alfred Tennyson Watt, 010839. The causes of death were listed as "a) Remote or earlier pathological or morbid condition: Melancholia; b) Immediate or Final Determining Cause: Suicide – Fracture of base of skull."

98 John Weaver and David Wright, *Histories of Suicide: International Perspectives on Self-Destruction in the Modern World* (Toronto: University of Toronto Press, 2009), 11.

 99 Anne Nesbet, "Suicide as Literary Fact in the 1920s," *Slavic Review* 50, 4 (1991): 827.
100 "Death of Dr. Watt," *Daily Colonist*, July 29, 1913, 4.
101 Ibid.
102 BC Archives, microfilm reel A1660, Women's Institute, Advisory Board of Women's Institutes of British Columbia, Minutes and Papers, 1911–1932, "Annual Meeting Advisory Board, September 10, 1913, Victoria." These minutes record that Watt was present, and "a resolution of sympathy with the secretary in her recent loss was passed and the hope expressed that she would continue in the work." When the board met again in May 1914, it was noted in the minutes that Mrs. Watt had not left all of her records behind, presumably because she left in haste sometime after the September 1913 meeting due to her travel plans. See also "Minutes of the Semi-annual meeting of the Advisory Board of Women's Institutes for British Columbia, held at the Parliament Buildings, Victoria, May 14–16, 1914."
103 LAC, RG 17, vol. 1190, file 232194, H.R.W. Moore, "Report of the Commissioner In the Matter of the Investigation of the Quarantine Station at William Head, B.C.," September 22, 1913, 5.

4. Role Reversal: From Colonial Widow to Imperial War Hero

  1 Adele Perry, "Interlocuting Empire: Colonial Womanhood, Settler Identity, and Frances Herring," in *Rediscovering the British World*, ed. Phillip Buckner and R. Douglas Francis (Calgary: University of Calgary Press, 2005), 159.
  2 Phillip Buckner, "The Long Goodbye: English Canadians and the British World," in Buckner and Francis, *Rediscovering the British World*, 187.
  3 Ibid, 197.
  4 Annie Walker, Edith M. Collins, and M. McIntyre Hood, *Fifty Years of Achievement: In Commemoration of the 50th Anniversary of the Founding of the Women's Institutes of Ontario* (Toronto: Federated Women's Institutes of Ontario, 1948), 46.
  5 *Ontario Women's Institute Story: In Commemoration of the 75th Anniversary of the Founding of the Women's Institutes of Ontario* (Toronto: Federated Women's Institutes of Ontario, 1972), 104.
  6 The papers of the National Federation of Women's Institutes are housed at the Women's Library (TWL); the reading room for TWL is now located in the Lionel Robbins Building at the London School of Economics. For more information on the collection see www2.lse.ac.uk/library/newsandinformation/womenslibraryatLSE.

7 Ancestry.com, *UK Incoming Passenger Lists, 1878–1960* [database online], Provo, UT, USA: Ancestry.com Operations Inc, 2008. Original data: Board of Trade: Commercial and Statistical Department and successors: Inwards Passenger Lists, Kew, Surrey, England: The National Archives of the UK (TNA), series BT26, 1,472 pieces. Class: BT26; piece: 554; item: 27. See also "First Turbine Steamer to Cross the Atlantic, *Victorian*, Meeting Bad Weather, Breaks No Record. Brought 1,500 Passengers Behaved Well in Heavy Seas and Her Captain Hopes to Make a New Record," *New York Times*, April 2, 1905. My thanks to Andrew Smith for pointing me toward this article.

8 Library and Archives Canada (hereafter cited as LAC), *Census of Canada, 1911*, Ottawa, Ontario, Canada: LAC, 2007, http://www .collectionscanada.gc.ca/databases/census-1911/index-e.html, series RG31-C-1, Statistics Canada fonds, microfilm reels T-20326 to T-20460, Census Place: *Metchosin, Nanaimo, British Columbia*. Page 3, Family No: 26; http://data2.collectionscanada.gc.ca/1911/jpg/e001938087.jpg

9 UK Incoming Passenger Lists, 1878–1960, Class: BT26; Piece: 554; Item: 27. For more on the relative cost of first-class transatlantic travel, see Mark Rennella and Whitney Walton, "Planned Serendipity: American Travelers and the Transatlantic Voyage in the Nineteenth and Twentieth Centuries," *Journal of Social History* 38, 2 (Winter 2004): 365–83, esp. page 368. My thanks to David Leeson for bringing this article to my attention.

10 The *Victorian* was capable of making the crossing in five days, and this longer travel time for the Watts most likely means that the ship encountered some stormy weather along the way. On the maiden voyage of *Victorian* in 1905, the weather did not cooperate, and rather than breaking a record for the speed of her first transatlantic crossing from Liverpool to New York, the ship was delayed for two days by bad weather, completing the voyage in seven days, rather than the expected five days. *New York Times*, April 2, 1905.

11 Cecilia Morgan, *'A Happy Holiday': English Canadians and Transatlantic Tourism, 1870–1930* (Toronto: University of Toronto Press, 2008), 36.

12 Ibid., 44–5.

13 Godman explains that her father left the diocese because some of his ideas were not acceptable to the local bishop. She provided three examples: 1) he once allowed his church to be used for the funeral of a Roman Catholic priest; 2) he performed a marriage ceremony "for a white man and his Chinese bride"; and 3) due to his "hatred of war, he had spoken out against the South African campaign as being unnecessary. Such unorthodox action Bishop Perrin felt could not be

tolerated." Josephine Godman, "The Ellison Family: A Pioneer of Port Renfrew," in *Footprints: Pioneer Families of the Metchosin District, Southern Vancouver Island 1851–1900*, edited by Marion I. Helgesen (Metchosin: Metchosin School Museum Society, 1983), 99–100.

14 Ibid., 101.

15 According to Josephine Godman's own account, her life was filled with tragedy: "The war came and my husband joined the Royal Sussex Regiment, and was taken prisoner at Mons. I had another son whom he never saw, as he died a prisoner of war, and I lost my eldest son to polio." Ibid., 101. The elder son died in 1918, and at their July 24 meeting that year, the executive committee of the National Federation of Women's Institutes passed a motion expressing their condolences to Mrs. Godman "in the sad loss of her little son." The Women's Library, National Federation of Women's Institutes (hereafter cited as TWL, NFWI), Complete Minute Book 1915–1919, GB 0106 5 FWI/A/1/1/1, vol. 1. As if that was not enough for one woman to bear, Godman explained that "[d]uring World War II, my younger son was killed on his ship after distinguished service. As he had no children, there were no descendants." Godman, "The Ellison Family: A Pioneer of Port Renfrew," 101.

16 For more on the Ontario roots of the WI movement, see Linda M. Ambrose, *For Home and Country: The Centennial History of the Women's Institutes in Ontario, 1897–1997* (Erin, Ontario: Boston Mills Press, 1996).

17 BC Archives, reel A 1660, Women's Institute, Advisory Board of the Women's Institutes of British Columbia, Minutes and Papers, 1911–1932. For information on the organization of the first WI branches in BC, see *Modern Pioneers: British Columbia Women's Institutes, 1909–1959* (Victoria: British Columbia Women's Institutes, 1959), 14–15.

18 Ambrose, *For Home and Country*; idem, *Women's Institutes in Canada: The First One Hundred Years, 1897–1997* (Ottawa: Federated Women's Institutes of Canada, 2000); Catherine C. Cole and Ann Milovic, "Education, Community Service, and Social Life: The Alberta Women's Institutes and Rural Families, 1909–1945," in *Standing on New Ground: Women in Alberta*, ed. Catherine A. Cavanaugh and Randi R. Warne (Edmonton: University of Alberta Press, 1993), 19–33; Terry Crowley, "The Origins of Continuing Education for Women: The Ontario Women's Institutes," *Canadian Woman Studies* 7, 3 (Fall 1986): 78–81; Carol J. Dennison, "They Also Served: The British Columbia Women's Institutes in Two World Wars," in *Not Just Pin Money: Selected Essays on the History of Women's Work in British Columbia*, ed. Barbara K. Latham and Roberta J.

Pazdro (Victoria: Camosun College, 1984), 211–19; and "Housekeepers of the Community: The British Columbia Women's Institutes, 1909–1946" in *Knowledge for the People: The Struggle for Adult Learning in English-Speaking Canada, 1828–1973*, ed. Michael R. Welton (Toronto: OISE Press, 1987), 52–72; E. Fletcher, *History of the Manitoba Women's Institute, 1919–1975* (Winnipeg: Manitoba Women's Institute, 1976); Marianne G. Otty, *Fifty Years of Women's Institutes in New Brunswick, Canada, 1911–1961: A History* (New Brunswick: Women's Institutes, 1961).

19 Perry, "Interlocuting Empire," 159.

20 Histories of the Women's Institutes published in the UK include J.W. Robertson Scott, *The Story of the Women's Institute Movement in England and Wales and Scotland* (Idbury, Kingham, Oxon: Village Press, 1925); Janet E. Courtney, *Countrywomen in Council: The English and Scottish Women's Institutes with Chapters on the Movement in the Dominions and on Townswomen's Guilds* (London: Oxford University Press, 1933); Cicely McCall, *Women's Institutes* (London: William Collins of London, 1943); Inez Jenkins, *The History of the Women's Institute Movement of England and Wales* (Oxford: Oxford University Press, 1953); Simon Goodenough, *Jam and Jerusalem: A Pictorial History of Britain's Greatest Women's Movement* (Glasgow and London: William Collins and Sons Company Limited, 1977); Piers Dudgeon, ed., *Village Voices: A Portrait of Change in England's Green and Pleasant Land, 1915–1990* (London: WI Books Ltd., 1989); Maggie Andrews, *The Acceptable Face of Feminism: The Women's Institute as a Social Movement* (London: Lawrence & Wishart, 1997); and Jane Robinson *A Force to be Reckoned With: A History of the Women's Institute* (London: Virago Press, 2011).

21 Andrews, "Identity Problems: A History of the Histories," in *The Acceptable Face of Feminism*, 41–57.

22 Ontario, Department of Agriculture, Women's Institute Branch, *Annual Report*, 1920, Mrs. Alfred Watt, "Evening Session Address," 126.

23 Ibid.

24 Ibid.

25 Ibid.

26 Ibid.

27 Mrs. Alfred Watt, and Miss Nest Lloyd, *The First Women's Institute School (Sussex 1918)* (Sussex Federation of Women's Institutes, 1919), 145.

28 Constance Davies, *A Grain of Mustard Seed: An Account of the First Women's Institute in Great Britain, with Extracts from Its Minute Book* (Denbigh: Gee and Son Denbigh Ltd., 1953), 11.

29 Watt, "Evening Session Address," 126.

30 Ibid.

31 Ibid.

32 The translation comes from a postcard mailed to the author from Bethan Williams, May 2007.

33 Davies, *A Grain of Mustard Seed*, 41–69. My thanks to Bethan Williams, former county chair for Ceredigion WIs and a NFWI board member, who told me about this book when we first met at the ACWW Triennial Meeting in March 2004 at Hobart, Tasmania; and to Audrey Jones, chair of the WI Federations of Wales, who sent me a copy of the book. Bethan and Audrey were our enthusiastic and gracious hosts when my husband and I visited North Wales in May 2008.

34 Davies, *A Grain of Mustard Seed*, 69.

35 On Cotton's contributions to the WI in the UK, see Davies, *A Grain of Mustard Seed*, 33–6.

36 Ibid, 54.

37 Ibid.

38 The report appeared in the *North Wales Chronicle*, June 18, 1915. It is reproduced in Davies, *A Grain of Mustard Seed*, 58 and 87.

39 Archifau Gwynedd Archives, The Agricultural Organization Society, Women's Institutes – North Wales, "Mrs. Watt's Report on Some Recent Work," 1. My thanks to Bethan Williams, who allowed me to consult her copy of this report.

40 Ibid.

41 Ibid.

42 Ibid.

43 On March 15, 1913, the deputy minister of the British Columbia Department of Agriculture wrote a letter to Henry Robertson, c/o Dr. A.T. Watt (Quarantine Station, William Head), to express his appreciation of the "very able manner in which [he] compiled the Rules and Regulations for Women's Institutes." Collingwood Museum, Untitled Scrapbook [Henry Robertson] (hereafter cited as Collingwood Museum, Robertson Scrapbook), 177.

44 Archifau Gwynedd Archives, The Agricultural Organization Society, Women's Institutes – North Wales, "Mrs. Watt's Report on Some Recent Work," 1.

45 Anne Stamper, *Sussex, the Cradle of the English WIs* (n.p.: Anne Stamper, 2004), 5.

46 On the growth of Ontario Women's Institutes in the early years, see Ambrose, *For Home and Country*, 39–41, and 228. For an understanding of how the Canadian Women's Institutes were financed through

government grants, see Linda M. Ambrose, "'Better and Happier Men and Women': *The Agricultural Instruction Act*, 1913–1924," *Historical Studies in Education/Revue d'histoire de l'éducation* 16, 2 (2004): 257–85.

47 Andrews, *The Acceptable Face of Feminism*, 22.

48 Ibid.

49 Anne Stamper, *Sussex, the Cradle of the English WIs*, 5.

50 Ibid., 9.

51 Ibid., 8.

52 "In Clubland," *Saturday Night*, August 18, 1917, 27.

53 Buckner, "The Long Goodbye," 188.

54 Katie Pickles, *Female Imperialism and National Identity: Imperial Order Daughters of the Empire* (Manchester and New York: Manchester University Press, 2002), 2.

55 LAC, MG 28 I 316, Federated Women's Institutes of Canada, vol. 7, file: Mrs. Alfred Watt, biographical notes, n.d., # 25

56 Janet S.K.Watson, *Fighting Different Wars: Experience, Memory, and the First World War in Britain* (Cambridge: Cambridge University Press, 2004), 3–4.

57 "In Clubland," 27.

58 Watson, *Fighting Different Wars*, 8.

59 Watt and Lloyd, *The First Women's Institute School*, 142.

60 Paul Ward, "Empire and the Everyday: Britishness and Imperialism in Women's Lives in the Great War," in Buckner and Francis, *Rediscovering the British World*, 268.

61 Anne Stamper, *Sussex, the Cradle of the English WIs*, 6–9.

62 Ward, "Empire and the Everyday," 268.

63 LAC, MG 28 I 316, Federated Women's Institutes of Canada, vol. 7, file: Mrs. Alfred Watt, biographical notes, n.d., # 25.

64 Ward, "Empire and the Everyday," 268.

65 Watt and Lloyd, *The First Women's Institute School*, 8.

66 Collingwood Museum, Robertson Scrapbook, 188, 189, contains a press clipping from *Saturday Night*, May 3, 1919.

67 Buckner, "The Long Goodbye," 193.

68 In the Collingwood newspaper, the *Collingwood Enterprise Bulletin*, a letter written from Lt. Robin Watt, son of Mrs. Watt, to his mother was presented under the headline "Grandson of Henry Robertson K.C. in offensive at Somme," Collingwood Museum, Robertson Scrapbook, 184. The press clipping does not include the date of publication.

69 Watt, and Lloyd, *The First Women's Institute School*, 8.

70 "In Clubland," 1917.

71 Watt, "Evening Address," 128.

72 Ibid., 136.
73 Mary MacLeod Moore, "A Canadian Woman's Work: What Mrs. A.T. Watt, M.B.E, of Victoria, B.C. Has Done in the Great War," *Saturday Night*, May 3, 1919, 31.
74 Mrs. Alfred Watt, *Women's Institutes* (London: Federation of Women's Institutes, 1919), 4. This pamphlet was accessed at The Women's Library, London UK.
75 Andrews, *The Acceptable Face of Feminism*, 1–15.
76 Watt, *Women's Institutes*, 2–3.
77 LAC, "Section of Women's Institute Organization and Technique Embracing Principles, Aims, and Methods of Work of Women's Institutes," MG 28I 316, vol. 8, file: Aims and Methods of Work of WIs, n.d.
78 Collingwood Museum, Robertson Scrapbook, 188, contains a clipping from the *Montreal Herald and Star*, February 12, 1919. Beginning with the May 1919 issue, the monthly WI journal *Home and Country* [UK] published a map of England and Wales on the front cover, showing the number of Institutes that were operating for each county. This map appeared regularly (though not every issue) until December 1920.
79 Watt and Lloyd, *The First Women's Institute School*, 62.
80 Ibid., 108.
81 Ibid., 53.
82 Ibid., 120.
83 Ibid., 121.
84 Ibid., 7.
85 Ibid., 11.
86 Ibid.,11, 92.
87 Ibid., 133.
88 Ibid., 45.
89 Ibid., 126.
90 Andrews, *The Acceptable Face of Feminism*, 48. A similar debate about the WI in Ontario is raised by Linda M. Ambrose and Margaret Kechnie, "Social Control or Social Feminism? Two Views of the Ontario Women's Institutes," *Agricultural History* 73, 2 (Spring 1999): 222–37.
91 "In Clubland," 1917.
92 Pickles, *Female Imperialism and National Identity*.
93 "An Appreciation of Mrs. Watt by the Lady Isabel Margesson," in Watt and Lloyd, *The First Women's Institute School*, 141.
94 *Home and Country* [UK], June 1919, 1.

5. On the World Stage: Forging International Networks

1 Leila J. Rupp, *Worlds of Women: The Making of an International Women's Movement* (Princeton, NJ: Princeton University Press, 1997).
2 Christine Bolt, *Sisterhood Questioned? Race, Class and Internationalism in the American and British Women's Movements, c. 1880s–1970s* (London and New York: Routledge, 2004), 182–90.
3 Ibid, 53.
4 Julia Bush, "Edwardian Ladies and the 'Race' Dimensions of British Imperialism," *Women's Studies International Forum* 21, 3 (1998): 277–89; Rupp, *Worlds of Women*, 53.
5 Laurel Lane-Moore, *Collingwood: Historic Homes and Buildings* (Collingwood, ON: Blue Mountain Foundation for the Arts, 1989), 98. It is not clear when this "extravagant trip around the world" occurred; however, in the fall of 1908, Robertson (aged 68 years) and a Mr. G.B. Westcott spent six weeks in England. See Collingwood Museum, Untitled Scrapbook [Henry Robertson], "Home from the Old Land," *Collingwood Bulletin*, November 12, 1908, 1, in Scrapbook, 153.
6 Mrs. Neve Scarborough, *History of the Associated Country Women of the World and of Its Member Societies* (London: The Rydal Press, 1953), 8
7 "W.I's Formed in Britain, Mrs. Alfred Watt Tells of Great Work Done There,' *Globe*, September 4, 1919, 8.
8 Estimates about the number of WIs in England at the end of the war vary between a total number of 900 and 1,200. See, for example, J.W. Robertson Scott, *The Story of the Women's Institute Movement in England and Wales and Scotland* (Idbury, Kingham, Oxon: The Village Press, 1925), 266; Janet E. Courtney, *Countrywomen in Council: The English and Scottish Women's Institutes with Chapters on the Movement in the Dominions and on Townswomen's Guilds* (London: Oxford University Press, 1933), 47; Inez Jenkins, *The History of the Women's Institute Movement of England and Wales* (Oxford: Oxford University Press, 1953), 22. In Canada, twenty-two years after the first WI was founded, 920 branches existed in 1919. Linda M. Ambrose, *For Home and Country: The Centennial History of the Women's Institutes in Ontario, 1897–1997* (Erin, Ontario: Boston Mills Press, 1996), 79.
9 "W.I's Formed in Britain, Mrs. Alfred Watt Tells of Great Work Done There,' *Globe*, September 4, 1919, 9.
10 Ontario Sessional Papers, 1920, 129.
11 Ibid, 129.
12 "Wait for Passage," *Globe*, September 4, 1919, 1.

13 *Globe*, September 4, 1919, 8.

14 Ibid.

15 Linda M. Ambrose, *Women's Institutes in Canada: The First One Hundred Years, 1897–1997* (Ottawa: Federated Women's Institutes of Canada, 2000), 13–20.

16 Mrs. Alfred Watt and Miss Nest Lloyd, *The First Women's Institute School (Sussex 1918)* (Sussex Federation of Women's Institutes, 1919), 45.

17 In Saskatchewan, until 1972, the provincially sponsored rural women's groups were known as Homemakers Clubs. In Quebec there were Les Cercles de Fermières, which were not affiliated with the FWIC at first, although they did join the ACWW in 1933. The Newfoundland and Labrador women's organizations, known as the Jubilee Guilds, joined the FWIC in 1951. See Ambrose, *Women's Institutes in Canada*, 99–132.

18 Linda M. Ambrose, "'Better and Happier Men and Women': *The Agricultural Instruction Act, 1913–1924*," *Historical Studies in Education/ Revue d'histoire de l'éducation*, 16, 2 (2004): 257–85.

19 Ontario Sessional Papers, 1919.

20 Library and Archives Canada (hereafter cited as LAC), MG 28 I 316, vol. 12, file: "Inaugural Meeting, February 1919, Winnipeg," 1–7.

21 Ibid.

22 LAC, MG 28 I 316, vol. 12, file: Minutes November 7, 1919, 1.

23 LAC, MG28 I 316, vol. 12, file: Minutes First Open Convention, November 11, 1919, 2.

24 Ibid, Minutes November 7, 1919, 5.

25 Ibid., 3–4.

26 Ibid., 6.

27 Ibid.

28 Ibid.

29 BC Archives, microfilm reel A1660, Women's Institute. Advisory Board of Women's Institutes for British Columbia, Minutes and Papers, 1911–1932. Minutes of Advisory Board of Women's Institutes for British Columbia, August 24 & 25, 1920, 2.

30 Ibid., 2.

31 "Women's Institutes Recommend Constitutional Amendments Giving Greater Independence of Government Control," *Victoria Daily Times*, December 11, 1920, n.p. Clipping included in BC Archives, microfilm reel A 1660.

32 Ibid.

33 Ibid.

34 Ibid.

35 BC Archives, reel A1660, Women's Institute. Advisory Board of Women's Institutes for British Columbia, Minutes and Papers, 1911–1932. Minutes of Advisory Board of Women's Institutes for British Columbia, May 10, 1921, 7.
36 Ibid.
37 Ibid., 7–8.
38 When Watt and Godman returned to BC, they directed their correspondence to the address of Mrs. Cleland, Rockland Avenue, Victoria, BC. *Home and Country* [UK], March 1920, 7. When Robin Watt was decommissioned by the British army in 1921, he planned to join his mother at an address in Esquimalt. See Ancestry.com, *Canada, Ocean Arrivals (Form 30A), 1919–1924* [database on-line]. Provo, UT, USA: Ancestry.com Operations, Inc., 2009. Original data: LAC. *Form 30A, 1919–1924 (Ocean Arrivals)*. Ottawa, Ontario, Canada: LAC, n.d. RG 76. Department of Employment and Immigration Fonds. Microfilm reels: T-14939 to T-15248. The Victoria Women's Institute membership list in the spring of 1921 recorded Watt and Godman's address as Lampson St., Esquimalt. See BC Archives, Women's Institutes, Victoria Women's Institute. Minute Book 1921–1922, Membership List.
39 BC Archives, Women's Institutes, Victoria Women's Institute. Minute Book 1921–1922., Executive Meeting, May 31, 1921.
40 Ibid.
41 Ibid., Special Meeting, May 9, 1921.
42 LAC, MG 28 I 316, vol. 3, file: FWIC Minute Book 1919–1939, Minutes of the Second Open Convention, University of Alberta, Edmonton, June 20–25, 1921.
43 Ibid.
44 Ibid.
45 Ibid.
46 Ibid.
47 Ibid.
48 *Home and Country* [UK], December 1921, 4.
49 Ibid.
50 *Home and Country* [UK], January 1922, 3.
51 "Blessings and Cursings," *The Woman's Leader and Common Cause*, March 2, 1923, 1–2.
52 The Women's Library, National Federation Women's Institutes (hereafter cited as TWL, NFWI) Complete Minutes 1921–22, GB 0106 5 FWI/A/1/1/5, vol. 5, Minutes of the NFWI Executive, February 14, 1922; TWL, NFWI, Complete Minutes 1922–23, GB 0106 5 FWI/A/1/1/6, vol. 6, Minutes of January 9, 1923.

53 TWL, NFWI, Complete Minutes 1921–22, GB 0106 5 FWI/A/1/1/5, vol. 5, Minutes of the NFWI Executive, February 14, 1922.
54 TWL, NFWI, file: Mrs. Alfred Watt, GB 0106-5 FWI/H/9, vol. 9, G. Denman to Mrs. Alfred Watt, June 14, 1922.
55 Ibid.
56 TWL, NFWI, Complete Minutes, 1923–26, GB 0106 5 FWI/A/1/1/7, vol. 7, Minutes of the NFWI Executive, May 12, 1925.
57 Ibid., June 19, 1925.
58 The first issue that bore that listing appeared in January 1923, just two years before the tenth anniversary of the founding of the Llanfairpwll Institute.
59 *Home and Country* [UK], December 1924, 841.
60 Ibid.
61 TWL, NFWI, Complete Minutes 1923–26 GB 0106 5 FWI/A/1/1/7, vol. 7, Minutes of the NFWI Executive, January 13, 1925.
62 LAC, FWIC, MG 28 I 316, vol. 3, file "Executive and Board Meetings – Minutes, 1919–1945," Minutes of the Executive Meeting of FWIC, Toronto, August, 1924, 6–7.
63 Ibid., 10.
64 Ibid., 10.
65 TWL, NFWI, Complete Minutes 1923–26, GB 0106 5 FWI/A/1/1/7, vol. 7, Minutes of the NFWI Executive, November 11, 1924.
66 Mrinalini Sinha, Donna J. Guy, and Angela Woollacott, "Introduction: Why Feminisms and Internationalism?" *Gender & History* 10, 3 (1998): 350.
67 TWL, NFWI, Complete Minutes 1927–29, GB 0106 5 FWI/A/1/1/9, vol. 9, Minutes of NFWI Executive, 13 December 1927. These minutes include a report of the International sub-committee that had been held on Monday, November 21, 1927.
68 The minute books of the NFWI Executive Committee, held at the Women's Library in London, are full of reports about the various international organizations that were attempting to make networks among rural women. The chain of events recounted here has been reconstructed by the author from those records.
69 *Modern Pioneers: British Columbia Women's Institutes, 1909–1959* (Victoria: British Columbia Women's Institutes, 1959), 8.
70 The Belgian correspondence to Watt stated that their intention had been "de reconnaître par une distinction honorifique vos grand efforts pour l'amélioration de l'agriculture par les Cercles de Fermières. Si pour les causes indépendantes de notre volonté, cette distinction ne pu être

accordé, nous n'en admirons pas moins vos merites." *Home and Country* [UK], May 1924, 530.

71 TWL, NFWI, Complete Minutes 1923–26, GB 0106 5 FWI/A/1/1/7, vol. 7, Minutes of the International Sub-Committee of the NFWI, October 13, 1925.

72 TWL, NFWI, Complete Minutes 1926–27, GB 0106 5 FWI/A/1/1/8, vol. 8, Minutes of NFWI Executive, February 9, 1926.

73 Ibid., Minutes of NFWI Executive, November 9, 1926.

74 Ibid.

75 "Canadian Woman Goes to Michigan," *Globe*, July 28, 1927.

76 TWL, NFWI, Complete Minutes 1926–27, GB 0106 5 FWI/A/1/1/8, vol. 8, Minutes of NFWI Executive Committee, June 14, 1927,.

77 TWL, NFWI, Complete Minutes 1927–29, GB 0106 5 FWI/A/1/1/9, vol. 9, Minutes of NFWI Executive Committee, January 8, 1929.

78 Ibid., Executive Committee Minutes, February 14, 1928.

79 Scarborough, *History of the Associated Country Women of the World*, 29.

80 TWL, NFWI, Complete Minutes 192729, GB 0106 5 FWI/A/1/1/9, vol. 9, Minutes of NFWI Executive Committee, December 13, 1927.

81 Dorothy Drage, *Pennies for Friendship: The Autobiography of an Active Octogenarian, A Pioneer of ACWW* (Caenarvon, UK: Gwenlyn Evans Ltd., 1961), 125.

82 Scarborough, *History of the Associated Country Women of the World*, 12.

83 Drage, *Pennies for Friendship*, 125.

84 Ibid.

85 No academic history of the ACWW exists, but in addition to Scarborough's *History of the Associated Country Women of the World*, for background see Drage, *Pennies for Friendship*; Mrs. John H. McCulloch, "The Formative Years of the Associated Country Women of the World," (London: Associated Country Women of the World, n.d.); Mariann Meier, *ACWW's Vital War Years* (London: Associated Country Women of the World, n.d.); Mariann Meier, *Thirty-Five Years and More* (London: Associated Country Women of the World, n.d.); Jean Robinson, *Three Women from B.C. and the A.C.W.W.* (Shirley, BC: Shirley Women's Institute, 1990); Associated Country Women of the World, *Working with Women Worldwide: Highlights of 75 Years of ACWW* (London: Associated Country Women of the World, 2004). See TWL, NFWI, Complete Minutes 1933–1935, GB 0106 5 FWI/A/1/1/11, vol. 12, Minutes of Special Meeting of NFWI Executive Committee, February 1, 1935.

86 Watt, Sholto., ed., foreword, *What the Country Women of the World Are Doing*, 3.

87 Scarborough, *History of the Associated Country Women of the World*; and Associated Country Women of the World, *Working with Women Worldwide*.

88 Drage, *Pennies for Friendship*, 132.
89 Ibid.
90 Ibid., 133.
91 Ibid.
92 Scarborough, *History of the Associated Country Women of the World*, 24.
93 Ibid.
94 "Constitution adopted by the Stockholm Conference, June 1933," in Scarborough, *History of the Associated Country Women of the World*, 151. That original constitution stood until it was amended in 1950 and expanded to seven pages to reflect new postwar realities. See ibid., 153–60.
95 Sinha, Guy, and Woollacott, "Introduction: Why Feminisms and Internationalism?" 147.
96 Scarborough, *History of the Associated Country Women of the World*, 128.
97 Ibid., 21.
98 Ibid., 27.
99 Ibid.
100 "Constitution," in Scarborough, *History of the Associated Country Women of the World*, 152.
101 Associated Country Women of the World, *Working with Women Worldwide*, 7.
102 Scarborough, *History of the Associated Country Women of the World*, 10.
103 Ibid., 9.
104 Scarborough, *History of the Associated Country Women of the World*, 21.
105 Drage, *Pennies for Friendship*, 138.
106 Ibid., 139.
107 Ibid.
108 Ibid., 140.
109 Ibid., 142.
110 Cornell University Archives, Rare and Manuscript Collections, New York State College of Home Economics Collection, 23/2/749, box 12, "President" to "All Delegates and visitors attending the Washington Conference," April 9, 1936.
111 Ibid.
112 Kathleen McLaughlin, "President to Talk Before Assembly," *New York Times*, May 31, 1936, 7; idem, "Country Women to Go to Mount Vernon," *New York Times*, June 4, 1936, 7.
113 David B. Danbom, "The New Deal and Rural America," in *Born in the Country: A History of Rural America* (Baltimore and London: The Johns Hopkins University Press, 1995), 206–32; and Arthur M. Schlesinger Jr., *The Coming of the New Deal*, Volume II, *The Age of Roosevelt* (Boston:

Houghton Mifflin Co., 1959), 366–8, and chapter 22 "War Against Rural Poverty," 369–81.

114 Associated Country Women of the World, *Proceedings of the Triennial Conference Held at Washington May 31–June 11, 1936* (Washington: United States Government Printing Office, 1937), 205. Hereafter cited as ACWW, *Proceedings 1936*.

115 "Roosevelt Lauds Rural Residents in Talk to 6,000 Women Delegates," *New York Times*, June 2, 1936, 29.

116 Ibid.

117 Kathleen McLaughlin, "Thousands to Attend Country Women of the World Conference Opening Tomorrow," *New York Times*, May 31, 1936, 7.

118 Cited in Drage, *Pennies for Friendship*, 147.

119 Ibid., 149.

120 Drage, *Pennies for Friendship*,148.

121 Rupp, *Worlds of Women*, 53.

122 Mark Shucksmith, "Conceptualising Post-Industrial Rurality," in *Towards Sustainable Rural Communities: The Guelph Seminar Series*, ed. John M. Bryden, (Guelph, ON: University School of Rural Planning and Development, 1994), 130.

123 ACWW, *Proceedings 1936*, 115.

124 Ibid.

125 Ibid.

126 Ibid.

127 Ibid.

128 The debate is described as "whether rural is a *geographical concept*, a location within boundaries on a map, or whether it is a *social representation*, a community of interest, a culture and way of life." See Statistics Canada, *Rural and Small Town Analysis Bulletin* 3, 3 (2002): 4. See also Keith H. Halfacree, "Locality and Social Representation: Space, Discourse and Alternative Definitions of the Rural," *Journal of Rural Studies* 9, 1 (1993), 23.

129 ACWW, *Proceedings 1936*, 181.

130 Ibid., 209.

131 Danbom, *Born in the Country*, 208; ACWW, *Proceedings 1936*, 209–10; See also FDR, Acceptance Speech, 1940, cited in Schapsmeier and Schapsmeier, 14. For more on Wallace, see Edward L. Schapsmeier and Frederick H. Schapsmeier, "A Prophet in Politics: The Public Career of Henry A. Wallace," *Annals of Iowa* 39, 1 (Summer 1967): 1, 20; Glenda Riley and Richard S. Kirkendall, "Henry A. Wallace and the Mystique of the Farm Male, 1921–1933," *Annals of Iowa* 48, 1–2 (1985), 32–55;

and Richard Lowitt, "Henry A. Wallace and Irrigation Agriculture," *Agricultural History* 66, 4 (1992), 8, 10.

132 ACWW, *Proceedings 1936*, 209–10.

133 Danbom, *Born in the Country*, 174. See also Lise Saugeres, "The Cultural Representation of the Farming Landscape: Masculinity, Power and Nature," *Journal of Rural Studies* 18,4 (2002), 373–84.

134 Dr. Ruby Green Smith recounted in a memo to her Cornell colleague Flora Rose that Watt took extra care to try to establish a personal bond with Smith. "Late the night before leaving Ithaca, Mrs. Watt came to our house and talked proudly of her two sons. One is on the editorial staff of a London paper and has had several of his poems included in an English anthology. The other son is an artist who is teaching in a school for 800 boys, where he is trying to develop appreciation of the art side of life among boys who are being trained for vocations. Mrs. Watt is returning to England by way of New Zealand. She was especially disappointed at not meeting Miss [Flora] Rose, whose career she has followed at long distance for many years." Cornell University Archives, Rare and Manuscript Collections, New York State College of Home Economics Collection, 23/2/749, box 12, Mrs. R.G. Smith to Miss Rose, June 30, 1936.

135 Drage, *Pennies for Friendship*,146.

136 Cornell University Archives, Rare and Manuscript Collections, New York State College of Home Economics Collection, 23/2/749, box 12, "Peace Bridge Ceremony of Farewell to Overseas Delegates to Conference of Associated Women of the World, June 16, 1936."

137 Ibid.

138 Drage, *Pennies for Friendship*, 149. Drage and the other delegates arrived back in Liverpool on July 4, 1936, aboard the Canadian Pacific Line's *Duchess of Atholl*. UK Incoming Passenger Lists, 1878–1960, BT26/1091/7. www.ancestry.co.uk (accessed July 24, 2010).

139 Drage, *Pennies for Friendship*,145.

140 TWL, NFWI, Complete Minutes 1933–1935, GB 0106 5 FWI/A/1/1/13, vol. 13, Minutes of NFWI Executive Committee, October 9, 1935.

141 Katie Pickles, *Female Imperialism and National Identity: Imperial Order Daughters of the Empire* (Manchester and New York: Manchester University Press, 2002), 75–90.

142 Lady Aberdeen to Mrs. Watt, February 7, 1930; letter reproduced in Associated Country Women of the World, *Working with Women Worldwide*, 9.

143 Scarborough, *History of the Associated Country Women of the World*, 151.

144 Ibid., 150.

145 "Part Two, 1936–1937: Around the World with Mrs. Watt, " in *Necessary Secrets: The Journals of Elizabeth Smart*, ed. Alice Van Wart (Toronto; Duneau Publishers, 1986), 86–7.

146 LAC, Alice Van Wart Collection of Elizabeth Smart Papers, 1928–1985, MSS 1990-3, 5 boxes. Box 2, Family Correspondence, files 1–4, and file 26; and Elizabeth Smart Papers (1925–1986), MSS 1983–5/1987–9, series C "Family," especially box 15, files 1–7; box 16, file 1; and box 37 "Watt, Mrs. Alfred Dec 1, 1934–Oct. 30 [1940]."

147 Van Wart, *Necessary Secrets*, 76.

148 Elizabeth Smart, in Van Wart, *Necessary Secrets*, diary entry July 26, 1933, 44–5, and October 17, 1936, 113.

149 Ibid., July 12, 1933, ibid., 37–8.

150 Ibid., September 2, 1936, 97; and July 7, 1933, ibid., 35.

151 Ibid., 35.

152 Ibid., November 6, 1936, 118.

153 Ibid., January 10, 1937, 128.

154 Ibid., June 21, 1933, 30.

155 Ibid., September 12, 1936, 99–100; October 9, 1936, 110; and January 10, 1937, 128.

156 Ibid., January 10, 1937, 128.

157 Ibid., 128.

158 Ibid., September 2, 1936, 97.

159 Ibid., September 12, 1936, 100.

160 Ibid., November 1, 1936, 117.

161 Ibid.

162 Ibid., October 11, 1936, 112

163 Ibid., August 19, 1936, 89.

164 Ibid.

165 Ibid., August 21, 1936, 91.

166 Ibid., August 24, 1936, 94.

167 Watt and Lloyd, *The First Women's Institute School*, 120.

168 *Home and Country* [Ontario], May 1937, 2. Watt was in New Zealand from October 8 to December 7, 1936, and arrived in Sydney, Australia, on December 12, 1936. Smart's diaries are quite sketchy for the next month, but they were briefly in Tasmania, then by December 21 in Melbourne. The next entry records that they were aboard the *Otranto* (an Orient lines ship) in the Indian Ocean, arriving in Ceylon (now Sri Lanka) on January 6, 1937. See Smart diaries, in Van Wart, *Necessary Secrets*, 110–126. See Muriel J. Pagliano, *Country Women: History of the First Seventy Five Years, Queensland Country Women's Association* (Brisbane: Queensland Country Women's Association, 1997), 443.

169 Smart, in Van Wart, *Necessary Secrets*, diary entries February 20, 1937, 148; and February 25, 1937, 150.
170 LAC, RG 17, vol. 327, file 504, Vincent Massey to J.G. Gardiner, March 17, 1939.
171 Ibid., M.R. Watt to "Dear Mr. Mackenzie King, " September 15, 1938.
172 Scarborough, *History of the Associated Country Women of the World*, 46.
173 Ibid., 47.
174 Ibid.
175 Drage, *Pennies for Friendship*, 151–2.
176 "London Triennial Conference Associated Country Women of the World," *Home and Country* [Ontario], Fall 1939, 1.
177 Ibid.

6. Sidelined by War: Waning Influence, Denial, and Death

 1 The Women's Library, National Federation of Women's Institutes (hereafter cited as TWL, NFWI) file: Mrs. Alfred Watt, GB 0106 5 FWI/H/9, "Luncheon in Honour of Mrs. Alfred Watt, M.A., M.B.E.," Frances Farrer to Members of the Executive Committee and to All Members of Sub-Committees meeting in July, n.d.
 2 "Hail and Farewell!," *Home and Country* [UK], July 1939, 245.
 3 Ibid.
 4 Leila J. Rupp, *Worlds of Women: The Making of an International Women's Movement* (Princeton: Princeton University Press, 1997), 4–5.
 5 *Home and Country* [UK], August 1939, 296.
 6 Alice Van Wart, *Necessary Secrets: The Journals of Elizabeth Smart* (Toronto: Deneau Publishers, 1986), August 19, 1936, 89. The Robertson family bible records that Katherine Robertson Arthur died on May 4, 1945. See Collingwood Museum, 008.21.2, Henry Robertson Family Bible, Volume 2, "Deaths."
 7 Josephine Godman, "The Ellison Family: A Pioneer of Port Renfrew," in *Footprints: Pioneer Families of the Metchosin District Southern Vancouver Island 1851–1900*, edited by Marion I. Helgesen (Metchosin: Metchosin School Museum Society, 1983), 101.
 8 Library and Archives Canada (hereafter cited as LAC), Elizabeth Smart Fonds, MSS. 1983–5/1987–9 box 15, file 2, Letter from Louise Smart to "My dear Betty," 11-12-43.
 9 Mrs. Neve Scarborough, *History of the Associated Country Women of the World and of Its Member Societies* (London: The Rydal Press, 1953), 54.
10 Ibid., 55.
11 Ibid.

12 On Gardiner's wartime leadership, see Norman Ward and David Smith, *Jimmy Gardiner: Relentless Liberal* (Toronto: University of Toronto Press, 1990), 231–68.

13 LAC, RG 17, vol. 337, file: 504-2, James G. Gardiner, Minister of Agriculture to Mrs. H. McGregor, President FWIC, August 11, 1939.

14 LAC, RG 17, vol. 327, file 504, M.R. Watt to Mr. Gardiner, Minister of Agriculture, September 7, 1939.

15 LAC, RG 17, vol. 327, file 504, Memorandum, Department of Agriculture, Minister's Office, n.d.

16 LAC, RG 17, vol. 327, file 504, "Memorandum of Services for Dominion Government by Mrs. Alfred Watt," n.d.

17 LAC, RG 17, vol. 3406, file 1500-6, M.R. Watt to Dr. Barton, September 27 [1939].

18 Ibid.

19 Ibid. Watt attached a two-page memorandum to this letter, further outlining her ideas.

20 LAC, RG 17, vol. 3406, file 1500-6, James G. Gardiner, Minister of Agriculture to His Excellency the Governor General in Council, March 30, 1940.

21 LAC, RG 17, vol. 3406, file 1500-6, Mrs. H. McGregor, FWIC President, to Dr. H. Barton, Deputy Minister of Agriculture, February 4, 1940.

22 LAC, RG 17, vol. 3406, file 1500-6, Mrs. H. McGregor, FWIC President, to Dr. Barton, Deputy Minister of Agriculture, February 23, 1940.

23 LAC, RG 17, vol. 327, file 504, Ian Alistair McKenzie, Minister of Pensions and National Health, to J.G. Gardiner, Minister of Agriculture, February 24, 1940.

24 LAC, RG 17, vol. 327, file 504, M.R. Watt to "Dear Mr. Gardiner," March 2, 1940.

25 Ibid.

26 Ibid., Handwritten postscript to the letter.

27 LAC, RG 17, vol. 327, file 504, M.R. Watt to "Dear Mr. Gardiner" handwritten note on Hotel Vancouver stationery, dated "Saturday morning" [March 2, 1940].

28 Ibid., James G. Gardiner, Minister of Agriculture to His Excellency the Governor General in Council, March 30, 1940.

29 The original idea was to continue Watt's funding for the first three months of 1940, but due to delays and cancellations during the election campaign, this was extended to six months. LAC, RG 17, vol. 3406, file 1500-6, "Memorandum with Reference to the Services of Mrs. Alfred Watt," n.d.

30 Watt prepared a report for J.G. Gardiner describing her activities in the fall of 1939 entitled "Federated Women's Institutes of Canada – October 9th to 13th." LAC, RG 17, vol. 3406, file 1500-6.

31 Ward and Smith, *Jimmy Gardiner: Relentless Liberal*, 237–48.

32 LAC, RG 17, vol. 327, file 504, M.R. Watt to "Dear Mr. Gardiner," November 29 [1940].

33 Ibid.

34 Ibid.

35 LAC, RG 17, vol. 3406, file 1500-6.

36 Ibid.

37 On Gardiner's imperialism, see Ward and Smith, *Jimmy Gardiner: Relentless Liberal*, 231.

38 Ibid.

39 LAC, RG 17, vol. 327, file 504, unsigned memo [to Gardiner], entitled "Department of Agriculture," Ottawa, June 11, 1941.

40 Ibid.

41 Cornell University, Rare and Manuscript Collections, New York State College of Home Economics Collection 23/2/749, (hereafter cited as CU, NYSCHEC), box 12, M.R. Watt, President ACWW to The Heads of the Constituent Societies Belonging to the ACWW in America, September 25, 1939.

42 Ibid.

43 Ibid.

44 CU, NYSCHEC, box 12, "Points to Consider Regarding Transfer of ACWW Central Office to USA," Attachment to M.R. Watt, President ACWW to The Heads of the Constituent Societies Belonging to the ACWW in America, September 25, 1939.

45 Ibid.

46 CU, NYSCHEC, box 12, Flora Rose to Mrs. Alfred Watt, November 8, 1939.

47 Ibid.

48 Ibid.

49 CU, NYSCHEC, box 12, M.R. Watt to Dear Miss Rose, November 18, 1939.

50 CU, NYSCHEC, box 12, RGS to Miss Rose, n.d. [emphasis in original]. Attached to M.R. Watt to Dear Miss Rose, November 18, 1939.

51 LAC, RG 17, vol. 3406, file 1500-6., M.R. Watt, report prepared for J.G. Gardiner.

52 Ibid.

53 This lecture was one of six that she had delivered while attending the convention of the New York State Federations of Farm and Home

Bureaus at Syracuse from November 27 to December 1, 1939. See the report prepared by M.R. Watt for J.G. Gardiner, LAC, RG 17, vol. 3406, file 1500-6. A copy of the speech is preserved in CU, NYSCHEC, box 1. Another version, which she circulated to the ACWW executive, is a document entitled "The Future of the Associated Country Women of the World," and is contained in the fonds of the Federated Women's Institutes of Canada, LAC, MG 28 I 316, vol. 8, file 14: "The Future of the ACWW 1939."

54 LAC, MG 28 I 316, vol. 8, file 14, Mrs. Alfred Watt, "The Future of the Associated Country Women of the World," December 19, 1939.
55 Ibid.
56 Ibid.
57 Ibid.
58 Dorothy Drage, *Pennies for Friendship: The Autobiography of an Active Octogenarian; A Pioneer of the ACWW* (Caernarvon: Gwenlyn Evans, Ltd., 1961), 154.
59 Scarborough, *History of the Associated Countrywomen of the World*, 50.
60 Watt, "The Future of the Associated Country Women of the World," 3.
61 Ibid.
62 Ibid.
63 Ibid.
64 Ibid.
65 Ibid.
66 Ibid.
67 Scarborough, *History of the Associated Countrywomen of the World*, 50.
68 Watt, "The Future of the Associated Country Women of the World," 3.
69 The NFWI was forced to leave the WI headquarters in October 1940 and to hold their executive meetings in Oxford. See Gervas Huxley, *Lady Denman G.B.E., 1884–1954* (London: Chatto & Windus, 1961), 168–9.
70 Watt, "The Future of the Associated Country Women of the World," 2.
71 CU, NYSCHEC, box 12, Susan Tweedsmuir to Eleanor Roosevelt, November 25, 1939.
72 Ibid., Eleanor Roosevelt to Flora Rose, December 12, 1939.
73 Ibid.
74 Ibid., Eleanor Cole, ACWW Vice-President, to Miss Flora Rose, December 13, 1939.
75 Ibid.
76 Ibid.
77 Ibid., M.R. Watt to Dear Miss Rose, December 9, 1939.
78 Ibid.

79 Ibid.

80 Scarborough, *History of the Associated Country Women of the World*, 51.

81 Ibid.

82 CU, NYSCHEC, box 12, "The Associated Country Women of the World Statement to Constituent Societies, Approved by Executive Committee at Emergency Meeting held 8th August 1940."

83 Ibid., Elsie Zimmern, Acting Chairman ACWW to Miss Flora Rose, College of Home Economics, August 26, 1940.

84 Ibid.

85 Ibid., M.R. Watt to Dear Miss Rose, September 24, 1940.

86 Ibid.

87 Ibid., M.R. Watt, President, to "Dear friends," Broadcast to the Constituent Societies of ACWW, December 1940.

88 Ibid.

89 Ibid.

90 Ibid.

91 Elizabeth Bailey Price, "What Women Are Thinking: The Women's Institute," *Chatelaine*, September 1941, 65.

92 Ibid., 66.

93 Ibid.

94 Mariann Meier, *ACWW's Vital War Years* (London: The Associated Country Women of the World, n.d), 7.

95 Scarborough, *History of the Associated Country Women of the World*, 61.

96 Ibid., 62.

97 Ibid.

98 LAC, RG 17, vol. 327, file 504, M.R. Watt "To Those Who Made the Ottawa Country Women's Conference a Memorable Event, in Gratitude for their Help."

99 Rupp, *Worlds of Women*, 180–204.

100 LAC, RG 17, vol. 327, file 504, M.R. Watt to Dear Mr. Gardiner, n.d. [rec'd in Minister's Office September 18, 1941].

101 Ibid.

102 Ibid.

103 LAC, RG 17, vol. 327, file 504, James G. Gardiner to Mrs. Alfred Watt, December 23, 1941.

104 Watt exchanged a number of letters with Gardiner and his deputy minister Barton from September 1941 through to January 1942 on the logistics of printing and distributing the conference report. See, for example, LAC, RG 17, vol. 327, file 504, M.R. Watt to Hon J. G. Gardiner, September 25, 1941; James. G. Gardiner to Mrs. Alfred Watt, October 13,

1941; James G. Gardiner to Mrs. Alfred Watt, December 23, 1941; M.R. Watt to Dear Mr. Gardiner, January 17, 1942; and James G. Gardiner to Mrs. Alfred Watt, January 24, 1942.

105 LAC, RG 17, vol. 327, file 504, M.R. Watt to Hon J.G. Gardiner, September 25, 1941.

106 "Britain to Use American Seeds," *New York Times*, January 26, 1941, 4.

107 Mariann Meier, *ACWW's Vital War Years* (London: The Associated Country Women of the World, n.d.), 5. For the American perspective on this initiative, see Ruby Green Smith, *The People's College: A History of the New York State Extension Service in Cornell University and the State 1876–1948* (Ithaca: Cornell University Press, 1948), 494–5.

108 TWL, NFWI, Complete Minutes 1940–43, GB 0106 5 FWI/A/1/1/19, vol. 19, Minutes of NFWI Executive Committee, Report of the Sub Committee on Agriculture, February 12, 1941.

109 Ibid., Minutes of NFWI Executive Committee, March 12, 1941 and May 14, 1941.

110 Rupp, *Worlds of Women*, 198.

111 Scarborough, *History of Associated Country Women of the World*, 66

112 Ward and Smith, *Jimmy Gardiner: Relentless Liberal*, 249. February 16, 1944, internal office memo; C.V. Parker, Private Secretary to Fred James, Assistant Director and Chief of Press and Publicity, March 3, 1944; Fred James, Chief, Press and Publicity Division of Department of Agriculture to Mr. Parker, Memorandum March 6, 1944; James G. Gardiner to Mrs. Alfred Watt, March 7, 1944; and MR Watt to Dear Mr. Gardiner, April 20, 1944. LAC, RG 17 vol. 327, file 504; MR Watt to Dear Mr. Gardiner, April 20, 1944. LAC, RG 17, vol. 327, file 504.

113 LAC, RG 17, vol. 3406, file 1500-6, MR Watt to Dear Dr. Barton, September 22nd [1944].

114 LAC, RG 17, vol. 3406, file 1500-6H, Barton, Deputy Minister Agriculture to Dear Mrs. Watt, October 6, 1944.

115 LAC, RG 17, vol. 3275, file 504 (1), Mr Watt to Dear Dr Barton, April 17, 1945.

116 Ibid.

117 LAC, RG 17, vol. 3275, file 504 (1), H. Barton, Deputy Minister to Mrs. Alfred Watt, April 23, 1945.

118 Dorothy Drage, *Pennies for Friendship*, 170.

119 Watt, cited Scarborough, *History of Associated Country Women of the World*, 71.

120 "Mrs. Alfred Watt and the Institutes," *Home and Country* [UK], July 29, 1947, 139.

121 "A Message from Mrs. Alfred Watt," *Home and Country* [UK], December 1947, 221.

122 Scarborough, *History of Associated Country Women of the World*, 71.
123 For more on the process of how this status was granted, and the difference between Category A and B, see Scarborough, *History of the ACWW*, 68–70.
124 Drage, *Pennies for Friendship*,173.
125 "A Message from Mrs. Alfred Watt," *Home and Country* [UK], December 1947, 221.
126 Ibid.
127 Rupp, *Worlds of Women*, 4–5.
128 "A Message from Mrs. Alfred Watt," *Home and Country* [UK], December 1947, 221.
129 TWL, NFWI file: Mrs. Alfred Watt, GB 0106 5 FWI/H/9, Sholto Watt to Lady Albermarle, July 21, 1948.
130 *Federated News* 5, 27 (October 1948): 1.
131 Knowles, *Inventing the Loyalists*, 6.
132 LAC, MG 28 I 316, vol. 4, file: FWIC Life Membership files, "Mrs. Alfred Watt, M.A., M.B.E.," n.d.
133 Ibid.
134 TWL, NFWI, file: Mrs. Alfred Watt, GB 0106 5 FWI/H/9, Mrs. Alfred Watt to Frances Farrer, September 2, 1948.
135 Ibid.
136 Ibid., Frances Farrer to Mrs. Alfred Watt, September 20, 1948.
137 "Mrs. Alfred Watt, M.B.E.," *Home and Country* [UK], January 1949, 1.
138 TWL, NFWI, file: Mrs. Alfred Watt, GB 0106 5 FWI/H/9, Sholto Watt, telegram to NFWI.
139 Ibid.
140 Ibid., F.M. Farrer, General Secretary NFWI to All County Secretaries, December 8, 1948.
141 *Home and Country* [UK], January 1949, 2.
142 TWL, NFWI, Complete Minutes 1947–49, GB 0106 5/FWI/A/1/1/1/21, vol. 21, Minutes of NFWI Executive Committee, December 16, 1948.
143 TWL, NFWI, Complete Minutes 1949–51, GB 0106 5 FWI/A/1/1/22, vol. 22, Minutes of NFWI Executive Committee, February 24, 1949.
144 Ibid.
145 TWL, NFWI, file: Mrs. Alfred Watt, GB 01065 FWI/H/9, "Mrs. Alfred Watt, M.B.E.," *Home and Country* [UK], January 1949, 1.
146 "Chairman's Address re: Mrs. Alfred Watt," *Home and Country* [UK], July 1949, 143.
147 Ibid.
148 Ibid.

149 TWL, NFWI, Complete Minutes 1949–51, GB 0106 5 FWI/A/1/1/22, vol. 22, Minutes of the International Sub-Committee of the NFWI Executive Committee, January 11, 1949, Attachment C in Minutes of the NFWI Executive Committee January 26, 1949.

150 Ibid., "Letters from Flintshire Federation Executive Committee and from Dyserth WI (Flints), Minutes of the NFWI Executive Committee, April 28, 1949.

151 See, for example, Sheila A. Munro, "Letters to the Editor Re: Lady Denman" *Home & Country* [UK], August 1946, 125.

152 "W.I. Hostel in London?" *Home and Country* [UK], March 1948, 42.

153 TWL, NFWI, Complete Minutes 1949–51, GB 0106 5 FWI/A/1/1/22, vol. 22, Minutes of the NFWI Executive Committee, January 26, 1949; and Minutes of the NFWI Executive Committee, April 28, 1949.

154 Anne Stamper, *Rooms Off the Corridor: Education in the WI and 50 Years of Denman College, 1948–98* (London: WI Books, 1998), 78.

155 Ibid., 79–80.

156 TWL, NFWI, Complete Minutes 1949–51, GB 0106 5 FWI/A/1/1/22, vol. 22, Minutes of NFWI Executive Committee, February 24, 1949.

157 "Re: Watt Memorial Fund," *Home and Country* [UK], June 1949, 139.

158 TWL, NFWI, Complete Minutes 1949–51, GB 0106 5 FWI/A/1/1/22, vol. 22, Minutes of NFWI Executive Committee, December 15, 1949.

159 On a site visit to Denman College in 2008, I learned that after the college sold off some of its acreage, the lime tree avenue was no longer the main entrance to the property. Sixty years after Watt's death, no clear marker was in evidence indicating that the trees were designated as a memorial to the WI founder.

160 TWL, NFWI, Complete Minutes 1949–51, GB 0106 5 FWI/A/1/1/22, vol. 22, Minutes of Denman College Sub-Committee, Attachment to Minutes of NFWI Executive Committee, October 27, 1949.

161 TWL, NFWI, file: Mrs. Alfred Watt, GB 0106 5 FWI/H/9, Sholto Watt to Miss F. Farrer, December 6, 1949.

162 Ibid., "Robin Watt to Miss F. Farrer," January 30, 1950.

163 Ibid., F. Farrer to Robin Watt, June 8, 1950; Anne Stamper, correspondence with the author, June 2008.

164 Frances Farrer, "Watt, Margaret Rose," in *Dictionary of National Biography: 1941–1950*, ed. L.G. Wickam Legg and E.T. Williams (Oxford: Oxford University Press, 1959), 930.

165 TWL, NFWI, file: Mrs. Alfred Watt, GB 0106 5 FWI/H/9, Sholto Watt to Dame Frances [Farrer], July 2, 1952.

166 Ibid.

167 *Federated News*, July 1949, 3. News of the appeal was repeated in *Federated News*, Fall and Winter 1949–50, 10.
168 *Federated News*, April 1950, 4.
169 *Federated News*, Overseas Tour Issue, February 1951, 10
170 The International Peace Garden maintains a website at www.peacegarden .com (accessed August 4, 2011).
171 *Federated News*, July 1952, 4.
172 *Federated News*, October 1953, 3.
173 *Federated News*, July 1955, 3.
174 Ibid.
175 TWL, NFWI, file: Mrs. Alfred Watt, GB 0106 5 FWI/H/9, Elsie Zimmern, "An Appreciation from Miss Zimmern," typescript from copy for the January 1949 issue of *Countrywoman*.
176 Mariann Meier, "Elsie M. Zimmern: Co-founder of ACWW – First Member of Honour," *The Countrywoman* (June/July 1967): 3.
177 Mariann Meier, "Why An Elsie Zimmern Memorial Fund?" *The Countrywoman*, March/April 1972, 3–4.

Conclusion: Interpreting the Significance of Madge Watt

1 The Parks Canada website lists Watt as a person of national historical significance: Parks Canada, "Watt, Margaret 'Madge' Robertson, National Historic Person," http://www.pc.gc.ca/apps/dfhd/page_nhs_eng .aspx?id=11470#tphp (accessed July 29, 2014).
2 Ibid.
3 Alan Gordon, "Heroes, History and Two Nationalisms: Jacques Cartier," *Journal of the Canadian Historical Association*, New Series, 10 (1999): 102.
4 Ibid.
5 Norman Knowles, *Inventing the Loyalists: The Ontario Loyalist Tradition and the Creation of Usable Pasts* (Toronto: University of Toronto Press, 1997), 171.
6 Ibid., 115.
7 An earlier version of this chapter was presented at the Canadian Historical Association 86th Annual Meeting in Saskatoon in 2007 as part of the round table discussion "Women's History as Public History."
8 Paul Litt, "Pliant Clio and Immutable Texts: The Historiography of a Historical Marking Program," *The Public Historian* 19, 4 (Fall 1997): 7–28.
9 Ontario Heritage Foundation, Toronto, Historic Plaques Program, file: "Associated Country Women of the World," (hereafter cited as OHF file), Mrs. Thomas Dyer to Mr. D.F. McOuat, April 14, [1958]. The Georgian WI

branch was founded in 1937, while the Mrs. Alfred Watt Memorial WI branch was founded in 1953. If Watt was in fact a member of Georgian WI, she must have joined in the fall of 1939 when she returned from England after hosting the ACWW convention in London. She did periodically spend time in Collingwood visiting with her sister, and it is plausible that while she was there, she became a member of the local WI. For dates of WI branch establishment, see Linda M. Ambrose, *For Home and Country: The Centennial History of the Women's Institutes in Ontario, 1897–1997* (Erin: Boston Mills Press, 1996), 234.

10 OHF file, Mrs. Thomas Dyer, Collingwood to "Dear Sir," May 31, 1957; and, D. F. McOuat to Mrs. Thomas Dyer, June 5, 1957.

11 OHF file, Elsie D. Bell (Mrs. John Bell) to The Honourable Bryan Cathcart, June 22, 1957.

12 Ambrose, *For Home and Country*, 172; and OHF file, D.F. McOuat to Mrs. Thomas Dyer, June 5, 1957.

13 Litt, "Pliant Clio and Immutable Texts," 22.

14 OHF file, D.F. McOuat to Mrs. T.H. Dyer, July 8, 1957.

15 Linda M. Ambrose, "Ontario Women's Institutes and the Work of Local History," in *Creating Memory: English Canadian Women and the Work of History,* ed. Alison Prentice and Beverly Boutilier (Vancouver: University of British Columbia Press, 1997), 75–98.

16 OHF file, D.F. McOuat to Mrs. T.H. Dyer, March 19, 1958.

17 OHF file, text of plaque.

18 Knowles, *Inventing the Loyalists*, 121.

19 OHF file, Elsie D. Bell (Mrs. John) to Ont. Archaeological Historical Board, August 29, 1967.

20 Ibid.

21 OHF file, Brian R. McLellan, Shaw McLellan & Melitzer, to Mr. Richard Apted, Director, Heritage Administration Branch, Ministry of Culture and Recreation, August 11, 1978.

22 Litt, "Pliant Clio and Immutable Texts," 7, 26–7.

23 Ibid, 22–5. Since 2005 Ontario's historic plaque program has been managed by the Ontario Heritage Trust. See Ontario Heritage Trust, "Provincial Plaque Program," http://www.heritagetrust.on.ca/Programs/Commemoration/Provincial-Plaque-Program.aspx (accessed July 29, 2014).

24 Collingwood Public Library, Local History Collection, box E: Prominent Citizens Collingwood and District, file: Watt, Mrs. Alfred, Press clipping. The photograph of the plaque that depicts Elliott, Marsh, and Lowe was originally published May 9, 1990, in the *Enterprise-Bulletin* newspaper in Collingwood.

25 OHF file, research notes signed "Phyllis," July 22, 1986.

26 OHF file, Shirley M. McKee (Mrs. Forrest), The Mrs. Alfred Watt Memorial WI Branch, to Nancy Kiefer, Consultant, Ontario Heritage Foundation, February 13, 1989.

27 Alan Gordon, *The Hero and the Historian: Historiography and the Uses of Jacques Cartier* (Vancouver: University of British Columbia Press, 2010), 189.

28 For more on the professional vs. popular influences in women's history, see Ambrose, "Ontario Women's Institutes and the Work of Local History," 75–98.

29 *Niagara Falls Evening Review,* July 30, 1936; *Home and Country* [Ontario], Fall 2000, 1.

30 "Peace Dramatized on Bridge over Niagara," *Niagara Falls Evening Review,* June 17, 1936.

31 *The Buffalo Courier Express,* July 30, 1936, n.p.

32 Marion Egerter, "A Mystery Solved," *Home and Country* [Ontario], Fall 2000, 1.

33 Email correspondence from Marion E. Egerter to Christine Reaburn, March 16, 2000. Copies of Egerter's research notes were supplied to the author compliments of Mary Janes, Public Relations Officer for FWIO. Many thanks to Janes and Egerter for generously sharing this material with me.

34 Email, Egerter to Reaburn, April 22, 2000.

35 For a list of ACWW triennial world conference locations up to 2004, see ACWW, *Working with Women Worldwide,* 60. The locations after that date were Turku, Finland, 2007; Hot Springs, Arkansas, USA, 2010; and Chennai, India, 2013.

36 Email, Egerter to Reaburn, April 22, 2000.

37 "The NPC [Niagara Parks Commission] funded the site, the garden design and stone, and an accompanying plaque describing the roles of our own Madge Watt, the 1936 ACWW president, and the 1936 presidents of the N.Y. State Home Bureaus and the FWIC." Letter, Marion E. Egerter, Hamilton PRO [Public Relations Officer], to "Dear Branch Members," undated. A copy of the letter was supplied to the author by Egerter.

38 Ibid.

39 Personal correspondence, Marion E. Egerter, to author, May 4, 2001.

40 Litt, "Pliant Clio and Immutable Texts," 27.

41 Alan Gordon, "Heroes, History, and Two Nationalisms," 88.

42 Photograph of grave stone supplied to the author by Linda Hoy, Quebec Women's Institutes.

43 Ambrose, *For Home and Country*, 213.
44 Knowles, *Inventing the Loyalists*, 171.
45 Gordon, *The Hero and the Historian*, 7.
46 Katie Pickles, *Female Imperialism and National Identity: Imperial Order Daughters of the Empire* (Manchester: Manchester University Press, 2002).
47 Leila J. Rupp, *Worlds of Women: The Making of an International Women's Movement* (Princeton: Princeton University Press, 1997), back cover.
48 Mrs. Alfred Watt and Miss Nest Lloyd, *The First Women's Institute School (Sussex 1918)* (Sussex Federation of Women's Institutes, 1919), 45.

Bibliography

Primary Sources

Archifau Gwynedd Archives, Caernarfon, Wales
- The Agricultural Organization Society. Women's Institutes – North Wales, "Mrs. Watt's Report on Some Recent Work."

Archives of the City of Edmonton, Edmonton, Alberta
- Emily Murphy Papers

Archives of Ontario, Toronto, Ontario
- Death Registrations, MS 935 reel 183.
- Ontario. *Revised Statutes of Ontario*, 1897.
- Ontario. Department of Agriculture. Women's Institute Branch, Annual Reports, 1900–1920.

BC Archives, Victoria, British Columbia
- Annual Reports of Dr. A.T. Watt, Superintendent of B.C. Quarantines
- Canada. Immigration Branch. Ships' Passenger Lists, 1905–1919.
- Canada. Department of Public Health, William Head Quarantine Station, 1902–1956, Reports of the Division of Quarantine – British Columbia, 1897–1956.
- British Columbia. Division of Vital Statistics, Volume 028, Death Registrations 010284 to 011002.
- British Columbia Women's Institutes, Advisory Board of Women's Institutes of British Columbia, Minutes and Papers, 1911–1932. Microfilm reel A1660.
- British Columbia Women's Institutes. Victoria Women's Institute. Minute Book, 1921–1922.

Collingwood Museum, Collingwood, Ontario
- Untitled Scrapbook [Henry Robertson]

- IIenry Robertson Family Bible. 2 Volumes.
- *1887 Jubilee History of the Town of Collingwood*

Collingwood Public Library, Collingwood, Ontario
- Genealogy Room, Family Histories, Box P-S, file: Robertson, Henry, Q.C.
- Local History Collection:
     Annual Report of the Collingwood Board of Trade for 1893
     Box E: Prominent Citizens Collingwood and District. File: Watt,
        Mrs. Alfred, press clippings.
     Cemeteries, Town of Collingwood, [Index], Section 3: Presbyterian
        Cemetery
     Gazetteer and Directory of the County of Simcoe, 1872–73

Cornell University Archives, Ithaca, New York
- Rare and Manuscript Collections. New York State College of Home
   Economics Collection, 23/3/749. Box 12.

Library and Archives Canada
- Alice Van Wart Collection of Elizabeth Smart Papers, 1928–1985, MSS
   1990–3, 5 boxes.
- Federated Women's Institutes of Canada, MG 28 I 316
- Department of Agriculture. RG 17. Volume 1190, file: Correspondence.
- Department of Agriculture. RG 17. Volume 1190, file: H.R.W. Moore,
   "Report of the Commissioner in the Matter of the Investigation of the
   Quarantine Station at William Head, B.C."
- Department of Agriculture. RG 17. Volume 1190, file: Transcript of Royal
   Commission
- Federated Women's Institutes of Canada. RG 28

Meaford Public Library, Meaford, Ontario
- Frank Harding Local History Collection. File 13 M: Newspapers, typescript.

Ontario Heritage Foundation, Toronto, Ontario
- Historic Plaques Program. File: Associated Country Women of the World. .

Presbyterian Church in Canada Archives
- *Annual Reports of the Women's Foreign Missionary Society, 1885–94*

Robarts Library, University of Toronto

Simcoe County Archives

The Women's Library, London Metropolitan University, London, England
- The National Federation of Women's Institutes Collection. GB 0106 5 FWI
   (Note: At the time of publication of this book, this collection had moved
      to the London School of Economics, London, England.)

University of Toronto Archives

University of Victoria Archives
- McPherson Library. University Women's Club, Victoria Branch, 1908–1993

William Head Federal Penitentiary Archives

Newspapers/Periodicals

The Buffalo Courier Express
Chatelaine
Collingwood Enterprise Bulletin
The Countrywoman
The Enterprise and Collingwood Messenger
Enterprise Messenger
Federated News
Frank Leslie's Weekly
The Globe
Harpers
Home and Country
Home and Country [UK]
Judge
The Ladies Pictorial Weekly
Life
The New York Times
Niagara Falls Evening Review
Saturday Night
Toronto Globe
Toronto Star
Truth
Vancouver Sun
The Varsity
Victoria Daily Colonist
Victoria Daily Times
The Week

Books

Adams, Mary. *The Confessions of a Wife*. Toronto: Copp Clark, 1902.
McEvoy, Bernard. *Away from Newspaperdom and Other Poems*. Toronto: G.N. Morang, 1897.
– *From the Great Lakes to the Wide West: Impressions of a Tour between Toronto and the Pacific*. Toronto: William Briggs, 1902.
Scott, J.W. Robertson. *The Story of the Women's Institute Movement in England and Wales and Scotland*. Idbury, Kingham, Oxon: The Village Press, 1925.
Todd, Mary Ives. *The Heterodox Marriage of a New Woman*. New York: Robert Lewis Weed Company Publishers, 1898.

Watt, Mrs. Alfred, and Miss Nest Lloyd. *The First Women's Institute School (Sussex 1918)*. Sussex Federation of Women's Institutes, 1919.

Watt, Sholto, ed. *What the Country Women of the World Are Doing*. London: The Liaison Committee of Rural Women's and Homemakers' Organisations, 1932.

Government Publications

Associated Country Women of the World, *Proceedings of the Triennial Conference Held at Washington May 31–June 11, 1936*. Washington: United States Government Printing Office, 1937.

Canada. Census of Canada, 1901.

Canada. Census of Canada, 1911.

Canada. The Civil Service List of Canada, 1885–1900, CIHM 46477–46492, fiche 1–3.

Canada. Royal Commission on Industrial Training and Technical Education, *Report of the Commissioners*, Ottawa, 1913.

United Kingdom. UK Incoming Passenger Lists, 1878–1960. Board of Trade, Commercial and Statistical Department and successors: Inwards Passenger Lists, Kew, Surrey, England. The National Archives of the UK (TNA), series BT26, piece 554, item 27.

Secondary Sources

Allen, Grant. *The Woman Who Did*. Oxford, New York: Oxford University Press, 1995.

Ambrose, Linda M. "'Better and Happier Men and Women': *The Agricultural Instruction Act, 1913–1924*." *Historical Studies in Education/Revue d'histoire de l'éducation* 16, 2 (2004): 257–85.

– *For Home and Country: The Centennial History of the Women's Institutes in Ontario, 1897–1997*. Erin, Ontario: Boston Mills Press, 1996.

– "Ontario Women's Institutes and the Work of Local History." In *Creating Memory: English Canadian Women and the Work of History*, edited by Alison Prentice and Beverly Boutilier, 75–98. Vancouver: University of British Columbia Press, 1997.

– "Quarantine in Question: The 1913 Investigation at William Head, B.C." *Canadian Bulletin of Medical History/Bulletin canadien d'histoire de la medicine* 22, 1 (2005): 139–54.

– "'What Are the Good of Those Meetings Anyway?' Early Popularity of the Ontario Women's Institutes." *Ontario History* LXXXVII, 1 (Spring 1995): 1–19.

– *Women's Institutes in Canada: The First One Hundred Years, 1897–1997.*
Ottawa: Federated Women's Institutes of Canada, 2000.

Ambrose, Linda M., and Kristin Hall. "A New Woman in Print and Practice:
The Canadian Literary Career of Madge Robertson Watt, 1890–1907."
History of Intellectual Culture 7, 1 (2007): http://www.ucalgary.ca/hic/
issues/vol7/1.

Ambrose, Linda, and Margaret Kechnie. "Social Control or Social Feminism?
Two Views of the Ontario Women's Institutes." *Agricultural History* 73, 2
(Spring 1999): 222–37.

Ammons, Elizabeth. *Conflicting Stories: American Women Writers at the Turn into
the Twentieth Century*. New York and Oxford: Oxford University Press, 1991.

Anderson, David D. "Another Biography? For God's Sake, Why?" *The Georgia
Review* 35, 2 (1981): 401–6.

Andrews, Maggie. *The Acceptable Face of Feminism: The Women's Institute as a
Social Movement*. London: Lawrence & Wishart Ltd., 1997.

Apthorp, Elaine Sargent. "Speaking of Silence: Willa Cather and the 'Problem'
of Feminist Biography." *Women's Studies* 18, 1 (1990): 1–11.

Ardis, Ann L. *New Women, New Novels: Feminism and Early Modernism*. New
Brunswick: Rutgers University Press, 1990.

Ardis, Ann L. "Organizing Women: New Woman Writers, New Woman
Readers, and Movement Feminism." In *Victorian Women Writers and the
Woman Question*, edited by Nicola Diane Thompson, 189–203. Cambridge:
Cambridge University Press, 1999.

Arp, B., ed. *Reflections: Collingwood, an Historical Anthology*. Collingwood:
Town of Collingwood, 1983.

Associated Country Women of the World. *Working with Women Worldwide:
Highlights of 75 Years of ACWW*. London: ACWW, 2004.

Barman, Jean. *Constance Lindsay Skinner: Writing on the Frontier*. Toronto:
University of Toronto Press, 2002.

– *Sojourning Sisters: The Lives and Letters of Jessie and Annie McQueen*. Toronto:
University of Toronto Press, 2003.

– *The West beyond the West: A History of British Columbia*. Revised edition.
Toronto: University of Toronto Press, 1996.

Beaumont, Caitriona. "Citizens Not Feminists: The Boundary Negotiated
between Citizenship and Feminism by Mainstream Women's Organizations
in England, 1928–39." *Women's History Review* 9, 2 (2000): 411–29.

Beddoe, Deirdre. "Towards a Welsh Women's History." *Journal of Welsh Labour
History* 3, 2 (1981): 32–8.

Beetham, Margaret. *A Magazine of Her Own? Domesticity and Desire in the
Woman's Magazine, 1800–1914*. New York: Routledge, 1996.

Beyea, Marion. "Research-Problems and Solutions: Archival Sources for Research on Nineteenth-Century Women Writers." In *Rediscovering Our Foremothers: Nineteenth Century Canadian Women Writers*, edited by Lorraine Mullen, 23–9. Ottawa: University of Ottawa Press, 1990.

Black, Naomi. "The Mother's International: The Women's Co-operative Guild and Feminist Pacifism." *Women's Studies International Forum 7*, 6 (1984): 467–76.

Black, Naomi, and Gail Cuthbert Brandt. "Il en faut un peu: Farm Women and Feminism in Quebec and France Since 1945." *Journal of the Canadian Historical Association* NS 1 (1990): 73–96.

Blaszak, Barbara. "The Gendered Geography of the English Co-operative Movement at the Turn of the Nineteenth Century." *Women's History Review 9*, 3 (2000): 559–83.

– "The Women's Cooperative Guild, 1883–1921." *International Social Science Review 61*, 2 (1986): 76–86.

Bolt, Christine. *Sisterhood Questioned? Race, Class and Internationalism in the American and British Women's Movements, c. 1880s–1970s*. London: Routledge, 2004.

– *The Women's Movements in the United States and Britain from the 1790s to the 1920s*. Amherst: University of Massachusetts Press, 1993.

Bonnes, Marie-Nöelle. "Les Anglaises et l'Effort de Guerre de 1914 à 1918." *Guerres mondiales et conflits contemporains* 198 (2000): 79–98.

Bono, Paola. "Women's Biographies and Autobiographies: A Political Project in the Making." *Resources for Feminist Research (RFR)/Documentation sur la recherché féministe (DRF)* 25, 3–4 (1997): 38–45.

Brekus, Catherine A. *Strangers and Pilgrims: Female Preaching in America, 1740–1845*. Chapel Hill: University of North Carolina Press, 1998.

Brouwer, Ruth Compton. *Modernizing Women, Modernizing Men: The Changing Missions of Three Professional Women in Asia and Africa, 1902–69*. Vancouver: University of British Columbia Press, 2002.

– *New Women for God: Canadian Presbyterian Women and India Missions, 1876–1914*. Toronto: University of Toronto Press, 1990.

Buckner, Phillip, and R. Douglas Francis, eds. *Rediscovering the British World*. Calgary: University of Calgary Press, 2005.

Burke, Sara Z. "'Being Unlike Man': Challenges to Co-education at the University of Toronto, 1884–1909." *Ontario History* XCIII, 1 (Spring 2001): 11–31.

– "New Women and Old Romans: Co-education at the University of Toronto, 1884–95." *Canadian Historical Review* 80, 2 (June 1999): 219–41.

Burns, Geoffrey W. *A History of William Head*. William Head: William Head Institution, 1982.

Burt, Roger. "Freemasonry and Business Networking during the Victorian Period." *Economic History Review* LVI, 4 (2003): 657–88.

Burton, Antoinette. "The Feminist Quest for Identity: British Imperialism, Suffragism and 'Global Sisterhood', 1900–1915." *Journal of Women's History* 3, 2 (Fall 1991): 46–81.

Bush, Julia. "Edwardian Ladies and the 'Race' Dimensions of British Imperialism." *Women's Studies International Forum* 21, 3 (1998): 277–89.

– "'The Right Sort of Woman': Female Emigrators and Emigration to the British Empire, 1890–1910." *Women's History Review* 3, 3 (1994): 385–409.

Butler, Judith. "Performative Acts and Gender Constitution: An Essay in Phenomenology and Feminist Theory." In *Performing Feminisms: Feminist Critical Theory and Theatre*, edited by Sue-Ellen Case, 270–82. Baltimore & London: The Johns Hopkins University Press, 1990.

Calder, Jenni. *Women and Marriage in Victorian Fiction*. London: Thames and Hudson, 1976.

Carbert, Louise. *Agrarian Feminism: The Politics of Ontario Farm Women*. Toronto: University of Toronto Press, 1995.

Carnes, Mark C. *Secret Ritual and Manhood in Victorian America*. New Haven and London: Yale University Press, 1989.

Chevigny, Bell Gale. "Daughters Writing: Toward a Theory of Women's Biography." *Feminist Studies* 9, 1 (Spring 1983): 79–102.

Clawson, Mary Ann. *Constructing Brotherhood: Class, Gender and Fraternalism*. Princeton: Princeton University Press, 1989.

Cohen, Yolande. *Femmes de parole: L'historie des cercles de fermieres du Quebec, 1915–1990*. Quebec: Le jour, editeur, 1990.

Cole, Catherine C., and Ann Milovic. "Education, Community Service, and Social Life: The Alberta Women's Institutes and Rural Families, 1909–1945." In *Standing on New Ground: Women in Alberta*, edited by Catherine A. Cavanaugh and Randi R. Warne, 19–33. Edmonton: University of Alberta Press, 1993.

Cole, Catherine C., and Judy Larmour. *Many and Remarkable: The Story of the Alberta Women's Institutes*. Edmonton: Alberta Women's Institutes, 1997.

Cook, Ramsay, and Wendy Mitchinson, eds. *The Proper Sphere: Woman's Place in Canadian Society*. Toronto: Oxford University Press, 1976.

Cook, Sharon Anne. "Letitia Youmans: Ontario's Nineteenth-Century Temperance Educator." *Ontario History* 84, 4 (December 1992): 329–42.

Cooper, Sandi E. *Patriotic Patriotism: Waging War on War in Europe, 1815–1914*. New York and Oxford: Oxford University Press, 1991.

Courtney, Janet E. *Countrywomen in Council: The English and Scottish Women's Institutes with Chapters on the Movement in the Dominions and on Townswomen's Guilds*. London: Oxford University Press, 1933.

Cox, Dwayne. "Alabama Farm Agents, 1914-1922." *Alabama Review* (October 1994): 285–6.

Crowley, Terry. "The Origins of Continuing Education for Women: The Ontario Women's Institutes." *Canadian Woman Studies* 7, 3 (Fall 1986): 78–81.

Culver, John C., and John Hyde. *American Dreamer: The Life and Times of Henry A. Wallace*. New York: Norton, 2000.

Cunningham, A.B. "The 'New Woman Fiction' of the 1890's." *Victorian Studies* 17, 2 (December 1973): 177–86.

Dagg, Anne Innis. *The Feminine Gaze: A Canadian Compendium of Non-fiction Women Authors and Their Books*. Waterloo: Wilfrid Laurier University Press, 2001.

Danbom, David B. *Born in the Country: A History of Rural America*. Baltimore and London: The Johns Hopkins University Press, 1995.

Davies, Constance. *A Grain of Mustard Seed: An Account of the First Women's Institute in Great Britain, with Extracts from Its Minute Book*. Denbigh: Gee and Son Denbigh Ltd., 1953. Second edition 1989.

Dee, Emma and Tanya Granich, eds., *Rural Women in the Colonial Context: Women as Workers and Homemakers in Rural New Zealand, Australia and North America in the Late Nineteenth and Early Twentieth Centuries*. Rural Studies Research Occasional Papers No 1. Wellington, New Zealand: History Department, Victoria University of Wellington, 2000.

Dennison, Carol J. "Housekeepers of the Community: The British Columbia Women's Institutes, 1909–1946." In *Knowledge for the People: The Struggle for Adult Learning in English-Speaking Canada, 1828–1973*, edited by Michael R. Welton, 52–72. Toronto: OISE Press, 1987.

– "They Also Served: The British Columbia Women's Institutes in Two World Wars." In *Not Just Pin Money: Selected Essays on the History of Women's Work in British Columbia*, edited by Barbara K. Latham and Roberta J. Pazdro, 211–19. Victoria: Camosun College, 1984.

Donovan, Josephine. *New England Local Color Literature: A Woman's Tradition*. New York: Ungar, 1983.

Dowling, Linda. "The Decadent and the New Woman in the 1890's." *Nineteenth-Century Fiction* 33, 4 (March 1979): 434–53.

Doyle, James. "Research-Problems and Solutions: Canadian Women Writers and the American Literary Milieu of the 1890s." In *Rediscovering Our Foremothers: Nineteenth Century Canadian Women Writers*, edited by Lorraine Mullen, 30–6. Ottawa: University of Ottawa Press, 1990.

Drage, Dorothy. *Pennies for Friendship: The Autobiography of an Active Octogenarian, A Pioneer of ACWW*. Caenarvon, UK: Gwenlyn Evans Ltd., 1961.

Dudgeon, Piers ed. *Village Voices: A Portrait of Change in England's Green and Pleasant Land, 1915–1990.* London: WI Books Ltd., 1989.

Dumenil, Lynn. *Freemasonry and American Culture: 1880–1930.* Princeton: Princeton University Press, 1984.

Edelman, Marc. "Transnational Peasant and Farmer Movements and Networks." In *Global Civil Society 2003,* edited by Helmut Anheier, Marlies Glasius, and Mary Kaldor, 185–220. London: Oxford University Press, 2003.

Enevist, Nile Erie. "The Biglow Papers in Nineteenth-Century England." *New England Quarterly* 26, 2 (June 1953): 219–36.

Farrer, Frances. "Watt, Margaret Rose (1868–1948)." In *Dictionary of National Biography 1941–1950,* edited by J.G. Wickham Leff and E.T. Williams, 930. Oxford: Oxford University Press, 1959.

Ferleger, Louis. "Arming American Agriculture for the Twentieth Century: How the USDA's Top Managers Promoted Agricultural Development." *Agricultural History* 74, 2 (2000): 214–15.

Fink, Deborah. *Agrarian Women: Wives and Mothers in Rural Nebraska, 1880–1940.* Chapel Hill: University of North Carolina Press, 1992.

Fitzpatrick, Ellen. Review of *The Challenge of Feminist Biography: Writing the Lives of Modern American Women,* edited by Sara Alpern, Joyce Antler, Elisabeth Israels Perry, and Ingrid Winther Scobie. *Journal of Interdisciplinary History* 26, 2 (1995): 348–50.

Fitzpatrick, John J. Review of *Emotional and Social Change: Toward a New Psychohistory,* by Peter N. Stearns and Carol Z. Stearns. *Journal of American History* 77, 3 (Dec 1990): 980–1.

Fletcher, E. *History of the Manitoba Women's Institute, 1919–1975.* Winnipeg: Manitoba Women's Institute, 1976.

Fowler, Robert Booth. *Carrie Catt: Feminist Politician.* Boston: Northeastern University Press, 1986.

Friedland, Martin I. *The University of Toronto: A History.* Toronto: University of Toronto Press, 2002.

Gabin, Nancy. "Revising the History of Twentieth-Century Feminism." *Journal of Women's History* 12, 3 (Autumn 2000): 227–34.

Gabriele, Sandra. "Gendered Mobility, the Nation and the Woman's Page: Exploring the Mobile Practices of the Canadian Lady Journalist, 1888–1895." *Journalism* 7, 2 (2006): 174–96.

Gambee, Budd L. *Frank Leslie and His Illustrated Newspaper, 1855–1860.* Ann Arbour: University of Michigan Press, 1964.

Garraty, John A. "How to Write a Biography." *The South Atlantic Quarterly* 55, 1 (1956): 73–86.

Gingras, Yves. "Pour une biographie sociologique." *Revue d'histoire de l'Amerique Francaise* 54, 1 (Été 2000): 123–31.

Godman, Josephine. "The Ellison Family: A Pioneer of Port Renfrew." In *Footprints: Pioneer Families of the Metchosin District Southern Vancouver Island 1851–1900*, edited by Marion I. Helgesen, 99–100. Metchosin: Metchosin School Museum Society, 1983.

Goodenough, Simon. *Jam and Jerusalem: A Pictorial History of Britain's Greatest Women's Movement*. Glasgow and London: William Collins Sons & Co. Ltd., 1977.

Gordon, Alan. *The Hero and the Historians: Historiography and the Uses of Jacques Cartier*. Vancouver: University of British Columbia, 2010.

Gordon, Alan. "Heroes, History and Two Nationalisms: Jacques Cartier." *Journal of the Canadian Historical Association*, New Series, 10 (1999): 81–102.

Gordon, Elizabeth. "Dr. and Mrs. Alfred Watt." In *Footprints: Pioneer Families of the Metchosin District Southern Vancouver Island 1851–1900*, edited by Marion I. Helgesen, 245–6. Metchosin: Metchosin School Museum Society, 1983.

Gordon, Lynn. D. "The Gibson Girl Goes to College: Popular Culture and Women's Higher Education in the Progressive Era, 1890–1920." *American Quarterly* 39, 2 (Summer 1987): 211–30.

Goyette, Julien. "Biographie, narration et philosophie de l'histoire." *Revue d'histoire de l'Amerique Francaise* 54, 1 (Été 2000): 81–8.

Grant, Gail. "That Was a Woman's Satisfaction: The Significance of Life History for Woman-Centered Research." *Canadian Oral History Association* 11 (1991): 29–38.

Grant, Philip A., Jr. "Senator Hoke Smith, Southern Congressmen, and Agricultural Extension, 1914–1917." *Agricultural History* 60, 2 (Spring 1986): 111–22.

Gray, Rachel. "Teaching: A Career . . . or a Little Hat Money? An Oral History with Alice Gray." *Ontario History* 84, 4 (December 1992): 315–27.

Grayzel, Susan. "Fighting for Their Rights: A Comparative Perspective on Twentieth Century Women's Movements in Australia, Great Britain, and the United States." *Journal of Women's History* 11, 1 (Spring 1999): 210–18.

– "Nostalgia, Gender, and the Countryside: Placing the 'Land Girl' in First World War Britain." *Rural History* 10, 2 (1999): 155–70.

Griffith, Elisabeth. *Her Own Right: The Life of Elizabeth Cady Stanton*. New York: Oxford University Press, 1984.

Halfacree, Keith H. "Locality and Social Representation: Space, Discourse and Alternative Definitions of the Rural." *Journal of Rural Studies* 9, 1 (1993): 23–37.

– "Talking about Rurality: Social Representations of the Rural as Expressed by Presidents of Six English Parishes." *Journal of Rural Studies* 11, 1 (1995): 1–20.

Hall, Jacquelyn Dowd. "Second Thoughts: On Writing a Feminist Biography." *Feminist Studies* 13, 1 (Spring 1987): 19–37.

Hall, Valerie Gordon. "Contrasting Female Identities: Women in Coal Mining Communities in Northumberland, England, 1900–1939." *Journal of Women's History* 13, 2 (Summer 2001): 107–31.

Hallman, Dianne. "Introduction to Special Issues on Biography." *Ontario History* 84, 4 (December 1992): 257–61.

Halpern, Monda. *And on That Farm He Had a Wife: Ontario Farm Women and Feminism, 1900–1940.* Montreal: McGill-Queen's University Press, 2001.

Harland-Jacobs, Jessica. "'Hands Across the Sea': The Masonic Network, British Imperialism, and the North Atlantic World." *The Geographical Review* 89, 2 (1999): 237–53.

Harrison, Brian. "For Church, Queen and Family: The Girls' Friendly Society 1874–1920." *Past and Present* 61 (1973): 107–38.

Harrison, Cynthia. Review of *Worlds of Women: The Making of an International Women's Movement*, by Leila J. Rupp. *H-Net Reviews in the Humanities & Social Sciences* (January 1999): http://www.h-net.org/reviews/showrev .php?id=2684.

Heap, Ruby. "From the Science of Housekeeping to the Science of Nutrition: Pioneers in Canadian Nutrition and Dietetics at the University of Toronto's Faculty of Household Science, 1900–1950." In *Challenging Professions: Historical and Contemporary Perspectives on Women's Professional Work*, edited by Elizabeth Smyth et al., 141–70. Toronto: University of Toronto Press, 1999.

Heilbrun, Carolyn. *Writing a Woman's Life.* New York and London: W.W. Norton & Co., 1988.

Hill, Patricia R. *The World Their Household: The American Woman's Foreign Mission Movement and Cultural Transformation, 1870–1920.* Ann Arbor: University of Michigan Press, 1985.

Hirshfield, Claire. "Fractured Faith: Liberal Party Women and the Suffrage Issue in Britain, 1892–1914." *Gender & History* 2, 2 (1990): 173–97.

Hoggart, Keith. "Let's Do Away with Rural." *Journal of Rural Studies* 6, 3 (1990): 245–57.

Holton, Sandra Stanley. Review of *Worlds of Women: The Making of an International Women's Movement*, by Leila J. Rupp. *American Historical Review* 104, 3 (June 1999): 872–3.

Hoover, Thomas O., Marion White McPherson, and John A. Popplestone. "Documentation, a Difference between Gossip and History." *Manuscripts* 26, 3 (1974): 184–9.

Hostettler, Eve. "Women's Work in the Nineteenth Century Countryside." *Society for the Study of Labour History* 33 (1976): 9–11.

Hufbauer, Benjamin. *Presidential Temples: How Memorials and Libraries Shape Public Memory*. Lawrence: University of Kansas, 2005.

Huff, Cynthia. *Women's Life Writing and Imagined Communities*. New York: Routledge, 2005.

Hunt, Karen. "British Women and the Second International." *Labour History Review* 58, 1 (1993): 25–9.

Huxley, Gervas. *Lady Denman G.B.E., 1884–1954*. London: Chatto & Windus, 1961.

Jeansonne, Glen. "Personality, Biography, and Psychobiography." *Biography* 14, 3 (1991): 243–55.

– "Teaching a Course in Writing Biography." *Perspectives* 26, 1 (1988): 13–15.

Jenkins, Inez. *The History of the Women's Institute Movement of England and Wales*. Oxford: Oxford University Press, 1953.

Jensen, Joan M. "Crossing Ethnic Barriers in the Southwest: Women's Agricultural Extension Education, 1914–1940." *Agricultural History* 60, 2 (Spring 1986): 169–81.

Johnson, Richard, Gregor McLennan, Bill Schwarz, and David Sutton, eds. *Making Histories: Studies in History-Writing and Politics*. London: Hutchinson & Co., 1982.

Johnston, Susan J. "Twice Slain: Sex-Trade Workers and Suicide in British Columbia, 1870–1920." *Journal of the Canadian Historical Association/Revue de la Société historique du Canada* 5, 1 (1994): 147–66.

Kane, Paula M. "'The Willing Captive Of Home?': The English Catholic Women's League, 1906–1920." *Church History* 60, 3 (September 1991): 331–55.

Karr, Clarence. *Authors and Audiences: Popular Canadian Fiction in the Early Twentieth Century*. Montreal and Kingston: McGill-Queen's University Press, 2000.

Kechnie, Margaret. *Organizing Rural Women: The Federated Women's Institutes of Ontario, 1897–1919*. Montreal and Kingston: McGill-Queen's University Press, 2003.

Keyser, Elizabeth Lennox. "Woman in the Twentieth Century: Margaret Fuller and Feminist Biography." *Biography* 11, 4 (1988): 283–302.

Kirkendall, Richard S. "Reflections of a Revolutionary on a Revolution." *Journal of the West* 31, 4 (1992): 8–14.

– "The Second Secretary Wallace." *Agricultural History* 64, 2 (1990): 199–206.

Kizer, George A. "Ralph W. Tyler – A Living Legend: Problems of Biography." *Vitae Scholasticae* 7, 1 (1988): 19–29.

Kleinman, Mark L. *A World of Hope, A World of Fear: Henry A. Wallace, Reinhold Niebuhr, and American Liberalism*. Columbus: Ohio State University Press, 2000.

Knowles, Norman. *Inventing the Loyalists: The Ontario Loyalist Tradition and the Creation of Usable Pasts.* Toronto: University of Toronto Press, 1997.

Lamonde, Yvan. "Problèmes et plaisirs de la biographie." *Revue d'histoire de l'Amerique francaise* 54,1 (Éte 2000): 89–94.

Lane-Moore, Laurel. *Collingwood: Historic Homes and Buildings.* Collingwood: The Blue Mountain Foundation for the Arts, 1989.

Lang, Marjory L. *Women Who Made the News: Female Journalists in Canada, 1880–1945.* Montreal and Kingston: McGill-Queen's University Press, 1999.

LaPierre, Jo. "The Academic Life of Canadian Coeds, 1880–1900." *Historical Studies in Education/Revue d'histoire de l'Éducation* 2, 2 (Fall/automne 1990): 225–46.

Lash, Joseph P. "The Roosevelts and Arthurdale." *The Washington Monthly* 3, 9 (1971): 22–37.

Law, Graham. *Serializing Fiction in the Victorian Press.* Basingstoke: Palgrave, 2000.

Lawton, Henry. "The Study of Emotion in History." *Journal of Psychohistory* 14, 4 (1987): 335–6.

Lévesque, Andrée. "Réflexion sur la biographie historique en l'an 2000." *Revue d'Histoire de l'Amérique française* 54, 1 (2001): 95–102.

Levi, Charles Morden. *Comings and Goings: University Students in Canadian Society, 1854–1973.* Montreal and Kingston: McGill-Queen's University Press, 2003.

Light, Beth, and Joy Parr. *Canadian Women on the Move, 1867–1920.* Toronto: New Hogtown Press, 1983.

Litt, Paul. "Pliant Clio and Immutable Texts: The Historiography of a Historical Marking Program." *Public Historian* 19, 4 (1997): 7–28.

Lowitt, Richard. "Henry A. Wallace and Irrigation Agriculture." *Agricultural History* 66, 4 (1992): 1–10.

– "Henry A. Wallace and the 1955 Purge in the Department of Agriculture." *Agricultural History* 53, 3 (1997): 607–21.

Maack, Mary Niles. "'No Philosophy Carries So Much Conviction as the Personal Life': Mary Wright Plummer as an Independent Woman." *The Library Quarterly* 70, 1 (January 2000): 1–46.

MacLaren, Eli. "'Against All Invasion': The Archival Story of Kipling, Copyright, and the Macmillan Expansion into Canada, 1900–1920." *Journal of Canadian Studies* 40, 2 (Spring 2006): 139–62.

MacMillan, Carrie. "Research-Problems and Solutions: Research in Nineteenth-Century Canadian Women Writers: An Exercise in Detection." In *Rediscovering Our Foremothers: Nineteenth Century Canadian Women*

Writers, edited by Lorraine Mullen, 49–54. Ottawa: University of Ottawa Press, 1990.

Mallory, J.R. "Biography, History and Social Sciences in Canada: Different Questions, Different Answers." *Journal of Canadian Studies* 15, 4 (Winter 1981): 125–8.

Mangum, Teresa. "Style Wars of the 1890s: The New Woman and the Decadent." In *Transforming Genres: New Approaches to British Fiction in the 1890s*, edited by Nikki Lee Manos and Meri-Jane Rochelson, 47–66. New York: St. Martin's, 1994.

Margadant, Jo Burr. *The New Biography: Performing Femininity in Nineteenth Century France*. Berkeley, California: University of California Press, 2000.

Marr, Lucille. "'If You Want Peace, Prepare for Peace': Hanna Newcombe, Peace Researcher and Peace Activist." *Ontario History* 84, 4 (December 1992): 263–81.

Marsden, Terry, Philip Lowe, and Sarah Whatmore, eds. *Rural Restructuring: Global Processes and Their Responses*. London: David Fulton Publishers, 1990.

Matthews, Jill Julius. "They Sure Had a Lot of Fun: The Woman's League of Health and Beauty between the Wars." *History Workshop Journal* 30 (1990): 22–54.

McCall, Cicely. *Women's Institutes*. London: William Collins of London, 1943.

McCulloch, Mrs. John H. "The Formative Years of the Associated Country Women of the World." London: Associated Country Women of the World, n.d.

McCullogh, Kate. "Mapping the 'Terra Incognita' of Woman: George Egerton's *Keynotes* (1893) and New Woman Fiction." In *The New Nineteenth Century: Feminist Readings of Underread Victorian Fiction*, edited by Barbara Leah Harman and Susan Meyer, 205–24. New York: Garland, 1996.

Meier, Mariann. *ACWW's Vital War Years*. London: Associated Country Women of the World, n.d.

– *Thirty-Five Years and More*. London: Associated Country Women of the World, n.d.

Miles, A. *The 'Chicago of the North': Anecdotes from Collingwood's Past*. Collingwood: Town of Collingwood, 2004.

Miller, Naomi. "Hugh Watt: Physician and Politician." *British Columbia Historical News* 37, 1 (Winter 2003), 18–21.

Mitchinson, Wendy. "Canadian Women and Church Missionary Societies." *Atlantis* 2, 2 Part II (Spring 1977): 57–75.

Modern Pioneers: British Columbia Women's Institutes, 1909–1959. Victoria: British Columbia Women's Institutes, 1959.

Moffatt, Aileen C. *Experiencing Identity: British-Canadian Women in Rural Saskatchewan, 1880–1950.* PhD thesis, University of Manitoba, 1996.

Montgomery, Maureen. "Hussies, Poachers and Pork-Packers' Daughters: Anti-American in Britain at the Turn of the Century." *Australasian Journal of American Studies* 6, 1 (1987): 22–34.

Morang, George N. *The Copyright Question: A Letter to the Toronto Board of Trade.* Toronto: George N. Morang & Company Limited, 1902.

Morgan, Cecilia. *'A Happy Holiday': English Canadians and Transatlantic Tourism, 1870–1930.* Toronto: University of Toronto Press, 2008.

– "'Of Slender Frame and Delicate Appearance': The Placing of Laura Secord in the Narratives of Canadian Loyalist History." *Journal of the Canadian Historical Association* 5 (1994): 195–212.

Morgan, Maggie. "Jam Making, Cuthbert Rabbit and Cakes: Redefining Domestic Labor in the Women's Institute, 1915–60." *Rural History* 7, 2 (1996): 207–19.

Mormont, Marc. "Rural Nature and Urban Natures." *Sociologia Ruralis* XXVII, 1 (1987): 3–20.

Morton, Suzanne. "Faire le saut: la biographie peut-elle etre de l'histoire sociale?" *Revue d'Histoire de l'Amerique Francaise* 54, 1 (2001): 103–9.

Moss, Jeffrey W., and Cynthia B. Lass. "A History of Farmers' Institutes." *Agricultural History* 62, 2 (1988): 161–3.

Nesbet, Anne. "Suicide as Literary Fact in the 1920s," *Slavic Review* 50, 4 (1991): 827–35.

Neth, Mary. *Preserving the Family Farm: Women, Community and the Foundations of Agribusiness in the Midwest, 1900–1940.* Baltimore: Johns Hopkins University Press, 1995.

Ontario Women's Institute Story: In Commemoration of the 75th Anniversary of the Founding of the Women's Institutes of Ontario. Toronto: Federated Women's Institutes of Ontario, 1972.

Otty, Marianne G. *Fifty Years of Women's Institutes in New Brunswick, Canada, 1911–1961: A History.* New Brunswick: Women's Institutes, 1961.

Pagh, Nancy, "Our Emily: A Review Essay." *BC Studies* 114 (Summer 1997): 89–91.

Pagliano, Muriel J. *Country Women: History of the First Seventy-Five Years, Queensland Country Women's Association.* Brisbane: Queensland Country Women's Association, 1997.

Painter, Nell Irvin. "Review Essays: Writing Biographies of Women." *Journal of Women's History* 9, 2 (Summer 1997): 154–63.

Passerini, Luisa. "Transforming Biography: From the Claim of Objectivity to Intersubjective Plurality." *Rethinking History* 4, 3 (2000): 413–16.

Pelletier-Baillargeon, Hélène. "La biographie. Un subtil alliage d'histoire et de littérature." *Revue d'histoire de l'Amerique Francaise* 54, 1 (Été 2000): 69–80.

Perry, Adele. "Writing Women into British Columbia History." *BC Studies* 122 (Summer 1999): 85–8.

– "Interlocuting Empire: Colonial Womanhood, Settler Identity, and Frances Herring." In *Rediscovering the British World*, edited by Phillip Buckner and R. Douglas Francis, 159–79. Calgary: University of Calgary Press, 2005.

Peterman, Michael A., and Janet B. Friskney. "'Booming' the Canuck Book: Edward Caswell and the Promotion of Canadian Writing." *Journal of Canadian Studies* 30, 3 (Fall 1995): 60–90.

Pfaff, William. *The Wrath of Nations: Civilization and the Furies of Nationalism*. New York: Simon and Schuster, 1993.

Pfeffer, Paula F. "Eleanor Roosevelt and the National and World Woman's Parties." *The Historian* 59, 1 (1996): 39–57.

Pickles, Katie. *Female Imperialism and National Identity: Imperial Order Daughters of the Empire*. Manchester and New York: Manchester University Press, 2002.

Prestwich, Patricia E. Review of *The New Biography: Performing Femininity in Nineteenth Century France*, by Jo Burr Margadant. *Histoire Sociale* 34, 67 (May 2001): 230–2.

Purvis, Jane. "Working Class Women and Adult Education in Nineteenth Century Britain." *History of Education* 9, 3 (1980): 193–212.

Putney, Clifford. "Service over Secrecy: How Lodge-Style Fraternalism Yielded Popularity to Men's Service Clubs." *Journal of Popular Culture* 27, 1 (1993): 179–90.

Pykett, Lyn. "Portraits of the Artist as a Young Woman: Representations of the Female Artist in the New Woman Fiction of the 1890s." In *Victorian Women Writers and the Woman Question*, edited by Nicola Diane Thompson, 135–50. Cambridge: Cambridge University Press, 1999.

– *The 'Improper' Feminine: The Women's Sensation Novel and the New Woman Writing*. London and New York: Routledge, 1992.

Reid, Debra. *Reaping A Greater Harvest: African Americans, the Extension Service and Rural Reform in Jim Crow's Texas*. Texas: A & M University Press, 2007.

– "Rural African Americans, Gender Roles, and Progressive Reform in Texas." Paper presented to the Rural Women's Studies Association Meeting, Minneapolis, Minnesota, June 2000.

Rennella, Mark, and Whitney Walton. "Planned Serendipity: American Travelers and the Transatlantic Voyage in the Nineteenth and Twentieth Centuries." *Journal of Social History* 38, 2 (Winter 2004): 365–83.

Richardson, Angelique, and Chris Willis, eds. *The New Woman in Fiction and in Fact: Fin-de-Siecle Feminisms*. New York: Palgrave-Macmillan Ltd., 2001.

Riley, Glenda, and Richard S. Kirkendall. "Henry A. Wallace and the Mystique of the Farm Male, 1921–1933." *Annals of Iowa* 48, 1–2 (1985): 32–55.

Robinson, Jane. *A Force to be Reckoned With: A History of the Women's Institute*. London: Virago Press, 2011.

Robinson, Jean. *Three Women of B.C and A.C.W.W.* Sooke, BC: Shirley Women's Institute Historical Research Group, 1990.

Rosenwein, Barbara H. "Worrying about Emotions in History." *The American Historical Review* 107, 3 (2002): 821–45.

Rupp, Leila J. "Challenging Imperialism in International Women's Organizations, 1888–1945." *National Women's Studies Association Journal* 8, 1 (1996): 8–27.

– "Constructing Internationalism: The Case of Transnational Women's Organizations, 1888–1945." *American Historical Review* 99, 5 (December 1994): 1571–1600.

– "Feminisms and Internationalism: A View from the Centre." *Gender & History* 10, 3 (1998): 535–8.

– "Is Feminism the Province of Old (or Middle-Aged) Women?" *Journal of Women's History* 12, 4 (Winter 2001): 164–74.

– "Reflections on Twentieth Century American Women's History." *Reviews in American History* 9, 2 (1981): 275–84.

– Review of *Reconstructing Women's Thoughts: The Women's International League for Peace and Freedom before World War Two*, by Linda K. Schott; *A World without War: How U.S. Feminists and Pacifists Resisted World War I*, by Frances J. Early; and *Women against the Good War: Conscientious Objection and Gender on the American Home Front, 1941–1947*, by Rachel Walter Goossen. *American Historical Review* 104, 2 (April 1999): 596–7.

– "Sexuality and Politics in the Early Twentieth Century: The Case of the International Women's Movement." *Feminist Studies* 23, 3 (Fall 1997): 577–606.

– *Worlds of Women: The Making of an International Women's Movement*. Princeton: Princeton University Press, 1997.

Rymer, Jeanne S. "Arthurdale, a Social Experiment in the 1930s: Foundations, Fantasies, Furniture and Failures." *West Virginia History* 46, 1–4 (1985–6): 89–102.

Sachs, Carolyn E. *Gendered Fields: Rural Women, Agriculture and Environment*. Boulder: Westview Press, 1996.

Sanborn, Josh. "More than Imagined: A Few Notes on Modern Identities." *Slavic Review* 59, 2 (2000): 330–5.

Saugeres, Lisa. "The Cultural Representation of the Farming Landscape: Masculinity, Power and Nature." *Journal of Rural Studies* 18, 4 (2002): 373–84.

Scarborough, Mrs. Neve. *History of the Associated Country Women of the World and of Its Member Societies.* London: The Rydal Press, 1953.

Schaffer, Talia. "'Nothing by Foolscap and Ink': Inventing the New Woman." In *The New Woman in Fiction and Fact: Fin-de-siècle Feminisms,* edited by Angelique Richardson and Chris Willis, 39–52. London: Palgrave, 2001.

Schapsmeier, Edward L., and Frederick H. Schapsmeier. "A Prophet in Politics: The Public Career of Henry A. Wallace." *Annals of Iowa* 39, 1 (Summer 1967): 1–21.

Schmidt, Jean Miller. *Grace Sufficient: A History of Women in American Methodism 1760–1939.* Nashville: Abingdon Press, 1999.

Schwieder, Dorothy. *75 Years of Service: Cooperative Extension in Iowa.* Ames: Iowa State University Press, 1993.

Scura, Dorothy, M. Review of *Telling Women's Lives: The New Biography* by Linda Wagner-Martin. *American Literature* 67, 3 (September 1995): 608–9.

Shapiro, Ann R. *Unlikely Heroines: Nineteenth-Century American Woman Writers and the Woman Question.* New York: Greenwood Press, 1987.

Shucksmith, Mark. "Conceptualising Post-Industrial Rurality" In *Towards Sustainable Rural Communities: The Guelph Seminar Series,* edited by John M. Bryden, 125–132. Guelph: University School of Rural Planning and Development, 1994.

Sinha, Mrinalini, Donna J. Guy, and Angela Woollacott. "Introduction: Why Feminisms and Internationalism?" *Gender & History* 10, 3 (1998): 345–57.

Smith, Ruby Green. *The People's College: A History of the New York State Extension Service in Cornell University and the State 1876–1948.* Ithaca: Cornell University Press, 1948.

Smitley, Megan. "'Inebriates', 'Heathens', Templars and Suffragists: Scotland and Imperial Feminism c. 1870–1914." *Women's History Review* 11, 3 (2002): 455–80.

Sperdakos, Sophia. "'For the Joy of the Working': Laura Elizabeth McCully, First-Wave Feminist." *Ontario History* 84, 4 (Dec 1992): 283–314.

Stamper, Anne. *Rooms Off the Corridor: Education in the WI and 50 Years of Denman College, 1948–98.* London: WI Books, 1998.

– *Sussex, The Cradle of the English WIs.* n.p.: Anne Stamper, 2004.

Steedman, Carolyn. "Difficult Stories: Feminist Auto/Biography." *Gender & History* 7, 2 (1995): 321–6.

Steinson, Barbara J. *American Women's Activism in World War I.* New York: Garland, 1982.

Stern, Madeleine B. *Purple Passage: The Life of Mrs. Frank Leslie.* Norman: University of Oklahoma Press, 1953.

Stetz, Margaret. "New Grub Street and the Woman Writer of the 1890s." In *Transforming Genres: New Approaches to British Fiction in the 1890s,* edited by Nikki Lee Manos and Meri-Jane Rochelson, 21–46. New York: St. Martin's, 1994.

Stevens, Donald G. "Organizing for Economic Defense: Henry Wallace and the Board of Economic Warfare's Foreign Policy Initiatives, 1942." *Presidential Studies Quarterly* 26, 4 (Fall 1996): 1126–39.

Stevens, Harry R. "Contemporary American Biographical Writing: Trends and Problems." *The South Atlantic Quarterly* 55, 3 (1956): 358–70.

Stiles, Deborah K. "Rural Women, Underdevelopment, Health Knowledge, and Modernity: Women and Family Farms as Part of a Broader Context of Change." In *Perspektive Žena u Obiteljskoj Poljoprivredi I Ruralnom Razvoju / Women Perspectives in Family Farming,* edited by Anita Silvana Ilak Persuric. Porec, Croatia: The Institute for Agriculture and Tourism, 2003.

Stiles, D., C. Rangel, J. MacLaughlin, L. Sanderson, and K. MacNeil. "Rurality, Gender, and Leisure: Experiences of Young Rural Women in a Nova Scotia Community." *Journal of Rural Community Psychology* E10 (2) (2007). Available: https://www.marshall.edu/jrcp/ARCHIVES/V10%20N2/stiles.pdf

Strong, Pauline Turner. "Feminist Theory and the 'Invasion of the Heart' in North America." *Ethnohistory* 43, 4 (Fall 1996): 683–712.

Styer, Sandra. "Exploring Women's Political Careers through Biographies." *The Social Studies* 73, 4 (1982):175–7.

Sullivan, Robert. "Evaluating the Ethics and Consciences of Museums." In *Gender Perspectives: Essays on Women in Museums,* edited by Jane R. Glaser and Artemis A. Zenetou, 100–7. Washington, D.C.: Smithsonian Institution Press, 1994.

Tallentine, Jenéa. "Strategies of Memory: History, Social Memory and the Community." *Histoire sociale/Social History* 34, 67 (2001): 197–212.

Taylor, Georgina. "Shall I Drown Myself Now or Later? The Isolation of Rural Women in Saskatchewan and Their Participation in the Homemakers' Clubs, the Farm Movement and the Co-operative Commonwealth Federation, 1910–1967." In *Women, Isolation and Bonding: The Ecology of Gender,* edited by Kathleen Storrie, 79–100. Toronto: Methuen, 1987.

Teather, Elizabeth, and Margaret-Ann Franklin, eds. *Country Women at the Crossroads: Perspectives on the Lives of Rural Australian Women in the 1990s.* Amidale, NSW: University of New England Press, 1994.

Thompson, Lynne. "'The Golden Thread of Empire': Women's Popular Education in the Lancashire Federation of Women's Institutes 1920–1939."*Journal of Educational and Administrative History* 28, 1 (1996): 42–57.
– "The Promotion of Agricultural Education for Adults: The Lancashire Federation of Women's Institutes, 1919–1945." *Rural History* 10, 2 (1999): 217–34.
Thorner, Thomas., ed. *A Country Nourished on Self-Doubt: Documents in Canadian History, 1867–1980.* Peterborough, ON: Broadview Press, 1998.
Tuchman, Barbara. "Biography as a Prism of History." In *Telling Lives: The Biographer's Art,* edited by Marc Pachter. Washington, DC: New Republic Books and National Portrait Gallery, 1979.
Tyrell, Ian. "American Exceptionalism in an Age of International History." *American Historical Review* 96 (Oct 1991): 1031–55.
Valenze, Debora M. *Prophetic Sons and Daughters: Female Preaching and Popular Religion in Industrial England.* Princeton: Princeton University Press, 1985.
van der Burg, Margreet. *'Geen tweede boer'. Gender, landbouwmodernisering en onderwijs aan plattelandsvrouwen in Nederland, 1863–1968* ('No second farmer'. Gender, Agricultural Modernisation and Education for Rural Women in the Netherlands). Hilversum: Uitgererij Verloren, 2002.
Van Voris, Jacqueline. *Carrie Chapman Catt: A Public Life.* New York: Feminist Press, 1987.
Van Wart, Alice, ed. *Necessary Secrets: The Journals of Elizabeth Smart.* Toronto: Deneau Publishers, 1986.
Vellacott, Jo. "Feminism as if All People Mattered: Working to Remove the Causes of War, 1919–1929." *Contemporary European History* 10, 3 (2001): 375–94.
Voss, Arthur. "Backgrounds of Lowell's Satire in 'The Biglow Papers.'" *New England Quarterly* 23, 1 (March 1950): 47–64.
Walker, Annie, Edith M. Collins, and M. McIntyre Hood. *Fifty Years of Achievement: In Commemoration of the 50th Anniversary of the Founding of the Women's Institutes of Ontario.* Toronto: Federated Women's Institutes of Ontario, 1948.
Walker, Ronald W. "The Challenge and Craft of Mormon Biography." *Brigham Young University Studies* 22, 2 (1982): 179–92.
Ward, Norman, and David Smith. *Jimmy Gardiner: Relentless Liberal.* Toronto: University of Toronto Press, 1990.
Ward, Paul. "Empire and the Everyday: Britishness and Imperialism in Women's Lives in the Great War." In *Rediscovering the British World,* edited by Phillip Buckner and R. Douglas Francis, 267–85. Calgary: University of Calgary Press, 2005.

Ward, Susan. "The Career Woman Fiction of Elizabeth Stuart Phelps." In *Nineteenth-Century Women Writers of the English-Speaking World*, edited by Rhoda B. Nathan, 209–19. New York: Greenwood Press, 1986.

Ware, Susan. Review of *Worlds of Women: The Making of an International Women's Movement*, by Leila J. Rupp. *The Journal of American History* 85, 3 (December 1998): 1122–3.

Washington, Margaret. "Sojourner Truth, Shadow or Substance: Writing the Life of a Legend." *Culture Front* 2, 3 (Fall 1993): 19–21.

Watcher, Phyllis E. "Bibliography of Works about Life-Writing." *Biography* 18, 4 (1995): 360–8.

Watson, Janet S.K. *Fighting Different Wars: Experience, Memory, and the First World War in Britain*. Cambridge: Cambridge University Press, 2004.

Weaver, John, and David Wright. *Histories of Suicide: International Perspectives on Self-Destruction in the Modern World*. Toronto: University of Toronto Press, 2009.

Weiland, Steven. "Biography, Rhetoric, and Intellectual Careers: Writing the Life of Hannah Arendt." *Biography* 22, 3 (Summer 1999): 370–98.

White, Graham, and John Maze. *Henry A. Wallace: His Search for a New World Order*. Chapel Hill: University of North Carolina Press, 1995.

Whiteley, Marilyn. *Canadian Methodist Women, 1766–1925: Marys, Marthas, Mothers in Israel*. Waterloo: Wilfrid Laurier Press, 2005.

Williamson, Samuel H. "Seven Ways to Compute the Relative Value of a U.S. Dollar Amount, 1774 to Present." *Measuring Worth*, 2009. URL: http://www.measuringworth.com/uscompare/.

Wilson, John. "Voluntary Associations and Civil Religion." *Review of Religious Research* 2, 2 (December 1980): 125–36.

Wilson, Shauna. "Manitoba Women Nurturing the Nation: The Manitoba IODE and Maternal Nationalism, 1913–1920." *Journal of Canadian Studies* 35, 2 (Summer 2000): 149–65.

Wood, Ann D. "'The Scribbling Woman' and Fanny Fern: Why Women Write." *American Quarterly* 23, 1 (Spring 1971): 3–24.

Woollacott, Angela. "Inventing Commonwealth and Pan-Pacific Feminisms: Australian Women's Internationalist Activism in the 1920s–30s." *Gender & History* 10, 3 (1998): 425–48.

–   "Maternalism, Professionalism and Industrial Welfare Supervisors in World War I Britain." *Women's History Review* 3, 1 (1994): 29–56.

Workman, Joanne. "Wading Through the Mire: An Historiographical Study of the British Women's Movement Between the Wars." *University of Sussex Journal of Contemporary History* 2 (2001): https://www.sussex.ac.uk/webteam/gateway/file.php?name=2-workman-wading-through-the-mire&site=15

Wright, Cynthia. "'Feminine Trifles of Vast Importance': Writing Gender into the History of Consumption." In *Gender Conflicts: New Essays in Women's History*, edited by Franca Iacovetta and Mariana Valverde, 229–60. Toronto: University of Toronto Press, 1992.

Wright, Donald. "Reflections on Donald Creighton and the Appeal of Biography." *Journal of Historical Biography* 1, 1 (Spring 2007): 14–26.

Zitter, Emmy Stark. "Making Herself Born: Ghost Writing and Willa Cather's Developing Autobiography." *Biography* 19, 3 (1995): 282–301.

Index